DEVILS IN AMBER- The Baltics

Other Books by Phillip Bonosky

A Bird in Her Hair (short stories) [1987]
Washington's Secret War Against Afghanistan [1985]
Are Our Moscow Reporters Giving Us the Facts About the USSR? [1981]
Two Cultures [1976]
Beyond the Borders of Myth: From Vilnius to Hanoi [1967]
Dragon Pink on Old White (China) [1962]
The Magic Fern (novel) [1960]
Brother Bill McKie (biography) [1953]
Burning Valley (novel) [1952]

DEVILS IN AMBER-
The Baltics

PHILLIP BONOSKY

International Publishers New York

DEDICATION

Dedicated to those Lithuanians, Latvians and Estonians who gave their lives for a better world. In particular for those Lithuanians I knew personally: Antanas Sniekus, Henrikas Zimanas, Justas Paleckis, Jonas Simkus, Juozas Baltusis and for those living who have not surrendered the dream nor lost their hopes that what has been won for their people will not be lost for ever.

Do not weep at the grave of brave comrades:
They who fell in struggle are heroes.
Every struggle must have its sacrifices–
They are fortunate who have died for freedom.
　　　　　　　　　　　　　　　　—Julius Janonis

© 1992 International Publishers, New York
United States and Canada, English edition, only
Manufactured in the United States of America

The contribution of co-editor Dr. Heinz Dieterich Steffan to this work was made possible by a research grant from the Center for International Studies, Mexico City.

LIBRARY OF CONGRESS CATALOGING-IN-PUBLICATION DATA

Bonosky, Phillip.
　　Devils in amber : the Baltics/Phillip Bonosky.—New York :International Publishers, 1992.
　　　　p.　　cm.
　　Includes bibliographical references and index.
　　ISBN 0-7178-0699-5 (pbk).- $9.95

　　1. Baltic States—Politics and government. 2. Baltic States— History—Autonomy and independence movements. I. Title.

DK502.7..B66　　1992　　　　947'4—dc20　　　　91-45096
　　　　　　　　　　　　　　　　　　　　　　　　AACR2 MARC CIP 1/92

Library of Congress

Table of Contents

GENTLE LITHUANIA

On my palm I bring you
Golden like the sun,
This pale piece of amber,
Gentle Lithuania,
The Baltic in my hand!
— Salomeya Neris

After a severe storm—it must be so severe that it plows up the very depths of the Baltic sea—it's the custom of vacationers at Palanga, a Lithuanian resort town on the Baltic, to stroll along the seashore with a stick probing among the tangled seaweed and algae the storm had torn loose and brought to the surface, for nuggets of amber. Amber is "northern gold," and once these shores teemed with it. Now only a monumental storm will pry it loose from its bed in the sea. There, sunk deep into alluvial soil, the resin from prehistoric pines has been molded and remolded by numerous seas and endless time into these pieces of hard petrified "stone," whose colors run all the way from deepest black to deepest white, with 200 shades in between. And, rarely but often enough, tucked inside the translucent stones, and waiting there for a thousand, even perhaps a million years, are bits of metal, a leaf, an insect, a small frog or snake, and even, from much later, a Roman coin.

Amber is the frozen past of the nation. It disappears into myth, and myth becomes all we know of her past. Then it was that the immortal queen Juraite fell in love with a mortal man, Kastytises, a fisherman. She brought him to her amber castle at the bottom of the sea. But, so the tale goes, Perkunas, god of thunder, jealous of their happiness, and of Juraite's daring to take a mortal as a lover, destroyed the amber castle (much like the Nazis would later), killed the fisherman and chained the queen to the ruins. These bits of amber that the stroller picks up today on the shores of Palanga are her tears....

For all history knows, it knows no better, and science stands almost mute before the tantalizing bits and pieces of startling evidence of another world caught in the frozen sunlight now being unearthed and mined and dug, cleaned and polished, and put under the microscope, and worn around one's neck.

Tears they might as well be: for they speak of a time when sorrow and woe were the common lot of these ancient people over whose land and through whose bodies armies have tramped. They speak of a time when this northern country of ice and snow (warmed however by the Gulf stream) had once known a tropical climate. On these shores too cold today for any fruit less hardy than the apple once grew olive and palm trees. Three Ice Ages had come and gone. Tribes had come and gone. Wedged into the center of some of these pieces of stilled resin are Roman coins, a bead, a bit from a bracelet, a sliver of bone.

The Roman historian Tacitus in 1 A.D. already speaks of Lithuanians as "hard workers who gathered amber..." It is similarly intriguing to hear an Indian speaking Sanskrit that shares words with Lithuanian. It's unnerving to learn that the names of some months in the Lithuanian calendar do not correspond with the season. The calendar says it's *vasaris*, which means summer; but the calendar also says it's February, which is winter. *Sausas* means dry, but it's January. Thus, in the language as in the amber, still lurk many secrets of the past waiting to be unraveled, if unraveled they can be. Both the Lithuanians and the Hindus who speak Sanskrit once worshipped the same god: "dieva," implying an affinity in the past supported by no other tangible evidence whatsoever. So, too, the language, as the oldest living European language, is also a kind of museum.

Immanuel Kant pleaded with the world to save the language even if the people themselves perished, as at the time it seemed they well might. Born in what was once Lithuanian Prussia, Kant had seen Prussian Lithuanian totally disappear by the 17th century as the language of that land. And Goethe, listening to the *dainos* of Lithuania, pointed out that there were no cradle songs among them. He might also have noted there were few songs celebrating war, warriors, victory—though many existed lamenting the loss of husband, son, or lover to the military. Untypical of any other nation, most of the Lithuanian and Latvian *dainos* were composed by women. For women war is loss, tragedy...

When a new home is built, even today, its gabled peak is crowned with a wreathe of oak leaves and rue. In this most Catholic of countries, the oak is an enduring symbol of survival. The rue is worn as a crown by virgins, and is Lithuania's national plant. Wearing it echoes an earlier period when Lithuanians were nature worshippers—they had not yet cut their ties to nature, worshipping as the god above all, Perkunas, the god of thunder. Christianized at the end of the 14th century, pagan rites, pagan memories and rituals remain intertwined with the more recent religious rites. Thus, even through pagan as well as Christian and socialist times, the stork transcends all religions, all ideologies, as it transcends mountain barriers and national borders. It rests on chimneys of the houses of "good men" and the Lithuanian farmer, responding to a past he no longer can name, shrugs his shoulders and builds another chimney. Storks know the few remaining centuries' old oak trees deep in the forest that have survived everything—kings and kaisers and hitlers.

Nomad memories haunt the countryside. Once you have left the cities, with modern plumbing and computers, there is still a countryside awaiting you in which time seems not so much to have stood still, inert, as to have proved immovable, stubborn. Weather-beaten shrines, enclosing and protecting little wooden figurines of Christ and Mother Mary from the wind and rain, will meet you at lonely crossroads. Peering inside, sometimes through glass, one is shocked to re-encounter in these wooden images of Christ and Mary the familiar faces of Juozas and Judita whom you had just left working in the field or in the barnyard. Whittling during the long winter evenings old men, whose gnarled hands had not lost their sensitivity, sought for models of a man and a woman no one living had ever seen and found them in people they did see: their family.

All of us are simultaneously as old as humanity itself, and as new as our grandchildren. Thus, Lithuanians trace their roots to a time when their identity as a people did not yet exist, and yet they existed. Christianized under duress, the shock of being forceably separated from Nature was so traumatic to them as a people, it would not be too extreme to say they have never fully recovered. If they continue to respect old, old trees it's because at one time they understood that their own flesh had once merged with the flesh of the tree. In the *daina* they sing:

> *There I swam in desperation,*
> *Firmly grasped the oak tree.*
> *Will you not be changed, oak tree,*
> *Changed into my father?*

But though the sources are lost in the mist of time, they know that nevertheless once they did exist. And, bit by bit, through centuries of struggle, of crossing and re-crossing lands unnamed and unknown, the myths they believed in became the substance of reality. A time came finally when the landscape they last looked on when they went to sleep was still the same when they woke next day—and the day after and after that day. Not only had they broken with Nature, they had begun to subdue her. They had acquired a home. They had become a people. They had a name. They entered history. Calamity knew where they were...

Different and yet sharing much that was the same, Latvia and Estonia nevertheless created their separate histories, and we shall deal with them too. But Lithuania is the largest of the three Baltic nations and often calls the tune. History is the biography of our world, but each nation has its own history formed by the whole and yet making its own contribution to the whole. Just as linguists search the language for clues to not only the Lithuanian past but to the past of mankind, so, too, we can hope that in their history, clues to something vital in humanity's progress can be found. The motor car pauses at the wayside shrine to look at the carved figures within and the passengers in the car find it difficult to reconcile these weather-beaten wooden figurines, speaking of another age, with their own contemporary selves. If the driver of the car is Lithuanian, does he see a glimmer of his own modern face in the old face of the wooden figure inside the shrine?

DYING LITHUANIA

The father brought up nine sons—
And she was the tenth, the little daughter...
The nine sons fell in battle—
But God kept safe the little daughter...
— Lithuanian *daina*

For centuries, Europe had watched Lithuania dying. Immanuel Kant, whose parents were (Prussian) Lithuanian, cried: "Lithuania ... deserves protection of the state. She must be preserved for her tongue possesses the key which opens up the enigmas not only of philology but of history."

As we have seen, both Lithuanian and Sanskrit share many words together—from "Perkunas" (god of thunder) to "Deva" (God). Just as in the golden grip of amber can be found shreds of palm trees that speak of a once-tropical climate, so tucked into the language itself philologists find tantalizing but frustrating clues to an early civilization—a time that fades into myth. Lithuanian is the oldest living language in Europe and was known to the Romans who borrowed words from it, and like the Sanskrit also shares words....

Yet little is known of its physical beginnings. It is surmised that the land now known as Lithuania was populated some 9,000 years before the beginning of our times by nomadic hunters. But hunters do not seek a place but the mobile auroch. They come and they go.

Firmer evidence exists to show that perhaps 5000 years ago, people of Indo-European origin invaded the land that did not yet have fixed borders and spread quickly over areas that extended all the way from the shores of today's Finland and Estonia to the Vistula and Dauguva. In their sweep north and south, they not so much conquered as merged with the native tribes, establishing what has been labeled by scientists as the Aistic or Baltic peoples. Of these there were many: from the Samgoitians (Zemiacia), Selians, Kursians, Skalvians, Suluvians, Yotvingians: a roll call of ghosts. Not until the 13th century were these tribes finally united in a feudal setting and began to think of themselves as Lithuanians.

The Latgalians, Zemagalians, and the Kursians were conquered in the 13th century by the German Knights of the Sword, the Livonian Order of the Crusaders, forming finally, under the power of the sword which turned

5

upside down became a cross, a people now known as the Latvians. They were close to the Lithuanians and their language is similar.

But not so with the Estonians. It is believed that hunting and fishing tribes of the Finno-Ugric group, for reasons unknown, left their origins in the Urals some thousands of years ago, moved westward until they reached the shores of the Baltic Sea and then stopped.

Later, some of the Baltic tribes came in from the south, and intermixing over a thousand years, separating into the southern areas now known as Latvia and Lithuania, nevertheless did not disappear but kept a separate identity from their southern neighbors, retaining the Baltic-Finnish pattern of speech, quite distinct from the speech of their neighbors. By the beginning of the 13th century, there were about 150,000 people who could be called Estonians. By this time they were a settled people already raising crops and cattle (very much what all the Baltic countries did up until modern times). Handicrafts were widely developed, and because they were located on the sea, they became seamen and tradesmen as well.

What is remarkable is that even as early as the beginning of the 13th century, all three Baltic countries had already acquired a language, and engaged in agriculture and husbandry. They already had learned to use iron. They knew how to manufacture bronze. But their land was poor in minerals (except in Estonia) and they had no coal, though much peat. But they early developed the barter system with their neighbors, and, indeed, almost from the dawn of their existence, the Baltic countries depended on trade with others to supplement and enrich what was a sparse subsistence economy.

The Lithuanians remained pagans long after the rest of Europe had become Christianized. Before their forced conversion to Catholicism, they worshipped nature—the sun, the moon, the stars were all humanized. Lithuanian *dainos* are full of pagan memory:

> *When the morning star was wed,*
> *Perkunas rode through the gateway*
> *And smote the green oak tree...*

For them the boundary between human and nature was fluid, and trees—oak trees—could change into their fathers and their fathers into oak trees. When Lithuania was finally Christianized at the end of the 13th century—as an act of survival—an entire interim period began in which Christian (Catholic) symbols and rituals intermixed with the pagan, much the way it happened later in Mexico and Peru and other Latin American countries, finally blending into something that was neither Catholic nor pagan.

Writes Fraser in *The Golden Bough*:

When the Missionary Jerome of Prague was persuading the heathen Lithuanians to fell their sacred groves, a multitude of women besought the Prince of Lithuania to stop him, saying that with the woods he was destroying the house of gods from which they had been wont to get rain and sunshine.[1]

The stubbornness with which pagan motifs persisted through Lithuanian culture merged with the stubbornness with which the Lithuanians clung to their language, though again and again an alien power lorded it over them, speaking a foreign tongue, and their own native ruling class scorned their native tongue as being vulgar. Ultimately, the language, the myths, the religion—all merged into one force geared to survival.

But the main threat to survival always came from the West—from Germany. The German Crusaders of the Knights of Livonia invaded Latvia and Lithuania repeatedly during the 13th century and into the 14th, occupying and converting by fire and sword the recalcitrant people. In their missionary zeal, they were ruthless. Nor did they hesitate to obliterate every vestige of "pagan" ritual and memory, and indeed came close to succeeding. In Prussian Lithuania they did succeed. By the 18th century, Prussian Lithuania had disappeared altogether, and with it not only its culture but a specific variation of the Lithuanian language, now a dead language, like Latin.

As Prussia disappeared, so all of Lithuania would disappear, it was then widely believed in Western Europe.

We were five brothers
On the green meadow.
The next day we were
The crusaders' spoil.

And when they seized us
Five youthful brothers
They fettered our feet
In chains of iron....

The crusaders' chief
Immeasurably cruel
Ordered green willow...,

Then they beat us
The blood began flowing
Down to the earth,
The earth began shaking....

Conversion did not come easily. Nor did conversion itself save Lithuania. Although the new priests, the Jesuits, launched a merciless crusade of their own against all vestiges of Paganism, nevertheless for years the Lithuanians resisted consciously accepting the symbols of Christianity, even returning the waters of their forced baptism back to the sea with the departing

Germans. The Jesuits tried, but tried in vain, to eliminate the *dainos* themselves. But the *dainos* were oral, invented on the spot, changed and modified as they passed from tongue to tongue. But the drive for cultural genocide was relentless, and it is extraordinarily depressing to read, seven centuries later, Alfred Rosenberg, Reich Minister of Nazi Germany, present his plans for the Baltic countries:

> The Reich's representatives in Estonia, Latvia and Lithuania should aim for the establishment of a German proletariat, so that in the future these regions may be incorporated into the German Reich, Germanizing the racially suitable elements and destroying the undesirable elements.

In the middle of the 19th century, with the consciousness growing among philologists and historians that in the disappearance of Lithuanian Prussia the world had lost a valuable source of history and culture, and fearing that all of Lithuania stood in jeopardy of the same fate, a cry was raised by a group of European scholars that "the Lithuanian language, one of the most important in philology, is quickly approaching extermination. Oppressed by Germans, Poles, Russians and Latvians, its existence will continue but a short time longer. With the disappearance will vanish the customs, legends, myths and poetry, of a nation which at one time was a sovereign power in Northern Europe." [2]

JESUS OVERPOWERS PERKUNAS

You gave us champions, Trakai,
Knew days of glory, when
You saw the Great Vytautas ride
Among the fighting men!
Where is the might we should inherit,
Where—the antiquity we cherish?
— Maironis, (1862-1932)

The impetus for survival, mainly against the German threat, was the power which began to weld the various conflicting forces within Lithuania and Latvia into a unity that foreshadowed the states themselves. It was Grand Duke Mindaugas who succeeded in subduing the recalcitrant dukes and boyars, forging a kingdom to which the hitherto warring nobles paid obeisance and in whose defense they pledged armed assistance.

By 1236, the new order was put to a supreme test when the Knights of the Swords invaded Lithuania. On September 22nd, they came to grief in a battle at Sula (Siauliai). A second invasion by the combined forces of the German Knights of the Cross and the Knights of the Sword came in 1237—one year later. They, too, were defeated. Again, in 1260, egged on by the Pope, they set out to convert the heathen with fire and sword, and again they failed. But in 1263, Mindaugas and his sons fell victim to conspirators and their death left the country without its royal head.

In 1316, the Grand Duke Gediminas inherited the throne and embarked on a vigorous struggle to clear Lithuania of the Germans. To do this he had to assure the Pope that he had indeed truly converted to Christianity and force was no longer necessary to persuade him to kiss the cross.

Indeed, Gediminas had struck a kind of *quid pro quo* with the Pope. In return for a pledge to restrain his over-pious German missionaries, who sent as many Lithuanians to the next world as they saved for this world as Christians, he assured the Pope that the Lithuanians were truly converted to Catholicism—late in Europe but finally convinced.

In 1323, he chose Vilnius* to be the capital of the country. Locating the spot, it was said, in a dream at the confluence of the Neris and Vilnele

* *Vilna* in Russian, *Wilno* in Polish, *Wilnos* in German.

9

rivers, Vilnius became, in the intervening centuries, a flourishing commercial crossroads for European trade but also a center of learning as well.

It was a time of expansion and conquest. At one point the Grand Duchy of Lithuania encompassed parts of *Rus*—of what is today's Belorussia, the Ukraine, Poland, and under Vytautas, the empire reached its furthest limits. It stood athwart the westward drive of the Mongols. For a time at least, it curbed the Germans by inflicting a major defeat on them at Grüenwald on July 18, 1410. By this defeat the Lithuanians were able to win back some lands and set up a more-or-less clear border between Lithuania and Germany, leaving Memel (Klaipeda) in the hands of the Germans.*

In 1447—still before the discovery of America—a new royal line appeared with the Grand Duke Kazimieras. Vytautas had died without leaving progeny. Kazimieras was clearly identifiable as the king of the boyars, whom he rewarded with grants of land and who, in turn, supported his claim to the Lithuanian throne. This was to include Poland where, in 1447, he moved to take up permanent residence. Wars were waged for more land, never enough to satisfy the appetites of the unappeasable boyars. With the acquisition—or the loss—of lands went the peasants as if they were the trees and stones, the unheralded, unconscious supernumeries in the struggles of the nobility. When they revolted—almost as a reflex action to their misery—they were attacked and suppressed mercilessly not only as traitors to their lords but as renegades to their faith. Their old god, Perkunas, had been overthrown and, with his ending, ended also that total unanimity between man and nature. The Christian, more explicitly, the Catholic God, now commanded the heavens.

The uses of religion had been quickly assimilated and understood by the boyars. God was automatically on the side of power—as he would return again on the side with the most cannon centuries later—and he was a stern God who invoked absolute obedience as defined by the Church.

All that the peasant uprisings achieved, besides death and devastation, was to force out of Zygimantas Augustas (1544-1572) a number of reforms, including an adjustment of grain deliveries somewhere near what the land worked by the peasant could actually produce. In addition, the time donated to the Lord (*Ponas*) as free labor was somewhat cut. But the question of just how big a single peasant's farm really was remained eternally in dispute. Attempts to measure it more accurately in order to determine more precisely how much tribute the peasant owed his lord often resulted in bitter quarrels and even bloodshed. The day of the surveyor, of those who could count and counted honestly, or counted dishonestly, had arrived and, indeed, would never leave the scene again. It was the lords who supervised

---

* It is this period—500 years ago—that is glorified in today's Lithuania where the medieval knights of that dim past are reincarnated in a setting of space travel and laser beams.

the measuring, and as in the American Southland, when it came to measuring the amount the serf produced, their arithmetic proved to be elastic; generous in the lord's favor, stingy in favor of the slave or peasant.

But whatever gains were won then, they were then and always short-lived. By the middle of the next century, peasants were once again giving their *Ponas* two free days of labor, with the rest of the time—whatever that was—their own. But later still, the two days expanded to six a week, with the one day Sunday when others could rest—when God rested—they could not.

And so set in the endless, unceasing, often underground warfare of poverty-stricken peasant against his Lord, which, as the Church itself became a holder of vast territory, against the Church, willy-nilly, as well. In fact, Church and landowners became one. Peasants would be punished in the church courtyard, where, as the years went by, the spires of the churches rose ever more splendidly to the sky from cathedrals whose magnificence rivaled the palaces of the Czars. State power and the power of the Church merged and continued in a tight embrace until modern times—until, in fact, 1939-40.

It is noteworthy that the peasant revolts always ended in defeat, with perhaps only some reforms conceded, but only on a tentative basis. These defeats confirmed the fact that, historically, peasants alone were incapable of winning power, as peasants, creating a specific "peasant society," for peasants in power became dukes and boyars and landowners themselves. The true liberation of the peasant had to wait until historically a working class could develop to the point where *they* could take power, and, unlike the peasants, indeed forge a new state, initiate a new civilization based on the new, relatively liberated relationship to the means of production that could now be feasible. Spartacus, the Roman slave, too, was foredoomed, for the liberation of Roman slaves in his time would have meant enslaving new peoples as they had once been. No other social alternative was historically available.

We sometimes dispose of the past by claiming that the pain and misery were, historically, inevitable, that progress demanded it, that where there was sweat there had to be blood. Sometimes we assure ourselves that just as the born deaf never miss sound, so those born in poverty and misery, knowing no other, never miss comfort and peace. Those living in squalor scorn clean clothes.... But the Lituanian peasant woman wept:

Who has heaped high
This lofty hill?
They are my sighs.

What little spring
Has formed this lake?
They are my tears...

Meanwhile, the oppressed were doomed to misery, early death, eternal poverty, blackest ignorance. History was not made by them, but by the "great men" in power. It was they who decreed that Lithuania and Poland would join together in one state on July 1, 1569, meeting in Lublin, Poland. That oxymoronic marriage between unassimilable states and peoples, forced by political circumstance, only bred endless distrust that continues to the present day.

The new state introduced the novelty of a king elected by the Polish and Lithuanian boyars who wielded power through the *sejm*, the parliament divided into two chambers, one seating the nobility and the other the bishops, governors and other eminent personalities. Lithuania, in this marriage, became a kind of lesser and more incompetent Poland—during which time the Lithuanian language fell into disuse, and became a kind of *patois* which only the peasants spoke, while Polish culture dominated the social scene. It is ironic, indeed, to note that the first Lithuanian catechism, called, in fact, the first Lithuanian book, published in Vilnius (then called Vilna) in 1595 was actually written in Polish. To learn Lithuanian one had to read Polish! As, later, under the Czars, one had to read Russian. Wrote the Lithuanian minister Dauksa, calling on the Lithuanian squires to publish the catechism in Lithuanian: "All of us see what scorn we have heaped on our own language!"[*]

All through its history, Lithuania (as well as Poland) would be oppressed by Prussia:

> Prussia, which was not a German region, had long before been a scene of activity of the Knights of the Teutonic Order. For a hundred years these "cur-knights," as Marx called them, waged a war of extermination against the native population, the Prussians. "By the end of the *thirteenth century*," said Marx, "this flourishing country bad been transformed into a wilderness; in place of village and cultivated fields—forests and quagmires; part of the inhabitants killed, part carried off, part forced to emigrate to Lithuania.... Where inhabitants were not exterminated, they were *enslaved*. The sacking of the towns and the ravaging of the countryside were the means of accomplishing the Germanization of Prussia, which was converted into a German military colony.
>
> The arrogant cur-knights began to apply their expansionist policy also to the contiguous Russian lands. But in the historic Battle of Lake Peipus, Alexander Nevsky, in 1242, routed the cohorts of the Teutonic Order which had invaded Russian territory, "as a result of which these reprobates were driven beyond the Russian frontier." When, at the beginning of the fifteenth century, the Teutonic Knights began to seize Polish and Lithuanian territory, the Slavonic people—the Poles, Russians, Ukrainians and Byelorussians, together with the Lithuanians—utterly routed these piratical hordes in the Battle of Tannenberg (Grünwald).[3]

Lithuanian Prussia however was lost forever and so was that branch of Lithuanian—Prussian Lithuanian—which today is studied as a dead language.

[*] As quoted in *The Daina, see* note 2.

WHEN LITHUANIA DISAPPEARED

"Great are the Crusaders' riches:
Spires of beaten gold
Grace the towers of their cities,
Silks their coffers hold.
I'll bring back a Prussian sword.
A silken scarf I'll bring..."
— Maironis–1903

Though Poland and Lithuania were united, it proved to be a marriage of convenience and not of love. Wars continued, most notably the 13-year war with Russia-Ukraine, until the Treaty of 1667. Before that, in 1655, Sweden, too, had made incursions into Lithuania and Poland.

This long devastating war was followed by still another war, this time between Sweden and Russia, into which Poland and Lithuania, still united as the Grand Duchy, were inevitably embroiled, since access to the Baltic seashore was one of the crucial issues. Indeed, Sweden seemed to be Lithuania's new permanent conqueror, but was ultimately defeated by the Russians in 1709 at Poltava. The Lithuanians followed this defeat with their own revolt against the Swedes whom they expelled from their country.

The Grand Duchy, in whose embrace Lithuania was almost smothered, nevertheless lasted for 500 years. In that period, the language almost perished, as indeed it did in Vilnius (Wilno) where Lithuanians made up only 2 percent of the city's population (1897). Only in the back regions of rural Lithuania among the illiterate peasants, the language persisted, ironically because the people were too uneducated to learn Polish or Russian or German but clung tightly to their own—not necessarily high or formal Lithuanian—but what was more typically a dialect. Prussian Lithuanian did perish. And, to all intents and purposes, so did Lithuanian in general, since the language did not appear in newspapers or books, and public affairs were conducted in Polish.

For many years, Lithuanians were never quite sure who they were—Lithuanian or Polish. After the publication of the Lithuanian catechism in Polish in 1595, it was still impossible for more than 500 years of Polish rule to publish any serious work in Lithuanian even if the subject dealt with Lithuania. What is factually the first history of Lithuania (1841) written by Teodor Narbutt was written in Polish. Adam Mickievicius, claimed both by Poland and Lithuania, was formally classified by birth as a Lithuanian but also wrote in Polish and his works, particularly his famous *Pan Tadeusz* (1894) whose setting is Lithuania, had to be translated into Lithuanian before Lithuanians could read it.

Wars bring plagues and famine with them. By 1709, a third of Lithuania's population had perished from both. Hardly had Lithuania made some recovery from so devastating a loss than civil war broke out into which the Russians, Prussians and Austrians intervened, plucking for themselves what territories suited them. So badly damaged was Lithuania, which was thus chopped up and distributed among the conquering powers, that its representatives sat for four years in the Sejm in Warsaw beginning in 1788 trying to decide what to do. The decision was once again to institute a monarchy, with certain changes in the powers of the delegates to the Sejm. But with the adoption of a new constitution Lithuania itself disappeared. Now only Poland existed.

Not until 1794, under the leadership of Taddeus Kosciusko (Lithuanian-born Pole) was Lithuania re-established and Vilnius recognized as its capital. But when the revolt of Jokubas Jasinkas was crushed that same year, Lithuania again was cut up, most of it becoming part of Czarist Russia, where it remained until modern times.

The following period in the history of the Baltic nations—spanning all of the 19th century—was characterized primarily by the fact that all were now incorporated into Czarist Russia and ceased to exist as specific nations. Their problems merged with the problems of the Russian oppressed. National liberation was most urgently felt, not by the bourgeoisie and landowners, who had adapted to Polish rule, but by the ordinary peasants and workers who had never lost their national characteristics. At times the Church was an ally in this yearning but an unreliable ally.

The Lithuanian language and native customs had almost disappeared between Polonization and Russification, although serfdom was not a Russian invention, but the general fate of all peasants in Europe and Asia. In feudal conditions the domination of the Catholic Church increased and finally became absolute. Nevertheless, simply by being Lithuanian the Church found itself the repository of what Lithuanian culture survived, the core of the language itself, and the remnants of historical memory.

However, though the destiny of the nation and the people was still being decided in the chambers of power where princes and kings held sway, by reading and listening to Lithuanian *dainos* of that period one can get a sense of the folk presence, of the voice of the voiceless. Most poignantly perhaps is the fact that most Lithuanian *dainos* were composed by the women and it is from their point of view that we see Lithuanian life.

Goethe was wrong in saying there were no cradle songs in Lithuanian. The Lithuanian mother sang as she rocked her child:

> *Maple groves within the garden*
> *Covered with green leaves.*
> *Underneath the little maple*
> *There is a little boy lying.*
> *Breeze is blowing up from eastward*
> *Breeze is blowing up from westward,*
> *Little breeze, blow softly,*
> *And don't waken my little boy.*

Or, she sang:

> *Choocha lioolia, little one,*
> *A-a-a-a, little one...*

But the typical day of a Lithuanian wife and mother left little time for cuddling children.

She awoke at 5 a.m. and fed the pigs, milked the cows and attended to the other farm animals. She then prepared her husband's and children's breakfasts. After cleaning up, doing laundry (by the river or stream) and attending to her children, she joined the other village women and together they worked at their weaving. They would sing together, the songs evolving according to the rhythm of the work....

At about noon, the wife prepared luncheon for the family. When many generations were part of the same household, all the women together were responsible for the feeding of all the men.

At about 4 p.m., the woman returned to her work at the loom until about 8 or 9 p.m. when supper was prepared. She then saw to the animals, put the children to bed and worked on her sewing and embroidering for the Lord. In the spring and summer she joined her husband in the Lord's field for several hours of work each night. She worked whether she was tired, ill or pregnant. In fact, many babies were born right on the field, often when no one was there to help her.[4]

They brought their infants with them to the field and there they lay wrapped in cloth, breast-fed by the mother from time to time, sleeping most of the day. They slept in their cradles only at night.

But if there are few cradle songs, there are many bitter songs of loss because of war. War, in these *dainos*, is always a calamity, producing only sorrow. *Varge! Varge!* (Woe! Woe!) As soon as boys were old enough to bear arms, they were conscripted into the Czar's army for an indefinite period—in fact, so long often, that they never saw home again.

> *Came a-flying*
> *A black crow*
> *Over the green meadow.*
>
> *—Hoi, crow, black crow,*
> *Hoi, you clever bird*

Where did you get
That little white hand with the gleaming ring?
—Over rivers,
Over seas,
A great battle raged...

There the water
Was congested
With young brothers.

There, more than
One mother mourns a son.

There, more than
One sister
Seeks her brother.

There, more than
One maiden
Sings of her lover...

And, the soldier, leaving home is questioned by his "maiden":

Where are you going,
My young fellow?
—To Paris hundreds of miles away...

Where will they bury you...
—Under the church tower.

For centuries the poor traveled to foreign lands only as instruments of conquest. They went to Paris, not to study, or to become an artist, but to die. What power tore the peasant lad out of his home village, from which up until then he had almost never wandered, and sent him to foreign lands? A great plow was plowing up Europe...

Nevertheless, incorporation into Russia brought Lithuania some benefits, primarily a nearby market for Lithuanian products. Lithuania's economy—as well as Latvia's and Estonia's—became interwoven with that of Russia proper, and, indeed, became identified with it in a single pattern—a fact of life which remains operative to this day, and which constitutes one of the objective factors that militate against forcible rupture.

In 1812, Napoleon, who admired St. Anne's church in Vilnius so much he longed to pick it up and take it home to Paris, began his ill-fated invasion of Russia, entering Russia through Lithuania—a route followed by the Kaiser and then by Hitler. But Lithuanians, too, resisted Napoleon whose revolutionary potential, which Beethoven had responded so fervently to, had spent itself. There was no liberating element left in his aim to conquer Europe. He made no attempt to enlist the peasantry on his side, just as Hitler made no such attempt, but plundered the country ruthlessly.

"War is the business of barbarians," he is credited with saying. His coming changed the status of Lithuania only insofar as he turned over part of her territory once again to Poland to become integrated into the Duchy of Warsaw.

The Napoleonic Wars inspired wars of independence all over Europe, inspired revolutions in France and Belgium, and uprisings in Poland and Lithuania. But these uprisings were foreshortened by class reality. Led by the aristocracy, the revolts were doomed in advance because they could not assure liberation from serfdom for the peasants. Nevertheless, feudalism itself was put on notice as the power of capitalism increased by leaps and bounds in England and France, and to a lesser degree in other countries of Western Europe. This period is rich in Russian culture which is inspired by the struggle for freedom—freedom from serfdom—in which the Decembrists played so heroic a role (1825). In the USA, where slavery (not yet serfdom) had been institutionalized for over 100 years despite the Declaration of Independence which declared that "all men are created equal," a truly liberating slogan for all but the American Blacks and Indians, it took a bitter civil war, in which over a million were killed, to resolve the contradiction between the fiction and reality.

All the uprisings, expressing peasant unhappiness, were but the preliminary stirrings of consciousness in the masses that a new era was waiting for them. Although the struggles of the peasants were also conducted under the slogans of liberty, fraternity and equality, the new economic system straining to be born would not grant those who fought for freedom the freedom they fought for.

Wars, foreign invasions, occupation, the presence of overlords to whom one was constrained to pay tribute—of *corvée*,"free" work, of goods, even the first night of one's bride—the reality of oppression as fate, the overwhelming pressure on one to accept himself as belonging to, and *deserved* belonging to, a lower order, were the dominant factors which molded the form of life for most peoples. There was no physical escape from it. Escape could only come in the imagination—in dreams.

Class divisions already existed, and the upper class not only did not deign to speak the common tongue but spoke Polish, Russian or French, and the common tongue was considered to be vulgar, too coarse to express the "finer" sentiments and thoughts of the nobility, and so not worthy of their care or attention. Over and over, through the annals of history of the Baltics, pleas to consider the language of the people as worthy of respect were raised, to be echoed by the most advanced intellectuals of the West, especially poets and artists and musicians who understood that the soul of the nation is to be found in its "common" people, and that soul is alive only in the native language.

Lithuania kept itself alive through its language. Speaking it, printing it, knowing it at all were considered evidence of subversion, and, indeed, every revolutionary in the Baltic countries raised as a fundamental condition for freedom the right of the language to be openly used by the people in its literature, schools, and discourse.

In this connection, the Catholic Church played a paradoxical role. Insofar as Catholicism was opposed to the orthodox Greek Catholic of the Czars it was, by that very fact, suspect as an expression not only of Vatican power but of Lithuanian nationalism. But the destiny of the Catholic Church was not to identify itself with the people, in the most fundamental sense of such an identity, but with the landlord class, of which it became itself a strong component—owning large tracts of land, buildings, businesses, and profiting from the labor of the serfs and workers. Seeking for allies, it found them among the oppressors of the Russian serfs—and struck up a *modus vivendi* with the Czar, after all. Thus, the struggle for liberation, which became finally a workers' struggle, inevitably found itself in conflict with the Church,* which put itself athwart the great liberating ideas of the 19th and later the 20th centuries.

By the beginning of the 20th century, we can begin to discern various of the elements that were interwoven in the pattern we recognize as the Lithuanian spirit. Survival was identified with possession of one's own language, the loss of which became even more poignant in periods of intense repression.

But the key elements in the character of the Lithuanian peasant—who, then, represented "the people"—were all contained in the poetry of the Lithuanian Luthern minister, Kristionas Donelaitis, born in what became known as East Prussia, in 1714, and who, in his epic poem, *The Seasons,* struck the chords of bitter lamentation and protest so familiar to the toiling peasant. But what was new was that he wrote the poem "in the peasant manner." He wrote "not in German, not in French" but in Lithuanian— which, in the first half of the 18th century was a remarkable affirmation of faith in the people, still years before both the French and American revolutions:

> *0, poor people, in your jacket patched with sheepskin,*
> *Who have watered borscht and plain potatoes for your meals*
> *Beggars, it would seem too poor for a gentleman's table*
> *Honored if you stand beside his chimney corner,*
> *And in felt shoes, his rich apartment, doff your caps.*
> *If some parasite smirks at you, don't feel ashamed!*
> *With his nose in the air, still he wears a stolen great coat,*

---

* *Popieziaus perkunavimas sutilo vien isjuokuma:* The curses of the Pope were turned into laughter—Folk saying.

In his gold perhaps the tears of orphans glitter.
Each day, as God knows, the sighs of women rise to heaven...

Before it is possible to recognize morally "the tears of orphans," or "the sighs of women," some glimmering of a different social system has to be present as a true alternative. The sense of justice is acquired historically and reflects the level of productive forces in society. Some still squirm at the connection between "justice" and "level of productive forces," but one remembers that the greatest philosophers and moralists of ancient Greece wasted no energy lamenting the fact of slavery (some individual slaves enjoyed a higher education and cultural consciousness than their masters) as long as they could see no social alternative to slavery. Thus, although the Lithuanian peasant saw in his life his ordained fate, and though he recoiled from suffering and pain, he could see no convincing alternative to the system which inflicted that pain upon him. In this sense, indeed, religion is the "sigh of the oppressed," for, at best, religion could promise escape from agony only through the door of death. "It is the opiate of the people," seen as a means of consolation, of how to endure misery, until the release of death to glory everlasting.

Only later, in the middle of the 19th century, did a more mundane exit to their fate seem to appear—emigration to America, where, it was promised, one could be "free," be one's own master.

The first printing press set up in Vilnius was established by Francisk Skorina in 1525. Intimations of the looming Reformation had begun to reach Lithuania and a university was established in 1579, with Jesuit monks as instructors.

Important dates in the history of Lithuania are 1410 when the Tuetonic Order was defeated at Tannenberg (Grünwald) and 1435 when the Livonian order was defeated at the Battle of Pabaisk, but probably the most important of these dates was 1385 when Jogaila (Jugiello) of the Gediminas dynasty was elected to the Polish throne and Lithuanians, up until then still pagan, were baptized as Roman Catholics. But it was not until 1570 that the first college of what would become Vilnius University was opened and, interestingly enough, the college was inaugurated with a Jesuit-sponsored debate in which the Jesuits challenged the supporters of the Reformation to debate Catholic doctrine with them. The college rose to university rank on July 7, 1578, later confirmed by King Steponas Batora on April 1, 1579. The university was planned to remain under Jesuit direction. This was all the more urgent because rival colleges under Protestant and Russian Orthodox churches were also planning to transform their colleges into universities, thus presenting the people with a choice.

Almost in spite of itself, the Jesuits' university grew, expanding, if gingerly, to meet the undeniable demands of science, whose development in Europe had proceeded apace. A university, by definition, deals with ideas, and even ideas that are to be refuted must however be stated. Thus students learned by reverse mirror-like process what the main intellectual currents of the times really consisted of. In fact, it was not possible to seal off Lithuania, particularly Vilnius, which became a commercial crossroads, from the rest of Europe, which seethed with rebellion. Rebellion finally threatened the Czar himself, and since many of the rebels were students, the university was shut down in 1831.

While Western Europe was throwing off the last fetters of feudalism, only Czarist Russia seemed not only to maintain but to cherish them. Russia became the great reserve of European reaction. Nevertheless, the march of liberating ideas, emanating from France, but also from America, could not be stopped. Still, for ideas to take hold, the material conditions which give them plausibility must first develop and ripen. Czarist Russia also felt the first tugs of those forces that had been let loose in England, and had supplied the means and ideas which had established England—that tight little island—into the strongest power on earth and certainly on the seas. Capitalism pulled at Russia and found its most profound obstacle to growth in the existence of serfdom. For capitalism to flourish it must have free workers—that is, free of the land. These workers are themselves shaped by the demands of industry, which works with machinery, with steam, and other complicated and involved processes which could not be comprehended much less complied with by the ignorant peasant. The first quality which distinguished the new worker—the *first* worker—was the fact that he needed to know how to read. His second distinction was his new relationship to *time*. The introduction of profit as a power in itself, as the source of social dynamism, is measured in terms of time, and profit (so to speak) put a price on time itself. If the peasant needed to know no more than that the sun rose and set, that the seasons came and went, and that his life was measured by their rising and setting, their coming and going, now, as a worker, he had to know that a working day did not follow the sun but the artificial measure of time—the clock. The clock took no notice of day or night. The worker had to get up by the clock, work by the clock, eat and sleep by the clock. His labor was evaluated, not by the sum of his efforts in general—in a harvest—but by how much he produced in a certain specific time period. Machines operated according to time schedules, and the worker had to set his physical processes according to time (being assigned precisely the time he had to eat, for his bowels to move, and when to die). He became an adjunct to the machine which ended by dominating him entirely, and he became "a fragment of a man...an appendage of the machine, destroying every remnant of charm in his work and turning it into a hated toil."[5]

But, at the same time, being congregated together in cities, and at work, in factories, mills or mines, and confronted by the same employer power, the worker also gradually became conscious not only of the power of his master but of his own latent power. He could not escape noticing, as he grew more sophisticated, and having been forced by the needs of his job to learn how to count, add and subtract, multiply and divide, that his labor produced a profit for his employer, but that, on the other hand, his payment for producing a profit for his employer fell far short of the value of what he had produced. We shall hear more of this historical discovery (which every child understands today but which took mankind an enormous effort to comprehend). But, at this point in the progress of mankind—the main burden of which would more and more be assumed by the working class—driving the peasant off his land into the towns where he labored inside foul-smelling and unhealthy buildings was seen as a monumental tragedy. In England, Oliver Goldsmith lamented:

> Ill fares the land, to hast'ning ills a prey
> Where wealth accumulates and men decay...
>
> A time there was, ere England's grief began,
> When every rood of ground maintain'd its man...
>
> But times are alter'd; trade's unfeeling train,
> Usurp the land and dispossess the swain...
>
> Ah, turn thine eyes
> Where the poor houseless shiv'ring female lies,
> She once, perhaps, in village plenty bless'd,
> Has wept at tales of innocence distressed;
> Her modest looks the cottage might adorn...
> Now lost to all; her friends, her virtue fled,
> Near her betrayer's door she lays her head,
> And, pinch'd with cold, and shrinking from the shower,
> With heavy heart deplores the luckless hour
> When idly first, ambitious of the town,
> She left her wheel and robes of country brown.[6]

The city was seen as the destruction not only of the peasant and yeoman but of the system of values, replacing the simplicity and, therefore, the virtue of a life in which man communed directly with nature, through God as an intermediary, with an altogether demonic imprisonment in airless cells chained to machines, to which were also sacrificed one's wife and children, and from which one could hope to be released only by an early and welcome death.

However, in the grim development of history, this movement from the land to the city is seen as progressive, if still in the paradoxical sense that progress, in general, rewards only the few and reserves misery for the many. In any case, once begun, the momentum could not be halted. And even in Czarist Russia, the force let loose in England from James Watt's (1736-1819) steaming kettle could not be caged. Serfdom had had its day. Serfs could not run machines geared to a time that had been meticulously divided into measured pieces that now functioned objectively as a force impelling man's energies. On February 19, 1861, serfdom was abolished in Russia. Simultaneously, a bitter civil war broke out in America—"the land of the free"—in the course of which the slaves were freed (also a gigantic act of expropriation of *property*) so that American industry could have available for its use the freed slave, now perhaps newly enslaved in a new kind of bondage but who at least was *theoretically* "free." Even as his individuality was being erased as he became lost in the anonymous masses of the working class, the concept of the individual as being the supreme worth of society, nevertheless became rooted in the general understanding of men. This led to the further concept, revolutionary in essence, and leaning on the belief that man was qualified to make fundamental judgments about his society, that if men must be governed, it must be only with their consent. Surrendering their individual will to the state, to the mass, had to be a voluntary act—or at least seen as an overriding necessity (in wartime, in moments of great national crisis, etc.) and, through it all, the sovereignty of the individual had to be cherished if only in prayers and dreams.

The idea that social power couldn't be usurped in the name of God or tradition, ownership of land, property, money, etc., and arrayed against the common man, confronting him as fate, grew slowly and painfully and remains a dream still for most of mankind.

Nevertheless, it existed. That the all-powerful Czar was forced by powers more mighty than he, more mighty than the God in whose name he ruled, was not lost on the common people, in whom myths and superstitions lingered stubbornly long after their viability as answers to unsolved questions had passed. In Russia, the liberated peasant could now sell his labor power freely, but his freedom did not extend to acquiring the means of ensuring his freedom. Land was not free. Seed was not free. Markets were not in his control. To work the land, he had to bind himself "freely" to his old masters, and the difference in his status before and after emancipation seemed, to many, to be worse not better. At least, before, the landlord was obliged to give him food and shelter. Now the landlord could turn him out of home and deny him food when he was ill, or worse—when the crops, because their market price had fallen, could not pay for his food and shelter. Similarly, the laborer discovered that when he worked he didn't earn enough to keep himself when he did not work. If before, calamity was the direct result of drought, of too much water, of crop failures, and therefore "understandable," now calamity arrived from mysterious sources, out of the machinations of unknown strangers, whose manipulations in the "market" followed laws that could not be confirmed in nature. A bumper crop logically spells abundance. But "on the market" it could be a calamity. It could cause (how?) the fall of prices and the farmer could begin to starve in the midst of plenty. *Scarcity* is what the market yearned for!

LITHUANIA STIRS AGAIN

Lithuania! Invaded by enemies dread
You must be like the hydra which, losing one head
At once grew five others instead...

— *To My Compatriots*, by Vincas Kudirka, (1858-99).

One concludes, from the meager historical evidence that is extant, that the shift from a nomadic, hunting era when men roamed the forests and sailed the seas (though hugging the shores) and had no stable home, to the era of fixed habitations, was a psychologically traumatic one. We know that when man discovered that he could find greater security in raising crops and domesticating animals, keeping both in one place and under control, he willingly surrendered his nomadic way of life and settled into one place. But in that shift, he began to enter a new historical period that would transform him as he transformed his environment. American Indians, still nomad, were not only perplexed but shocked at the white man's drive to *own* things—land. How could you own the land, which belonged to everybody? they asked. What *kind* of human being is it that must *own* things?

Identifying security and survival with a *place*—with land—which matured early in the history of man, is surely the source of nationalism and patriotism—two faces of the same coin. In the beginning, where one raised one's crops and husbanded one's domestic animals was where one took one's existence. To remain in the place where one had prospered—at least acquired enough food and shelter to survive—was eminently logical. The process by which identity with a particular place developed into identity with what one accepted as one's country—nation—is what history tells us took place and why.

But when did a natural identity and love of one's source of livelihood and survival develop into that monstrous aberration, *nationalism*, which elevated ownership of land as proof of one's natural superiority over others simply because one *was*? History has been tight-lipped about how this transformation took place, but we know now that when land became property and had both a use and exchange value, as *capital*, it lost its original, even innocent (historically speaking) role and function. Wars of conquest became wars not merely to augment one's own territory but to increase one's wealth. Patriotism, a legitimate feeling, became distorted into its caricature—nationalism. Nevertheless, even in extreme nationalism, its faraway origin in the need to survive, and *only* to survive, can be detected.

But today, nationalism—the extreme nationalism especially of small nations—is objectively absurd. No small nation supports itself or can support itself by its own production. If it lacks oil, it lacks freedom. If it lacks access to the sea, it is "locked." If it cannot grow corn and wheat enough, it must buy them on the market or find satisfying substitutes. It cannot dictate the price of its own labor, but must accept the price put on it by foreign, i.e., powerful nations. Planes cross entire countries in minutes. Looking down on those patches of land with names and histories lovingly preserved by the natives, one is struck at how quickly they lose their distinctive character and become part of the massive contour of the continent itself. From a space rocket, they disappear entirely. Only by coincidence does nature follow political boundaries. She distributes forests and mountains, lakes and seas according to her own laws. She has no real barriers, not even seas and mountains. And she ignores man-made barriers on top of the land with her enormous "faults" along which speed gigantic powers convulsing the oceans and shaking the land, with no reference to social systems anywhere. It is man who carves up areas of land, erects barriers between trees on this side and trees on that side, giving a name to the trees on that side which is different, and often hostile, to the trees on this side.

And yet, as we've seen, the struggle for precisely that distinction, that land, in which one was born and which nourished one, is almost as old as mankind itself.

Nevertheless, with the onset of the 19th century, communities settled for centuries began to stir. Tied to the "mother land," reared with a sense of ultimate identity with it—culturally, with one's language, often with physical likeness to one another so that one could distinguish between a dark Italian and a blonde Swede—millions of people left their birth places and went elsewhere to live out their lives and raise their children—mainly to the USA.

An ordinary person does not easily pull up his roots and set out, for all practical purposes blindly, for an unknown land. He needs a powerful spur—poverty, war, oppression. The great emigration from Europe to America in the 19th century followed by a couple centuries the forced emigration of tens of thousands of Africans in chains. Europeans came to America without visible chains, but chained they were nevertheless, into wage slavery.

The entire period spanning the second half of the 19th century was characterized by internecine struggles taking many forms in Europe, but the end, never realized, but glimpsed in dreams, in utopian fancies, always involved attaining some greater degree of freedom—that is, power over one's own life. In Lithuania, a peasant uprising broke out in February, 1863. This uprising achieved a level of consciousness and/or organization that all previous uprisings had lacked. This one had a specific goal: the peasants wanted to break the legal bond tying them to the landlord. Defeated by the Czar's army at Gudiskia, in May, the rebellion continued stubbornly but by 1864, it was crushed.

Nevertheless, in the struggle itself, which was supported actively by the ordinary peasants, a consciousness that their struggle was at the same time a struggle for human liberation in general took on a wider and deeper scope than ever before. It domestically was a struggle against the rule of the boyars. In the spirit of the times, this struggle was seen as a blow for human—all human—freedom. But it accomplished only minor reforms, including the lowering of the price of land. But the consciousness that it had not been limited to merely fighting to lower the price of land but to liberating mankind as a whole did not escape the peasants, or at least their most sophisticated leaders.

Although in theory, buying land was within the reach of an industrious and lucky peasant who saved, borrowed, or even stole money to buy it, in actual fact he was able to buy less than 20 acres, or hardly enough to support much more than a garden. With only this, he remained still at the mercy of the landowner who established the price of crops, extended or didn't extend credit, bought or didn't buy what the independent peasant produced at a price the independent peasant could not control. In the relentless logic of economics, even those peasants who enjoyed a momentary independence had eventually to mortgage or sell their lands, which wound up in the hands of the landowners, or usurers, where they had originally been before. It was theoretically possible for a peasant to buy up additional land, and thus himself become a rich landlord, but a practical impossibility.

The "liberated" peasants without land became proletarians, who were not yet workers, but who went from town to town offering their labor at the prevailing price for odd and seasonable work. The ex-peasant commuted between the town and country, being at home in neither. He worked for the landowner on a seasonable basis and worked in town for the factory owner when factories were working. But the price of his labor was never set by him but by his employer. His employer, too, complained that prices were not set by him but by mysterious forces commanding "the market." Maxim Gorky drew the plight of the homeless proletarian whose equivalent in the USA was the "emancipated" Black slave sent on the labor market after the end of the Civil War, 1865—unforgettably in many of his short stories and particularly in his play, *Lower Depths.*

Nevertheless, the second half of the 19th century saw the worldwide advance of capitalism which, with the great leap forward in new technology, marked by the harnessing of steam, overwhelmed the western world. The advent of the railroad—a creature of steam—accelerated the internationalization of capital as it extended the boundaries of the world market, and brought into existence the phenomenon of international finance capital with its unforeseen but revolutionary consequences. With economic power no longer confined to national boundaries, with the world, or at least the western world, mainly confined to Europe, no longer bound to a subsistence level of industry and agriculture, and with production of raw material and finished products, now spurring each other, dramatically rising, added to by outright plunder like Spain of Mexico, a huge capital surplus was accumulated in the hands of a few entrepreneurs in a few countries (Western Europe, then the USA, and ultimately Japan). Such capital was not inert—to lie in banks as solid gold. This capital was enormously restless and, inspired by an inner necessity sought only to multiply, and indeed, and not too slowly, developed a greed that would devour everything before it—whole countries, even continents. The great cities, the civilization we now hail, were no more than a by-product of this insatiable greed, which at its apogee seemed to prevision those later hypnogogic monsters out of the deep that devoured or destroyed everything in their path for no other reason except their demonic need. As we know, millions would be sacrificed to this Mammon, this half-mad god, at whose bloody altar the entire human race seemed (when the atom bomb appeared) to be an inevitable sacrifice.

In any case, its power was awesome and escaped the confines of hitherto accepted human morality. *Crime* became declassified in the anonymous working-out of economic "laws" which, though they committed enormous havoc, misery and danger, possessed no human agent who could be "blamed," could be stigmatized in terms of human, individual crime. It became a commonplace among the people that it was a crime only to steal little; no crime to steal big. It was a crime to kill your neighbor, not a crime to kill unknown neighbors in huge impersonal wars. *Business* established the social rules patterned on its own necessity.

The point is that this enormous power—this Golem-Mammon set loose on the world—seemed to be in the uncertain hands of men who, from every point of view but one, were intellectual and moral lilliputians. The one respect in which they transcended all others was in the size of their financial appetites. Even so, they had no real control over the monster they helped bring into existence. That monster had escaped their clutches.

Railroads entering and leaving one's country raised the question of borders, for railroads cut through mountains and crossed impassable rivers, and thus jeopardized the unity of nation and geography, which had helped identify and characterize nations hitherto. Doing commerce with other nations, allowing their vehicles to penetrate one's borders, forced a certain modification of sovereignty—the foreign business partner had to be assured rights in your land. The internationalization of capital began invisibly to erode the integrity of national states, and in due course, the spread of capital across all borders and through all states made more and more obsolete national borders, whose persistence was due more to tradition and even nostalgia, than to necessity. True, separate states continued to perform certain functions in the international division of labor that remained valid. But more and more often the world seemed to be the domain for tourists, who visited foreign climes to view the exotic, while cashing in their travelers checks in a bank in New Delhi or Peking or even Lhasa as easily and conveniently as they did in New York, Paris or London. And strictly for the delectation of the tourists, the natives doffed their normal suits and hats and put on costumes, sang folk songs and did native dances—then went home and turned on their radios to listen to rock and roll or went out to a cafe to dance the twist or hully-gully.*

For Lithuania—which also celebrated holidays when the "natives" dressed up in Old Folks costumes and sang folk songs and danced folk dances, which the city-raised young had to be particularly taught—the advent of capitalism in Russia meant an increased demand for her agricultural products, and for the raw materials she produced to service the industries of other countries.

But capitalism itself also made its appearance in Lithuania. By century's end, Vilnius counted 157 industries with 4700 workers. Kaunas, the second major city, had 2000 workers. Ultimately, half of the population of the big cities in Lithuania could be classified as belonging to the working class. Nevertheless, farming remained dominant, and mainly dairy farming—though by 1900 there were some 400,000 farm hands working for wages or being paid in kind or as sharecroppers.

Thus, along with the spread of capital and the birth of modern industry, not only did a modern capitalist class appear but so did the modern working class. Everything comes into existence bringing along its negation, however disguised or embryonic. Being disinherited as peasants, the class that had nothing to sell but its labor power felt no instinctive bond either to the land, where many had been born, nor to the town or city in which they were driven to seek work. Their roots to the land were cut and, essentially, once again they became nomads, moving from place to place—

---

* It's remarkable how this dance—the hully-gully—spread all over the world, although it originated on New York's Fire Island and was characterized by couples dancing without touching one another because the dance, originated by homosexuals, would have broken the law if male had danced with male. But who knew that in Vilnius?

and even country to country—looking for work. Their "country" became the place where they found a job. (Millions to this day leave their homes to travel to foreign lands to work, where they exist as transients on sufferance, at the same time that they no longer fully identify with the village in which they were born.)

Replacing, and eventually joining, the landowner as direct exploiter was now the factory owner, who in turn owed allegiance to a class of financiers whose tentacles reached all over the world. As we know, in the very nature of things, the factory owner (and financier behind him) did not confine himself merely to matters directly concerning the factory. Too many forces had been let loose in the world which could ruin him—and it was essential to his survival that his interests be safeguarded and nurtured by some force outside his own means—i.e., the state. Indeed, before long the interests of the state, which was supposed, at least in theory, to represent the interest of the entire people, coincided with and became one with the interests of the capitalists. If Louis XIV could claim that *he* was the state, eventually General Motors could also claim that "what helped General Motors helped the country." The state became identical with capital. The historical substance of nationalism had been supplanted by a new substance—which more and more totally filled up the content of the state that had been systematically emptied of its former substance. States became more and more hollow shells fronting for a power that dared not advertise itself. Kings and parliaments remained but state decisions were made increasingly and as a matter of course in the board rooms of corporations rather than in the cabinet rooms of countries, which often were interchangeable in any event. (Most Presidential cabinets of the USA are nothing but the duplicates of corporation board rooms.)

Thus the national character of a country tended to be diminished and "realized" more and more through its costumes, songs, language, manners—attractive to tourists—than in its actual power, which had become internationalized. Who has not seen, as a tourist, American Indians dressed in Indian war-dress, hawking beads and blankets from roadside stands, the once proud faces of bygone warriors hardly visible in their faded and defeated expressions, and even the memory of their pasts totally obliterated by Hollywood where, if lucky, they could get a day's work mimicking an Indian?

It was inevitable, in the progress of history, that the state should become the instrument of finance capital and do its bidding. Through the power of the state, not only could commerce be adjusted to the needs of finance capital but the state could also regulate and control the supply of labor.

With the state—in particular the Czarist state—presumably representing the people as a whole, it had the power to suppress labor and peasant discontent in the name of defending the national interests. "National interests" were, in practice, the interests of the upper ruling class.

Lithuanian economic power was divided between the capitalist entrepreneurs in the cities and the rich landlords in the countryside. Significantly, in the cities where wealth was concentrated and immediately available through banks, as liquid venture capital, foreign speculators also had access to it, and it tended to fall into the hands mainly of Germans but also of Jews. The land itself remained in the hands of Lithuanian landowners, on the whole, though not exclusively.

By the last half of the 19th century, the working classes as we know them in the modern sense, had made their appearance. But they came on the scene unrecognized as what they ultimately became—a threat to entrenched power. The working class emerged out of the sea of disinherited peasants, bankrupted handicraftsmen, and de-classed clerks and small businessmen. The arcane workings of economics had produced them. In their early form of *proletarians*—as Rome knew them—they were a mass of the disinherited, of ex-slaves, out of whom petty criminals emerged, who lived by their wits, and who were kept in order with "bread and circuses." They consumed but did not produce. They drained the resources of society. They were courted by would-be dictators who used them as mobs to gain power.

Balzac who saw the future demise of the bourgeoisie even as they replaced royalty could not see, in Paris' *sans-culottes*, the future "stormers of heaven" that Marx would live to see. Few in Balzac's day saw anything but tragedy in the proletarianization of the peasantry. Nevertheless, by 1848, not only had the explanation for their appearance and their role in history been recorded but the rationale for their existence and the function they were to play in history was outlined with devastating logic by two men whose names would forever be connected with the history of the working class from thence on forward—Karl Marx and Friedrich Engels. And their declaration of human rights was titled *The Communist Manifesto*.

By the turn of the century most of the world had been parceled out to a few great powers—chiefly Britain, France, Spain. Hurriedly, the USA took what it could just as the century ended—the Philippines, Cuba, some Carribean islands, Puerto Rico. It had already through the Monroe Doctrine (1823) posted No Trespassing signs on all of Latin America, which it reserved for itself. Indeed, for those latecomers on the world scene—Japan, Germany, Italy—there seemed to be no colonial pie left to carve up. It had all been taken. And if one wanted some of it for one's self, one had to take it from those who already possessed it. Futile attempts to do just that by military might consumed the energy and lives of millions of ordinary Japanese, Germans and Italians for the next almost hundred years. With few results. The map of the world remained relatively the same until WWII.

If WWII proved that the world could not be re-carved in the old-fashioned imperialist way, it also proved something else that was even more dramatic. Such carving-up was no longer necessary. Instead of obtaining markets, piece by piece, the whole world became one market, and to exploit the workers and peasants of Brazil or Indonesia it was no longer necessary to occupy these countries with tanks, but with computers. Economic power knew no borders. It penetrated and bound millions of human beings to one source, to which they paid fealty, more effectively than whole armies could.

Ideas precede deeds, but are born of the deeds that preceded *them*. Preliminary to the battles on the barricades are the battles in men's minds, often conducted on terrain as bloodless as cafes and coffee houses normally are, in fueilltones made of only paper, on lecture lecterns that hold only a glass of water, or on street corners, or wherever men gather and think. In (Polish) Vilna, the young Adam Mickievicius joined the Philomaths, founded in Vilinius in 1817, or the lovers of learning, dedicated to regenerating their homeland through service to the "Fatherland, Learning and Righteousness."

In 1848, heading a delegation of Poles to Rome, Mickievicius would take hold of the Pope's hand and cry: "Know that today the spirit of Christ is to be found in the humble garb of the common people of Paris."

Swept along by the revolutionary tides of Europe, which seemed to have their source in Paris, Mickievicius, though seeing in Poland an instrument for the revolutionary liberation of Europe, nevertheless refracted in his own personality and writings the main forces in contention on the continent. Born in what was then Polish Lithuania, and having studied in Vilnius, his great epic poem, *Pan Taduez*, celebrates the life of the Lithuanian peasant (which he both romanticized and described with unerring realism) but in whose spirit he himself continued his own struggle, eventually espousing socialism as he understood it.

"Modern socialism" he would write in 1849, one year after the publication of the *Communist Manifesto*, "is only a manifestation of a feeling as old as life itself, a manifestation of sensing that which in our life is incomplete, cut off, abnormal and consequently unhappy. The socialist feeling is the spirit's aspiration towards a better existence, not individual but in common..."[7] He cried:

> *Litva, my country, like art thou to health,*
> *For how to prize thee, he alone can tell*
> *Who has lost thee....*

Exile, emigration, the last half of the 19th century and to 1914 would witness 253,000 Lithuanians leave their homeland, driven by famine, wars, oppression, and reconstitute "little Lithuanias" in widely separated parts of the world—Australia, Argentina, Canada, the USA—*Neturin kur galvos priglausti*, I have nowhere to lay my head.

In their homeland, which existed incognito, they resisted, rose, and always fell. In 1863, the Czar finally crushed what he had reason to hope was all resistance and the spirit to resist. The teaching of Lithuanian was forbidden in the schools and banned was the publication of all books and periodicals in the native language. Again, the spirit of resistance could be preserved only in the language itself, which being forbidden officially, became the vehicle through which Lithuanians kept their sense of nationhood alive.

Despite the banning of Lithuanian—or perhaps because of it—Lithuanian poets and writers were stirred to express their opposition to Czarist oppression by persistently writing in the forbidden language, bringing to the surface such writers as Bishop Antanas Baranauskas; the remarkable peasant woman, who started to write only at the age of 50, Julia Zemaite; Vincas Kurdirka and the poet Jonas Maironis and others. Since the efforts of Lithuanians alone could not overthrow the Czar, the hopes of Lithuanian revolutionaries—or just dreamers of liberty—coincided with the struggle of the Russian workers and peasants themselves. It was understood that liberation of Lithuania would come on the same dish as the liberation of Russia itself.

Strike after strike broke out in Lithuania's main cities. The amorphous, ungainly and unfocused mass of proletarians began to find a focus at last in their common struggle for their rights. Working hours were long and working conditions inhumane. Women and children worked long hours as well. In 1861, 45 stone-cutters who worked for the railroad went on strike, holding out for three weeks. In the end, their strike was broken by the Czar's police and both leaders and workers were jailed—and whipped. Later strikes broke out in Vilnius by the tobacco workers (1871) and metal workers (1874) in Kaunas, resulting in modest concessions from the employers—but concessions, nevertheless. The first farm workers' strike was in 1883. Marxist books appeared in 1883-84, spread by the Liberation of Labor group.

In light of the later history of Lithuania, it is important to note that Vladimir Lenin first appeared in Vilnius in 1895 and sought to connect the Lithuanian Social Democrats with the Russian Association for the Liberation of the Working Class of Russia proper. Thus, revolution was possible—in Lenin's view—only when all forces of Czarist Russia united into one organization. Significantly, Lenin failed to achieve that end in Lithuania at that time. Lithuanian stubbornness, long recognized as a Lithuanian national trait, managed to frustrate even Lenin, even as it would later manage to frustrate Gorbachev.

As far back as the late 1890s, the Lithuanian exceptionalists insisted that liberation could be won by the Lithuanians alone, in this idea sharing the one-eyed view of politics typical of the Jewish *Bund*, which also chose to go it alone. Unity of the two parties—Bolshevik and Lithuanian Social Democratic—would not take place until the revolutionary upsurge of 1917–18, helped to attain that unity by such outstanding revolutionaries as Felix Derzhinski and others.

FIRST SUCCESSES

A forbidden way they show
To the joy we long to know...
Poppies flourish in my heart,
Ever brighter red they are...
          —*Red Poppies*, by Liudas Gira

The hundred days of the Paris Commune in 1871, when the French communards again "stormed heaven," was like the flare of a struck match that lasted but for a moment in the night of European oppression. It was drowned in blood. But History is frugal, and no experience is so totally negative, so hopelessly lost, so bleakly sterile that the people cannot glean at least a grain of useful knowledge from it. Just as matter cannot be abolished but only transformed, so the experience of the people cannot be abolished but only transformed. European socialism read the bloody script written by the Communards and drew proper conclusions. The prime lesson that Marx and later Lenin would learn in the defeat was the absolute need of the working class to forge its own weapon in the shape of its own party of a different type. Only today is this lesson, and conclusion, being questioned as having spent itself.

Marx and Engels had their French 100 days. Lenin had his Russian revolution of 1905. It was this latter event that had the most explosive effect on Russian history. It came directly on the heels of the ignominious defeat of the Czar's navy, exposing for the whole world to see the inner weakness and social obsolescence represented by the Czarist oligarchy. That the Russian colossus could be brought to its knees by Japan, militarily untested up until that moment in major combat, was a profound humiliation as well as a national tragedy. As always, the perpetrators of the calamity escaped with no penalties. Only the people paid—some 400,000 Russians who were killed, wounded or taken prisoner. Russia's defeat also announced the appearance on the world scene of another ambitious and growing imperialism in Japan, which had already tried out its powers in a war with China in 1894-1895, beginning an unending war of attempted conquest that would continue for a good part of the following century. (Japan would acquire Korea and Manchuria.)

Though the monarchy continued as before, still the truth could not be hidden. The war with Japan had ended in *defeat*, and such defeats are not

34

only public proof of the weakness of the state, or the class embodied in tl power of the state, but of the state's supporters and beneficiaries as well— the Church, the intelligentsia, of the landlord class. It was clear even to the most ignorant peasant that in such a defeat not only lay proof of the weakness of the system, but of God himself. If the Czar's god, whose power the Czar invoked, could not prevail over the Japanese (Shinto) god, then indeed Czarism stood naked before the people. Even Tolstoy challenged the Czar's god.

Frightened by the reaction of the people to the monumental defeat, the Czar began to make those very concessions he had spurned before. In Lithuania, for instance, he lifted the ban against printing books and periodicals in the Lithuanian language. But by then the people had moved beyond demanding the mere right to speak and read Lithuanian. When the Czar drowned the demonstration of 150,000 in St. Petersburg in blood on January 9, 1905—some 1000 were killed outright and a thousand more injured—"Bloody Sunday," became the by-word for Czarist tyranny and a rallying cry for revolution.*

Those who have blanked out the revolutionary history of the Lithuanian working class cannot "remember" that all Lithuania was ablaze with horror and anger at the news of "Bloody Sunday" and protests, "sympathy" strikes, broke out in all the cities of Lithuania, as well as in Latvia and Estonia, and, even more significantly, farm hands in the big country estates also joined in with their city brothers. It was not lost upon even the backward, superstition-ridden peasant that the St. Petersburg demonstrators were led to the slaughter by Father Georgi Gapon, who persuaded them that their complaints would be heard by their "father," the Czar. The Czar had instead fled the capital for his country residence, and left his "children" to the mercy of the guns.

Now, we hear the name "Bolshevik" for the first time. For it was the "Bolsheviks" of the Social-Democratic party, which had its contingent in Lithuania, that supplied the leadership and direction of the strikes. In Lithuania, the principle strike leader was Vincas Kapsukas, whose name would be associated thenceforth with the revolution in Lithuania.

All over Russia, the spirit of rebellion spread, involving at its height some 2 million workers—an unprecedented outpouring, and most impressive of all, a vivid demonstration of the fact that the working class had entered history in a dramatic and convincing form, exhibiting a conscious-

---

* "Bloody Sunday" was a monstrous act of provocation. Father Gapon, on whose assurance that the Czar would listen to them, led the demonstrators straight into the trap previously set for them. Later, it was learned Father Gapon was a police spy for the Czarist Ohkrana and a provocateur.

ness of its own power and revolutionary potential never seen or felt before by so many.

On January 10, 1905, five strikers were killed by the Vilnius police and 30 wounded. Their funeral drew a vast moving sea of 40,000 mourners, who expressed in their silent march a determination that was all the more terrifying to the Czarist forces because of its restraint.

So terrified, in fact, was the government that it issued a proclamation promising political reforms and greater democratic concessions than ever before. Although the movement did not stop at reforms in Russia itself, in Lithuania the momentum of the revolution which would have carried the people to complete victory, starting with the overthrow of Czarism itself (which had to wait 12 more years), was deflected by a combination of bourgeois forces and—as charged by the Bolsheviks—those forces within the Lithuanian Social Democratic Party that opposed the Bolshevik wing.

In any case, much was gained. Perhaps what was most lastingly gained was the realization the people now possessed as an ideological fact—having seen themselves in massive movement throughout the country—that real power lay in their hands and not in the throne. This realization spurred critical revisions and restructuring in the ideas of the intellectuals, which was reflected in literature, art and even music—with the opening of the first Lithuanian theater, which produced the opera *Birute*. Books now in Lithuanian poured off the printing presses. Bold inquiries into Lithuanian history, tradition, culture began to be made. Hearing themselves speak Lithuanian to each other openly on the streets, in schools, theater, etc., intoxicated the Lithuanians with the miracle of speech restored.

Lithuanian consciousness rose to a level it had never reached before. But what distinguished this awareness from all previous attempts to kindle Lithuanian consciousness was the new, overwhelming fact that it was spurred by revolution—by the masses come to consciousness as a power. Nationalism was defined by working class power.

WORLD WAR I

There I saw for the first time
How troops go off to war...
          — Julius Janonis, 1896-1917

One of the prime liberties which bourgeois-democratic societies point to with pride is the granting of suffrage. Never, it is true, certainly in the beginning, is it *universal* suffrage. Always, it is hemmed in with sometimes paralyzing restrictions. Property qualifications, educational requirements, payment of a poll tax, residential requirements, age, race—and most notoriously—sex: all to larger or greater extent limited, or even denied totally, the right to vote to large sections of the population. Women, for instance, did not win the right to vote until comparatively recent times in most countries. African-American people in the USA were not allowed to vote for centuries, and are hampered to this day. And so on.

Nevertheless, winning suffrage, even limited suffrage, was no small thing in itself, and marked a great advance in the general struggle for human rights. With suffrage, at least the principle was established, if observed more often only in the breach, that the consent of the governed was required before a nation could justly be ruled. Positive as that was, nevertheless suffrage gave rise to many illusions: the one, for instance, that the people *would* be allowed to nominate and choose freely their own representatives to speak and act for them in parliament or congress. But practice soon showed that it was quite possible to control the election process almost as surely as though none existed.

In the case of Russia, however, the euphoria that followed acquisition of the (limited) right to vote was brief. The 1905 revolution forced the Czar to allow the people to participate in elections to the Duma, and indeed a number of Left deputies were elected to the Duma. But even though the Duma had restricted powers to govern—actually, none at all—the new Duma brought into existence by the expanded suffrage of 1906 panicked the Czar. He promptly dissolved it, and the following one as well, sending all the Social Democratic deputies to Siberia, thus inaugurating a period of intense reaction, under the leadership of Prime Minister Stolypin, whose repressive measures were noted for their cruelty. Actions were taken against the peasants, forcing them to move out of villages and to set up

37

homes on what land was available. Most could not manage such a shift, and unable to make the move, they sold their land back to the kulaks who had owned it all to begin with. Thus, the absolute monopoly of land under kulak power moved ahead rapidly.

Lithuania was part of Russia. And what happened in Russia happened in Lithuania. More and more visibly, Lithuania was becoming a peasant country whose land, however, was not owned by the peasants but by the rich landlords. Along with Lithuanian landlords we must note the phenomenon of German barons, protected by the Czar, a bastion of absolute reaction, whose power existed in a real way until it was ended by the 1917 revolution, or rather, only scotched. Its real end came in 1940-45.

In this conscious attempt to remake Lithuania as a peasant land construction of factories and industries came to a halt. Only small factories were built—one of them in Kaunas, opened up by the Germans Schmidt and Tilmannis, employing 1300 workers.

In 1913, on the eve of the first world war, the Lithuanian revolutionaries, led by Kapsukas, Angarietis, and Eidukevicius, started a newspaper, *Vilnis*, patterned on the Russian Bolshevik's *Pravda*, which itself had begun publishing in 1912.

War had always threatened Lithuania's national survival. World War I came closest to destroying the country altogether. Lithuania almost immediately became a battleground—and again in 1941. Then, as later, German occupation was brutal and merciless, leaving in its wake not only death but destruction that would take years to repair. Then, as later, the Germans stole everything that could be moved—piled into freight cars and sent West. Taxes were imposed on the people. All the factories were closed, and many of them transported bodily to Germany itself.

Then, as later, Germany's policy toward Lithuania amounted to genocide. In 1914, conquest was to be followed by colonization. Meanwhile, steps were taken to reduce Lithuania in advance to a state of colonial dependence.

Then, as later, the people resisted, and formed organizations that fought the deportations and forced enlistment in the German army. Partisan detachments—the "forest brothers"—of escaped prisoners and rebellious civilians engaged the Germans from their hideouts in the forests. In many ways, the reaction of the Lithuanians to German occupation in 1914-1918 was a rehearsal for 1941-1944.

In both instances, not all Lithuanians resisted the Germans. In fact, the bourgeois landowners moved even closer to the Germans after the 1917 revolution in Russia. In that event, they foresaw the shadow of Lithuanian revolutionary upsurge as well. But their fear of their own people was not unique, and their class interests led them to look upon foreign invaders as their protection. In 1871, the Paris bourgeoisie, under Thiers, saw in the oncoming Prussians not the enemy but their defenders. This would be repeated in 1940 when the Germans invading France found only token opposition in the French upper class, the so-called "200 families," whose army was led by a Vichyite general, Maxime Weygand, an admirer of Colonel de la Roque, French führer of the fascist Croix de Feu, and who put up only nominal opposition to the oncoming Wehrmacht. In fact, he feared his own soldiers more than he feared the Germans, and begged the German High Command to give him their protection. France fell in six weeks.

The 1917 revolution in Russia, which moved rapidly in nine months, as though giving birth, from a bourgeois revolution under Kerensky in February to a workers' revolution under Lenin in November, raised hope in the breasts of the oppressed and fear in the breasts of the Lithuanian oppressors. The latter turned in every direction for salvation, and believed they had found it in the Germans themselves. They collaborated with them, even to the point of organizing a Lithuanian Council that would promote German aims in Lithuania through Lithuanian means.

The Lithuanian Council, formed in September, 1917, with 20 hand-picked representatives to which Professor Augustinas Voldemaras was added in July of 1918, was totally subservient to the Germans, and in its declaration of independence, December 11, 1917, after "bravely" asserting its sovereignty, noted:

> In the formation of this state and for representation of its interests at the peace talks, the National Council requests the protection and help of the German Empire. Since the vital interests of Lithuania require a prompt establishment of lasting and close relations with the German Empire, the National Council advocates close, *permanent* (my italics—P.B.) ties between the Lithuanian State and the German empire, by way of a treaty implemented mainly in the form of a military and traffic convention, and a customs and mint community.

This open and shameless subservience to Germany, Lithuania's historic enemy, whose soldiers had just finished devastating Lithuania in a bitter war, aroused a storm of criticisms and protests. This almost universal opposition forced the Council members to adopt a new Declaration, February 16, 1918, in which they declared Lithuania to be independent, this time leaving out an open statement of dependence on Germany, although—as we would see in the years following—this declaration of independence was adopted—as they say—with "their fingers crossed behind their backs."

In the USA, efforts were made by the extreme Nationalist Knights of Lithuania to raise a Lithuanian Legion to fight the Bolsheviks. Their emblem was the Knight on a rampant horse, lately resurrected by the present squatters in Lithuania.

In their statement to the Paris Peace Conference in 1919, a delegation from the Lithuanian Council made its aims clear, noting that "rioting and revolts against the German occupation, which took place in 1916 and 1917, made Germany look for a way out of the situation. Germany hoped to form a state body of Lithuanian representatives which could be trusted to serve as mediator between the German government and the Lithuanian people. For that purpose the government of Germany addressed some well-known Lithuanian politicians asking them to help to choose suitable members for that reliable council."

Among those Lithuanian negotiators, we see the name of Antanas Smetona—a name that will persist through all the ensuing governments until the very end in 1940 when he fled his own native land to a safe haven in Germany, and then to a safer one in the USA.

His sinister role in the politics of this period has been studiously ignored or downplayed. And yet, in many ways, it was a foreshadowing of the role he would play again and again, confronting almost the same alternatives and choices in 1940 that he first confronted in 1920. Then, too, the Byzantine rationale was invented which tried to justify de facto surrender to Germany on the grounds that Germany guaranteed Lithuania's independence—but, in the real terms of the times, such an "independence" could only be *against* revolutionary Russia and revolutionary Lithuania, and *with* authoritarian and later fascist Germany.

The Lithuanian Council was made up of rich landowners, priests who were also landowners, capitalists, peasants who were already rich, or even worse, *hungered* to be rich, and of intellectuals who discovered the logic of reaction in the syntax of reason. Giving them their cue, Smetona argued: "We cannot remain completely neutral. We have to say openly whom we incline to." And, indeed, the Council openly "inclined" to the German authorities who had no sentimental illusions about their role. Nor did the people, who dubbed the Council the "Kaiser Council."

Almost with eerie repetition, some 20-odd years later, and the Germans once again in occupation, another "Council" was set up, under the leadership of Juozas Ambrazavicius, whose aim was to overthrow the then fledgling socialist government and "restore free and independent Lithuania, emphasizing friendly relations with Germany and their will to become part of Europe under the new regime of Adolph Hitler..."[8]

Here, we must pause to review once again the circumstances in which the new revolutionary government issued, with Lenin's approval, its "Declaration of Rights of the Nations of Russia," in which it was declared that the peoples of Russia had the right to national and state sovereignty, which included the right to self determination, including secession, if it came to that, and the establishment of independent states, including within those states the autonomy of distinct minorities. Under the Czar, Russia had been known as the "prison house of nations," and it was Lenin's aim to establish a free and equal community of nations, drawn together by mutual agreement and for reciprocal benefit. Lenin's sincerity was tested in the case of Finland, which was given its independence.

In 1917, peace negotiations between revolutionary Russia and Germany began at Brest. Speaking for the cause of Lithuania, Vincas Mickevicius-Kapsukas demanded that the Germans leave occupied Lithuania and that all minorities in the Baltics be given the right to choose the way they wanted to live by national referendum. This proposal, which was the only way in which to assure true independence, was vigorously opposed by the Lithuanian Council, whose position was cited by the Germans as representing the will of the Lithuanian people. The German spokesman, Kühlmann, declared that there was no need for a special referendum since "the legally convened representatives of these countries (Poland, Lithuania and Kurland) had long ago decided to secede from Russia, and to submit the question of their future State system to the discretion of Germany."[*9]

Speaking against this position, Vincas Mickevicius-Kapsukas declared that the "Lithuanian workers and peasants in Lithuania and Latvia, workers and peasants in America, protest vigorously against it..." [10]

All in vain. The Germans were not in the mood to surrender what they had not lost. However, news that Lithuania would become a satellite of Kaiser's Germany aroused profound resentment in Lithuania, and against the Lithuanian Council which had collaborated with the Kaiser. Opposition cut across political and class lines. And yet Smetona was saying that "Our attitude cannot be changed." When at a Council meeting the issue was brought up for a vote, Smetona confronted the Council members with a blackmail threat that if they repudiated his position he would resign. The threat worked. Smetona obtained the 12-vote majority of the 20 members of the Council. Still, with four members resisting, and four abstaining, ultimately Smetona was forced to resign and his position was assumed by Jonas Basanavicus. But this was temporary. Under Basanavicus' leadership, the Council adopted another resolution which, in words, asserted Lithuania's independence, though no such independence became a reality. Nevertheless adopted on February 16, 1918, and hailed as Lithuania's Declaration of Independence, it became the official declaration of independence, celebrated during the bourgeois period, and reasserted under the authority of the Lithuanian government headed by Landsbergis.

* Practically the same language and logic were used by the Landsbergis forces in March, 1991 to refuse submitting the future status of Lithuania to a national referendum.

Having done his work—producing a plausible facsimile of independence—Basanavicus now resigned (agreed to beforehand) and Smetona, who had never left the leadership ideologically, returned officially. On February 28, 1918, the Council sent a statement to the Germans asserting that the Declaration of December 11, 1917, had been adopted, and on March 23, 1918, Kaiser Wilhelm signed a statement agreeing to the species of "independence" which the Lithuanian Council now proffered him. But it was a sham. The Kaiser had no real intention of accepting a really independent Lithuania and had no reason to. Indeed, Germany had tied Lithuania so tightly to itself in an economic knot that it could not be untied by a mere declaration. Nor was Lithuanian "independence" taken seriously by any of the parties involved. In fact, hardly had the agreement been inked than the Council issued a decree (June 4, 1918) announcing that Lithuania was to become a monarchy, and its king would be the German Prince Wilhelm Herzog von Urach, Graf von Nurttemberg who, to make him legitimate, would be dubbed, "Mindaugus the Second"! To have foisted a king on Lithuania—and a German at that—in the name of "independence" was so bizarre that all it did was feed the revolutionary fires already spreading throughout the country. Wrote *Vairas*, a monthly: "The election of a German as a king could not be popular in Lithuania..." In fact, it amounted to a provocation, and graphically underlined both the desperation and irresponsibility of the nationalist forces in the saddle at the time. But so convinced was Smetona and his confederates that Germany would win the war, and so profoundly a lackey he and his supporters were in their souls, they could not envision how repulsive the idea of a German king—or really any king—was to the ordinary Lithuanian. And then to compound the obscenity—to give this German the name of Lithuania's early king was too much! It violated the very soul of their love for their homeland.

All it did, finally, was to strengthen the resolve of the revolutionaries (who expanded enormously), that to secure genuine freedom for Lithuania they would have to depend on their own efforts. Willy-nilly those efforts would be revolutionary, not because revolutionaries dictated that they be so, but because events made them so. In this struggle, the Communist Party of Lithuania played a key role.

FIRST SOVIET REPUBLIC

Men's rebirth we shall be celebrating
For the first time with one-sixth of the world.
Victory songs we'll sing, a new sun blazing
From the bright-red banners we've unfurled.
—Joyous Days, Liudas Gira

The uprising of the Russian workers in Petrograd, storming the Winter Palace, putting the Kerensky government to flight (with Kerensky making good his escape disguised as a woman) and establishing a workers' and peasants' government under Lenin, all of it accomplished with a minimum of bloodshed, inspired not only the workers and peasants of Lithuania but the oppressed the whole world over. In the USA, among many, Eugene Debs, the head of the Socialist Party, hailed it, as did Mother Jones, the legendary leader of the coal miners, and so did Helen Keller, world famous already for her incredible feat of overcoming the handicaps of blindness, deafness and muteness.

Revolutionary winds were blowing everywhere. A savage war for the division of markets had raged in Europe for four years* with unprecedented casualties, the barbarism of gas warfare, unparalled destruction of European architecture and culture, exposing to millions finally that all governments were nothing but the compliant tools of the interests of classes opposed to the interests of the people in general.

The open and shameless betrayal of the Smetona forces to Germany had appalled honest Lithuanians everywhere. With the model of the Bolsheviks before them, workers formed—almost spontaneously—organizations pledged to the principle of Bolshevism, of Communists, as they were to become known, taking the name from the French communards.

On October 1, 1918, the newly organized Communist Party—breaking with the orthodox leadership of the Social Democratic party—opened its first congress, illegally, in Vilnius. It met literally within the shadow of the German occupation troops. It was at this convention that the Party organ-

---

* "Why, my fellow citizens, is there any man here or any woman—let me say is there any child here—who does not know that the seed of war in the modern world is industrial and commercial rivalry? ... This was a commercial and industrial war. It was not a political war."
— September 5, 1919, speech in St. Louis by President Wilson.

ized itself on the basis of principles which committed it to a revolutionary transformation of the nation.

On November 9, 1918, the Kaiser was overthrown and Germany surrendered. German occupation soldiers in Lithuania broke free.

The Red Army formed several contingents of Lithuanians, then as it would again in 1941-42. By the end of the year, 1918, Lithuania was swept with revolutionary revolts, with strikes everywhere, and clashes with the Germans, who were being forcibly pushed out of the country, occurred daily. At this critical juncture, with the fortunes of the Germans waning, the Council decided not to make Urach king after all and moved to organize a new government on November 11, 1918, under the leadership of Augustinas Voldemaras, a Lithuanian, it would turn out, who was more German than the Germans themselves. His name will occur over and over in Lithuania's subsequent history as leader of the most malevolent force in its entire experience.

But this last-ditch effort of the Smetona forces to misdirect the forces now in full motion got nowhere. In fact, efforts that extended through the sessions of the victorious powers at Versilles in 1920 to win international recognition of their independence also got nowhere, with its delegation, headed by this same Voldemaras, forced to cool its heels outside the conference door. (Soviet Russia had already recognized its independence.)

On December 18, 1918, the Communist Party resolved to establish a provisional government headed by V. Mickevicius-Kapsukas, and local revolutionary councils sprang up all over Lithuania in response. On December 16, the provisional government had officially declared that the power of the German occupationists was ended and, along with it, the Council of Lithuania, which had been nothing but a German puppet, and proclaimed that all power was now in the hands of the Soviets of Workers, Landless and Poor Peasant deputies. Thus was born Soviet Lithuania—an event which was indeed historic as an expression of the profound desire of the Lithuanian working class and peasantry to rule themselves. Soviet Russia recognized the new regime on December 21, 1918, as it did similar regimes in Latvia and Estonia, acknowledging their independence and freedom.

This first establishment of Soviet power in Lithuania remains controversial. In the eyes of the bourgeoisie and international capital, *no* government established by and for the working class and poor peasants is ever legitimate. But the fact remains that the monumental horror of the European war, with its enormous slaughter (10 million in all), totally exposed the reality of Czarist power as not only autocratic but grossly inefficient and monstrously indifferent to the loss of life. The grotesque and even farcical nature of the Czarist regime was perhaps summed up no better than in the incredible relationship of the Czarina to the mad monk Rasputin, whose influence on state affairs was appalling.* Capitalism growing in Russia could not develop normally under the medieval grip of a Czar and Czarina and their Rasputin. But unbelievably cynical and criminal was the jousting for hegemony among European powers, which saw in the sacrifice of millions nothing but the means by which Europe and the markets of Africa and Asia and the rest of the world could be divided up. To the victor belonged not only the spoils but the medals. And yet it was impossible to take fire into your bosom without burning your clothes....

Lenin's decree recognizing Soviet Lithuania specified an independent sovereign Lithuania. The people had won power through their own efforts at a time when the Red Army had not yet appeared on the Lithuanian scene itself. In fact, Lithuania was still occupied by German troops when the Soviets were established, and the Lithuanian Council still ostensibly functioned. Only late in 1918, in December, did the Red Army, along with its Lithuanian divisions, enter Lithuania, forcing the Germans out. The Council and its cabinet of make-believe ministers reconvened in Kaunas, but it was now no more than a conductor without an orchestra....

The Soviets had de facto power. The new government of workers and peasants launched a series of measures that began to change the course of Lithuania's social life. Its decrees specified complete equality of all races and peoples, instituting universal suffrage at the age of 18 (23 would be the age under Smetona), established the legal right of workers to form and join unions and other people's organizations, reopened Vilnius University, which had been closed down on the Czar's orders since 1832; and bravely, if too optimistically, began the slow, hard work of restoring the economy on a new basis, helped to do so with loans of gold and goods from Russia.

But the ease with which the workers and revolutionaries took power in Lithuania was misleading. The Entente powers had no intention of letting Lithuania slip out of the orbit of imperialism into the hands of the people. In erecting a united front against socialism, former enemies became de facto friends. In the Compiegne-Ture Agreement, signed by Germany, 1918, the Entente powers (plus the USA) had already designated the Baltic countries to be a *cordone sanitaire*, whose function was to keep the "bacillus of Bolshevism" out of Europe proper. The cordon followed roughly the Curzon line, drawn at the request of the Powers, by Lord Curzon. The Agreement Clause to the Treaty ordained that German troops would be stationed in Lithuania to control the situation, and to give the counter-revolutionaries time and material with which to launch a counter-attack.

---

* Like the influence of a psychic on Nancy Reagan and on her husband, the unbelievable Ronald Reagan.

Hard beset by interventionist forces, revolutionary Russia couldn't come to Lithuania's assistance against the forces of Yudenich, Deniken and Kolchak, and their local White Guard janissaries, who would wreak such havoc and spread such devastation over all of Russia for the next three years, causing stupendously more deaths and damage than the revolution itself—a matter of weeks and a handful of deaths—had caused.

Americans are little aware of the fact that as early as 1918, the U.S. actively intervened in Lithuanian affairs, working in concert with Great Britain, Finland, Sweden, France and the Netherlands to suppress the revolutionary forces in power. The Americans, that same year, would send a full expeditionary force of 9,000 to Siberia, actively aided Lithuanian reaction with provisions and even tried to recruit a Lithuanian Legion from among American Lithuanian immigrants. But since most of these immigrants had fled a reactionary Lithuania, owned and ruled by a clerical-landowner clique, they were in no mood to take up arms to restore the old order. Given huge tracts of land, as far back as 1387, by the Grand Duke Jogaila—more Polish in his sympathies than Lithuanian—the Church, beginning with a gift of much of Vilnius to the Bishop, in addition to "plots of land and houses, their inhabitants, and all their possessions" assumed a power in Lithuania that was to endure for centuries. This was in addition to the requirement forced on the regents to "supply the priests and churches, both in the cities, as well as the outlying villages, with money, acreage, and facilities for every parish priest to build a tavern for himself. These gifts of Jogaila, as well as those of succeeding Grand Dukes, served to promote a privileged class of clergymen, concentrating large real estate holdings and other wealth in their hands. The wealthy Church extended its hierarchy throughout the country though it was not able to suppress the paganism that persisted several ages." [11]

This was the beginning of the power of the Church, which increased with the years and remained the core around which reaction built its political power, and indeed, which persists to this day. "Religious freedom," in the mouths of Lithuanian reaction, means the return of most of the land to the Church, along with "their inhabitants," no matter how nominally free they seem to be.

These forces had something material to fight for. They were against "independence," which under the circumstances, no matter who came to political power, could only mean the adoption of measures that in some way would curtail the power of the Church.

Not only was the Church against independence—and we are speaking of "independence" under bourgeois rule. So was the USA.

It was Lenin himself who, in February 1920, revealed the contents of coded, secret telegrams exchanged between B.A. Bakhmetev, who was the counterrevolutionary Kolchak's representative in the USA, to his representative, Gulkevich in Sweden. Bakhmetev, who had access to the State Department, wrote (from Washington) to Gulkevich (October 12, 1919):

> The State Department acquainted me verbally with the instructions given for Gade [John A., U.S. Government commissioner to the Baltics]. He is not accredited to any Russian government. His mission is to observe and his behavior must not lead the local population to expect that the American government could agree to support separatists trends going beyond autonomy. On the contrary, the American Government trusts that the population of the Baltic Provinces will help their Russian brothers in their work of general state importance .... Gade had been given extracts from the recent speeches of the President in which he fulminates against Bolshevism.

Indeed, starting with Wilson, the declared champion of the right of small countries to self-determination, the true policy here announced would never deviate in the decades to come; small nations, particularly the Baltic nations, were no more than a pawn in the anti-Soviet struggle. At that moment, Estonia was making a bid for independence, taking Wilson at his announced word; nothing could have been more naive.

In a subsequent telegram this secret policy was spelled out even more succinctly. Another Kolchak agent, I. Sukin, writing to "Minister" Gulkevich (October 9, 1919):

> [Alfred] Knox [British general, heading the British military mission to Kolchak] has given the Supreme Ruler the message of the British War Office in which the latter warns of the inclination of the Baltic states to conclude a peace with the Bolsheviks who guarantee them immediate recognition of their independence... We replied to Knox that the conclusion of a peace between the Baltic states and the Bolsheviks would be undoubtedly fraught with danger since this would permit the release of part of the Soviet forces and would clear the way to the infiltration of Bolshevism in the West. The mere fact that they are ready to talk peace is, in our opinion, evidence of the utter demoralization of the parties of these self-governing entities which cannot protect themselves from the penetration of aggressive Bolshevism.
>
> Expressing the conviction that the Powers could not approve of the further spread of Bolshevism we pointed to the necessity of withdrawing all aid from the Baltic states since this would be a real means of exerting influence by the Powers, and is more advisable than competition in promises with the Bolsheviks who have now nothing to lose.

These and other telegrams made it clear that the Powers were concerned, not with self-determination and independence, though in all three countries the aim was to establish a bourgeois republic (modeled on the West), but with stopping the spread of Bolshevism, and key to stopping it was the continuation of the war. Lithuanians, Latvians and particularly Estonians were expected to keep fighting the "Bolsheviks," if they expected even ordinary supplies, including food.

Meanwhile Poland, under Pilsudski (Lithuanian by birth), was casting covetous eyes on Lithuania as well. Poland, in the grip of a hopelessly reactionary landowner class, dreamed of erecting a "great Poland" which would include large areas surrounding Vilnius (still called Wilno) and which at one time had, in fact, "belonged" to Poland. And, indeed, Polish troops moved in now and reconquered Vilnius with no opposition—in fact, with the connivance of the Western powers.

But the main agent for overthrowing and suppressing the movement toward socialism and independence, (which were seen as one) was the Germany that had been denounced in a thousand speeches as barbarian, the very essence of militarist reaction. Some 40,000 German troops, later persisting in the so-called *Freikorps*, in whose service many a future SS man first tasted blood, moved into Western Lithuania, supplemented by Polish and Kolchak White Guards elsewhere.

At this point, Voldemaras would lead a delegation to Versailles in an effort to win recognition from the Big Powers, and had to cool his heels in the anteroom to the palace. In any case, counter-revolution, backed by Allied men and ammunition, launched an attack in February 1919 against the fledgling Lithuanian Soviet Republic, with Polish and German troops leading the assault.

Soviet Lithuania had not yet had time to organize its defense adequately. One must remember that all the astonishing accomplishments then as later, in Lithuania, as well as in Russia, were the accomplishments of *amateurs*. Once, when a peasant came to Lenin complaining that he, a peasant, was unequipped to govern in his own village, Lenin told him that *none* of them, including himself, had any training in conducting affairs of state. They were all nothing by experience and training but agitators and would have to learn how to govern by governing, which included mastering the mysteries of economics and other vital sciences.

In any case, at this crucial moment in Lithuanian history, Russia was beset by numerous enemies and was fighting for its life. On April 21, 1919, the Poles retook Vilnius and capitalism was restored. The "government" of Lithuania under Voldemaras, meanwhile, existed on sufferance. The Germans ruled. The American member of the international mission to the Baltic States, J.B. Dawley, characterized Voldemaras' government as a government "only in name." With the Germans and the Poles in the saddle, plunder and robbery became the rule. Efforts to rid themselves of such predators came to nothing. In fact, the triumphant Western powers had plans of their own for Lithuania—in their plans Lithuania was to be joined to Poland which then would become an even stronger anti-Soviet bastion.

Here one encounters in an early form the one-dimensional anti-Sovietism which willingly sacrificed all other principles of democracy (a dim vision in any case), of sovereignty, of independence (even if severely limited) in order to erect what was hoped would be an iron curtain between eastern and western Europe. Wilson's malign influence was manifest here. A past master at phrase-making, he introduced into world politics the style which mixed pharisaical middle-class Sunday preacher's piety with bullets and bombs, an American attitude that had traditionally defined the world outside of America as a world of aborigines, all of whom needed converting instantly to "Christianity." Indeed, irritated at Wilson's 14 points (by which Wilson expected to reorganize the world) France's Clemenceau, who understood that it all boiled down to which corporation group would get which rich market, growled: "Why, God had only ten commandments."

The position of the bourgeois Lithuanians then as now was extremely difficult. They seemed always to be between the devil and the deep blue sea. Despite the fact that Soviet Russia offered to recognize the Baltic bourgeois governments, and even to extend to them what economic aid it could, they hesitated. They had not been given the go-ahead signal by their Western sponsors. Decision was finally precipitated by the turn of military events. The Red Army succeeded in throwing the Polish forces out of the country in the summer of 1920. A peace treaty with Soviet Russia and Lithuania was signed in Moscow on July 12, 1920. Soviet Russia turned over the Polish-conquered area of Vilnius, and Vilnius itself, to the Lithuanian bourgeois government, then headed by Kazys Grinius,* and a leader of the Peasant Populists. It also extended a loan of three million rubles in gold. Indeed, Lithuanian independence was assured by Soviet power. No doubt the Western forces chose Lithuanian independence as a lesser evil to a socialist Lithuania. But the ironic fact remains that independence for the Baltics was due to the Russian revolution of 1917.

This fact, of course, remains a bone in the throat of nationalism.

---

* Later, in 1940, he would be one of a number of eminent Lithuanians to sign a telegram of greeting to Hitler, hailing him as a "Liberator" of Lithuania.

FASCIST LITHUANIA

Why do millions, like martyrs
Slave all day and every day?
Why are wealth's producers starving
And in groaning poverty stay?

Being kind will gain us nothing.
Rise to battle, set fly sparks!
We'll win happiness through struggle
Taking as our leader Marx.

From A Worker's Catechism—Julius Janonis

But what does "independence" mean, *really* mean, in the real world? Political independence, or at least the form of it, cultural autonomy, or at least what's left over after—to anticipate—American TV is finished with it, important and even basic elements in the concept of independence, nevertheless do not decisively determine a nation's independence. The fact is that unless a nation is large enough, with sufficient energy resources to run its own industries, with a population that is more or less homogeneous (or at least not divided into hostile camps) and is able and willing to defend its autonomy with arms, no such thing as real independence is possible. There are, in reality—except for the largest countries—only different grades and forms of dependence. Decisive in every relationship of one country to another is its economic power. If, as with Ghana today, the main crop on which a country depends for its livelihood—like Ghana on cocoa—can be put to the mercy of the international finance markets, then it's pointless to speak of independence. All that's relevant is the market for cocoa and what one has to do to maintain it and exploit it. True, there sometimes occur, in the international balance of forces, what one might call "pockets" which, for various reasons, remain at least physically untouched—like Switzerland, Hong Kong, Macao, etc. But their functions are so unique and special and useful that the big powers find it more opportune to leave them relatively undisturbed for the service that they perform.

No such role was cut out for the Baltic countries. They had no special, unique function to perform that benefitted all parties and acted as a clearing house for antagonistic forces, which nevertheless had to do some amount of business with each other.

Parliamentary government, based on Western models but midwifed by the Entente at Versailles, had a brief career. It endured for about six years and choked—to use an inelegant but accurate image—on its own vomit.

It is one of the ironies of history that the independence of bourgeois Lithuania was recognized and backed up by Soviet Russia, which extended recognition in July 1920, despite the fact that the government had come to power over the bodies of its own Lithuanian revolutionaries and after having overthrown the first Soviet republic with German arms.

This recognition by Soviet Russia appalled the West for it assumed autonomy of both Lithuania and Soviet Russia at a time when the Entente powers were still scheming to overthrow revolutionary Russia and force the Baltic countries to rejoin their "natural" motherland, Czarist Russia.

Poland's continued occupation of Vilnius and the Vilnius district, with open Vatican support, remained a major obstacle to Lithuanian independence. Appealing to the League of Nations for bread, the Lithuanians received a stone. The League's Hymans Commission proposed a monster of a plan: Vilnius was to remain autonomous (as the Vatican wanted) but "federated" to Lithuania which itself would be "federated" with Poland! But Lithuania would be divided into two semi-autonomous areas: Vilnius and Kaunas, although Vilnius would be declared the Lithuanian capital, once the Poles agreed to leave.

Nothing came of the plan, as nothing was intended to come of it. Poland remained in control of the Vilnius area until once again Vilnius was liberated by the Red Army in 1939.

Meanwhile in April, 1920, the first Constituent Assembly was elected, with 112 deputies divided among eight parties, with the Christian Democrats (Catholic) and the Peasants Union winning 59 and 28 seats respectively and together forming a majority. In this election, the Party that was to become sole ruler of Lithuania from 1926 to 1940, Antanas Smetona's and Agustinas Voldemaras' Party, the National Progress Party, or as it would be better known by its later name, Tautininikas, won *no* seats. As for the Communists, they were outlawed.

This government lasted a mere six months as the Poles retook Vilnius that October. The government, headed by Ernestas Galvanauskas yielded to Dr. Kazy Grinius, who formed a new cabinet based on a coalition between the Christian Democrats and the Peasants Union. This coalition fell apart in January of 1922, and was trying to function out of Kaunas. Nevertheless, the government managed to draw up a new constitution, modeled on the West's, in which a number of elementary democratic rights were included, particularly relating to suffrage. Lands previously owned by absentee landlords, or grants from the Czar, etc., were nationalized. A Lithuanian currency was adopted. Indeed, much of what is today proposed was first tried out then.

On October 10–11, 1922, the first seimas was elected, with 78 deputies. It lasted until March of 1923. The second seimas gave the Christian Democrats a majority. But it, too, could not function. The third, elected in May 1926, had only three members of Tautininkai.

Under the leadership of Mykolas Slezevicius, the Peasant Populist representative, the government tried to curb the growing power of the church, and incurred the church's wrath, being denounced as agents of Bolshevism. On December 16, 1926, a group of officers, led by Col. Povilas Plechavicius, staged a coup, taking over a number of governmental buildings. This apparently so stunned the government that it seemed to lose all will to resist. Slezevicius resigned, and president Grinius called on Voldemaras, whose party had no more than three representatives in the seimas, and who was back of the coup, to form a new government, and he himself resigned. On December 19, Smetona was "elected" President—and so died the feeble experiment in parliamentary democracy, of "independence" in Lithuania, blessed by the Western democracies and crucified on the unholy cross of anti-Bolshevism. Smetona, though he parted with Voldemaras in 1929, remained "president" until his precipitate flight into the haven of Hitlerite Germany in 1940, and thence to another democracy that had had so large a hand in Lithuania's demise as a parliamentary democracy—the USA.

Before he departed, Smetona had turned Lithuania into a fascist dictatorship, based more or less on Mussolini's concepts of a corporate state. Elections became frauds, and the President, who held office officially for seven years, was "elected" by a college of electors, under the direction of Dr. Vladas Mironas, the priestly head of the Tautininkai. Lithuania has the odious distinction of first introducing gas chambers for executing dissidents in the First Fort.

The truth was that the landowning class, the clergy, the capitalists had no interest in defending or functioning through a parliamentary system, which, in their eyes, contained many perils. The very word *democracy* was suspect. It is only one of the continuing ironies of history that this very suspect word, *democracy*, is being employed today toward anti-democratic ends as the struggle to overcome socialism continues.

In any case, WWI had devastated Lithuania. Some 1,200 villages with 14,270 dwelling places were ruined. Some 2,000 homesteads and 50 towns were devastated. Altogether about 57,000 inhabited places were destroyed, leaving Lithuania a wasteland.

The road back was daunting. But to rebuild the country at the expense of its working class while making a profit for its own entrepreneurs, but even more so, for foreign investors, was not only cruel but foredoomed to failure. Putting their entire faith on the positive workings of the international financial market—even pegging the Lithuania *litas* to the American dollar—bespoke a touching reliance on foreign capitalists and in the equally touching belief that it really would work miracles and reward all its acolytes unfailingly. Nobody expected the Stock Market to collapse in New York City, and even so, if it collapsed in New York City—so far away—how could that possibly harm *Lithuania's* farmers and workers?

By 1940, Lithuania was deep in debt to her chief creditors. She already owed banks in the USA some $6,864,801. She owed Sweden, which had large investments in Lithuanian industry, $4,157,350. To Great Britain, the debt came to some 50,000 pounds, and to Germany to 1,493,184 Marks, with smaller indebtedness to other European countries, or rather to financiers, like Belgium, amounting finally to about 19 percent of her annual budget.

In the light of current proposals to privatize the Lithuanian economy, it is instructive to note that Lithuania's entire economic system was, by 1940, dominated by foreign capital, mainly through joint-stock companies and other economic devices (loans, banks, etc.). In their anti-Sovietism, they moved to cut off their noses to spite their faces, and abandoned the flourishing business with Russia in metal working and wood working. The decline of these industries struck a blow to Lithuanian economy.

But being able to produce goods and dispose of them freely on the world market did not solve Lithuania's problems, then as it does not now. In any case, the world market is not "free." For domestically manufactured or produced goods to compete with similar goods produced elsewhere, one's own products had to have some marked superiority to theirs. But even when they did, this alone did not assure buyers. For such goods often could not penetrate trade barriers erected by other countries to keep foreign competition out of the domestic market. Again, what operated here was not "free competition" but the advantages assured by monopoly. The direction of "free competition," as far as history tells us, is toward monopolization. Colonial countries become mere dumping grounds for the overpriced goods of the dominating imperialist country, or the source of cheap labor or both, a condition that more than half the world is in today.

No law rises higher than the all-powerful economic law that operates in the financial markets of the world, where investments are still possible. Just as water seeks its own level so, too, investment funds—capital—seeks the area which promises the highest rate of profit. Thus, foreign capital flowed into those industries that promised the greatest return, but which did not necessarily mean of most use to the people. Profitability was assured not by making needed goods cheaper but by creating conditions which meant, among other things (low taxes, for instance) keeping labor costs low. But keeping labor costs low means low income for the workers, therefore a constricted domestic market, which breeds discontent, with all the familiar consequences. The pattern has always historically been: first the trader, then the soldier....

Foreign capital took over Lithuania's electrical resources—of 21,000,000 *litas* invested in electricity, foreign capital owned 20,850,600. In the chemical industry, it came to 6,950,000 *litas* as a whole of which 6,476,000 were in foreign hands. In metal and machine working, the figures were 6,700,000 and 2,135,000 respectively. In textiles, it came to 4,725,000 as a whole with 2,350,000 foreign. Paper, printing, publishing—vital industries to any independent nation—280,000 *litas* were owned by Lithuanian capital and 167,300 by foreign.[12]

It paid off. From 1924 to 1932, Lithuanians, through their sweat and blood, paid 60 million *litas* to foreign investors in interest and dividends. (Actually indirectly more was paid.) Of course the drive to make higher and higher profits is remorseless, and the means are classic, mainly instituting a longer work day, lower wages, the introduction of labor-saving machinery replacing workers, and even importing badly paid foreign labor. And of course, always higher prices coupled with a smaller and smaller percentage of taxes paid to the government.

So extreme and irresponsible was the greed of foreign investors that the hike in the electrical rates to Lithuanian consumers actually drove the people of Kaunas to revolt in 1939. Thousands deliberately refused to use electric lights and burned candles instead. The revolt succeeded in forcing a reduction in the rates. Even so, the foreign investors lost nothing. Each year they could count on an average of 1.5 million *litas* ending up in their pockets out of the labor of Lithuanian workers.

One of the great advantages that a powerful country has over any country less powerful lies in its ability to fix prices. Ever since colonialism was a historic fact, we know that the "mother" country always dictated to the "dependent" country what prices were to be paid for raw material produced by the colonial countries and what prices the colonial countries would be obliged to pay for the finished products coming out of the "mother" country fashioned from the goods they had to sell cheap. A stronger country could always blow smoke into the face of the weaker one.

Where a foreign power dictates prices it also, by that same process, dictates wages. Thus, to the most "glorious" period of Lithuanian independence, the Lithuanian working class lived the life of an Oriental coolie. At a time when advanced countries were cutting hours of labor to eight, in Lithuania workers continued to put in a ten-hour, twelve-hour, and even fourteen-hour day. Wages were kept close to the subsistence level, or fell below. There were no social safeguards—"safety nets"—no unemployment protection, no old age pensions, and indeed no pensions of any kind, no health services. Employment was chancey. Since most key factories depended on foreign orders to function, when those orders failed to come or to come in sufficient quantities, they cut down production, sending their workers home to wait for "better times."

What was typical of the workers also affected the small peasant. Farm prices were at the mercy of economic forces controlled in the stock markets of the West. In this period, thousands lost whatever fragile hold they had on the land and were forced into the cities where they endured as a kind of half-peasant, half-worker: a human hippogriff.

In 1926, the Lithuanian trade union movement—*Lietuvos Darbininku ir Tarnautoju Profesinu Sajunga*—with 17,000 members joined the Amsterdam International Federation of Trade Unions, then under Socialist control.

At its Brussels Congress, August 5-11, 1928, among other resolutions, the International particularly noted:

> The march of Fascism and of reaction in a series of countries (Italy, Hungary, Bulgaria, Lithuania and others) is not only forcing down the standard of living of the workers and threatening all their social gains, but also through the abolition of democratic rights and political liberties, is introducing a regime of despotism which is reverting to the worst methods of absolutism and of executive justice, using mass imprisonment, internment under inhuman conditions, banishment by decree, concentration camps for its own citizens, and often indeed not shrinking from the death penalty.[13]

The '20s are today being romanticized, as the truly democratic period of Lithuanian, Latvian and Estonian history. True, there was a semblance of democracy at least until 1926, in the existence of parliamentary forms and severely curtailed elections, but elections nevertheless, and opposition parties were allowed to function. In fact, the Socialists increased their vote in the Diet (1926) from 8 to 15 in the May election. The opposition then had 40 representatives, and the Nationalists had 38.

On December 17, 1926,

> The followers of Woldemaras (*sic*) and Smertona (*sic*), nationalists, clericals, landlords and army officers, effected a Fascist coup. They proceeded to shoot, imprison, or exile trade union leaders, Socialist and Communist functionaries. They consolidated their regime by dissolving the Diet, revising the constitution, and by establishing a personal dictatorship for the president.
> The number of political prisoners runs into the hundreds. On October 12, 1928, 40 of them went on a hunger strike to compel humane treatment.[14]

In Latvia:

The left coalition government with 4 members of the Social Democratic party, resigned on December 13, 1927, over the treaty with Russia. In the elections of October 1928, the Communist Party made a gain, while the Socialists lost 7 seats.

Social-Democrats received 26 seats (previously 33), the independent Socialists 3 (previously none), the Mensheviks 26 (previously 4) and the Communists 5 (previously none). There are 100 seats in the lower house.

In August 1928, the government suppressed 19 Communist unions. The Communists retaliated with a general strike in Riga, which was not fully successful.[15]

Meanwhile, at the 6th Congress of the Communist International held in Moscow between July 17 and September 1, 1928, Nikolai Bukharin in his report to the delegates stated:

The experience of recent years, the small wars of plunder continuously waged against the colonial peoples, and the events of the last year; intervention against the Chinese revolution, sharpening conflict between the powers for a new division of China, the mobilization of troops in Poland, the immediate menace to the independence of Lithuania—and in connection there with the constantly growing menace of war against the Soviet Union by an imperialist bloc under the leadership of Great Britain recalls all these facts as illustrating the criminal war policy of the imperialists, which may suddenly burst into a terrible world conflagration.

The dictatorship imposed on Lithuania in 1926, with Voldemaras and Smetona as its architects, put a decisive end to any dreams that Lithuania would model itself after the "democracies" then extant, except in a strictly symbolic way. One should note in all this, that despite the fact that he became a total autocratic dictator, Smetona never lost his title of "president."

So what, in reality, could independence mean? When you come down to it, the Baltic countries had very little to sell to others. And, indeed, what they did sell—mainly the products of the dairy industry—they often sold at the expense of their own population. The well-to-do in England and Sweden could eat Lithuanian butter and cream. The Lithuanian peasant had "duonas bet ne Sviesta"—bread with no butter. The Lithuanian peasant who produced these products often had to be content with thinned out skimmed milk, varske, or "poor man's soup," sugared bread in hot water.

The now-ruling class of Lithuania chose a course which seemed pre-programed for disaster. The talent most prized in diplomats of small countries is the talent to maneuver. Unable to impose their will on any other people, the people of a small country must, ordained by fate, learn the art of dealing with others stronger than they are. They can't even deal with strangers in their own language but must learn the language of those with whom they are compelled to deal. No other people are obliged to honor their heroes, pay respect to their household gods, or accept their money.

What military forces they have seem to visitors from powerful nations like nothing but colorful supernumeries better suited to a musical comedy.

These (and other) humiliating realities cannot be magicked away. The mouse can never really roar. Small countries survive on sufferance and sufferance alone. At most, they can console themselves with the only consolation allowed them—malicious wit. They find their oppressors ridiculous, but this observance, too, in the final analysis is just consolation, not power. They still have to be careful that they're not stepped on, which means, diplomatically speaking, they have to be adept, nimble, masters in the art of flattery, feigned obeisance, imitators, adapters: all passive skills in the art of survival. These necessary skills also have their corrupt aspect expressing itself in envy, self-contempt, and readiness to do the dirty work of those above them to curry favor and because they no longer feel any sense of national or personal pride.

The worst side of the need to survive came out in their relationship to Germany. Though Germany had been the stick that had beaten them over and over, nevertheless it seemed that the ruling class of Lithuania never resented it fully but, in fact, managed to turn those beatings into a virtue and even in a desire to merge themselves with their oppressors. In actually moving to make a German king of Lithuania—and not in darkest medieval times but in modern times—those who spoke in Lithuania's name touched bottom. For years, Lithuania allowed the German barons a special role in Lithuanian affairs and, indeed, saw the last of them only as they disappeared over the horizon pursued by Ivan.

Toward Germany, toward Kaisers and toward *führers*, the ruling clique had only smiles. Toward *Soviet* Russia (not toward Czarist Russia) they pursued a policy of hostility, suspicion, double-dealing, and betrayal.

Toward Soviet Russia, they violated the elementary law of survival— adapt. Trade, which benefited thousands of Lithuanian workers, was sabotaged. Lenin's policy of coexistence with all other states, friendly and unfriendly, extended to the Baltics as well, but was grossly misinterpreted and misapplied. Lenin's sincerity was proven beyond cavil by his action in granting Finland its independence on December 31, 1917, when he signed the Decree of the Council of Commissars. He had also recognized the independence of the Baltic states, when they became momentarily socialist, and even after their overthrow, despite the cruel repression of all working class and progressive forces, not only the Communist Party but all unions as well. The only condition Moscow asked to be observed was one that the Lithuanians should have been happy to comply with—a pledge from those in power that they would not enter into any secret agreement with any third power (specifically Germany) threatening the security of the USSR. The security of the USSR automatically meant the security of the Baltics.

In July 1920, the Poles who had invaded Lithuania and annexed Vilnius, were thrown back by the Red Army and Vilnius was returned to the Lithuanians. But in October, the Poles were back again and again they took Vilnius. In the face of the Polish threat, the Lithuanian authorities displayed the ambivalence that would be visible in the governments of Western Europe a few years later when faced by the Hitlerite threat. With the Poles already in Lithuania, the commander-in-chief of the Lithuanian army, General Silvestras Zukauskas, was away from his post hunting boar at Rokstskis as the guest of the Polish Count Prezezdziecki.

Although finally when resistance, mainly in response to the alarm of the people, was given to the Poles, it remained halfhearted. The fact was that the Great Powers, acting through the League of Nations, did not back Lithuania's claim to Vilnius but chose to leave it under Polish control. Soviet offers to join with the Lithuanians to repulse the Poles were rejected—and would continue to be rejected up until the house itself began to burn.

Lithuania's first experience with the League of Nations, into which it was accepted on September 22, 1921, was a sobering one. Instead of finding a sympathetic response to the claim to Vilnius, the Lithuanians were ordered by the League to form two autonomous areas, one around Vilnius and one around Kaunas, and enter into a federation, with Poland to determine economic and military matters. Lithuania got nothing out of this "bargain." The Poles got free access to Lithuania's main river, the Nemunas, to its Baltic seaport, Klaipeda, and its railroads. The Church agreed.

This deal was concluded by the Belgium diplomat Paul Hymans, and was known as the Hyman Plan. In essence, it meant the virtual surrender of national sovereignty, but the then government of Lithuania, which was a coalition of Christian Democrats and Peasant Populists, speaking through its premier, Kazys Grinius, was inclined to accept it anyhow.

Word on what the Plan consisted of brought widespread reaction among the people, who made their wishes known in various demonstrations. The Communist Party of Lithuania, illegal and underground, issued a warning to the people, charging that representatives of the rich peasants then ruling the country were preparing to turn Lithuania over to Poland. Vincas Mickevicius-Kapsukas, then General Secretary of the Lithuanian Party, declared in his report to the Third Congress, October 24-29, 1921, that such an alliance (with Poland) meant "... an even fiercer reaction, a more disgusting oppression and exploitation of the workers, a heavier burden of taxes and high prices, and an involvement of Lithuania into an adventurist war against Soviet Russia..." [16]

This warning was taken up by the masses, including sections of the Lithuanian army itself, whose soldiers had been wondering where their generals were hiding. Afraid that compliance with the Plan would arouse the people to mass opposition, the government backed down and on December 24, 1921, informed the League of Nations that it had rejected the League's recommendations.

But they had both underestimated and misunderstood the role of the League. As we know, it would finally founder on its inability to openly promote what the Great Powers which controlled it secretly considered to be its real function. Lithuania would suffer in advance what Abyssinia would suffer a few years later. The League was adamant. In its private plans, Poland had a far more important role to play in European politics than Lithuania. In its eyes, Poland's visceral hostility to the Soviet Union qualified her as the key element in erecting a strong buffer belt that they had drawn between the USSR and the West—the so-called *cordone sanitaire*, running from Estonia in the north down to the Balkan peninsula. "In February, 1919," Marshall Ferdinand Foch, in command of the allied troops at victory's end in 1918, would write in his memoirs, "... in the early days of Leninism I declared to the Ambassadors Conference meeting in Paris that if the states surrounding Russia were supplied with munitions and the sinews of war, I would undertake to stamp out the Bolshevik menace once and for all."[17]

The decision of the League (read: Great Britain and France, with the USA—not a member—in the background) came as a blow to the Lithuanians. It would be only one of many underlining Lithuania's relative unimportance as an independent state—in fact, a liability—as compared to Poland's importance in the overall scheme of things. Lithuania—i.e., its political ring master—was to learn that its importance was very narrowly defined and was related directly to the permanent aim of "stamp(ing) out the Bolshevik menace." The dream of some idealists of a nation that was truly independent—could make its own political decisions and suffer no punishments—withered: instead of the League actually championing and defending the right of small nations to self-determination it became clear, with decision made or no decision made in case after case, finally culminating in what amounted to connivance with Italy to invade Abyssinia in 1935, the League was the instrument of the Big Powers and their imperialist ambitions, and nothing else. Its *raison d'etre* became clear by its actions if not by its high-minded pronouncements: it was to "stamp out the Bolshevik menace."

November 9, 1925, was declared a national day of mourning in Lithuania—mourning the loss of Vilnius. The Lithuanian government ostensibly broke off relations with Poland—but only ostensibly. It was this same government which had already "resigned" itself to the loss of Vilnius, and as "realists," understanding that the entire West (as defined by those who held power) was against them, they felt they had no choice but to capitulate. (This pattern had already been followed elsewhere or would be followed in the years to come as in the cases of Czechoslovakia, Austria, the Rhineland, etc.).

The Lithuanian "realists" entered into various negotiations with the Poles in an effort to work out a *modus vivendi* by which, while conceding the substance to the Poles they could manage to hold on to the shadow of sovereignty. At Copenhagen, in September 1925, they reached an agreement with the Poles in which the Poles would be allowed to raft Lithuanian timber down the Nemunas on its way to Poland, as well as to reestablish all communication systems keyed to facilitate Polish business. Polish citizens would be allowed to live in Lithuania as well, with rights even better protected than those of native Lithuanians.

Once the substance of the agreement was made known, a storm of protest erupted, strong enough to bring the government down.

All through the 1920s, international intrigue against the Soviet republic continued. Churchill had never ceased to regret what seemed to him, early on, a golden opportunity to "strangle the (Bolshevik) baby in its crib," and he had masterminded various schemes of intervention, the most notorious of which was one under the international spy Sidney Reilly, whose grandiloquent plans included staging a putsch on the Kremlin itself. In these plans Poland always played a key role. She was seen as a "corridor" for Western forces on their way to cross the Soviet border.

Part of Poland's efforts to magnify her role in European affairs always involved in one way or another acquiring hegemony over Lithuania. In these intrigues, more often than not, she had the backing of England. Polish ruling circles approached Germany with a promise to grant Germany access to the corridor and to Danzig in return for her support of Poland's proposed invasion of Lithuania, which was set for the summer of 1926. In May, 1926, what was still alive in Lithuania took part in what was a free (if limited) election, bringing Slezevicius to power.

It was to forestall this threat of Polish invasion that the Soviet Union now proposed concluding non-aggression pacts with the Baltic countries, which, after many delays and pretexts for postponing the signing, were finally signed in Moscow in September, 1926.

The signators agreed not to enter into any alliance with any third party directed against either of them. With the pact, the Soviet Union formally recognized that Vilnius and the area around Vilnius belonged to Lithuania. It implicitly and explicitly accepted the factual independence of Lithuania under its bourgeois form of government, led, or soon to be led, by men profoundly hostile to socialism itself.

The terms of the Pact could hardly have been more reasonable. They reaffirmed the integrity of Vilnius as part of Lithuania at a time when this fact was denied not only by Poland, which actually held the territory of Vilnius, but also by the Allies—England, France and the USA, which had supported Poland's annexation.

In view of this action of the Soviet Union, one would think that even bourgeois historians would now hail this Pact as an act of true generosity, extremely rare in politics. Even more significant, especially in view of later events, was the fact that the Pact was proposed and carried through under Stalin's auspices and was an expression of the Leninist concept that each nation had the right to choose its own form of government. Of course, the provision included in the Pact that Lithuania should not enter into any anti-Soviet conspiracies did not sit well with many in the governing circles of Lithuania, who proceeded to intrigue against the Soviet Union, in the endless effort to forge a Baltic Entente (1934–1939), with the ink on the Pact still wet. Of course, the line that Lithuanian nationalists had a moral right to dissemble, conspire and deceive—since all these means were legitimate in the opposition to "tyranny"—did not go well with the Kremlin. Nor is it sufficient today to cite anti-"Stalinism" as an automatic absolvent of all acts which, if they could not be cited as opposition to "Stalinism," would be considered as nothing but crimes. In 1926, Lenin was two years dead. Events had not yet developed to that extreme level where fascism put the very future of European civilization in peril. Lenin's foreign policies remained in force in the USSR even with Stalin now at the head.

Nationalism, like all history's movements, had its variations, nuances, stages and contradictions. Sharing the same roots as genuine patriotism, love of one's homeland, it could and did take on monstrous forms as the world would see with the rise of Hitler. The only model of successful fascism of a major country that existed in Europe in 1926 was in Italy. Mussolini was hailed in the bourgeois world as a hero. Churchill himself praised him for having found the key to stopping the spread of Bolshevism. Nobody was condemned for proposing to remodel his own country on corporate lines. Mussolini had come to power by force. And now, in 1926, on December 17, led by the ever-invulnerable Smetona, the Nationalist Party he headed took over power in Lithuania by a *putsch*. Although a complete dictatorship was now instituted, as we've already noted, Smetona nevertheless retained the title of "president." But that was all he retained of any symbol that could be connected with formal democracy. On the contrary. Smetona introduced a fascist dictatorship, openly modeled on Mussolini's in Italy. Smetona viewed even a truncated democracy which existed in some countries as nevertheless dangerous to the interests of the class he represented. In a speech at Kaunas, December 18, he elaborated:

The freedom of parties must be curbed. A firm united government has to subdue incited crowds. A united nation headed by a single leader; this slogan was advanced in Italy ... Italy was the first to proclaim the new State system called fascism.... Other countries, such as Poland, Yugoslavia, Lithuania, came after Italy.[18]

Thus, Smetona openly declared that Lithuania was now a fascist country. This meant, first of all, an open dictatorship based on terror, the elimination of even the limited freedoms gained by the people under the bourgeois systems, the dissolution of all competing parties, even those only nominally competing, elimination and incorporation of unions into the fascist order, shutting down of all, even the mildest, dissenting newspapers, the closing of the universities, and the outlawing of the Communist Party, etc. The most intense terror was reserved for the Communists. Four of the leaders of the Communist Party were executed, arousing the horror of Thomas Mann, who denounced the Smetona government for it.* Thousands of others, both members and "sympathizers," were imprisoned. A gas chamber for executing prisoners was introduced—marking the first time a gas chamber was used for this purpose in Europe.

Smetona, in his foreign policy, would serve as a laboratory example of how nationalism leads to anti-nationalist acts and decisions. Instead of firmly insisting that Vilnius must be returned to Lithuania, he signed the Concordat Pact with the Vatican, which brought into existence the "Church Province of Lithuania" which excluded Vilnius and the surrounding area as an integral part of Lithuania, thus giving de facto recognition to Poland's occupation of Vilnius.

Even as Lithuania was being partitioned with the approval of the Pope, high-ranking members of the Catholic hierarchy retained posts in the Smetona government. Archbishop Mecislovas Reinys was Foreign Minister from September 25, 1925 to April 21, 1926. Msgr. Mykolas Krupavicius, also a Catholic prelate, was Minister of Agriculture from 1923 to 1926.

Supporting Smetona all the way were the ruling circles in England, the USA, and of course the Vatican. "Solving" the Lithuanian problem by giving Vilnius and large areas of her land to Poland met with their approval. For, in their long-term plans, Poland was scheduled to play a decisive role. Poland was like a permanently cocked pistol aimed at the heart of Soviet Russia.

Heading the Lithuanian Church Province, established by the Pope in his *Lituanorum gente* on April 4, 1926, was a man of whom we shall hear more in days to come: Archbishop Juozas Skvireckas. In accepting the role, Skvireckas was agreeing to ceding Vilnius and the surrounding area to

* Executed were Karolis Pozela, Juozas Greifenbergis, Kazys Giedrys, Rapolas Carnas.

Poland, thus arousing the anger, not to say the contempt, of most patriotic Lithuanians. Agreeing with the Entente powers that the future lay with Poland as the most reliable and powerful opponent of Bolshevik Russia, the Vatican was more than ready to let Lithuania disappear once again in a "unity" with Poland as it had done centuries before. And, as for the Bishop, already schooled in deserting Lithuania, he found no problem of conscience in welcoming the Nazis to Kaunas in 1941 and factually ceding the nation over to *them*. Indeed, as his own diary would reveal, he was a great admirer of Hitler.

RISE OF HITLER

Cafe full of smoke and gossip,
Bored, the bourgeois sips his lager—
Bare breasts, legs in silken stockings
Creep up closer, gleam and sparkle...
Bored, the bourgeois sips his lager...
Dollars, Marks...
Bored, the bourgeois sips his lager...
                The City— Balys Srugoa, 1896-1947

A new period opened for Lithuania—as indeed it opened for the entire world—in 1933. In 1933, Hitler at last came to power—handed that power practically on a platter, the Chancelorship of the State—by von Hindenberg himself, representative par excellence of Germany's past Prussian nobility, directly reaching back to Bismark.

In Germany's last parliamentary election, on November 6, 1932, the results showed a sharp drop, 2,000,000, in the Nazi vote—from 250 to 196 representatives to the parliament. The Communist vote had risen from 89 to 100, representing a rise of 275,000. The Social Democratic vote totaled 121. Together the votes of both working class parties could have defeated Hitler handily if they could have been coordinated. It is the tragedy of Germany that hostility between the two parties was so intense that no such coordination could be achieved.

Even so, the election results proved that the German people did not want the Nazis to rule them. Handing the chancelorship over to Hitler and thus legitimizing him was an act of class treachery. Indeed, there was hardly a country in all of Europe that was not seething with upper class plots to forestall or suppress the revolution that so many were convinced was now on the political agenda.

Looking back from a perspective of over 50 years, and particularly after the catastrophic defeat of German, Italian and all other fascisms, it might seem strange that forces in the smaller countries should have seen in Hitler not only a power to ally themselves with but, in fact, seen in his Germany a model for reorganizing their own countries. In the first few years after Hitler came to power, it seemed that he had found the key to solving the major political dilemma facing Europe. Not only did he manage to suppress opposition in his own country, and even win the support of the masses, including sections of the workers previously influenced by the Left, but he had won the support and approval of ruling powers in the West, particularly in England and France. Arousing the people by a strident and mystical nationalism, he even succeeded in unifying them for the purpose he had in mind. In fact, Hitler's achievement seemed to Western political leaders, including Churchill, to be nothing short of miraculous. Mussolini's fascism lacked the elan, the spirit of a mission, the dynamism which Hitler's facism seemed to have, especially in the beginning. In addition, say what you will, Italy could not become a stronger force than it really was by puffing itself up with Mussolini's speeches. It always remained vulnerable and, in fact, could have gone under in 1926 if the Bank of Morgan hadn't come to its rescue with timely "loans" of millions.

So, Hitler's "model" seemed very inviting to many in Europe, especially to small countries and, in due course, a number of smaller European countries, climaxed by Spain in 1936, took up the Nazi salute. As Hitler was handed victory after victory by the West, smaller politicians, the notorious pragmatists, the "realists," drew the conclusion that not only was fascism the wave of the future (as Anne Morrow Lindbergh, wife of the American Charles Lindbergh, ecstatically saw it) but that it had the backing and approval of Western imperialism and the blessing of the Pope.

Against European fascism stood only the apparently fatally weakened Soviet Union, whose dogged policy of trying to reach some form of "collective security" among European powers against Hitler was constantly frustrated and even mocked by spokesmen for those powers. In his speeches at sessions of the League of Nations, the USSR's Maxim Litvinov pounded away at the theme that war would be aimed not only at his own country, the USSR, but would envelop the "democracies" as well, that "peace was indivisible." But his warnings fell on deaf ears.

During the entire decade of the '20s and early '30s, forces in all the Western and East European countries were busy with endless intrigues. The new element, the element which Great Britain as the arbiter of the balance of powers in Europe could not handle in the same way and by the same means—bribery, buying off one internal force to pit against another, waging war by proxy, and so on—was the emergence of revolutionary Russia on the world scene. Even more frustrating was the fact that the Russian revolution had been guided, then led, by a set of most remarkable men and women who, among other assets, possessed this most extraordinary quality of all: they could not be bought or trapped by any of the hallowed means employed with such virtuosity by the web-spinners in London. The magnitude and volcanic nature of the revolution, which purified itself like a forest fire, transcended such petty means of influencing the agents of these forces. For Lenin and his closest associates the glitter of ruling class prestige, the hunger for gold, the thrust for power dimmed into insignificance when placed against the overwhelming regenerative energy released by the revolution, with its promise of reshaping the world.

This same power of revolution that helped purge the revolutionaries of petty ambitions also inspired an entire generation of just "ordinary people" with the same ideals, which then became the moral norm, shaped the people's character, which has remained basically intact ever since, and is visible even today in a period of storms and upheavals.

Germany had always been the greatest threat, not merely to Lithuania's independence but to her very existence. The total disappearance of Prussian Lithuania was an example of what fate awaited the rest of little Lithuania and the other two Baltic countries if Germany should once again engulf their lands.

Why did the Nationalists conspire with the actual and proven enemies of their countries? The explanation can lie only in the fact that the appearance of revolutionary Russia on the world scene, and proof that it could survive and, by example, encourage other countries to follow suit, was indeed a coming to life of the Manifesto's declaration that a "spectre is haunting Europe." This ghost, magnified a thousand times by fears arising from knowledge of guilt, galvanized reaction into a defense of their power and privileges *and very nature*, in all its psychological and cultural aspects, like no other force on earth. It seemed, at that time, that the Revolution would indeed sweep over the world, as revolutions broke out in Germany, Hungary, and seemed imminent in Italy and other countries, including in the Orient.

The fear of socialism was a class fear. It transcended moral boundaries. Smetona and his group represented not the national interests of Lithuania, if "Lithuania" is to be understood as its *people*, but the interests of the established landlords, newly spawned capitalists, even the German barons. Their loyalty was not to *this country* but to the highest rate of profit *anywhere*. This phenomenon of the upper classes in a nation essentially surrendering to a foreign tyrant to fend off their own revolutionary working class was not confined to Lithuania. France's "200 families" feared their own workers more than they feared Hitler, and the swift collapse of France in six weeks—though France had the largest army in Europe—was due to class treachery. General Weygand, scion of the upper class, admirer of the fascist Colonel de la Roque, leader of the Croix de Feu feared a revolution from his own soldiers more than he did the oncoming troops of Hitler whom he begged for assistance.

The flight of European capital and European business to America before and after the war was different from all other earlier emigrations. It was the money that went first seeking a safe haven. The well-to-do European "refugees" of the late '30, '40s and the postwar had nothing in common with "Europe's refuse" (unless morally) welcomed to America by an America that still remembered the pain of labor and still earned its bread by the sweat of the brow, if only as a myth.

This phenomenon—fear of socialism—was at the heart of European politics of fear and proved to be fatal in the opposition to Hitler, who played ever contemptuously on those fears, so sure was he that every ruling class in every bourgeois country in Europe was up for sale. After all, he had been the beneficiary of German upper class largesse. If the German Junker class imagined that it was using him, Hitler, as many aristocrats believed, they found out soon enough that it was he, Hitler, who used them. But by that time it was too late. In any case, Hitler knew that in every bargaining session with the West he always held the top card, not guns but ideology. His power over the German masses was worth something—a great deal, in fact. He had shaped an entire people into a weapon, and this weapon, intended to be aimed at the East, could also be turned on the West—at least for purposes of blackmail.

The attitude of the Big Powers toward the future of the Baltic states was clearly expressed in a number of decisions taken by the Entente early in the '20s. Conference after conference was held, sponsored now by the French, now by the English, to consider the "Baltic Problem." Always the aim was to form a "bloc of Baltic states" to serve as a barrier to the "spread of Bolshevism." In the eyes of the conspirators in France and England, Poland was assigned the key role in the coming struggle to isolate and hopefully to undermine Soviet Russia by means of an economic blockade and military intervention. In 1926, Britain, itself menaced by a "Bolshevik"reneral strike, was in full possession of the "Baltic problem," and in Geneva tried to hammer out a policy for the Baltic bloc that would more reliably contain the Bolshevik menace. Internationally, the policy of relentless terror and persecution of anti-fascists was applied by the Smetona group in Lithuania with unexampled zeal. This policy of internal repression more and more openly paralleled, even imitated, Hitler's own. It was inevitable that at a certain point these policies would merge. In politics, as in mathematics, things equal to the same thing are equal to each other.

A review of Hitler's policy toward the Baltics has the virtue, if nothing else, of clarity. It left no ambiguity to cloud any point. Hitler did not pursue anti-democratic aims with the slogans of democracy. The critical test of what Nazi intentions toward Lithuania were became clear in the key question of Memel, now Klaipeda, Lithuania's main opening to the Baltic Sea. Hitler had already achieved his *anschluss* with Austria on March 11, 1938. This remarkable coup was also the result of upper class treachery. Only the Austrian workers and revolutionaries had opposed giving in to Hitler and many of them paid for this premature patriotism with their lives. One should also remember that many of the Nazi's military officials, who manned the S.A., won their bloody spurs in the *Freikorps*, which had been a paramilitary force, made up of Germans who did not disband after defeat but continued (and were allowed by the Allies to continue) their depredations in Lithuania long after the end of formal hostilities. Many later S.A. leaders would recall their early years in the Baltics and the fierce fighting that took place in Lithuania with no prisoners taken. "The fighting in the Baltic States," confessed Rudolph Hoess, commandant of Auschwitz as he awaited execution, "was more savage and more bitter than any I had experienced in the World War or in the *Freikorps*. There was no real front, for the enemy was everywhere. When it came to a clash, it was a fight to the death, and no quarter was given or expected..."[19]

At Munich, in September 1938, Hitler gave assurances to France's Daladier and England's Chamberlain that if they gave him Czechoslovakia he would make no further requests for *lebensraum* after that. He was given Czechoslovakia and as a tidbit, Memel. This "appeasement" of Hitler was sold to the people of France and England as having secured "peace in our times." The image of Chamberlain arriving in England waving a piece of paper, signed by that "gentleman," Hitler, which assured Chamberlain that Hitler was a decent fellow after all, remains indelibly burned on the memory of mankind. Everyone in Europe presumably let out a sigh of relief at the news. Leon Blum, then France's Socialist leader, hailed the agreement with Hitler, declaring in *Le Populaire*: "Life has become normal. One can go to work again and sleep comfortably; one can enjoy the beauty of the autumn sun."

However Western Europe greeted Munich, as far as the Polish ruling clique was concerned, Munich was a signal that now the West would not interfere with Polish demands on Lithuania. After all, serving up Austria to Germany on a diplomatic platter could hardly be misinterpreted. The Polish government decided the iron was hot and they should strike. They began to make fresh demands on the Lithuanian Smetona group, organizing demonstrations with planted agents carrying signs and chanting slogans, "On to Kaunas!" Poland now wanted all of Lithuania and moved three Polish divisions to the Lithuanian border to emphasize her demands.

Nazi Germany supported (if indeed it did not inspire) the Polish moves. In fact, if it came to war with Lithuania, Germany expected to take over that part of Lithuania west of the Nemunas up to Dubysa and the Klaipeda territory.

It was at this point that the Soviet Union (March 16, 1938) advised Poland in sharp terms that any invasion of Lithuania would mean the abrogation of the Non-Aggression Pact that Poland had signed with the

Soviet Union in 1932. It was this threat that made Poland pull back its forces. But nevertheless it raised the demand—issued as an ultimatum—that Lithuania establish full diplomatic relations with Poland, which would have meant de facto recognition that Vilnius and environs legally belonged to Poland.

In view of the great hubbub made by the Allies over Lithuanian "independence" since, and especially since 1940, it is instructive to note that the Allies then (1938) advised the Lithuanian government to accept Poland's demands. The British government made it clear where it stood, informing the Lithuanians that unless it accepted Poland's demands "it (England) could bear no responsibility in case the ultimatum was rejected."[20]

Again (March 18, 1938), the Soviet government warned the Poles against taking action against Lithuania. Meanwhile, word of the secret negotiations had gotten out to the people and they reacted with consternation. They understood that giving in to Poland's ultimatum meant not only losing Vilnius but surrendering Lithuania's fragile independence as well. Nevertheless, on March 19, 1938, the government capitulated. The Lithuanian Communist Party issued an appeal: "Lithuania's independence is in danger!" Demonstrations broke out all over the country. And, more than a footnote to the times, is the incident that happened at a performance of *Samson and Delilah* at the State Theatre in Kaunas, on March 20, 1938, when a man from the audience rose up and denounced the action of the government, demanding its resignation. His name was Justas Paleckis. He was immediately arrested. But a day would come when he would be elected president of the republic....

Meanwhile, opposition to the Smetona government sellout spread, with huge rallies in Kaunas and elsewhere, with Smetona's police dispersing the crowds. Indeed, so unpopular was the capitulation of the Smetona government to Poland that in addition to the Communist Party, which was the first to react, now other parties joined in, including the Christian Democrats and Social Democrats. The demand was for Smetona and his clique to resign, to be replaced by a coalition government. It is important to note also that even out-and-out nationalist organizations and parties, caught by surprise, also reacted—at least their ordinary membership reacted—with confusion and consternation, some of them backing the demand for Smetona's resignation, to be replaced by a coalition government of various parties.

Social conflicts multiplied as the economic situation worsened, including among the "middle class": teachers, for instance. Wrote *Lietuvos Zinos*, a liberal paper:

The lot of a teacher who has a family is becoming truly tragic; he who devotes all his energy and his health to the children of other people, cannot hope to educate his own children... Teachers are menaced by illness—tuberculosis is a frequent guest among them...

In fact, social tension rose to such a pitch that some action on the part of Smetona became obligatory. On March 24, 1938, the sitting government with Juozas Tubelis as premier resigned, only to be replaced by a new nationalist government led by the Catholic priest, the Reverend Vladas Mironas. To gain acceptance, this "new" government called itself a "labor government," which seemed sufficient to calm the opposition of most bourgeois parties, since with a priest at the head of the government, it seemed that the Vatican was now backing Smetona, who remained president.

But hardly had Mironas assumed power than he reaffirmed the policy of the previous government, which the Communist Party scorned as a case of change that brought no change. Lithuania, under the Nationalists, had graphically proven that, from the Nationalist point of view, "independence" as such was a chimera for Lithuania. Its own real choice was between the "West" and the Soviet Union—and for them this did not present a viable alternative. Nevertheless, the Lithuanian military attache in Moscow, Colonel K. Skucas, grasped the fact and realistically wrote to his government in March 1938, that "Small states are once more given a lesson that ... their own strength is not enough for maintaining their independence and defending their interests; they need support from one of several great powers..."

He recommended that "It might be useful to seek for such support from Moscow."

But this advice fell on deaf ears. National feelings were ruthlessly suppressed by a nationalist government. Singing patriotic songs became subversive. *Tiesa*, the often underground newspaper of the Communist Party, commented:

This year (1938) not a single state office hoisted a flag, only the population, expressing their hatred for the actions of Polish imperialists, hoisted flags. Thus the fascists, making friends with Beck and Co., [who ruled Poland] today give up the Vilnius area.

To drive the point home, on November 29, 1938, the police shut down the Union for the Liberation of Vilnius and stopped the publication of its magazine, *Musu Vilnius*. In fact, even to mention the word "Vilnius" made one suspect.

Surrendering Vilnius meant—although it was not put so directly then—also surrendering Klaipeda.

When, in due course, after Munich (September 1938), Smetona was confronted by the German demand that he cede Klaipeda to Germany, he hardly wavered: he gave in very shortly after the required ritualistic language of regret had been voiced. The fact was that Germans had been engaged in various intrigues in Klaipeda for years and their activities had been well known to the police, but little had been done to stop them. The Nazis by this time had refined their tactic of "boring from within": of sending Germans or collaborators ahead into a targeted country, under the guise of "tourists" or a cultural organization of sports, the notorious *Kulturverbund*, which then acted as saboteurs and, on the arranged-for signal, "rose" and took over—usually without any but token opposition.

Klaipeda (Memel) had been just such a target from the moment Hitler came to power in 1933. He already sent his agents—the Nazi Dr. Ernst Neuman, a veterinary surgeon, and Pastor von Sass—into Klaipeda with instructions to prepare the ground for Nazi annexation. Here we might pause to note that all the over-worked language of spy novels acquired their original reality with the appearance of the Nazis. Hitler indeed sent "agents" ahead into unsuspecting, or even suspecting, countries, where they were instructed to lay the groundwork for a future takeover. He indeed planted spies wherever he could, recruited by blackmail or by manipulated ambition, or ideological zeal, and got them to carry out subversive assignments. His agents used money to buy up newspapers and journalists, to bribe politicians. No means were ignored nor considered too contemptible (or even childish)—from concocting stories of oppression of German nations in the Sudenland to dressing up German prisoners in Polish uniforms in order to perpetrate a provocation used as a pretext for invasion (as in Poland). Often the puppets were then disposed of.

The Neuman-Sass clique working with Voldemaras in Klaipeda was well-known to the police who monitored their activities. In fact, they were arrested in 1934 in an attempted *putsch* that failed. Their sentences were light and in 1938 they were in any case set free.

Hitler was a master in intimidating and bringing to heel particularly heads of governments, ranging all the way from Dollfuss and Schuschnigg, of Austria, to Benes of Czechoslovakia. Included, now, were Smetona and Juozas Urbsys. True, none of the bourgeois political leaders who bowed to Hitler's ranting and raving had the stomach to oppose him, not on military grounds (for Czechoslovakia along with her ally, France, possessed enough troops to stop Hitler), but on political, ideological grounds.

Smetona, too, was dominated by ideology. He needed neither lures nor threats. He met Hitler more than halfway. This would be illustrated vividly by the Klaipeda episode which, like all the other European governmental surrenders climaxed at Munich, was also a rush to surrender—almost as though into the arms of a lover—when no surrender was mandatory. To increase the pressure on Lithuania, Poland signed a non-aggression pact with Germany on January 26, 1934. Although the intentions of Germany toward Lithuania were clear to anyone awake at all, it was nothing short of amazing to see how studiously the leaders of the country most in peril labored not to see the obvious. As Hitler saturated Klaipeda with German agents—German residents outnumbered Lithuanians by 59,337 to 37,625*— still Lithuanian officials, like the then Foreign Minister Dr. Dovas Zaunius, insisted that Lithuania had nothing to fear, since they were sure Germany had no plans to take Klaipeda over. So said *Lietuvos Aidos*, a Nationalist organ, and so said Nationalist Party magazine *Vairos*. *Lietuvos Aidos* made its sentiments clear when, on May 22, 1933, it wrote: "For our sake, we are glad that communism did not win in Germany." For fascists all over Europe, the resounding May 22, 1933 triumph of German fascism headed by Hitler was a bugle call for victory. What was most impressive was that Hitler had managed to gain enormous concessions from France and England *without firing a shot!* The message could not be misunderstood: the West *supported* Hitler's aims. This message was not even subliminal. In Spain, the West had stood aside as Franco (with Mussolini and Hitler backing him with arms and troops) assassinated Spanish democracy. But even before Spain, the signs were unmistakable.

Hitler's successes encouraged and activated all the nationalist forces in all of Europe. They began to imitate the Nazi party even in detail. In Lithuania, led by Augustinas Voldemaras, and supported by Staff General Petras Kubiliunas, the Nationalist Party (Tautininkai) began to take steps to distance itself from its agreement with the USSR and to open up avenues of accommodation with Nazi Germany itself. The still underground, but rapidly growing in influence, the Communist Party of Lithuania issued a warning that "Nazi Germany is the main enemy," and described the situation then obtaining in these prophetic words:

> Intensification of Nazi activities in the Klaipeda territory, as well as the plot guided by the Nazi agents, especially increased the danger for Lithuania. On the other hand, Lithuania's strength has been weakened by the Smetona-Mironas government, which under cover of alleged neutrality, is step-by-step surrendering to Nazi Germany: this policy has already led to giving up Lithuania's position in Klaipeda.

In *Tiesa*, as the whole world hailed the Munich Pact, as bringing "peace in our time," the Communist Party of Lithuania declared:

---

* Also, there were 38,404 native "Memelanders" who had been born in Memel (Klaipeda) and considered themselves the only true natives. There were also 5,278 "aliens" and 900 "others," according to the 1925 Lithuanian census.

No peace has been won, the danger of world war has increased. The hour is approaching when the fascist aggressors, having torn Czechoslovakia, will turn their bloody paws to the small nations and first of all Lithuania.[21]

In March, 1938, the Swiss *Der Weltwache* had already declared: "Lithuania is forced to her knees. Kaunas cannot pursue an independent policy any more."

Indeed, the bourgeois concept of "independence" was being subjected to severe tests. The most elementary principle underlying the reality of independence is a country's ability to defend itself. Small countries had only the option of maneuvering. Only when mass demonstrations forced its hand did the government move to arrest the well-known German agents conspiring to detach Klaipeda from Lithuania and turn it over to Germany. The *putsch* was nipped in the bud, and 126 of the chief conspirators were arrested, though none were given severe sentences, or in those cases where severe sentences (for four) were given (death), their sentences were later commuted by Smetona, and finally they were freed. Neuman was given 12 years and von Sass, 8. Voldemaras, who had been up to his neck in the conspiracy—this man had once been Premier of the country and Smetona's political crony—was also arrested and sentenced to 12 years. He died in prison in 1944.

The process by which the Lithuanian government of Smetona gave in to Hitler is vividly described in a telegram from the Soviet charge d'affaires in Lithuania to Moscow:

March 22, 1939.
At 12:10 midnight I was called in by Lazaraitis who communicated to me following: Ribbentrop had said to Urbsys [Lithuanian foreign minister] that the incorporation of Klaipeda into Germany was vital and urgent for the Klaipeda Germans. Unless the Lithuanian Government gave up Klaipeda voluntarily, riots would immediately break out there, making it necessary for the Reichwehr to intervene. Should one German be killed in the riots, the Reichwehr would go into Greater Lithuania. Ribbentrop suggested that Urbys (*sic*) promptly get in touch with Mironas [then premier] and make a decision over the telephone. Urbys promised to give a reply immediately after his return to Kaunas. As soon as Urbsys arrived on March 21 the German Minister called on him to say that a Lithuanian delegation was expected in Berlin not later than March 22. The Cabinet decided, Lazaraitis said, to yield to force and took a decision to transfer Klaipeda to Germany. A delegation headed by Urbsys is leaving for Berlin today. Along with the German Minister, the French, English and Italian Ministers have also been notified of the Cabinet decision.[22]

On March 20, "it was the turn of Foreign Minister Joseph Urbsys to sit where Tiso and Hacha had sat and receive the same treatment." Both Tiso and Hacha—Tiso of Slovakia and Hacha, Czech president—were Nazi collaborators and were executed after the war. But Urbsys survived everything, and in 1990 in his 90s, he was resurrected by the Landsbergis forces in Lithuania and like a ghost returned to haunt Lithuanian democracy, which he had every reason to believe he had sold forever to Hitler in 1939. Even so, an observer of today's Lithuania saw him as a man "intimidated" by the Sajudis forces. He has died since in disgrace.

Soviet Russia proposed to the Lithuanian government to send troops to defend Klaipeda with the Lithuanians but Smetona turned the offer down, claiming (according to the British diplomat in Kaunas) that "passage of Russian troops might result in Communist Party uprisings."

It was an already familiar formula. Obsessive fear of the Soviets made the Germans seem attractive. On March 22, 1939, Nazi troops goose-stepped into Klaipeda, which instantly became Memel again, wildly welcomed by some 60,000 German residents (including recent "tourists") while 40,000 Lithuanians and others watched from their windows with apprehension if not yet fear. The Lithuanians, instructed by Smetona, put up no resistance, even some joined in the welcome, waving little flags with the swastika on them. Very soon they were to be honored by the presence of the Führer himself, who had come to Klaipeda-Memel on the pocket battleship *Deutchland* through a rocky sea and, though desperately seasick, forced himself to make an appearance despite the cold and his heaving stomach. Once again, Hitler had achieved a great victory without firing a shot—in fact, by simply speaking on the telephone. With Memel in German hands, and the Finns, under Mannerheim openly hostile, it could now be confidently assumed that the Baltic Sea was closed to Soviet shipping, or could be closed at any moment.[23]

All this took place with the benevolent "neutrality" of the Allied powers. None of them protested the move, including the American Secretary of State, Sumner Welles. Wrote the Lithuanian ambassador to the USA, Povilas Zadeikas, to his government in Kaunas, March 31, 1939: "It is clear to me that the State Department was interested in attributing Memel to Germany as soon as possible."

The loss of Klaipeda to Germany and of Vilnius to Poland left the "independent" government of Lithuania, now seated in Kaunas, nothing but an empty plain with a string of villages between Vilnius and Klaipeda to govern.

The Smetona government—though it hardly deserved the dignity of the title—did not mourn the loss of Klaipeda for long but accepted it "philosophically," grateful that Germany allowed them to use the port. An agreement signed with Germany on May 20, 1939, was advertised as being a "solution" to the crisis.

To step back a moment. In July 1935, the Comintern had met in Moscow for its Seventh Congress and there evolved the strategy for resisting the drive of fascism toward war. The policy then adopted indicated a sharp turn in Communist tactics from those followed up until then. Instead of "class against class," or, as the Chinese would put it later, "spear against spear," now, faced with the common and growing menace, the working class of the world held out a hand of cooperation to every class in each country which was threatened by fascism and wished to resist it, a turn in tactics that became known as the "united" or "popular front." This "front" included sections of the patriotic bourgeoisie, even those sections of the ruling class that recoiled against being swallowed up by the Nazi shark. Most significantly a conscious attempt was made to heal the split between Communists and Socialists.

In Lithuania, (as in Latvia and Estonia), the Communist Party adapted its tactics to the broader, more basic tactic of popular resistance to fascism, which was seen as heading the world towards war. It was the Bulgarian Dimitrov, who had won world acclaim for his masterful and courageous opposition to German fascism while a prisoner in a court trial at Leipzig in 1933, who made the classic definition of fascism as the "open terrorist dictatorship of the most reactionary, the most chauvinistic, the most imperialist element of finance capital." Germany was characterized as the "spearhead" of international finance capital in its supreme bid to destroy the working class movements everywhere in the world.

The Congress destroyed all lingering illusions that there was anything revolutionary, truly revolutionary, in Nazi theory and certainly none in its practice. Despite the demagogic Nazi attacks on "plutocrats" and the rabid use of the world "revolution," Hitlerism posed no real threat to the "plutocrats" of Germany and their "revolution" was a *counter*revolution. The Congress also made clear its position on the key question of nationalism, declaring in an adopted resolution that "While Communists are irreconcilable opponents, on principle, of bourgeois nationalism, of every variety, they are by no means supporters of national nihilism, of an attitude of unconcern for the fate of their own people."

In Lithuania, the Communist Party called on all true patriots, every Lithuanian who had the survival of his nation and (in view of the genocidal policies of the Nazis) his people at heart, to join with all others in resisting the danger of fascism and therefore war and subordinating all other considerations to this single overwhelming one. Communists had to penetrate through the demagogic covering of the Nationalists to its fascist heart, warning that nationalism was not nor could it be a form of government that was somewhere in between "red" and "brown." It showed that Lithuanian nationalism was fascism in disguise.

Where the policy of the united or popular front was adopted, as in France and Spain, the masses rose to the call. In Spain they resisted the attempt of Franco fascism to gain power by treason, and in that struggle international capital educated the world's masses in the meaning of class loyalty, as France, England, the USA, though "democracies" stood aside and watched their sister democracy in Spain go down in flames. As always, they resorted to a legal fig leaf: in this instance declared a "neutrality" in the war, the benefits of which "neutrality" fell on the side of Franco. Hitler, Mussolini, and Franco could ask for nothing better: a hands-off policy while they brought all their power to bear on the Loyalist government, whose election by all the totem means supposedly held sacred by "democracy" helped it not at all. Leon Blum, whose diatribes against the Communists reeked with democratic rhetoric, refused to help the Spaniards in their eleventh hour. Indeed, France even closed its border to keep out the Spanish refugees fleeing for their lives into France, and those who managed to get in were confined to concentration camps where they were treated like animals.

If France itself did not go fascist, though it threatened to with the rise of the Croix de Feu, led by de la Roque, most admired by General Weygand (who fought the Red Army in Poland in 1920 and later was instrumental in leading the French forces not so much to defeat as to betrayal to the Nazis), it was because of the uprising of the people in huge popular front demonstrations in which the Socialist and Communist Parties united against what was seen as a common threat.

This proved not possible in Lithuania. The Smetona clique was already deep in conspiracy with fascist Germany. But the people, as they watched Hitler come closer and closer to their borders, were alarmed. They had watched with dismay the march of Nazi troops, almost without even token resistance into the Rhineland, into Austria, into the Sudenland, into Czechoslovakia, into Klaipeda, and finally into Poland. Without needing to be told, most Lithuanians—*all* Lithuanians—knew that Lithuania itself was next. Over 100 Lithuanian volunteers fought Franco in Spain in 1936, with 36 dying there.

To resist the German army, the Lithuanians had no more than a fictional army of their own. It was crucial that they seek allies—and the most available potential ally could come only from their neighbor, Soviet Russia. But that way was barred. The menace from Germany was real, and proven; even so, in the eyes of the Lithuanian governing group it seemed less morbid than did the danger implicit in any relationship of trust and reliance with the Soviet Union. One cannot say that they entered into relationships, both hidden and open, with Nazi Germany with their eyes closed. On the contrary, it was Nazi Germany's dramatic success in suppressing its working-class parties, both the Communist and Social Democratic, taking over the enormous union structure in the so-called Labor Front under Dr.

Robert Ley and making it no more than an obedient servant of the ruling powers, that entranced them so much. Today, as revisionists are busy remaking that past, when "everybody" was both anti-Communist and anti-Nazi, such reminders of what really happened, though not welcome, are nevertheless obligatory. Possibly it requires both a wrench of the memory and of the imagination to reproduce the ideology of the Smetona group that made it possible to see in the German concentration camps, crematoria, and genocide the dawn of a new order in which they felt at home. Nor can it be pleaded that they acted in ignorance, and even if they did, ignorance of the laws of history is no excuse before the bar of historic justice.

No doubt they were not conversant with the diaries of Goebbels which fell into the hands of the allies only after victory, and his plans for the Baltics were not precisely known. But the truth is that if not the precise plans certainly the *attitude*—the contempt which the Germans showed, and had showed, and with their *Freikorps* massive murders in the '20s and even '30s in which no quarter was given—could not be misunderstood. In any case, Goebbels was writing in his diary (which he intended for eventual publication but not when and how it was) for March 16, 1942:

> In the East, nationalistic currents are increasingly observable in all former Baltic States. The population there apparently imagined that the German Wehrmacht would shed its blood to set up a new government in these midget states, which at the end of the war, or possibly during the war, would veer over to the side of our enemies. This is a childish, naive bit of imagination which makes no impression upon us ... National Socialism is much more cold-blooded and much more realistic in all these questions.... It does only what is useful for its own people, and in this instance the interest of our people undoubtedly lies in the vigorous establishment of German order within this area without paying any attention to the claims, more or less justified, of the small nationalities living there.

Did the Smetona government know that this was the real thinking of the Nazi overlords?

Theodore Oberlander was put in charge of the Plan for the East, under Alfred Rosenberg, Reich Minister (who had been born, incidentally, and grew up in Czarist and bourgeois Estonia) who succinctly expressed the essence of this "Plan":

> The Reich's representatives in Estonia, Latvia and Lithuania should aim for the establishment of a German proletariat, so that in the future these regions may be incorporated into the German Reich, germanizing the racially suitable elements and destroying the undesirable elements.

"Undesirable elements" was code language—and not too obscure code language—for Communists, Social Democrats, liberals and Jews. Oberlander, made *Reischleiter* of the "Union for the German East," had the job of organizing Fifth Columns within the Baltic countries, as well as within Poland and the Ukraine. His tactics were to provoke Nationalist and anti-Semitic agitation among the people, launch criminal attacks on workers and all democratic organizations, and so profoundly undermine the morale of the people that when the moment of invasion struck, they would be so disorganized that they would be unable to put up effective resistance.

As director of the "Institute for East European Economy," located in Königsberg, he laid elaborate plans for Lithuania's future, along with the future of other East European countries, which was a future limited to agriculture and stock raising, to producing the raw material for the mills and factories of Germany.

Oberlander traveled often and freely to Lithuania. Even as early as 1923, the then-Lithuanian government felt it necessary to check on his activities. He met too often with known spies and paid agents. During the trial of the Nazis in Klaidpeda in 1934, it was established by the court that Dr. Oberlander had been the moving spirit behind the subversive activities of the Nazi underground, which had organized and carried out the rebellion, using the considerable German population as a base.

If the attempt to seize power failed in 1934, it did not fail five years later. For on March 22, 1939, the Nazis took over Klaipeda, calling it Memel then and, hopefully, forever. With Oberlander as *gauleiter*, the Nazis, far better organized and armed now with the impressive record of Nazi triumphs already under their belt, launched a campaign of terror against those who resisted. Whatever resistance there was, however, did not have the support or approval of Smetona and his group. Boasted Oberlander in a lecture delivered at Greifsweld University, soon after taking Klaipeda without firing a shot:

> The Jews are already leaving Memel ... Today the new S.A. batallions march through Memel. But inasmuch as the Lithuanian authorities have not yet fulfilled all the conditions of the Memel Statute, they had better do this, and soon, according to the spirit and working of that document. Kauen [Kaunas, where the Smetona government had parked itself] must now take the initiative. Hitler, in Berlin, will make the decision.

In his lectures to his German—and also to his "honorary" German Lithuanian audience—he referred always to Lithuanians as "Eastern subhumans" who had to be exterminated. In speech after speech, he reiterated the theme that the "border" regions of Germany would have to be annexed to Germany and the native population subjugated, sorted out according to how closely individuals met Nordic physical standards, absorbing them, and branding the unlucky ones as "undesirable elements" and making real slaves of them, or exterminating them.

Among his arguments, he constantly repeated that "The low birth rate of the German people, in comparison with the high one of the Slavic people, is a political factor of the very first importance. The increase in the Slavic population may become a serious threat not only to the German East, the first bulwark of the Western world, but also to all of Europe...." (*German Work*, vol. 10, October 1936).

Malthus was brought back to life and squeezed once more for whatever juice was left in him. Death was all the information and wisdom he produced, and the Nazis admired him. But further with Oberlander:

> The fight for nationalism is nothing but the continuation of war by other means and under the cover of peace.... It is a fight which lasts for generations. Its only aim is: Extermination.[24]

These Nazi "intellectuals" had half-digested Clausewitz, as well as Machiavelli, not to speak of Nietzche and de Sade, all of which was regurgitated by a certain Adolf Schickelgruber But mainly they felt that they had blackmailing power over the bourgeoisie for they had ferreted their secret out, and knew their bourgeoisie inside and out. With this knowledge that at the heart of the upperclass rule was nothing but power based on the submission of the masses, and that they would pay anything to anybody who could guarantee keeping the masses submissive, they understood that, like an impertinent blackmailer, indeed, they could even tease their panicked betters now and then with threats that implied they might betray them. All of German nobility had gone over to the Nazis, safe in the fatuous assumption that these one-time servants of theirs who came when they were called and went when they were dismissed would remain servants through everything. It was no accident that after March 1933, a large number of aristocrats and upper middle class intellectuals from the universities joined the SS. In 1938, 18.7 percent of the Obergruppenführer (generals) of the SS had titles.

Of course the aristocrats did not completely depend on what they supposed was the inherent instinct of the lower classes to come to heel when ordered. If they needed Hitler, Hitler needed them—or rather their money. And it was the leading banks of Germany (with their international connections) that funded his party. Presumably they believed that what they could give they could as readily also take away. The fact is that at no time did they try. (And when in 1944, they tried to assassinate Hitler, they bungled the job. It was too late anyhow.)

Oberlander was the very embodiment of both the knowledge that Hitlerism was in secret in a panderer's league with riches and of the arrogance such knowledge bred. He fit the formula for a certain *untermench*, described in *The Nazi Legacy*:

Throughout history, societies have maintained a staff of untouchables, those who do the dirty work without which civilization could not function, and who are despised, sometimes even persecuted, for undertaking it. There have always been night-soil carters, pawnbrokers, [illegal] abortionists, unlicensed peddlers, smugglers of brandy in times of prohibition. The caste gets no thanks from the society [class] that employs them. In response, they have developed a sour solidarity among themselves.[25]

This list would now be extended in a mordant way. To it would be added *Kapos*—those brutal guards in the camps—police spies, Nazi collaborators, low-level officials who stole the boots from the executed, executives swollen with distinction and pride as accepted servants of the Nazis in their conquered countries, German hausfrau who never asked where the French nylons came from, or the Polish ham, or even the Polish children she "adopted"—all of these were contemporaries of Hoess who "did not have the breadth of view" of his Nazi superiors to question the "correctness" of a policy which condemned half of Europe to the ovens or to sudden death on the battlefield.

Oberlander helped lay the groundwork for the attack on Poland, which followed on September 1, 1939, and largely due to his previous subversive activities, including staging the bizarre provocation on the evening before with Germans dressed in Polish uniforms "attacking" a German radio station, but more decisively the Polish government of Colonels refusing assistance from the Soviet Union, Poland fell in six days. Of the 300 military airports, the Soviets discovered that 292 faced the Soviet border—eight defended Poland from Germany.

What transpired then in Poland—unrestrained terror, the erection of extermination camps everywhere, a relentless search for Communists and Jews—all this was there for any who wished to know what lay in store for them. The Soviets marched into Poland from the east to mark the line beyond which the Nazis understood they could not go, and to rescue as many Poles, Belorussians, Jews and Ukrainians as possible. Once again, they liberated Vilnius, which had been in Poland's control for almost two decades, and restored it immediately to Lithuania—it was still Smetona's Lithuania, but no word of gratitude exists as coming from that government for the restoration of its historic capital.

Nevertheless, Georgi Dmitrov, whose defiance of the Nazis in the Nazi court in Leipzig after the staged Reichstag Fire in 1933, had set the model for Communist courage in the face of the enemy on his home grounds, and who now headed the Communist International, declared:

There never has been nor is there today in the world any state, other than the Soviet Union, which has, of its own accord, ceded a whole region to a small people living on its borders, out of regard for the national interests of the people.

In return for giving Vilnius back to it, the Soviets expected the Smetona government to abide by the Mutual Assistance Pact, which forbade negotiations with Hitler. But apparently Smetona interpreted the return of Vilnius, not as an act of generosity but as further proof of Soviet aggressive intentions. The constant in his schemes was hostility to the "East," and Smetona did not hesitate to enter into secret negotiations with the Nazis, following out the logic of his obsession that everything the Soviets did for Lithuania was a threat and salvation lay only with Hitler. This culminated in the final denunciation of the liberation of Lithuania in 1944 as "occupation" and "aggression" and "annexation."

But however Smetona and his clique saw things in the reverse mirror of their ideology, the Lithuanian people, already alerted by the Klaipeda takeover of what fate lay in store for them, feared for their lives. Once before, just after the end of WWI which, however, did not end for them, they had suffered the untold agonies wreaked on them by the German *Freikorps*, that training ground for future SA and SS Nazi officers. The *Freikorps* were "mercenary units formed to replace the disintegrating army of the (German) empire. (These units) fought in the Baltic region during 1919 in the often ferocious postwar clashes of Germans, Poles, and Russians, as each national group sought to establish or maintain its authority in an area where prewar boundaries were no longer valid and new ones had not yet been defined."[26]

Veterans of this savage period graduated by a natural progression into the Nazi SA, which "was made up of those informal militias that were organized after 1919 by communities and counties, as well as by the government as a protection against Communist terror which, beginning in November 1918, continued to create disturbances in one region or another. When the Baltic venture was brought to an end by the inter-allied Baltic Commission created for the purpose, the hopes of the Communists—churned up and financed by Moscow—were re-awakened. Even the Reichstag parties felt it essential to establish security divisions beyond the army and the police, so that, if necessary, attempts at a *putsch* from the left could be countered. Thus, these militias were legalized and supported by the state, and some of them were even provided with arms by the government. I need only remind you of the Organization Esherich, which acquired something like a hundred thousand guns. Today we have the Reichsbanner Black, Red, Gold as the governmental security troop against the left and right." So spoke Hitler's one-time chief of the Nazi Storm Troopers Otto Wagener, confidant of Hitler and unrepentant Nazi to the end.[27]

This version of events is crammed with the type of euphemisms we became even more familiar with in the ensuing years, like establishing "security divisions behind the army and police" which were the marauding, murderous bands that lay waste to postwar Lithuania and formed the basis for Hitler's SS in 1933.

But the prelude to this was being shaped by acts perpetrated by the Smetona government still in ostensible power. The Soviet government requested more tangible proof of Smetona's sincerity in his sworn pledge to uphold his part of the Mutual Assistance Pact. With invasion imminent, the Soviet government asked for permission to return Red Army troops to take up defensive positions on the German border in Lithuania (as well as Latvia and Estonia).

The Soviets had good reason to be on the alert. The *Kulturverbund* was notorious as a sports coverup for infiltrating Nazi fifth columnists into a targeted country who, at the prearranged signal, would drop their bats and balls and uncover their guns. Even so, such large-scale appearance of "tourists" of course had to be known to the Smetona government, who might quite likely have planned on their support to repel the Soviet units entering the country to defend the borders. That this ploy failed is quite possibly another reason why Smetona felt so naked before the oncoming Soviet troops, especially when his demand that the Lithuanian army oppose them was turned down by the generals.

God knows he had tried! When the war between Finland and the Soviet Union broke out in November 1939, not only was reaction the whole world over re-inspired with hope—and the phoney war long stalled on the Western Front gave every indication of coming alive, with men facing each other across No Man's Land now joined together to march east—but the Baltic fascists, nationalists and reactionaries of every stripe also took on new hope.

In December 1939 (one month after the war started), and March, 1940, the month it ended, leaders of all three Baltic countries began to conspire in earnest. They were sure their hour had struck, and indeed, Ulmanis, Latvia's head, informed members of the Latvian army that "the hour of decision" had arrived. He was aware that the Allies had ready a force of 57,000 to march East. Smetona openly called for action against the Soviet Union at a fascist-organized congress held in March. He felt secure enough—and fatuous enough—to mock the Russians referring to them in a contemptuous way as "Slavs," which Lithuanians, of course, are not. Neither are Eskimos.

Now opened up a series of provocations against Soviet personnel and soldiers, reminiscent of the same tactics to be used 40-odd years later by the Landsbergis forces, calculated to precipitate a bloody clash with Soviet troops which could then be used to incite mobs by waving the bloody shirt. But these provocations only resulted in the Soviets demanding that their troops be allowed to take up their stations on the borders. As we know, after a bitter and heated discussion among Smetona's entourage, consent was finally given especially when the head of the army, General Vincas Vitkauskas and former head, General Stays Rastikis, refused Smetona's demand that they resist the Russians.

Regardless of how this move, and the sequence of events that preceded it, has since been pictured—and no doubt Nationalists and those in the West wishing to preserve an irredentist feeling among the Baltic peoples did not hail it—the fact of the matter is that the sight of Red Army contingents moving up to the border brought great reassurance to the Lithuanian population. However the 1939 pact between Hitler and Stalin is to be read, there was no ambiguity about the purpose of these troops—they were marching to stand as a barrier to the march east—*Drang nach Osten*—of Hitler's forces.

"NEUTRAL" ON THE SIDE OF FASCISM

These nights are so dark and frightening,
These thoughts are so grimly disquieting ...
Ballad–Vincas Mykolaitis-Putinas, 1893-1967

Smetona had already signed a treaty with Germany right after the fall of Poland, in September 1939. In this treaty, the Lithuanian government pledged that "Lithuania stands under the protection of the German Reich."[28]

All during the first part of 1939, the Soviets had conducted almost desperate negotiations with Great Britain and France in what proved to be a forlorn attempt to forge an anti-fascist united front, aimed at stopping Nazi expansion. For years the USSR's Foreign Minister Maxim Litvinov, had been crying in and out of season for "collective security," and had been snubbed at the foreign offices of Britain and France. To the cry for "collective security," he was answered by Roosevelt's pallid, "quarantine the aggressor," a slogan with no content, or rather, it already had a morbid content, for it had already been put to the test with Franco. Toward the Spanish war, which was clearly a war instigated by fascist treason, the allies chose to be "neutral." This was a case of being "neutral" on the side of the aggressor. In damning both sides–the innocent and the guilty–only the guilty benefit. Germany and Italy did not feel inhibited by any qualms of conscience, or legal restraints, and intervened directly on the side of Franco, sending him arms while countries friendly to the Loyalists were forbidden to send arms to the Loyalist government. The world is constantly reminded of how effective this "even-handed" treatment of Spain proved to be in viewing Picasso's *Guernica*. *Guernica* had been reduced to rubble by Germany's Condor Legion, which bombed it literally non-stop as the Americans later bombed Dresden and seeing in Franco's war a valuable training ground for World War II, as indeed it turned out to be.

When it became clear, in weeks of futile negotiations with lower echelon representatives from France and Great Britain who, it turned out, had not been authorized to reach any binding agreement with the USSR, the Soviets concluded the negotiations which, in any case, at least in the opinion of their ambassador to France, was less an attempt to reach an agreement than it was a fishing expedition "to find out the state our army is in."[29]

It had taken the British 17 days to reach Moscow by boat, when a plane could have brought them there in hours, and the Soviets, sitting down to conduct serious business even with these unimportant representatives, soon realized that the talks would have very little to do with concrete plans, but would be "talks about talks." The Soviets were very anxious to get assurances on a number of key matters—cooperation with the Poles (refused) and with an allied assurance that they would come to the assistance of the Baltic countries if they were attacked by Hitler. Refused. The British explained to the by now disillusioned Soviets that they couldn't convince the Poles to cooperate with the Soviets—to let the Red Army cross its borders—nor could they convince the leaders of the Baltics—all of them fascists and dictators of their own countries and secret or open friends of Hitler—to accept the help of the Red Army in case they were attacked by the Germans—a dead certainty. In fact, the allies' refusal to commit themselves to the defense of the Baltics was nothing more than an invitation to Hitler to march east, an "invitation" which the Soviets read to mean that if the Nazis kept on marching "east," all the way to Moscow, incorporating the willing armies of the three Baltic countries as they went, it would not particularly worry France and Great Britain.

It was at this point, when all hope of reaching a true military alliance with the West had gone by the board, that the Nazis offered the Soviets a non-aggression pact. And, reading all the signs to mean that they were being trussed up as a sacrificial lamb in the coming war which the British hoped would be limited to war between Russia and Germany alone—and such hopes were liberally expressed in reactionary quarters all over Europe and America—while the other powers remained on the sidelines cheering each other on to greater and greater mutual slaughter, the Soviets took what looked to them like the only way out. They signed.

This act, and this period, remains a sensitive one to this day. Some see in it Soviet treachery, particularly those whose sense of honor could not be appeased unless the Soviets went down to defeat with all flags flying! Western hagiography excuses Chamberlain who is described merely as a naive old man who "was deceived and cheated by a wicked man," very much like little Red Riding Hood meeting the wolf in grandmother's clothing. Chamberlain was no naif. He understood precisely what he wanted to achieve—the destruction of the USSR—and his eagerness to bring it about was so extreme that he was willing to serve up country after country to Hitler's appetite so long as he believed he could achieve that purpose. If he was deceived, it wasn't by an "evil man" only. It was largely self- (class) deception. Hitler knew how to manipulate class obsessions and did not choose to be Number One in Europe after England. He wanted to be Number One *over* England, or at least equal to England. And he chose his own way of doing it. Nobody was deceived because of honorable motives acting as blinders to evil. One evil man simply outmaneuvered another evil man.

Any objective student of the times can hardly avoid concluding that the Soviets bargained in good faith. In fact, they seemed to be inspired with the same hope of reaching a binding agreement with their class enemies that has seemed to inspire Gorbachev in our day. But when the question becomes a question of national survival only one law operates—national survival. The Non-Aggression Pact was, incidentally, not unprecedented: at one time or another almost every European country seems to have signed some kind of non-aggression pact with their neighbor only to violate it when the situation seemed to demand it. Also, hardly a treaty existed which did not have its secret clauses. But admittedly, though adding secret clauses to advertised "open" treaties was not unusual for bourgeois countries dealing with each other against a third, that a *socialist* government would also indulge in the same deception seemed to violate proclaimed socialist morality enunciated by Lenin who had, in his time, denounced such practices, concurring in Wilson's hope that governments would sign "open covenants openly arrived at."

But hard choices often come up in life. Between a rock and a hard place, the Soviets chose the only course they felt won them time. And time was what they badly needed.

The Soviets had watched the European powers consolidate and shape their anti-Soviet plot, starting (to date it only from then) with the Anti-Comintern Pact signed between Germany and Japan, November 25, 1936. Italy signed a year later on November 6, 1937, and then, on February 24, 1939, it was also signed by Horthy's Hungary, and on March 27, 1939, by Franco's Spain.

Quite a line-up already—and impossible to misunderstand. Missing still were the two key European powers—France and England. But in October 1939 that was repaired when France's Daladier, and the "innocent" Chamberlain signed with Hitler and Mussolini the treaty which has gone down in history as the infamous Munich treaty, investing the word "appeasement" with a far more sinister content than it had ever had before.

Nevertheless, the immediate effect of the Soviet-German Pact on both Poland and the Baltic countries was positive. When the Red Army crossed into eastern Poland, it was greeted with wild enthusiasm and mass demonstrations by the populace, largely made up of Ukrainians and Belorussians and Jews. A contemporary account saw it this way:

Not a shot was fired, not a bomb was dropped, and villages and townspeople, free from the terror of German air attacks, hailed the Red Army as deliverers.

Russian troops themselves contributed to this feeling of relief by saying they came as comrades. Many inhabitants in this part of Poland are Jews whose number has been swelled by thousands of Jewish refugees fleeing before the Germans. Their joy was great at finding themselves safe from Nazi hands.[30]

The Red Army stopped at the Bug River, which coincided with the Curzon line, and most Jews were sent to safety beyond the Urals. Among them was a young man by the name of Menachim Begun, later to become premier of Israel, and an inveterate enemy of all things socialist. Still, in his UN speech, December 10, 1945, Albert Einstein expressly noted that only the Soviet Union opened its borders to Jews in 1939 and saved tens of thousands from the Holocaust, almost at a time when a ship seeking safety in Cuba, under Batista, was turned back to Germany. In 1938 the Poland of the Colonels refused to repatriate thousands of Polish Jews from Germany, thus dooming most to death. Choose your morality: immoral to cross the Polish border or moral to save the lives of thousands of Jews?

Not only that but almost immediately, Moscow returned Vilnius, occupied by Pilsudski's Poland since 1920 (by agreement with the Big Powers and the Lithuanian Smetona government) to Lithuania. There is little gratitude in politics. Whether one reads this action by the Soviet government (under Stalin) as generous, as Georgi Dimitrov did, or as a Machiavellian move by the arch-villain Stalin, still the fact remains that Vilnius was returned by Soviet Russia to bourgeois Lithuania. The only condition the Soviets made—one which one imagines needed no special emphasis—was that the Lithuanians refrain from secret negotiations with Hitler—which is precisely what Smetona and his group continued to do, as they had been doing all along.

Later, when the secret sections of the Soviet-Nazi Pact were revealed, a great hubbub was raised over the immorality of such secret dealings. But even if the agreement had been open, nobody at the time who stood to benefit from it would have protested. Secret or open, thousands of Jews *were* rescued, Vilnius *was* returned to Lithuania, Ukrainians and Belorussians who had been taken over by Poland in WWI *were* reunited with their homeland. The Bug was the line at which the Red Army stopped, and one can interpret that as proof of a prior agreed division of Poland or—as later proved to be the case—the farthest defense line against the Nazis that the Soviets were able to set up. If looked at as a whole, of which the 1939 period is just part, it is difficult in view of the Soviet Union's later action in defending Poland's return of western territory taken from it by Nazi Germany and drawing the Western border along the Oder-Neisse, to see something devious in it. After all, Poland had been abandoned to its fate by England and France. The USSR rescued it.

As for treaties, the walls of the world can be papered with treaties that have been broken, and whose secret clauses became known only long after the facts when they were nothing but historical curiosities. Merely recall the dozens of treaties with the American Indians broken by the U.S. government. Nationalist Lithuania, for instance, had made treaties with Nazi Germany (May 20, 1939 and July 10, 1940) pledging economic and other aid to Germany. In its treaty of April 17, 1940, it secretly agreed to concessions which tied it directly to Hitler's Germany. In February 1940, it met with Latvian and Estonian fascist government agents *secretly* to annul the treaties with the USSR.

The May 20, 1939 treaty had been worked out between Lithuania's Juozas Urbsys and Germany's Joachim Ribbentrop. It tied Lithuania economically so tightly to the Germans that the Germans themselves commented that "The agreement concluded attained our object of the integration of Lithuania with the Reich."[31]

Cernius had headed the government then but his policy in no decisive way differed from Smetona's. Cernius had publicly spoken of opposing alliances with anyone, proposing to remain neutral. During the vital negotiations that the USSR conducted with England and France during 1939, Cernius (in response to the known wishes of the allies, answering messages that only ears ideologically attuned to receiving them could pick up) refused to accept any offer from the three, if they should extend it, of guaranteeing Lithuania's security. The Latvian and Estonian governments—by now totally under Nazi influence—also refused such guarantees. It was this refusal which the British and French pointed to as the reason why they could not agree with the Soviets in the Soviets' offer to defend the Baltics (with the Red Army) when Hitler attacked. How could you *force* a country to be protected by you?

Well, means had been found at other times. True, the British and French were more experienced in refusing to aid onetime allies, turning over Austria and Czecholovakia and, to be blunt about it, Poland to Germany, even when they did have treaties presumably committing them to a military defense. Thus, even if they had a signed treaty with the Soviets intended to protect the Baltics from Hitler, once Hitler moved they would conveniently have "forgotten" the treaty with all its clauses, public and secret both.

And as for Lithuania itself, it openly declared its "neutrality" which, in the political context of the times, was a proclamation that the country was there for anyone's plucking. Lithuanian Deputy Prime Minister Kozys Bizauskas had put it clearly (June 28, 1939): "Lithuania wants to be and remain neutral. As for guarantees for the country [referring to the USSR] the Government of Lithuania has not taken and is not going to take any diplomatic steps."*

It had refused to take any steps, diplomatic or military, in opposition to Poland when Poland marched in to take over Vilnius and the Vilnius area. It had done the same when confronted by the Klaipeda crisis. The Lithuanian ambassador to London protested that the Lithuanian policy of neutrality was "a passive one," and he felt it would be "better for them to take an active part," and concluded on a note of bewilderment: "It is difficult for me to understand why none of the Baltic States takes such initiative."[32]

Although it is cursed today for being so far-sighted then, the Lithuanian Communist Party declared that the Cernius government, which was a coalition of Christian Democrats and Populists, had "come to power... (giving) many promises. It promised to unite all the nation's efforts and defend every inch of Lithuanian soil against any invaders. From the very beginning, however, the new government began breaking its promises [which had all] turned out to be mere words."[33]

* Quoted by Dr. Kostas Navickas in *The Struggle of the Lithuanian People for Statehood*, p. 119.

SECOND LITHUANIAN SOVIET REPUBLIC

A car wreck
For the scrap-yard bound.
Your hopes
Of more loot!
   Bourgeois,
   Crash
You loved to hear
The cash-bell sound.
Those days are over—
It's not your cash.
May my poem be a shot
At you....
      A Poem-Shot— Vytautas Montvila, 1902-1941

Seen through the haze of Nationalist nostalgia, the past as it really was totally disappears and in its place a facsimile of Nationalist hopes and aspirations is erected. It is built entirely out of bitter defeats, frustrations, a warped sense of class superiority that does not deign to recognize any truth related to justice for the lower classes. Everything that happened in the year 1939-40 was, in their fevered imaginations, the work of the devil—some, as in the Church, literally thought so, and others gave it a secular name—now a name which would amply substitute for the devil—Stalin.

This is not the place to reassert the historical balance in which the man Stalin is correctly positioned. Suffice it to say that if indeed he was personally responsible for all the evils attributed to him, then even the devil would envy his prowess.

Few witnesses to the events of that short period remain who can speak freely—though there are some. But no witness is more reliable than one who is no longer alive, but her testimony still vibrates with the immediacy of her experience. She is Anna Louise Strong, an American journalist. She was born in a parsonage in Friend, Nebraska in 1885. She died in China in 1970 and was buried in the Revolutionary Martyrs Cemetery there. Her biography can be quickly sketched: "She knew everyone—Big Bill Haywood, Roger Baldwin, Jane Addams, 'Mother' Ella Bloor, Emma Goldman, Max Eastman, FDR and Eleanor Roosevelt, Trotsky, Stalin, Litvinov, Borodin,

Mao Tse-tung and Chou En-lai—and she went everywhere. She worked with the Wobblies on the West Coast when she was still in her twenties, and she marched with revolutionary armies in Russia, Mexico, Spain and China.... She was a peculiarly American revolutionary and the millions of words that she wrote as a journalist were all to show her fellow Americans the 'truth' about what was going on in the world. Passionate, indefatigable and sometimes impatient with the opinions of others, she was nonetheless dedicated to the cause of humanity and the betterment of the world."[34]

Indeed, few contemporaries were better equipped to observe, understand and interpret the revolutionary events of the first half of the 20th century than was this remarkable American woman, in whose character all the finest traits of American Puritanism and the pioneering spirit of the West were embodied.*

Of course she was "biased"! She was frankly and openly "biased" on the side of the millions of abruptly awakened "little people" the whole world over who were propelled into the revolutionary cauldron of our times without, so to speak, time to dress, without necessarily choosing, and yet, *being chosen*, performed as though the script for revolution had already been inscribed in their genes.

"I stopped in Kaunas for a day on my way to Moscow," she begins her account. "A day," she added, "would do for Lithuania, I thought. In all its twenty years it had never been important. And now, with war shaking Eastern Europe and Eastern Asia, little Lithuania lay still more outside the stream of world events."

Indeed, as far as the "world" was aware of Lithuania at all, it was in the kind of impertinent reference to it as an exotic, almost totally invisible nation, that the song writer Cole Porter made in a song he wrote for the 1926 Broadway musical, *Paris*: "Lithuanians and Letts do it, let's do it, let's fall in love...." Or ironic references by well-known historian Frances Hackett, who in an essay (1919) on culture, "The Sickbed of Culture," pointing out how "superior Americans" looked on all foreign cultures wrote: "If the ignorant foreigner 'immigrants who bring no personal traditions,' come from countries of oppression, she must decline to believe that they had a literature and a culture. There is only one culture, our own. Perhaps in steerage you can evoke noises from a Lithuanian that sound like human speech. Yes, but soon that Lithuanians will have 'the locutions of the slums.' Beware of Lithuania. Do not pat the strange dog. He might bite a piece out of your culture."[35]

---

* I met her in New York City and again in Peking where she lived in the onetime Italian embassy and presided over the American colony there—and was often on the phone with Mao Tse-tung and Chou En-lai.

Probably the only other Lithuanian shown to the public (and yet not known) was the Lithuanian boxer, Juozas Zuhauskas, who became heavy-weight champion of the world in 1932 under the name of Jack Sharkey. Finally, Upton Sinclair had presented America with the Lithuanian, Jurgis, in his novel, *The Jungle* (1906).

In fact, most Lithuanians in America who achieved some distinction were not known as Lithuanians; most had "Anglicized" their names. As for the country itself, as far as Americans were concerned, Lithuania could as well have been on the moon. The same for Latvia ("Letts do it") and Estonians; who, in fact, had ever *met* an Estonian?

Louise Strong had heard "rumors" that Lithuania was "being Sovietized."

"After the first hour I knew that I just had to stay longer." And she did. "The day grew to a week, the week to a month. Lithuania had become important. It had become even epoch-making." Today's public that believes that little Grenada was a Soviet threat to America has to brace itself for the reason: "A sovereign state was changing from capitalism to socialism quite constitutionally without destruction of life or property. *This thing had never happened before.*" (My italics).

Indeed, "everything was so orderly, even so decorous, that it was hard to think of it as a revolution. The talk was all of trade unions, of elections, of protecting public properties. What could be more sedate than that? Yet a new speed had hit this quiet land, and in a few short weeks, it was traveling into the first stages of socialism, nationalizing land, banks and industries, workers' control, Soviets....

"'And without firing a shot,' boasted editor Zimanas of the Communist *Tiesa* (Truth) which had grown in three weeks from an illegal sheet the size of your hand to an eight-page paper printed in Kaunas' biggest plant. 'Without even stopping a wheel,' the 'revolution without violence' that the liberals always prayed for. But the capitalist's world won't like it any better for that.'"

Strong remarks: "He was right. They didn't. Up at the foreign embassies they spoke of it as the 'death of Lithuania.' One of the American legation staff was more frank: 'It wouldn't have been so bad if the Red Army had merely seized the country and established a protectorate. But they've started something going among the lower classes that is undermining the whole social structure. You should see my janitor.'"

Oh, what those innumerable janitors, housemaids, gardeners, street cleaners, house painters, etc., whom one could comfortably tell to go and they went, to come and they came, now answered!

Something had started among the lower classes!

Strong went on:

The events of the previous days may be briefly summarized. In early June the Soviet Union had presented an ultimatum, demanding the formation of a government in Lithuania which would fulfill the treaty of mutual assistance signed the previous autumn. The ultimatum was accepted and, on June 15, a considerable force of the Red Army entered the country where smaller units had been present since the signing of the treaty. Tanks, cavalry, infantry in trucks rolled through the streets of Kaunas and passed on to appropriate camping places. They did not mix with the Lithuanians' internal life at all. The Red Army gave concerts and dances to the Lithuanian army, as allied armies should. Otherwise it was known to be out in the woods near the border.

But long-oppressed Lithuanians, whose champions had been thrown into prison for the fourteen years of the Smetona dictatorship, took heart and began to talk and organize. President Smetona fled; Prime Minister Markys thus became president, appointed Justas Paleckis, a brilliant progressive journalist, as prime minister and himself resigned. Thus Paleckis* in turn became president and appointed a cabinet of ministers consisting of well-known intellectuals, later adding a few Communists.

It was all highly constitutional.

And so the first days of the second socialist government in Lithuania began. "Paleckis' first decree set free about a thousand political prisoners—including Communists and Communist sympathizers. Within a week after Paleckis came to power, the first of the big popular demonstrations took place. Tens of thousands of workers marched through the streets of Kaunas demanding the legalization of the Communist Party, and secured it."

And so, seeing this much, she wanted to see it all. Few are fortunate enough to be there at the very birth of a new society like John Reed in Russia a few years earlier, and she was one of those fortunate few.** With pad and pencil as her only weapons, she started out:

> I found that fiery, energetic organizer, Motiejus Shumauskas—who like many of the leaders I was meeting was only a few days out of prison—in a beautiful, well-equipped building, full of assembly halls, committee rooms and secretarial offices.
> "Our present from the plutocrats," laughed the workers whom I met on the steps. This building, the Darbo Rumai, had barely been finished when Smetona's dictatorship was finished too.

Why had Smetona built "Workers' Rooms"? It was a "bureaucratic attempt ... to keep them (workers) quiet, and later a tool of the secret police to spy on their activities." The idea came straight out of Mussolini's corpo-

---

* Sitting years later, in socialist Lithuania, on the same platform with Paleckis in Kaunas, I couldn't resist the drama of it and leaning over toward him I asked: "Did you think when you were in prison in the 1930s that one day you'd be sitting here as president of the republic?" Looking so much like our own George Washington, he only smiled.

** I myself would witness the birth, or soon after the birth, of a number of socialist-oriented countries, like Afghanistan, Vietnam, North Korea, China.

rate state program. "It was supposed to receive workers' complaints and to act on them in the workers' interests, but the workers had soon learned that their complaints were sent directly to their employers so that these might know with which workers to take suppressive measures. They had avoided Darbo Rumai after that."

So much for democracy a la Smetona! *Real* democracy looked quite different. "There was no special decree passed, but as soon as the Red Army came and Smetona fled, the workers knew that they were free to organize and began to do so at once."

Shumauskas, who later would become Chairman of the Council of Ministers (1956-1967) invited Miss Strong to attend a meeting in Kaunas:

> More than 300 workers, of whom perhaps a fourth were women, gathered in the well-equipped hall. Straight from the factories, women in old cotton gowns, men mostly in blue denim shirts.

Nothing probably proved how deeply democratic the revolution really was than the spontaneous participation of the women, who had played no part in society before, except as drays and bearers of children who were oppressed not only by the State but by their husbands who themselves were oppressed but passed on their misery to their wives.

> Shumauskas spoke: "To secure a better life for us all, the working class must be organized. Kaunas workers have always been leaders; now you must organize the whole land...
> "Choose from your ranks your best organizers to go to all parts of Lithuania over the weekend...."
> Hands went up and questions piled in by the dozens. One question suggested another, and the vast variety of them indicated the initiative of the Lithuanian workers and the wide expanse of their problems.
> "In factories where committees are already elected, do these stand?"
> "For the present, yes," said Shumauskas. "We have already our wage demands for our factory. Shall we present them directly to the boss or bring them to the union meeting?" "The union will make a wage scale for all the factories at once," was the reply....
> "The boss is hiring new people, not serious workers but gangsters. Must these be accepted into the union?" "What are the rules for accepting or rejecting members?" "Is membership voluntary or compulsory?" "So far the Communist Party fraction does the organizing in our factory. Will this now be done by the trade union or the Party?" "What shall we do if we see that the owners are trying to close down the factory? This will throw us all out of work."...
> "You take the third floor balcony and choose your organizing committee with delegates on it from every textile factory. By tomorrow this committee should be everywhere at work enrolling members and holding elections of factory committees where these have not yet taken place ... Railroad workers to the fourth floor; leather workers the third floor offices; metal workers second floor balcony; printers...."

This is how it went; they organized spontaneously but also consciously. Indeed, this is how it went in every country where the revolution triumphed; the workers spontaneously organized themselves into committees ready to assume direct control of their lives. History offers *nothing* more democratic than such periods, such moments; and if they lead into stabilized and later institutionalized forms of self-rule which are susceptible to bureaucratic ossification, this is not fore-doomed. It is a tendency wherever power has to be delegated for the delegates sooner or later, almost in the nature of the beast, to usurp and take personal possession of the power which is only delegated to them. But one knows how insidious the process is, extending even to the man who has limited tickets to sell to some special occasion and succumbs to the temptation to sell them at a bit more, which he then pockets for himself. But for this there must also be buyers ready to bribe him!

In any case, what Lenin called the "festival of workers," i.e., the revolution, in its early days, was intoxicating, not as an observed emotion but as one *lived*. Only later, as they looked back, did they realize at what peak of exhiliration they then had functioned, forgetting to eat, forgetting to sleep, intoxicated by an alcohol no inebriate had ever tasted. In its power all problems yielded. Historians of culture would note later how, in what was a relatively short period of time—the active period of taking power—mere boys and girls, adolescents, solved artistic problems as if by magic—problems which had paralyzed mature artists for decades, for centuries. But before the need to express, the obdurate obstacles of habit, tradition, stratified forms, etc., simply dissolved. The young Eisenstein made movies which solved cinematic problems on the run, so to speak, that are still exploited by cinema-makers to this day. Who, but a Russian revolutionary cinema maker, discovered the whole secret of montage? "Everyone took to art with passion," wrote Grigori Kozintsev, the Soviet filmmaker, speaking of *his* revolution. "That was real happiness! ... And the thing that was most amazing in this new life was that I, a mere lad, could take part in it... We organized EEKS (the Factory of the Eccentric Actor). I was then sixteen. Although we had absolutely no material means, we decided to mount a production ... It was a case of trying to demolish all the usual theatrical forms, and to find others, which could convey the intense sentiment of the new life. Unless this last point is recognized, our creations of that period would become incomprehensible. All these experiments, all these quests for new forms came because we had an intense feeling of an extraordinary renewal of life. We felt profoundly the impossibility of translating this sensation of the marvel and the importance of events through the means offered by the art of the past, which to our eyes appeared dreadfully academic."[36]*

This extraordinary sense of vitality was communicated to young artists—but not only to young artists but to all the young and the young in spirit—by the revolution, and the fact that this extraordinary level of heightened response to and participation in the events of the times could not be maintained is not a criticism of it, or of them. Ecstasy is brief.

Lithuanian artists, too, were infused with the electric power of events. They were not destined to have the time to develop what they had so auspiciously begun. Indeed, among the other crimes to be laid at the door of the Nazis, was the inexpressible crime of killing off art and the artists.

Kostas Korsakas would write in the middle of the war (1942):

> *To the Liberators of Lithuania:*
>
> *My brothers, soldiers from the Ukraine,*
> *From the sunny steps of Kazakstan,*
> *From the golden fields of the Kuban,*
> *Where your fast horses fed on grain,*
> *From Georgia's hills, from Hayastan,*
> *Where grapes are ripening on the vines*
> *And wine is flowing through the veins*
> *Of earth: men of the south, men of the north,*
> *All you who by red banners stand—*
> *You're fighting for my native land...*
>
> *My native land you've never seen,*
> *Yet I address you as my friends—*
> *He is my brother who defends*
> *Old Lithuanian land from the foe ...*
> *Brothers, I wish you'd hold as dear*
> *This land, as if it were your own ...*
>
> *Red Army soldiers, brothers dear,*
> *Come, free my land. Don't you hear*
> *Her calling out to you, "Come soon!"*
> *The light of freedom, like the sun,*
> *Comes from the east. And when you've won*
> *Her freedom, she will wipe the tear*
> *Of happiness from tortured eyes...*
>
> *Then will she be to you as dear*
> *As your own land, my brothers-in-arms.*
> *She'll be to you, as she is to us,*
> *Our gentle mother, Lietuva.***

---

* Later, I met Kozintsev after his triumph with *King Lear*, and in *him*, in any case, the vitality of the revolution that had taken place a generation ago still continued.

** Translated by S. Roy.

This remarkable elan and sense of brotherhood that Miss Strong personally witnessed in Lithuania she had also been witness to in Russia in its early days. Also, in beleaguered Spain as later in China. In America, the high moment of workers' creativity occurred in the '30s, and there was a kind of reprise in the '60s when a similar outburst of vitality poured out of the generation that cried, "Hell, no, we won't go!" and "We Shall Overcome!"

So, in actual fact, such moments in history are not rare. Nor can they be ordered, programmed, specified. Thus, when Miss Strong met with the philistines in the American Legation a few days later after her experiences in Lithuania, she was surprised to hear them speak of "the new drive the Russians had started." Not a Russian had been anywhere on the premises!

"Would you like to go with one of the new organizers to see how the trade unions start in the provinces?" asked Shumauskas, and she went.

She visited far and near places, witnessed innumerable meetings, saw the people take shape as organizers of their own lives. They functioned by committee—they elected their own fellow workers and neighbors to serve on them. The multiplying meetings developed a momentum and build-up of their own and it all converged into a powerful force.

This is how *all* revolutions develop, regardless of how they start. Those who preach loudest of "democracy" fear it most when it shows itself in this truly democratic way. Attempts to launch counterrevolutions under the guise of revolutions always come up against the basic fact that they are not *democratic in their souls*, and inevitably expose themselves. (This is what is happening now in Eastern Europe and the Baltics as I write.)

When the mansions of the rich are turned into rest homes for the poor, one knows something has radically changed. Miss Strong went on:

It began, of course, with the coming of the Red Army. [Which the poet hailed.] The foreign embassies claimed that the Red Army did it all. The capitalist press abroad wrote of it as an "army of occupation," imposing its will ... But you can't build a Soviet Socialist Republic that way.

A Soviet Socialist Republic has to be built from the inside, by the will of its workers and peasants. It has to be built freely, without a sense of compulsion. Soviet Lithuania really arose that way. Nine-tenths of the Lithuanians will tell you that. They know, for they felt themselves built it.

Nine-tenths, yes—but it's not the nine-tenths who own the land, the printing presses, the banks and the police, and have international connections, and so are able—with the magnifying power of electricity—to mount a chorus of lament so loud that it drowns out the modest tales of modest people who are Carl Sandburg's "the people, yes." True, one-tenth *were* forced to give up "their" property, "their" privileges, "their" many-roomed mansions, and "their" wails have assailed the ears of mankind until they are deaf.

But to go on with Miss Strong, with the authenticity of an eye-witness:

> The most applauded folk in all Lithuania during the months of my visit were the Red Army boys. At concerts, dances, popular demonstrations, and meetings of the new trade unions, I heard them mentioned scores of times, and never without cheers. In the earlier weeks they were not yet become Soviet. But they were looked upon as "Our Great Ally," which had marched into the Baltic States to strengthen their defenses and protect them from Europe's war.
>
> This, of itself, was enough to make them accepted, for the Baltic peoples like all peoples, dread the war which is today sweeping Europe and threatening to engulf the world.

It must be remembered that Miss Strong is still writing of an Eastern Europe not yet "engulfed" in the war, but feeling it draw near, and dreading it. Poland had been invaded, and those near the Polish border could whiff the odor of dead bodies and shivered with fear. How many times had fire and pestilence come from across the border to Lithuania? The Germans were widow-makers. Hardly a Lithuanian household had forgotten them in 1914-1919 and the pitiless forages and murders of the *Freikorps*, which ravaged Lithuania with the consent of the Allies, even after formal hostilities had ended.

Miss Strong:

> But the Red Army swiftly added to its popularity by its behavior. They won the envy of the Lithuanian soldiers by their superior equipment; yet they treated them as equal allies. They amazed the peasant by their scrupulous consideration for his property, even to the last fence post. They startled the intellectuals by their culture and knowledge of world affairs ....

But it's not necessary to strain the resources of language to picture convincingly a revolutionary army coming as liberator to the same kind of people they themselves had been (and still were): peasants, unemployed workers, etc.

The lords of privilege fled West before them and their places in society were filled by those whom they were used to ordering to go and to come.

Said Miss Strong:

> A tall, bony peasant woman whom I met bringing strawberries to Kaunas told me: "Rich folks frightened us about the Red Army. They said the Army would take our lands from us and steal our food. But they take no food from us, not even if we offer it...."

Miss Strong goes on:

> Even those foreign legations which have tried for years to organize the Baltic States against the Soviet Union and which bitterly hate the present Soviet

transformation in those states will admit to you in conversation that "the Red Army men have done nothing rough."

An American relief worker, who has spent the past six months in Vilna (*sic*) also told me: "In all these months I have not heard of a drunken soldier or of any scandal with women. Any army in the world—no, any group of cultured gentlemen in the world—might be proud of the record they have made."

Ah—but is it so rosy as all that? Says Strong:

It should not be assumed that the whole Lithuanian population cheered the Red Army from the beginning. Some of them cheered but most of them wondered and waited. For twenty years they had been filled with tales of horror about the Soviet Union, and they did not yet know what to believe. Besides, the people who cheered the Red Army when it first came in September of 1939 were later arrested by the hundreds by the Smetona regime. So, the second time when the Red Army came in numbers on June 15, 1940, many of the people waited to see when it would be safe to cheer...

The most complete account was given to her by (Henrik) Zimanas, editor of *Tiesa*:

"We thought it would be easier for workers' organizations after the mutual assistance pact was signed. The ministers were so scared that they even promised amnesty for Communist prisoners. But then there came the worst terror we had ever known. Nobody was allowed to see the Red Army when it came into the country; it went to its post by night and stayed there. Hundreds of workers were arrested for just talking to Red Army men. In Vilna, which the Soviets gave to Lithuania, the Smetona government at once staged a pogrom against those people who had welcomed the Red Army. When Kaunas workers marched to the Soviet legation to thank them for Vilna, they were beaten by the police right in front of the Legation."

And further:

"We knew at one o'clock by the Moscow radio that the ultimatum* had been accepted. At three o'clock the Lithuanian radio admitted it, and by seven o'clock the Red Army was already on the streets. The people at first stood silent, just watching, hardly knowing what it all meant. Then some began to clap and then to cheer and then to sing ... Then the people understood that the Red Army had come as Allies, to protect us from war. More and more they began to cheer them as they came—tanks, cavalry, infantry in trucks—strong and endless."

And:

"The cheers were in our hearts," said a Jewish journalist of that city, "but we remembered the pogroms. The Vilna police were still reactionary and for several days arrested people who cheered the Red Army. I knew a boy who was arrested more than a week after Smetona fell for saying: 'Hail to the Red Army.' His father went to the police and they asked a bribe of 100 lits but they finally bargained to let him go for 25 lits, for they knew they would not be in power long."

* To permit the Red Army entry into Lithuania.

And then:

The coming of the Red Army and the fall of the Smetona dictatorship which accompanied it released forces among the working class, the peasants and progressive intellectuals which had been suppressed for fourteen years. A thousand political prisoners were almost at once released from prison; a large part of them were Communists. After their years in prisons and concentration camps they were in various stages of ill health. The most exhausted were sent at once to rest homes. The others threw themselves immediately into work.

But what of Vilnius itself, what was it really like when it was under Polish control?

Vilna was the cheapest place in Poland to live. Hordes of retired Polish officials on small government pensions moved here, where they could still be lords, with plenty of half-starved servants. They spent their time dreaming of a Greater Poland....
    Vilna contained seven nationalities. All lived in full separation and hated each other. Nobody really knows the numbers of them. There had never been an honest census. The Jews claim a majority in the city's center, but the Poles created a Greater Vilna with suburbs and claimed a majority there. They took the census not by race but by religion. All Roman Catholics were considered Poles. Thus the Lithuanians and many of the Byelorussians were simply eliminated from the census returns. Their language and their schools were suppressed. From time to time Vilna had pogroms, both under the tsar and later under the Poles.
    Into such a Vilna last September (when the Nazis crossed into Poland) came tens of thousands of Polish refugees fleeing from the German bombs.... The real wealthy bourgeois got to Stockholm and London.

And then:

When the Red Army first came into Vilna on September 19, 1939, the common people met it with cheers. After six weeks it withdrew, and Vilna was given to Lithuania. Promptly the Smetona government staged one of the worst pogroms in Vilna's history attacking under the name of "Jews" all persons who had shown sympathy with the Red Army. Some 20,000 of Vilna's workers, especially the Jewish, didn't wait for this pogrom. They went with the Red Army into the U.S.S.R.....
    As soon as Smetona's government got Vilna, he set up a Lithuanian nationalism as exclusive and oppressive as the Polish had been. Nobody could be a citizen or have the right to employment unless he could prove that he had resided in Vilna before the Polish seizure of 1920.* So much red tape and so many documents were demanded that of 250,000 persons living in the city, only 30,000 were able to qualify... Smetona's governing officials received people only in the Lithuanian language, which most of Vilna's people could not speak....
    A city hungry and jobless, full of long-embittered national hates, where the government refused to talk in the languages understood by the people....
    Such was the Vilna into which the Red Army came again in 1940....

* Compare similar provisions for citizenship in Landsbergis' Lithuania.

Everywhere in Vilna I saw the shocking heritage left by the Polish lords. A large proportion of the children and young people had never been to school at all. Even those who got some schooling had been taught 80 to 90 in a single room. Teachers often got tuberculosis from the strain on their lungs and the bad food which was all they could afford.

It was from this that the Red Army, which was conscious of itself as a people's army, rescued Vilnius. More:

Vilna workers had been even more suppressed than those in the rest of Lithuania. As late as the spring of 1940 there were factory owners who beat their workers with sticks like Asiatic despots. Such was the owner of a small, primitive glass factory in which I saw a trade union election held. The speaker stood on a cart in the factory enclosure, a great space with low walls and high sloping roof. The owner sat on the balcony of his house which looked down on the factory yard.

"Comrade workers," said the speaker. "You have here a building and raw materials, you have here machines. You have here working hands. Why do you need an owner?"

All of them cheered.[37]

Indeed, it seemed quite clear and even simple then. Few at this occasion had any hint of the devilishly complicated and pitiless future that awaited them. For "cheering" many of them signed their death warrants.

Miss Strong interviewed Karolis Didziulis, "not long since out of prison," who had been appointed governor of Vilnius. "We must end this evil process where first Poles suppress Lithuanians and then Lithuanians suppress Poles," he told her. "Under Smetona, only 30,000 people here had the vote. We have given it at once to everybody." This included, for the very first time peasant women who "had no vote under Smetona unless they were tax-paying heads of families."

We [Strong, Venclova and Cvirka] came next to a small volost center (ownership center) in the heart of the Swualki district. Of 2,900 voters listed here, 2,100 have already voted, though it is barely noon. I asked them why their district had such a good turnout, and they answer: "Because there is very good feelings and we like the new government a lot."

Venslova* (sic) gives me a clearer explanation. "This was the Center of the peasant uprising in 1936. Losing their farms because of debts, the peasants struck against the low prices and heavy taxes, and refused to sell their products or pay their taxes. When Smetona sent in the police, the peasants fought them with pikes; many were shot and hundreds arrested. That is why this district is so much more active than the others."

Miss Strong sums up the election:

Very democratically, very informally, very frankly and very effectively the whole thing was done. Seldom have I been in a meeting of such good feeling where the results so accurately mirrored the choice of all. The thing that surprised me most

* Later to become Minister of Education.

was how these workers took it. The chairmen in most of the meetings were just out of prison.* The workers had not been allowed to hold meetings until the past few weeks. Here they were raising their hands and getting the floor and electing Soviets like veterans. Just like ducks to water!

What surprised me next was how sensible and prosaic it all seemed. They were just telling decent, respectable workers to keep on with their jobs and protect property and elect reliable representatives. The recent election of a Working People's government had made it possible for the workers to uphold the laws instead of opposing them; it had given to the Revolution the weapons of stability and law...

Thus, all through the week in all parts of the country the tide set ever stronger towards the Soviet Union, and toward the whole revolutionary program of the Communists, which included four points for the coming People's Sejm.

1. Lithuania a Soviet Socialist Republic
2. Incorporation into the Soviet Union
3. Nationalization of land, with users' rights for all actual soil tillers
4. Nationalization of banks and industries....

At 3:30 o'clock in the afternoon of July 21, 1940, Lithuania became a Soviet Socialist Republic by unanimous vote of the People's Sejm. Two hours later, also by unanimous vote, the Sejm voted to apply for admission... [into the Soviet Union].

So the event was reported *at the time* by a first-hand observer.

"Back in Kaunas," Miss Strong noted, "they were counting the votes.... In most cities and towns of Lithuania, from 90 to 95 percent had voted, ... even in the rural districts, in spite of the rain, there had been a turnout of more than two-thirds."

The turn-out had been even more significant in view of the fact that an active and "dirty tricks" campaign had been waged by the opposition Christian Democrats through church sermons and other means including rumors that only one candidate could be voted for, when in fact eight or ten were there on the ballot. The Poles were told that they could not vote in a "Lithuanian" election, and because under Smetona they had not been allowed to vote in a "Lithuanian" election, they had believed this tale—at least for the moment. Some were told that they should not vote for the Jews. And some had to be assured that they could vote at all—though they were propertyless, and under 23 years of age. Eighteen-year-olds had to be convinced they, too, were now old enough to vote!

When the votes were counted, it was found that 95.5 percent of the total adult electorate had come to the polls.

Indeed, over 1,386,509 had voted in this country with a population of less than 3 million. And they voted overwhelmingly for the Workers Peo-

---

* In country after country, which had adopted a socialist orientation, I kept meeting men and women in high places who, sometimes only months before, as in Afghanistan, had been in prison, some condemned to death.

ples Union, which was a united front of all patriots, progressives, anti-fascists, Communists.

Of the 79 representatives in the new parliament only 38 were Communists. The final makeup of the new parliament (seimas) consisted of 24 peasants, 21 workers, 30 intellectuals, 4 soldiers. By national origin they broke down into 67 Lithuanians, 4 Jews, 3 Poles, 1 Russian, and 1 Latvian. The Seimas met on July 2, 1940 and adopted a declaration that read:

> All the land of Lithuania, her natural resources, forests and waters belong to the people.
>
> For centuries the peasants of Lithuania fought for land and freedom.... Many of the finest sons of the people gave their lives in the struggle for freedom...
>
> When the cruel rule of the landowners was removed, the Lithuanian people hoped to build a better life for themselves. But the Lithuanian capitalist who came to power, oppressed and robbed them no less...
>
> The peasant was losing his land, which was soaked in the tears and sweat of his fathers and forefathers, to speculators and exploiters. A new class of landlords and exploiters came into being while the peasant sank even more deeply into poverty and misery...
>
> Now this nightmare of history has ended. The working people have become the masters of liberated Lithuania. The hour has come when the hopes and dreams of their fathers have become reality, when working people are building a new form of government, a new bright and happy life....

Some 76,346 peasants were given land "not to exceed 74 acres."

Then, on July 21, 1940, the People's Parliament by a *unanimous* vote proclaimed itself a Soviet Socialist Republic and sent a delegation to Moscow, including Justas Paleckis, Karolis Didziulis, General Vincas Vitkauskas, (who had opposed Smetona), the poet Salomeja Neris, the writer Petras Cvirka, and 15 others, including freshly elected MP's (some of whom later repudiated their actions), to petition the Supreme Soviet for entry into the USSR. Latvia and Estonia followed suit.

This vital moment in the history of Lithuania has been burlesqued and (it's correct to say) slandered particularly recently as memories of the reality fade and a grotesque Nationalist-shaped mask is bolted over that decisive act. That entire historical period is summed up in the predigested, bought-and-paid-for prose of *New York Times* correspondent Craig Whitney, who had the distinction of being found guilty (along with a journalist from the Baltimore *Sun*) in July 1978 of slandering Soviet TV, was fined (and paid) 1,144 rubles:

> After the Stalin-Hitler Pact of 1939, which divided Eastern Europe into spheres of influence, the Soviet Union *intimidated* the Baltic lands—Lithuania, Latvia and Estonia—into accepting military bases in their territory. In 1940, Moscow forces *occupied* all three Baltic republics, and they were *incorporated* into the Soviet Union after rigged elections that same year.[38]

All the words I've italicized are, one can say who has even a slight acquaintance with the history of the period, at best gross distortions, at worst outright lies. Mr. Craig Whitney wasn't even alive during that period and imbibed his twisted concepts along with his mother's anti-Soviet milk.

Miss Strong (and including the writer) were most certainly alive at the time, and Miss Strong bore witness on the spot, and I (with the whole progressive world) watched events from afar but emotionally and ideologically not from a distance: we were there too on the spot.

Perhaps the best answer to all such slanders is to be found in the poem of Vytautas Montvila who, as it happened, had actually been born in Chicago and taken back to Lithuania as a child, where he became a revolutionary, spending time in Smetona's prison from 1929 to 1931. In 1940-41 he was active in the socialist reconstruction of the country, and was part of the resistance when Lithuania was invaded by the Nazis, who arrested him and shot him. On proclamation of the Soviet Socialist Republic he wrote in 1940:

> *Here ends the bloody feast of wrong*
> *And Justice comes unbound.*
>
> *Ring out with joy our freedom song,*
> *Released from underground*
>
> *We who all suffered yesterday*
> *Locked up in prison chains*
>
> *By fire and steel are freed today*
> *To stand for freedom's gains.*
>
> *0 freedom, cherished as a dream,*
> *We hail you with full voice.*
>
> *You move us like a mighty stream*
> *And make our hearts rejoice*
>
> *Our comrades who faced death at night*
> *Salute us from the grave.*
>
> *People once shorn of every right*
> *The way ahead now pave.*
>
> *0 Lithuania, you are free,*
> *To see your brighter day!*
>
> *Now shall the crimson banners be*
> *Your guide upon the way.*

The translator may have felt constrained to sacrifice feeling to the exigencies of rhyme. But we are free to recreate the true emotion behind the awkward English words unused to expressing sincerity in such an uncorrupted way. In 1940, when this poem "Freedom Song" was written, only men and women who had actually spilled their blood to win it had the unassailable right to choose the way they would express it. All subsequent scribblers should, in all decency, hold their peace!

THE RED ARMY ENTERS

He is my brother who defends
Old Lithuanian land from the foe...
             To the Liberators of Lithuania–Kostas Korsakas

On June 15, 1940, Smetona, after his efforts to commit Lithuania openly on the side of fascist Germany failed, precipitately fled with his immediate entourage, including his Defense Minister Gen. G. Mustakias, along a route already well paved by earlier such hasty departures and to be even more heavily traveled in the days to come as events turned against them. Smetona sped to Hitlerite Germany with the trained nose of a hound dog. To him, this Germany bristling with guns, already with tens of thousands of prisoners working in its mines, mills and factories as no more than slaves, and spotted with concentration camps and crematoria, was a "haven." Even as he passed into the protection of *der Führer*, other Lithuanians (Latvians and Estonians) were packed into cattle cars on their way to the extermination camps. Possibly their trains passed each other. In any case, Smetona and his group were extended every privilege, and while in Germany, he helped direct and coordinate the "underground" resistance in Lithuania. Eventually, when all was lost, he and his entourage were allowed to pass into West Germany, and there into the understanding hands of the Americans who fixed up entry permits for them, doctored to taste, making it possible for Smetona to take up residence in Cleveland, Ohio, where (it is said) he died in 1944 in his attempt to rescue his wife's fur coat from their son's burning home. Some fled to safety in the USA or Latin America (like the infamous Nazi, Klaus Barbie.) Some–50,000 of them, according to the American War Refugees Board–died in Auschwitz. Others still entertained delirious dreams of once again returning to Lithuania and composed a tatterdemalion "government-in-exile" which then subsisted on American rations for decades to come.

On July 14, 1940, seeing the approaching storm already quite visibly on the horizon, the Soviets had asked permission to return troops into Lithuania to take up defense positions on the Lithuanian-German border. It was this demand that precipitated the crisis. Although the Smetona group hated the Soviets more than they hated (if hated is the word) the Nazis, this animosity to the Soviets was not shared by the people. The people *feared* the Nazis. They had absolutely no illusions about them. They knew if they went to Germany, it would be as slaves—not honored guests. Not only had they already seen the Nazis at work in Klaipeda, but they had also been terrorized by the native *Savandoriai*, the para-military Nationalist forces whose terrorization of the population paved the way for the entry of the Nazis. Indeed, looking back, there is hardly a period in Lithuanian history, dating from the Middle Ages, when they had no reason to fear the Germans. Nobody in Lithuania doubted that after Poland, Lithuania was next. What was inexplicable was the fact that there were some Lithuanians who looked with favor on the oncoming Germans and could hardly wait to hail them.

All that year—1940—feverish behind-the-scenes activity turned the capitals of the three Baltic nations into buzzing beehives of rumor and paranoia. At the instigation of Smetona, an attempt was secretly made to forge a Baltic military opposition to the Soviets, indeed, a decades' old attempt to forge a Baltic Entente, which failed. Indeed, behind-the-scenes doings, secret clauses added to ostensible legal treaties written in invisible ink taking away at the bottom of the text what seemed to be granted at the opening, seemed to be the norm. Always the reactionary cliques of all three countries were in close contact with Berlin...

The Red Army troops that he could not prevent from entering the country, Smetona nevertheless subjected to every kind of abuse and provocation. Lithuania swarmed with Nazi secret agents and the Voldemaras group of gangsters, the Iron Wolves, were brought out of jail and hiding and given to understand that their services were urgently needed. Red Army soldiers were waylaid and murdered as were true patriots protesting the fatal direction in which Smetona was exerting his whole effort to drive the country. At a much later hearing (1965) into that period of government-sponsored and protected criminality, it was clear—as one of the perpetrators admitted—that the purpose behind the rampage of murders and incitements was "to surround the (Red Army) bases in such a way that in case of emergency these could have been liquidated."[39]

Thus, Smetona did his worst to annul in life what he had given lip-service to when he signed the Mutual Assistance Pact with the Soviet Union in October 10, 1939, which was then hailed by the people as a guarantee of their safety at a time fraught with peril. The Pact made clear that the USSR restored Vilnius and the Vilnius area to Lithuania—the ages-old dream of Lithuanians the world over finally realized. The two parties to the Pact agreed to render each other every assistance which included military aid in case of an attack on either of the parties from a third source. In order to ensure Lithuania's safety and make clear to Germany where it could not hope to go, the Lithuanian government (with Jonas Cernius, who was also a Brigadier General and Chief of the General Staff of the Lithuanian army, as its premier) agreed to let the Soviets garrison the frontier areas facing Germany.

Perhaps most typical of the popular reaction to the news of the Pact was that of Petras Cvirkas, Lithuania's outstanding writer, who said, "All the Lithuanian nation rejoices at the restoration of Vilnius to Lithuania and especially at the Mutual Assistance Pact between the Soviet Union and Lithuania." (*Tass*, October 12, 1939).

Seeing nothing but disaster for their plots ahead of them, Smetona asked Cernius to resign, and in his place put in Antanas Merkys, a reliable defender of bourgeois power, a leader of the Lithuanian Nationalist Union, which represented the rich landowners, and openly espoused the views of Mussolini and then Hitler. Both Smetona and Voldemaras had been (and Smetona still was) in the party's leadership. It was the Nationalist Party that had successfully engineered the coup in 1927 which instituted Lithuanian fascism ("fascism" used here not as an epithet but as a precise description of the political and ideological system which was now put into operation, wiping out all democratic gains and ruling by diktat and terror).

The so-called "opposition" parties, the Christian Democrats and the Populists, lined up behind Merkys. The first act of the "new" government was to arrest the leaders of the Communist Party, including its general secretary, Antanas Snieckus, who later would head the postwar government and whose death on Jan. 22, 1974 was mourned by tens of thousands.

This was the opening gun for a desperate, last-ditch campaign instigated and waged by the Smetona forces. Smetona was prepared to go the whole road—up to and including open hostility to the Soviet forces hoping to perpetrate bloody incidents which could be blamed on the soldiers (much as the Landsbergis forces were to do later). The government refused to supply the Red Army units with provisions and charged high rents for the buildings and other property used by the Army. They refused to work on and, in fact, sabotaged previously agreed construction projects meant to house the Red soldiers. They arrested any Lithuanian who wanted to fraternize with the soldiers. They flooded the information media with slanderous tales about the soldiers, missing none, from rape to riot, particularly the most imaginative ones originating in Berlin. (Then , but now it's New York and Washington.)

Red Army soldiers were under strict orders not to respond to provocation, even to murders. Meanwhile, the Germans were rolling over Europe. By the beginning of summer, 1940, the Wehrmacht had already conquered Denmark, Norway, Holland and Belgium, and in six weeks it had destroyed the French army, led by a Nazi-sympathizer, Weygand, who deliberately sabotaged resistance. Along with the destruction of the French Army—up until then the most powerful in Europe—went the destruction of the British

Expeditionary Force, which had to content itself with the "victory" of Dunkirk. Caught like geese in a trap, they were all trussed up for total slaughter. But Hitler countermanded the order to General Ewald von Kleist, who was poised to close the trap, on the notion that he needed the British as a future ally against the USSR. The Belgian army had surrendered without (in effect) firing a shot, on orders of King Leopold.

All these remarkable "victories" had one thing in common, not lost on those political weather cocks whose noses were tilted into the air sniffing opportunity. For who could avoid wondering why these huge armies either surrendered without firing a shot or collapsed after what was no more than token resistance—and if they wondered that, how could they escape the conclusion that the Great Powers, precisely "the enemy," actually connived at their own defeat? This was a clear signal to those looking for signals. When the master himself breaks his sacred word, deceives and wallows in treason, his servants need feel no compulsion to remain pure where they sinned, loyal where they betrayed. To Smetona and his co-conspirators in Latvia and Estonia, it seemed that the brazen words of the Horst Wessel song were literally coming true: "Germany today—tomorrow the world!" And what was even more impressive, it was clear that nobody they recognized as the lords and masters of the world, in whose presence they were used to scrape and defer, seemed to be over-worried at the prospect. So, when Hitler marched into Lithuania, Latvia and Estonia, they intended to be there welcoming him with bread and salt!

If Nazi successes left them smiling, they aroused in the Soviets intense alarm. At this point, as they watched France—impregnable, undefeatable, Maginot-line defended France—fall in six weeks, they realized that everything had speeded up and was rushing to a climax. Though they had a Pact with Germany, nobody in the Soviet leadership believed for a moment that the Pact was any more than a stratagem, a resting-point, for the Nazis. They asked the Smetona government to let more troops go to the border to thicken the defense lines in Lithuania (also in Latvia and Estonia).

Corroboration of the effect that the entry of the Red Army had in Lithuania (for one) comes from an unexpected source, a weekly American newsletter, *In Fact*, which (August 12, 1940) wrote:

> An authoritative source in Lithuania air mailed *In Fact*:
> "When the Soviet Army began strengthening its bases in Lithuania recently, several hundred German airplanes used as Stukas or dive bombers, which had just landed in unoccupied airfields, disappeared. Soviet authorities discovered, after their garrisons occupied all available strongpoints, that a great mobilization of 80,000 German 'tourists' for a national sports festival had been called to take place in the capital (Kaunas). The day set was the fourth after the Soviet troops reinforced the original garrison. It was not held."[40]

And, indeed, it wasn't. The pattern was already clear to any who needed to know it. The Nazis typically organized the native Germans in each country they were about to invade, using them as a fifth column, or as the "voice of the oppressed," as a native "welcoming committee." Smetona was, of course, well aware of who these "tourists" were (80,000 tourists!) and had obviously given the Nazis permission to land hundreds of Stukas on Lithuanian soil.

However the demand of the Soviets to garrison the Western borders of Lithuania is pictured today, the fact of the matter is that the entire peace-loving world looked upon the move of the Soviets to fortify any border facing Germany *as the only evidence* that there would be serious resistance to Hitler in Europe.

The world had watched, in stunned disbelief, as country after country surrendered to Hitler, some without firing a shot, and some putting up only half-heartedly—one cannot even call it "resistance." Oddly enough, Smetona was given undeserved credit for resistance to Hitler by accepting the entry of the Red Army troops. The truth was he had resisted accepting them "with fury." And it was only the refusal of his own cabinet to back him, including the commanders of the army, which forced him to grit his teeth in assent.

REVOLUTION IN LITHUANIA

A cell of a room. Table, chair, a maze
Of wrinkles on a hard bony face.
"Comrades, party organizer, tonight again
The Kulaks will try to burn the grain."
        Party Organizer—Vladas Mozuriunas, 1922-1964

"Lithuania's path to socialism is the easiest ever known," cried the new President, Justas Paleckis exultantly. Paleckis had addressed the crowd of delegates to the new *Seimas* at the Grand Opera House in Kaunas. Said he then: "Our so-called independences was always a myth. Our country was the football of foreign imperialists; its fate was decided in London, Geneva, Warsaw, but never in Kaunas. It was oppressed by its own capitalists and by international capitalists.... Never again will capitalists exploit Lithuania!"

This vow was greeted—it need hardly be added—with stormy applause. Meanwhile, they had the formidable job of building a new society. Fortunately for them, they were all—as Lenin explained to a visitor who came to see him in the Kremlin and who recoiled from the prospect of self-government—nothing but amateurs at the unprecedented and historically decisive responsibility of organizing a new society. "We were nothing but agitators," Lenin explained. Few of the Bolsheviks who came to power in Russia in 1917 really knew how to read a blueprint, let alone draw one. They were not engineers, architects, businessmen, agronomists. All they were were men and women with a vision. Indeed, if they had had some hint of the daunting proportions of the task ahead of them, they might have lost heart at the very beginning. Instead, men and women who had met in secret cellars to draw up leaflets and pamphlets calling on the people to resist the Smetona dictatorship now had to draw up calls to the people to keep calm, protect their factory machinery, exercise self-discipline, and begin to study, study, study.

Assistant Minister Maimin, who was put in charge of taking over the factories (not many of them), and make sure that there would be no interruption in production, noted: "The taking over is proceeding in fullest order. No country ever went to socialism before without destruction of property and life." And why was this so in the present instance? "The chief cause of such orderly proceeding is the presence of the Red Army. Next is the fact that our bourgeoisie is not strong or well organized. Most of it is actually active in industry in a productive sense; we have few people living on dividends and interest... Besides this, we are proud that the office and technical staff of our factories did not split away from the industrial workers, as they did in the Russian revolution in 1917. They are fully cooperating; because of this we have practically no sabotage, thus far...."[41]

The revolution in Lithuania, Henrikas Zimanas, editor of *Tiesa*, which had had an underground existence during the bourgeois period when Smetona ruled, had been achieved "without firing a shot. Without even stopping a wheel. The revolution without violence that liberals always pray for. But the capitalist world won't like it any better for that."[42]

Indeed, the transition from capitalism to socialism—or, more accurately, to the beginnings of socialism—took place "without violence," and Zimanas was correct in adding that the capitalist world "won't like it any better for that." Hungary, too, had gone over to socialism under Bela Kun in 1919, but the socialist republic was short-lived, drowned in the blood of revolutionaries killed by the invading troops of the Allied powers. For a brief historical moment Bavaria, too, had a "soviet republic," but that, too, perished in the storm of counterrevolutionary bullets.

No doubt, the triumph of socialist forces in the Baltic was received with enthusiasm by the people—certainly at first—and this enthusiasm was part of the euphoria which swept the country. History did not provide up until then too many examples of triumphant socialism, and Lithuania's earlier attempt to establish socialism during and after WWI was also drowned in the blood of working class martyrs. Counterrevolution came with German bayonets. Paris's Commune of 1871 lasted only three months and that, too, ended with thousands of Commundards falling before the death squads of Thier.

The *only* successful revolution which had not only been able to institute socialist principles and build a new social system, but could also *defend* it, was the Russian. But it, too, had lived a precarious life, expecting any day to hear the second shoe drop—the "second shoe" being the second attempt to carry out Churchill's dream of "strangling the baby (now quite a lusty youth) in its crib." All of the USSR's leaders, from Lenin, Stalin to Trotsky, accepted as a matter of fact that the Western imperialists would one day launch a do-or-die attack on their socialist state. While Lenin and Stalin believed the socialist state could defend itself, even in the absence of world revolution, Trotsky did not. It is no exaggeration to say that almost from the day of its birth until that fatal day, June 22, 1941, when the long-awaited attack finally came, the young socialist state sacrificed *everything* to build itself up in preparation for the inevitable onslaught. This period prior to war was like a historical pressure cooker, in which all the social ingredients—food, clothing, housing, "democracy," etc.—were subjected to intense implosive force which, from the abstract point of view of "normalcy," produced only distorted products, cooked for one purpose alone: self-defense. Anyone who rummages about in Soviet history from any other point of view, setting up "democratic" standards against which to "judge" it, are either ignoramuses or cynics or both. The cardinal assignment facing every leader in the USSR from 1917 to 1941 was to survive. What came out of that period was survivors, not winners of schoolboy essays on democracy.

In fact, the Republic's ability to create a system which not only succeeded in developing a huge heavy industry from what was practically zero but also was able to convince the overwhelming majority of the people that the goal of establishing full socialism in the future was worth the present sacrifice. Many today give Stalin the main credit for that, "forgiving" him his mistakes and even crimes as part of the inevitable price of building a society in which they were free—free in the socialist sense. In any case, "blaming" anyone or anything for the tragedies that took place in the course of gigantic historic upheavals was like blaming the Atlantic Ocean for sinking ships with women and children.

Be that as it may, in any case, Soviet accomplishments were impressive. By 1939, the Soviet Union had attained a level of production which brought it close to the level obtaining in the West. Admittedly, the cost had been great. It was a forced march all the way. In order to achieve industrial independence and erect an industrial foundation for a socialist state, the Soviets had had to exert a monumental effort, foregoing and postponing the luxuries of consumer production, as well as a fully expanded democracy. It was openly admitted that the Union was a dictatorship—but a dictatorship of the working class. Nevertheless, a dictatorship is a dictatorship. Force is applied to somebody and that somebody doesn't like it.

Still, the dictatorship had been imposed. Menaced by outer and inner enemies, boycotted and blockaded by the West, which spawned innumerable conspiracies and plots for palace revolutions and widespread sabotage, a siege mentality had inevitably developed. In a siege there is no room for two policies. Defense has to be in the hands of a single command. This single command became, in effect, the command of one man and his closest advisers. It was the era of no second chance, which imposed on the participants the *absolute necessity to win the first time*. There would be no reprise for losers.

It is useless to pretend today that *no* threat existed from the West. (Events proved otherwise.) It is arguable whether some in the leadership did not exaggerate that threat for opportunist reasons. It is easy to understand a psychology developed in the midst of intense combat, political or military, whose simple standard applied to everyone was—are you with us or, if you are not with us, you're against us. A minority vote was, as the guns stared you in the face, treason.

Winston Churchill, inveterate enemy of socialism to his dying day, was sensitive to the hypocrisy of those in power, with whom he mixed cigar ashes in the same ash tray, when they mouthed political pieties for the press that they profaned ten minutes later in the Club. Wrote he in his book, *The World Crisis: the Aftermath*, long before WWII, as he measured allied intentions toward the young Soviet Union:

> Were they (the allies) at war with Russia? Certainly not: but they shot Soviet Russians on sight. They stood as invaders on Russian soil. They armed the enemies of the Soviet Government. They blockaded the ports and sunk its battleships. They earnestly desired and schemed its downfall. But war—shocking! Interference—shame! It was, they repeated, a matter of indifference to them how the Russians settled their own affairs. They were impartial—bang![43]

Churchill himself had a large hand in conspiracies (of which there seemed to be a new one hatched every month) directed against the young Soviet republic. Here is a graphic sampling of one:

> In the course of their regular duty, the Lettish Guards would be stationed at all the entrances and exits of the theater during the Bolshevik meeting.... At a given signal, Berain's guards would close the doors and cover all the people in the theater with their rifles. Then a "special detachment" consisting of (Sidney) Reilly himself and his "inner circle of conspirators," would leap on the Bolshevik Party!
>
> Lenin and the other Soviet leaders would be shot. Before their execution, however, they would be publicly paraded [Lenin in his undergarments] through the streets of Moscow "so that everyone should be aware that the tyrants of Russia were prisoners."[44]*

Although this plot failed, others did not, including the assassination attempt on Lenin himself, in which he was gravely wounded. Other leading Bolsheviks *were* killed. Sabotage *was* rampant, schemes of counter-revolutionary uprisings *were* being hatched in every Western capital in the world. Millions of dollars *were* spent to bribe and buy up political leaders and adventurers.

In this atmosphere of intrigue, treachery and murder, it is naive to think that the possible targets for a *putsch* could sleep peacefully at night. It's said that Stalin constantly changed his own sleeping quarters. And yet, in spite of these and other conspiracies, added to the fact that socialism was being inaugurated by a population which was still illiterate or barely literate—and smelled more of the barnyard than of the salon—it should occasion little surprise that the enormous difficulties faced by the first generation of revolutionaries also included grave miscarriages of—if not historic justice,

---

* It is almost unbelievable that the BBC produced a glorified version of Sidney Reilly's life, forgiving him even counterrevolution for his prowess in bed.

then of personal justice. Some individuals of the class were innocent, the class was not .... It is notable, too, that Lenin, while grudgingly conceding spending scarce funds to preserve the Bolshoi theatre, that gaudy, gold-leafed jewel of the Czars, wished he had money to send to the villages to educate the illiterate who knew nothing of the Bolshoi.

But the tremendous upheaval through which the Russian revolution had to go (in its second phase: its first phase, the insurrectionary phase, had been relatively peaceful and almost bloodless) was not mandatory of all countries moving into socialism.* Indeed, the very fact that the USSR existed guaranteed that some of the new countries would not need to experience violence,** as was true of the Baltic countries. The role of the Red Army was to see to it that revolutionary forces were free to function. Those who believe that the natural place for revolutionaries is in prison or before a firing squad may boggle at this formulation. But Lithuanian experience proves it out.

Perhaps no greater testimony to the truth of the Russian revolution—to its historical necessity—has been given than that by George Kennan, long-time enemy of socialism, and father, as "X," of the postwar policy that blossomed into what the world knows now, to its cost, as the Cold War. Since then, Kennan has repented. In 1967, he wrote in *Foreign Affairs*, October, under the title "The Russian Revolution Fifty Years After":

> In creating a new order ... in clinging to power successfully for half a century in a great and variegated country where the exertion of political power has never been easy; in retaining its own discipline and vitality as a political instrument in the face of the corrupting influence the exercise of power invariably exerts; in realizing the many far-reaching social objectives; in carrying to the present level the industrial-ization of the country and the development of new technology; in giving firm, determined and in many ways inspired leadership in the struggle against the armies of German fascism; in providing political inspiration and guidance to many radical-socialist forces of the world... in these achievements the Communist Party of the Soviet Union has not only stamped itself as the greatest political organiza-tion of the century in vigor and will, but has remained faithful to the quality of the Russian Revolution as the century's greatest event.

---

* This phraseology must be taken with care. "Socialism" was not a product brought to the people already baked and ready to consume. It was a process which Marx saw as covering an "epoch" and going through various phases, unfolding its inner dynamic according to its own laws, as yet really not fully understood. It is still in the process of development and self-discovery.

** Revolutions in our days *followed* violence, were in reaction to violence—the massive, all-destructive violence of war. Revolutionaries always sought for peace in which to stabilize their countries and begin to rebuild them, for revolutions almost always inherited a devas-tated country.

COUNTERREVOLUTION

Remember!
Bid Time
Stop.
Remember!
Those who will not return
Ever.
Remember!

(Inscription on memorial plaque at Skuodas where 3,000
Lithuanians were killed by Nationalists in 1941)

So now you had a country! Heady thought! What should you do with it?
Only one country before had had a successful workers revolution, which it
had proven not only capable of creating but, even more importantly, of
defending. All revolutionaries are amateurs, even supremely naive dreamers, who lack practical competence to build and then to administer a social
system. But once propelled into power, they had to deal with it. And so
they looked for models. As of then, there was only one model extant: Soviet
Russia—next door.

And yet, though they studied the model, they did not imitate it literally.
Give them credit. For those early revolutionaries understood that allowances for historical differences must be made. They were keenly aware of
the national roots of their people and, indeed, had suffered at the hands of
those ultra-cynics, the Nationalists under Smetona and Voldemaras, who
posed as true representatives of the national spirit of the country.

Nevertheless, a new Constitution was adopted by the new parliament on
September 25, 1940, in which the guidelines for developing socialism as
they understood it were clearly marked out. Paragraph 1 stated flatly that
"The Soviet Socialist Republic of Lithuania is a socialist state of workers
and peasants."

Further on: "All power in the Soviet Socialist Republic resides in the
working people of the towns and countryside, as expressed through the
representatives of the people's councils." And: "The socialist system and the
socialist ownership of the means of production constitute the economic
base of the Soviet Socialist Republic of Lithuania." And: "The land, water,
forests, large shops, factories, mines, ore deposits, waterways and airways,

banks, municipal works and large buildings in towns and industrial places are state property, that is, the property of all the people."

Uniquely different from all other (bourgeois) constitutions were the following: "Citizens of Lithuania have a guaranteed right to work, that is, a right to a job, paid for according to the quantity and quality produced."

This *guarantee* was of course historic. For workers, it was all-important. It was followed by "Citizens of Lithuania have a right to rest." Also unique! A *right* to rest! This meant paid-for vacations and the construction of vacation areas, mainly in the choicest parts of the country. "Citizens of Lithuania have a right to old-age pensions, to health and disability insurance"–then also pioneering and unique constitutional *guarantees*, expanding the areas of human rights beyond all previously set limits. The best the American Constitution would *guarantee* was the right to *pursue* happiness, the race going to the swift. Although pensions were not unknown in the West, they were secured only after bitter struggle, and were never incorporated in law or contract as a basic human *right*, and always endured fragilely on sufferance.

Equally unique in 1940, was the paragraph: "Women are guaranteed the same rights as men in all economic, governmental, cultural and socio-political spheres of life." But Lithuanian women had already been granted this right in the first socialist, briefly lived, republic of 1920, and even in 1940, women everywhere had managed to achieve not too much more than the right to vote, and only in the advanced countries. Such unconditional equality was specifically guaranteed to all minorities, "regardless of their national or racial origin," which was indeed the beginning of the liberation of Jews and the classic minorities in Europe who were always scapegoats for reaction.

Important for Lithuania was the provision in the Constitution that "the church is separated from the state and the schools are separated from the church," a provision violently opposed by the church, which had played a dominant role in the political, as well as the educational life of the country. The church has never reconciled itself to this blow at its power, though even bourgeois states had taken steps to separate church and state early on.

The Constitution goes on to list a variety of guaranteed personal freedoms, including personal security from arbitrary arrest, protection of personal property, the secrecy of the mails and integrity of the home. For the first time in any country, except Russia, all citizens 18 and over are "elected by universal, secret ballot." And perhaps for the first time, too, the slogan "one man, one vote" was introduced.

Each of the three Baltic constitutions which more or less duplicated each other also contained (as the Lithuanian Constitution did, in Article

69) a section on the right to secession: "The Lithuanian Soviet Socialist Republic shall retain the right to secede from the USSR."

Just that. At that time, the provision was included almost *pro forma*, for in the very process of building socialism in consort with the USSR, nobody was thinking of how to secede from it, which quite likely would also mean reversing the socialist process. Nevertheless, it was there, insisted on by Lenin:

> We want a voluntary union of nations—a union which precludes any coercion of one nation by another—a union founded on complete confidence, on a clear recognition of brotherly unity, on absolutely voluntary consent.

The new Constitution was hailed even in previously hostile quarters. Wrote the organ of the Liberal Party, *Lietuvos Zinos (News of Lithuania)*: "The 13 years of the Smetona regime will remain as a tragic era in our history. But Smetona is no more. Today we are marching towards a new life..."

But only for a year!

Nevertheless, before the onslaught of the Nazi forces in June of 1941, the new government had taken a series of steps that set the foundation for what was hoped would be a socialist Lithuania.

A significant date comes up—May 9, 1941. By that date it was possible to say that unemployment had been wiped out in Lithuania! Wages were raised 85 percent. The 8-hour working day was introduced everywhere. Paid vacations. Health care, special accommodations for children, etc.

On August 5, the Seimas passed a law setting 85 acres as the maximum size of the privately owned farm. Land owned by the rich landlords, including the church, much of it by absentee, was confiscated, and turned over to the working peasants. Some 75,000 landless peasants were given land—for most of them a dream they had never believed could ever come true. Some 1,482,600 acres were thus turned over to them. It's true that under a previous bourgeois administration there had been some half-hearted land reform measures, but the land that fell into the hands of any but the very rich landowners sooner or later had to be surrendered for back taxes or unpaid mortgages, and the bulk of it wound up where it had all been before: in the possession of the kulaks.

Collectivization also began at about the same time the land was distributed, but the move to join several small farms into several big farms, and thus cultivate them more economically, was voluntary. It caught on and spread throughout the countryside.

Civilization judges a society by the provisions it makes to care for its children, particularly in educating them. During the bourgeois period, almost 24 percent of the population between 9 and 49 were illiterate. Illiteracy was even higher in the countryside. But literacy itself did not guarantee work, as Anna Louise Strong testified at first hand, meeting impoverished and sickly teachers obliged to teach classes with 60 or 70 pupils.

In this respect, all the Baltic countries, now at the portals of socialism, (still a great unknown!), performed brilliantly. The first step was to eliminate illiteracy completely. At its peak, 100,000 adults in Lithuania were enrolled in literacy classes.* The second step was to provide schools staffed with dedicated teachers, constructing a network that covered the entire country so that even the remotest hamlet was near enough to a school to which to send the children.

The third step was to introduce a curriculum that met the standards of education required to equip the people with the tools to understand their times and to make a contribution in developing and mastering their lives. Church was separated from school. This very fact alone meant freeing thousands of young minds from the binding cloth of superstition, and bringing reason to bear on the key problems of their lives. Religion itself was protected—one was free to believe what one chose—but the people were also protected *from* religion, especially as it tried to impose its directives on their social lives. People were allowed to make their own religious choice, or none at all.

Books became available in big and cheap editions. In one year, 113 new libraries were opened. Seven new theatres were also opened. Art institutes, musical ensembles and orchestras multiplied and, on January 16, 1941, the first Academy of Sciences in Lithuania was inaugurated.

This first attempt to establish socialist (in large part, no more than democratic) relations in the nation had won the support not only of the working class and poor peasants but of the intellectuals as well. Among them would be listed Petras Cvirka, Salomeja Neris, Liudas Gira, Vytautas Montvila, Antanas Venclova, Teofilis Tilvytis, Jouzos Baltusis, Kostas Korsakas, Jonas Simkus—all writers who found themselves in the struggle for socialism. Veteran writers who had established reputations in bourgeois Lithuania also supported the new regime. And there were some who did not.

Indeed, it was a brave new world that was being built in the very teeth of the dragon. For the plans worked up in the various committee rooms were not to be more than glimpsed still in the planning stage before war shattered them to bits. On June 21, 1941, the Nazis, indifferent to all previous promises to observe Lithuania's integrity as a nation, sent hun-

---

* I would witness the same phenomenon in Vietnam in 1965 when the whole nation literally had gone to school. In traveling about the country, one encountered letters of the alphabet painted on trees and poles, so that even as one traveled, one learned.

dreds of Nazi Stuka bombers across the Lithuanian border catching the
summer vacationers at Palanga unawares and splashing its white beaches
with the blood of children. Right on the heels of the Nazi invaders came
the Lithuanian fascist collaborators.

Long before the fatal day had struck, Lithuanian fascists had already set
up headquarters in Berlin under Kazys Skirpa acting in concert with
Smetona, and had worked out a network of Nationalist agents within
Lithuania itself, awaiting orders to strike on *Der Tag*. Orders were sent to
them via couriers, originating with the Lithuanian Information Bureau.
Typical of those orders was the one sent on March 19, 1941—*three months
before the Nazi invasion*—by the LIB to contacts in Lithuania:

> As has been mentioned, the hour of Lithuania's liberation is close at hand.
> Immediately the campaign from the West starts you shall be informed of it over
> the radio and otherwise. Local uprisings must be started in the enslaved cities,
> towns and villages of Lithuania or, to put it more exactly, all power must be seized
> the moment the war begins. Local Communists and other traitors of Lithuania
> must be arrested at once, so that they may not escape just punishment for their
> crimes. (The traitor will be pardoned only provided he proves beyond doubt that
> he has killed one Jew at least)...
>
> As soon as the action starts, capture bridges, main railway junctions, airports,
> factories, etc. Do not destroy them and prevent the Russians from destroying
> them, especially bridges in particular since they are of great strategic and
> economical importance.
>
> Already today inform the Jews that their fate has been decided upon. So that
> those who can had better get out of Lithuania now, to avoid unnecessary victims.
> As soon as fighting starts, paratroopers will be landed in the country's rear.
> Immediately establish contact with them and, should the necessity arise, give help
> to them.
>
> German troops will soon be marching through villages, towns and cities. In
> their ranks you will see many of your fellow countrymen. Make them welcome
> and give all help they may need. By this time the organization of the Lithuanian
> Provisional Government must be completed in the whole of Lithuania....[45]

Thus, the day of attack—the beginning of this monstrous incalculable
crime—was well known to the Lithuanians in Berlin. If they had possessed
even a breath of national concern, instead of helping the Nazis to pillage
their own country, they should have given warning to the world. But no.
They had their own plans. In their messages, statements and bulletins they
seemed to assume that the Germans had already conceded power to them
to rule Lithuania. If so, they were profoundly deluded. But to be deluded so
profoundly by the Germans had to be preceded by *self*-delusion. The Germans had no intention of ceding power to this gang of ultra-fascist Lithuanians whose visions of glory, and the return of the days of "Greater
Lithuania" they saw through a haze of blood. What they did not understand was that criminals have only contempt for those who serve them.

Not only were they villains, these "patriotic" Nationalists, they were also incredible fools. Indeed, they hurried to set up a "Lithuanian Provisional Government," with Juozas Ambrazevicius as its "premier." And, indeed, they worked around the clock to "eliminate undesirables." We know that in the three months which the "Government" was allowed to exist, the members of the Lithuanian Activist Front had murdered thousands of Jews, as planned. They also murdered Communists (whom they considered regardless of their nationality as "Jews") and suspected Communists and in fact all dissidents. As described in *Blowback* by Christopher Simpson:

> ... municipal killing squads employing Lithuanian Nazi collaborators eliminated 46,692 Jews in fewer than three months, according to their own reports, mainly by combining clock-like liquidation of 500 Jews per day in the capital city of Vilnius with mobile "clean up" sweeps through the surrounding countryside.
>
> Such squads were consistently used by the Nazis for their dirty work that even the SS believed to be beneath the dignity of the German soldier.[46]

Another witness, Kaze Malukiene, who was a nurse during the war at the Skuodus Hospital, testified:

> When a Red Army man, wounded in the leg, was brought in (to the hospital), I wanted carefully to wet his bandage before I took it off, because it was stiff with congealed blood, but at the moment the priest Jankauskas bawled: "There is no need!" He tore the bandage off with his own hands and asked the soldier: "Who are you?" The wounded soldier remained silent. Jankauskas went on: "Where are your documents?" The Red Army man answered: "If you want them, look for them." The priest was furious and together with another armed man took the soldier away. Presently I heard the soldier calling, "Liudi pomagite!" ("People help me!"), and then I heard the shots from the direction of the dairy...[47]

The soldier's poignant last cry, "People, help me!" fell on ears that had been receptive to Bishop Vincentas Brizgys of Kaunas's early command to Lithuanians not to give aid and comfort to the "enemy." Brizgys was to sponsor a conference of "people's representatives" in 1943 at which he publicly called on Lithuanians to join the Nazi army as "volunteers."[48]

Both Brizgys and Lionginas Jankauskas (among 300 other priests) managed to escape Lithuania as the Red Army, led by its Lithuanian division, re-entered Lithuania in 1944. They escaped to Nazi Germany. Most of Lithuania's priests however did not "escape," because, as they maintained, they were guilty of no crimes and had clear consciences. They had only contempt for those who had "escaped." Of those who did "escape" most, like Brizgys and Jankauskas, ended up in the USA, where they lived cozy lives excoriating the "Communists" for suppressing religious freedom in Lithuania. It is perhaps only an ironic footnote that this sudden flood of several hundred priests to the USA caught the Lithuanian hierarchy there by surprise. They didn't know what to do with them, since there weren't enough Lithuanian parishes to go around. Most ended up in non-Lithuanian parishes, "fitted" in.

The moment the word arrived from Berlin that war had begun, the Nationalists, hidden till then (much the way Landsbergis describes himself and his confederates 'hiding' during the socialist period, much as his Nationalist father had hid before him), now emerged wearing white arm bands, and started rounding up and killing people on their prepared lists. Many Jews fleeing East* to escape the oncoming Nazis were caught by them. Many others, ranging all the way from minor officials in the socialist regime to heads of collective farms, were ferretted out by Nationalist cadres and turned over to the Nazis.

"As soon as the Germans entered Skuodas," Pranas Guze, who was a survivor witness testifying at their trial in Klaipeda in March, 1964, "the priest Jankauskas appeared. He was armed, and he was making out lists of people and was pronouncing death sentences on them. It was on his, Jankauskas' orders, that my brother Alfonsas was arrested and shot."[49]

Witness after witness at that trial (and other trials) testified to the episodes of unrestrained sadism with which this priest ordered, and himself carried out, the most bestial tortures and murders. He spared no one he considered to be "bolsheviks" which included their children, even babes in arms. He became known as the "Black Commandant" and took a special pleasure in killing Red Army prisoners. "The picture of the killer, clad in cassock, stands before my eyes even now, as I speak. He is a degenerate—I have no other word for him—he is a man execrated by the people of Skuodas," pronounces Jonas Sonklodas, who, as a child, remembered Jankauskas well.

> Even while working as the chaplain in Skuodas the priest Jankauskas was not distinguished for his honesty and humanity. He treated the pupils cruelly. I will never forget how he beat me on the hands with a metal ruler for my failure to learn my prayers and how he terrorized my parents about my unwillingness to learn my lessons in religion.[50]

When some of the executioners were caught, the people stood them up in court and almost desperately tried to extract a clue from these creatures that would explain their crimes in some at least minimally recognizable sense. But the replies they got were the replies of small-time merchants, of rag-pickers, of second-hand clothes dealers, small-time stock speculators, etc. "After the shooting," one of them, Ignas Velvacius-Vilius testified in court, "part of the departing Gestapo men and soldiers of the Simkus group loaded the better clothes onto cars and took them away. The remaining clothes were taken away on the following day by the officials of the Nationalist Party..."

---

* Like the parents of the American-Lithuanian artist, Rudolf Baranik.

For *them*—the Nationalists—cast-offs! One of them, Juozas Duda, would testify: "We took the clothes of the shot to the barracks and there we divided the whole lot among us. I got an overcoat, a towel, and a cap and a pair of socks..."

The commander of the 9th Fort, which had become a monstrous slaughter house, Juozas Sliesoraitis, speaks as a father. "I admit," he said, "having taken an overcoat, a suit, shoes, underwear, several dresses, boots and other articles ... for the children." But 1,800 Lithuanian children, in what was called "operation kindergarten," were slaughtered here in the first days of the Nazi invasion.

One wonders if he felt this display of fatherly concern for *his* children would melt the hearts of the jury whose own children it might have been whose clothes he stole from their bodies soon to become bones buried in limestone?

"What is right? What is wrong?" asked that modern Pontius Pilate, the commandant of Auschwitz, Rudolph Hoess, who supervised the murder of 2 million people including 50,000 Lithuanians. Even as he sat in a prison in Poland writing his memoirs as he awaited his own execution, still he could find no answer to that ancient question. "The reasons behind the extermination program seemed to be right. I did not reflect on it at the time. I had been given an order, and I had to carry it out. Whether this mass execution was necessary or not was something on which I could not allow myself to form an opinion, for I lacked the necessary breadth of view..."[51]

It is worth continuing with Hoess's confession and further revelations,* for they summed up in the voice of this compliant mass murderer the heart of the ideology that supplied him with the rationale to commit crimes unnumbered. In him we see the signal bankruptcy of that conscience supposedly formed by 2,000 years of Christianity. That "conscience" had been usurped by the class for which Hitler spoke when he assured the German middle class that they could put their consciences in his care. Within a mausoleum in Weimar, just five miles from Buchenwald,** one may still find the coffins of Schiller and Goethe, modestly stuck in among the gold-encrusted coffins of the last Hollenzollerns. Inside the town itself still stands the home of the Bachs (father and sons) and of the Hungarian-born Franz Liszt. These expressed the best of the German soul. But within smell of the burning corpses, is the camp whose entrance is marked *Jedem*

---

* Particularly in view of the distortions contained in William Styron's *Sophie's Choice*, which itself chose to concentrate on the psychology of the man without seeing it as a reflection of the psychology of a class.

** For a graphic account of life in Buchenwald, read *Naked Among Wolves* (1960) by Bruno Apitz, who spent 12 years there as part of the resistance. I interviewed him in 1965 in Berlin.

das Seine: to each his fate—where numberless intellectuals indeed met their fate and the entire civilization embodied in Goethe, Schiller, Bach, Franz Liszt failed at its crucial, ultimate test. In this camp they murdered Ernst Thaelmann, after years of imprisonment, and though he died, his murderer survived. Denounced by others, the murderer received a sentence of four years.

It was all there in the personality of Rudolph Hoess, including the banality which so surprised later commentators, but shouldn't have. That banality in crime is precisely brother to the banality of choices, decisions and virtues of bourgeois life.

Searching his mind in prison facing execution, finding only the stub of conscience left from his upbringing but unable to identify it further, Hoess could not see what his leaders had done that was morally wrong, or what was wrong in what he had done in loyally obeying them.

He was what's called fatuously a "family man," and expressed parental feelings for his own children that are a distillation of the bourgeois soul: "It would often happen, when at home [located on the grounds of Auschwitz] that my thoughts suddenly turned to incidents that had occurred during the extermination. I then had to go out. I could no longer bear to be in my homely family circle."

But this was no attack of conscience, it was merely fear of his own loss. "When I saw my children playing, or observed my wife's delight over our youngest, the thought would come to me: how long will our happiness last? My wife could never understand these gloomy moods of mine, and ascribed them to some annoyance connected with my work..." Is it too macabre to suggest that "annoyance" might have been some prisoner's recalcitrance or cry of despair as he was being marched to the ovens? In any case, "My family..." he would relentlessly go on, "were well provided in Auschwitz. Every wish that my wife and children expressed was granted them. The children could live a free and untrammeled life. My wife's garden was a paradise of flowers. [Fertilized by the ashes of the victims?] The prisoners never missed an opportunity for doing some little act of kindness to my wife and children and thus attracting their attention."

Immune to even the slightest hint that he was drawing the portrait of a monster, he continued to picture himself as a fond, middle-class father, with a flower-loving *hausfrau* of a wife, and his typical happy family. In the middle of Hell, he preserved the image of middle-class Germany as Heaven. "The children always kept animals in the garden, creatures the prisoners were forever bringing to them. Tortoises, martens, cats, lizards: there was always something new and interesting to be seen there. In summer they splashed in the wading pool in the garden... But their greatest joy was when Daddy bathed with them."

Daddy! Daddy! His work left little time, however, for his children and he regrets: "Today I deeply regret that I did not devote more time to my family. I always felt that I had to be on duty the whole time. This exaggerated sense of duty has always made life more difficult for me than it actually need[ed] to have been. Again and again, my wife reproached me and said, 'You must think not only of the service always, but of your family, too...'"

And finally: "Let the public continue to regard me as the bloodthirsty beast, the cruel sadist, the mass murderer; for the masses could never imagine the commandant of Auschwitz in any other light. They could never understand that he, too, had a heart and he was not evil..." For he had started life with "one object for which it was worth working and fighting, namely: a farm run by myself, on which I should live with a large and healthy family. That was to be the content and aim of my life!"* And through it all—through the gassing and burning of 2 million people—he retained his belief in God, and the virtues of a middle-class German remained intact... Hoess and the priest-murderer, Longinas Jankauskas, both Catholics, found such reasoning fully satisfactory.

Hoess was not unknown to Lithuania. At the end of WWI, between 1918 and 1921, he had joined, like so many other rootless German ex-servicemen of that time, the *Freikorps*. He explained: "The *Freikorps* of the years 1918-21 were peculiar phenomena of the times. The government of the day needed them whenever trouble started either on the frontiers or within the country, and then the police force, or later the army, was too weak to deal with the situation or for political reasons dared not put in an appearance." *Needed* them, the soulless mercenaries! The bourgeois, "democratic" *Reich* with its parliament and ordered elections, its regular voting days and its "free press," still *needed* a band of cut-throats to serve its purposes!

"The fighting in the Baltic states," Hoess writes, "was more savage and more bitter than any I had experienced either in the World War or later with the *Freikorps*. There was no real front, for the enemy was everywhere. When it came to a clash, it was a fight to the death, and no quarter was given or expected..." [52]

Indeed, that period at the end of WWI, when German troops were sent into the Baltics to prevent those countries from going socialist, were savage days, and service with the *Freikorps* proved to be the training ground out of which so many of the later members of Hitler's SA graduated, already fully formed as killers.

These murderers, allowed status by the Allies, would return to the Baltics some 20 years later, and again found that there was "no real front,

---

* Precisely the same as Lithuania's Landsbergis. *See* pages 258, et seq.

the enemy was everywhere." They waged total war against the Lithuanians, Latvians and Estonians. But now as before they had their native helpers—the Nationalist bands which had waited for this moment.

In their blindness, hatred and self-poisoning, the Lithuanian Nationalists had immediately set up, as we have said, under the auspices of the Lithuanian Activist Front, a "Provisional Government of Lithuania," headed by the Christian Democrat, Juozas Ambrazevicius, who explained:

> The Lithuanian Activist Front, acting in constant contact with activists in Berlin and their headquarters as well as with their own leader Colonel Skirpa [ambassador to Nazi Germany] whose activity was favored by the German military and political departments, prepared and secretly organized an uprising [directed from Berlin] of Lithuanians during the Bolshevik occupation of Lithuania. The uprising was intensely planned [at a time when the Smetona government had signed a Mutual Assistance Pact with the Soviet Union expressly forbidding "secret" dealings with Germany] for the moment when, with the outbreak of war, the German troops would turn against the Bolsheviks. According to the plan [known to Smetona, et. al. all the time] on the very first days of the war the activists and partisans started fighting against the Russians ... while in Kaunas, as early as on June 23, at 9:30 a.m. the Activist Front, standing at the head of the nation and determined to restore free and independent Lithuania, emphasizing friendly relations with Germany and their will to become part of Europe under the new regime of Adolph Hitler, proclaimed the Provisional Government of Lithuania.[53]

Here, in this statement, recurs the same irrational juxtaposition of ideas like "free and independent" with their opposite, "part of Europe under the new regime of Adolph Hitler" that strikes us as already familiar from Hoess' "confessions." Hoess had brushed aside crimes beyond number to claim respect as a "family man." And such oxymoronic combinations, like grotesque miscarriages preserved in alcohol for medical students, like two-headed human embryos, occur over and over in the writings of Nazis and Nationalists—between whom by this time it was impossible to draw a distinction. And, in truth, when one examines the reality of their positions, especially with history having knocked them on the head, the attempt to express opposite ideas in the same context forced them into semantic gymnastics. Today, "democracy" of the Nationalists is combined with the suppression of democracy.

But what of the "independent" government? It certainly had all the outer accoutrements of a government. It had a "president," a "cabinet of ministers," courts and lawyers, even armed forces at its disposal. It started bravely enough, and "took steps to establish close contact with German troops with a view of cleansing the country of the savage Bolshevik bands that were active in many parts of Lithuania [that is, the anti-Nazi partisans]..." but quite soon it ran into trouble with the German occupiers. It seems that the leading personalities had set aside a prominent role for the traitor, "Prime Minister Col. Kazys Skirpa,"* who had engineered the "up-rising" from his sanctioned quarters in Berlin. But he failed to arrive to assume his duties. No explanation offered, but waiting for Kazys to arrive was like waiting for Godot. It paralyzed the "government" in Kaunas. While waiting, "the Provisional Government of Lithuania took pains to establish immediate relations with appropriate German military authorities that had arrived in Kaunas." But the eagerness to embrace the German authorities was not returned by the German authorities. In fact, Gen. Pohl, the German military commandant of Kaunas, "did not consent to the German army being greeted on behalf of the Provisional Government of Lithuania." Then came the shocker: "From this moment it was evident that the German military headquarters, apparently acting under certain instructions, did not recognize the Provisional Government of Lithuania, did not address it officially, and, naturally, sought no contact with it."

The coldness—actually, the contempt—of the German military authorities was a crushing blow to the Lithuanian "Government," which indeed was "provisional," but much more so than they had ever dreamed. They were literally orphans, and kept on tapping forlornly at the door and scratching at the window of German Power asking to be let in: "The provisional Government, however, went out of its way to clear up all its problems with Gen. Pohl and though the German military commandant kept declining official interviews with representatives of the Government—" But, thank God, "practical requests, especially those concerning food and police, he did take into account."**

They weren't going to starve at least. And the Germans needed the Lithuanian police to control the people, ferret out hidden revolutionaries and anti-fascists and herd prisoners into the various Prison Forts where they were exterminated in due course. This kind of work the Germans allowed them to do.

But when it came to "such questions as currency, organization of a partisan force, complaints as regards taking goods from storehouses," etc.,

---

* Kazys Skirpa died in August, 1979, at the age of 84 in Bethesda, Maryland. According to the creatively rewritten version of his life in the New York Times obituary, "Mr. Skirpa became premier of Lithuania shortly after German forces invaded the Soviet Union in June, 1941. During his brief term, he urged his countrymen to resist the Soviet domination that began when the Soviet army occupied Lithuania in 1939 and established a Communist government. Six weeks after Mr. Skirpa came to power, Germany invaded Lithuania. Mr. Skirpa's government was deposed and he later was imprisoned. He left Lithuania after World War II and came to the United States in 1949 ... Mr. Skirpa worked for 16 years for the Library of Congress as a senior librarian. In 1965, he wrote 'Restoration of Lithuania's Sovereignty,' published in Lithuanian in 1973."

** Compare this treatment to the way in which the CIA trussed up and salted away in a house deprived of telephone or outer communication a band of Cubans the CIA had custom-shaped to take over the Cuban government once Castro's government had been overthrown at the Bay of Pigs in 1961.

they spoke to deaf ears. The "independent" government representatives fared no better with their "request(s) to set free the interned Lithuanian soldiers, to give their consent to organize a national corps, that would take part in the struggle against the Bolsheviks, also to strengthen the action of cleansing the country of Bolsheviks, to allow the Government to use the means of transport and the telephone in order to communicate with the provinces, etc ... only a small part of these requests were complied with."

Worse: "Part of the soldiers who had belonged to the former corps were deported as prisoners of war—" and most likely *they* went straight into the ovens at Auschwitz— "some were sent home on furlough and those in Vilnius were turned in to the police." And the police sent *them*, in their turn, to prisons in Germany...

The Germans, the "Government" went on complaining, had "no intention of permitting the organization of a national Lithuanian corps" [as they would allow General Andrei Vlasov to organize a Russian "army" later made up of deserters, of POW's, but never fully trusted by the Nazis. Vlasov was eventually caught by the Allies, turned over to the Soviets and hanged ... only to find resurrection and rehabilitation in the pages of *New Times* in 1990]... despite the fact that the aforesaid soldiers had to give written undertaking to participate in the campaign against Bolshevism."

German suspicion of the Nationalists was liberally tinged with all but open contempt. As Goebbels had confided to his diary: The Germans had no intention of "setting up a government in these midget states," only to see them, "at the end of the war, or possibly during the war ... veer over to the side of our enemies." Traitors once, why not twice? The Germans wanted from their Lithuanian traitors nothing but total obedience—when told to beg, they were expected to beg, and told to sit, to sit. They were expected to perform tasks considered beneath the dignity of a German soldier—to carry out their slop buckets, conduct the slaughters of women and children, stoke the ovens into which other Lithuanian mothers and fathers had been shoved. And when it came to getting a share of the spoils of ... murder, they had to wait until "the Gestapo men and soldiers of the Simkus group" had their chance to "load the better clothes on to cars and took them away." As for *them*, they could have what "remain(ed)," presumably much of it too spoiled by blood stains for immediate use....

Insult could hardly go further than when the Germans not only denied the "government" ... "any kind of facilities to travel," but "all the motor vehicles were taken from it. The Government was deprived of the simplest means of performing its official duties."

Nevertheless, the Nazis in Kaunas received nothing but the warmest cooperation, ranging all the way from the Catholic Lithuanian authorities, Archbishop Juozas Skvireckas and his assistant Bishop Vincentas Brizgys, to the lowliest school janitor who acted as a government spy on the teachers and pupils. But in return for their subservience they got nothing but insults. Still, no insults could discourage these diehard ex-landlords who thirsted for "Bolshevik" blood, which included the blood of Bolshevik babies as well. "But even being in want of any communication service, the Provisional Government of Lithuania went on with the hard work of reconstruction." Hard work it was indeed. For "it was unable to use either the press or the radio,* which had been at the disposal of the Germans since June 25, to announce its decrees and laws."

We are here treated to the vision of earnest "law-makers" passing laws in solemn conference assembled—but unable even to let the people whom they were supposed to be governing know what laws they had passed. It began to sound like a page from *Alice in Wonderland* and a perpetual Mad Hatter's tea party. A handful of men furiously passed "laws" which nobody even heard of let alone obeyed, though it must be said that it's doubtful if the people *had* learned what laws were passed they would have been overjoyed, especially the law "on the denationalization of urban houses and plots of land, on the denationalization of industrial enterprises, on the reforming of the court system, laws concerning the University [it was closed down] and other schools, etc."

Deprived of the use of press and radio, the Government had to rely on word of mouth to advertise its actions "through people arriving from the provinces." Sadly: "On the whole the Government was detached from the people."

But did this discourage the members of the "Government?" Not in the least, even though the obstacles continued to mount: "The German military authorities continued to officially ignore and to avoid dealing with the Provisional Government of Lithuania, though—" and here is where all reason, all persuasion reached an impenetrable brick wall—"the collaboration [they themselves characterized themselves as collaborators], especially from the economical point of view, as on numerous occasions the German authorities were informed, would have only been to their benefit."

They were ready to sell the heart and soul of their people to the Germans and the nation itself at bargain prices. But the Germans didn't need to bargain with them. Only to order. At a later meeting with a German representative of the Ministry of Home Affairs, a Dr. Greffe (who was from the Gestapo), "made it clear that the Provisional Government of Lithuania was formed without Germany's knowledge" and so, "in its present form (it)

---

* However, the radio was available to Bishop Brygys who broadcast soothing sermons to the people assuring them no harm would come to them from the Nazis who were to be cooperated with fully.

was not acceptable to the Germans. The present Provisional Government of Lithuania was to be reformed into a national committee or council, attached to the German military headquarters..." Dr. Greffe was even clearer: "Emphasizing that the Germans possessed sufficient means to liquidate the Provisional Government of Lithuania ... Dr. Greffe suggested that they should reconstitute themselves into a kind of committee or council mentioned."

How the mighty had fallen! They had been looking in vain for the arrival of Dr. Skirpa from Berlin, only to learn that that master intriguer, having done his work for them, was now "arrested" and in German hands. Still not giving up all hope, the Provisional Government–still calling itself that–decided to send a delegation to Berlin to see if matters could be improved. But before setting out, they ran into further domestic difficulties. Although it seems hard to imagine any organization to the right of the "Government," there actually was one: the Voldemaras Iron Wolf, which, disagreeing with the Activist Front, finally "on the night from July 23 to 24, Voldemarites took over the Kaunas Commandant's office, the battalion and the Lithuanian police by force." And so ended the "Government"...

Ended, but its ghost lingered on. Attempts to make contact with the German authorities continued, always being met with rebuffs, incapable of taking offense or of being insulted. "Individual departments and ministries did their utmost to meet the economic demands of the Germans, tolerating injustices, etc. In July the state farms were taken over by the corresponding German authorities. The same attempts were perceptible in the sphere of woods, which in July were taken over by the Germans." And here is the anti-climax, which bears what was now the typical mixture of farce and self-delusion. "Such tendencies(!) suggested (!) that it was not desirable that the Provisional Government of Lithuania should manage the economic affairs of Lithuania. Its decrees [which nobody had even noticed] were cancelled."

Finally, after taking over all the ministries, offices, and "expelling the Provisional Government itself from its premises (August 4), [the Germans] created impossible conditions for its activity."

It had taken a lot of convincing but finally when even the office clerk had no telephone to use, and the "president" had to communicate his government's wishes by ectoplasm, "in the face of these facts the Provisional Government of Lithuania holds that its activity is stopped against its will." The momentous day was August 5, 1941.

The "Government" had lasted three months. But although in those three months it had been unable to persuade a mule to cross the road, it did have the resources to kill tens of thousands of Jews and "Communists," as Christopher Simpson would document in his book, *Blowback*.

As for Ambrazevicius, the "premier" of the Provisional Lithuanian Government, he managed to "escape" through German assistance which brought him safely in due course to the USA, into which he found no difficulty entering. There he changed his name to Brazaitis where his past was re-stitched into a more comfortable cover. Here is how reactionary America's Lithuanians portrayed him:

> Juozas Brazaitis, mentioned before as a member of the *Darbininkas** editorial staff, was a dedicated resistance leader against Bolshevik and Nazi alike. When the unholy alliance of Nazi Germany and Soviet Russia ended in war in the early summer of 1941, the Lithuanians proclaimed the revival of their independence and set up a provisional government with Juozas Brazaitis as the head [any attempt to locate "Brazaitis" as the head of the provisional government is bound to fail; no such man existed. There *was* an Ambrazavicius, but for some obscure reason the Americans re-christened him as Brazaitis—P.B.] The resurgence of Lithuanian freedom was brief. The dream of independence was shattered by the Germans after only two [factually, three] months.
>
> The underground council (the Supreme Committee for the Liberation of Lithuania) continued to function during the German occupation [as energetic collaborators], went into exile with the stream of refugees in 1944 [the year Lithuania was liberated by the 16th Lithuanian Division of the Red Army], worked secretly in Germany [planning to overthrow the new socialist government], came out into open at the end of the war, and finally came to the United States. Brazaitis remained at the heart of it all....
>
> Having found a haven in the United States, Brazaitis went on working for Lithuanian liberty with lectures, articles, books and general involvement in Lithuanian affairs. In 1964, saddened because the world seemed to have forgotten the tragic plight of the Baltic Nations, he published, "Vienu Vieni" (All Alone). It is the story of all the forms of Lithuanian resistance against foreign oppression and is an ardent call to continue resistance.[54]

What a pity that he gave in to pessimism! If he had survived to 1990, it's quite possible—no, certain—that the present "president" of the also provisional government of Lithuania would have welcomed him "home" on a red (or perhaps green, black and orange) carpet, as so many long-time exiles, whose bloody pasts have been sanitized by time and American power to redefine the vocabulary of the world, turning yesterday's fascist into today's "democrat."

---

* Here is the official reaction of the World Jewish Congress to *Darbininkas*: "The WJC said that base anti-Semitism was evidenced in many of the publications of the emigre group, a sampling of which it released to the press today. The WJC cited as one example the Lithuanian-language weekly, *Darbininkas*, which has asserted that 'the Jews murdered not six but seventy million innocent people' and has condemned what it referred to as the 'Jewish Eichmanns.' *Darbininkas* has led the fight against the exposure and deportation of Lithuanian war criminals, advising possibly guilty Lithuanians not to 'answer any, even the simplest questions about yourself' if confronted by the OSI. *Dirva*, another Lithuanian newspaper advised: 'Let us chase these (OSI) interviewers from our homes.'"

RESISTANCE

Red Army soldiers, brothers dear
Come, free my land...
To the Liberators of Lithuania– Kostas Korsakas, 1942

Though the "government" had fallen–or more correctly, been carried out with the trash–individual Lithuanians, some directly as members of the Iron Wolves, some intoxicated with the idea that Nazism was the "coming thing," and some just carried along with the tide, continued to serve the Germans. Later, at his trial, Kazys Mickevicius, leader of the Schutzmannshafts battalion, would confess candidly: "I enjoyed shooting," and a fellow "shooter," Stasys Bezius, confided with the air of someone confessing to an endearing fault that he preferred to shoot women and children only with his personal revolver–white-handled and dainty.

Before they–and their collaborators–were through, they would have managed to murder some 700,000 Lithuanians. They killed about 200,000 Soviet POW's as well. Following out their voluntary personal collaboration with the Nazis on economic matters, they supervised the rounding up and transporting to Germany of two million head of cattle–robbing the country of its main source of food and income–and cooperated in ferreting out hidden grain and seeing it carted off to Germany. They helped demolish 20,000 homes, 53,000 public institutions. They helped burn down whole villages, like Pirciupe, on the rumor that the villagers harbored partisans. (In this instance, they crowded the people–old men, women and children– into a barn and set it on fire, shooting anyone who managed to run out). They demolished the Evangelist-Calvinist library constructed in 1611, destroying rare books, irreplaceable manuscripts. They closed down Vilnius University. They restored the medieval ghetto into which all the Jews were herded, and which was systemically destroyed, with the Jews–except those who escaped into the forests–sent to their deaths at Panavyz, where an estimated 60,000 perished. (Some 200,000 Jews were killed in Riga.) In Kaunas, which had a Jewish population of 40,000 in 1941 when the war began, all but 8 or 9 thousand who managed to flee with the Red Army were killed. Jews perished in the monstrous Ninth Fort, as well as at mass execution sites outside of it. Jews from all over Europe–Berlin, Vienna, France, Holland, etc.,–ended up here.

The first pogrom began on June 25th or 26th in the suburb of Slobodsk, densely populated by Jews. The Nazi thugs burst into the apartments; using their rifle butts, they smashed in the heads of women and old men. Infants were bayonetted...

The Germans forced them to dig their own graves with their bare hands. Hundreds of Jews...were herded into the Letukisa garage on the Vitautasak Avenue opposite the Catholic cemetery. Here the German cannibals perpetrated their bloody orgies. To the sound of accordion music they advanced upon their helpless victims. With pincers, they tore their sexual organs from their bodies, cut out their tongues, chopped off their legs and gouged out their eyes.[55]

All this took place in Kaunas, where both archbishop Juozas Skvireckas and his assistant Bishop Vincentas Brizgys presided, issuing statements over the radio (whose use was refused to the "government") counseling the people to "behave quietly and pursue their daily business with confidence, without fear that they might be harmed."[56]

Indeed, collaborators were not "harmed." But those who opposed, even in the mildest form, Nazi barbarism were "harmed"—if that is the word. "Any contact with the Lithuanians," we read in the *Black Book*, "provoked the most ferocious wrath on the part of the Germans. Disregarding anti-Semitic badgering and cruel penalties, some Lithuanians did their best to help Jews escape from the ghetto. They supplied them with food and assisted them in every possible way. Despite all barriers, Jews and Lithuanians managed to meet in the city, and the latter welcomed them warmly and gladly. When the German police discovered these 'crimes,' the Jews were hanged, while the Lithuanians were exiled to Germany—all their goods and chattels confiscated." And, it hardly needs adding, they ended up in Auschwitz.

Organized Lithuanian resistance to the Nazi occupation began as early as 1941, immediately after the war broke out in June. It is well known that this resistance was initiated and organized first by the Communists, including the resistance inside the ghetto. Under the leadership of Antanas Snieckus, first secretary of the Communist Party of Lithuania, the partisan movement, which was to grow into a great force, was first coordinated and directed. Future partisans were flown in by glider at night behind German lines and those who survived the blind landings formed the core of the partisan forces.

Eventually, there were 90 separate partisan groups in Lithuania, and their role was to harass, sabotage and engage where feasible the German soldiers in battle. In this they did signally well. The Germans were forced to detail considerable energy, time and soldiers to deal with the partisans. Despite them, the partisans managed to derail 364 trains carrying Nazi soldiers to the front and their supplies, destroyed 300 locomotives, 2,000 railroad cars, tore up miles of track, blasted or bombed supply dumps, destroyed enemy garrisons, killing some 10,000 Hitlerite soldiers and their collaborators. They rescued prisoners from camps and prisons, and trains carrying them to Germany.

They often managed to cut German communication lines. They even "liberated" certain pockets which they held until the Red Army could arrive. Units of the regular Lithuanian army, which the Nationalists had tried in vain to enlist as part of the German army, also fought, most of them as soldiers with the Red Army. A Lithuanian division of the Red Army was formed on the banks of the Volga in December 1941. It was made up of anti-fascists who had retreated with the Red Army out of Lithuania, the members of the 29th Territorial Corps—those who had survived—as well as some Lithuanians who had served in the Soviet army before Lithuania had become socialist.

The new unit formed out of these Lithuanian soldiers was the 16th Lithuanian Rifle Division, and it was sent to the front in 1943. It fought the Nazi invaders on the plains of Russia, in Belorussia, and finally in Lithuania itself, battling the Nazis in the western part of Lavia—Kurland.

It liberated Siauliai in September, 1944. In October, it helped to liberate Zemaitija and in January 1945, took part in the liberation of Klaipeda, which had been given to the Nazis by the Nationalist Smetona government in 1939. The Division was awarded the Red Banner for heroism and given the right to be called "The Klaipeda Division" as the liberators of Klaipeda. Thousands of individual soldiers and partisans were awarded medals for heroism, and ten received the highest award of all—Hero of the Soviet Union.

After three years of Nazi occupation, liberation came to Lithuania in the summer of 1944. In early July the Soviet forces entered the territory of Lithuania and after a five-day battle, the armies of the Third Belorussian front liberated Vilnius (once more), and by October all of Lithuania was cleansed of the Nazis.

The people of the entire country celebrated victory. But not all. Incredible as it sounds, there were nevertheless forces within Lithuania for whom the victory of the Red Army (including its Lithuanian division) was not cause for joy but for sorrow. Even today, 45 years after liberation, Lithuanian Nationalists unabashedly admit, in literature published by the Lithuanian-American community in Chicago, that "From 1944 to 1952, well-organized military units of the Lithuanian resistance movement waged a protracted guerilla war against the Soviet occupants in which about 50,000* lives were lost on each side. A large Soviet military force and

* A gross exaggeration. Quote is from an undated brochure published by the Lithuanian-American community in Chicago (in the author's possession).

massive deportations of innocent civilians to Siberia (10% of the population) were used to contain the resistance movement."

As this self-volunteered testimony reveals, fascist forces in Lithuania never laid down their arms, but continued their war supplied by American money and guns under the direction of the CIA. Absolutely no proof of Nationalist resistance to the Nazi occupation exists before or during the war years. On the contrary, it was they who supplied the Nazis with collaborators, executioners and spies. They organized the so-called "Liberation Army of Lithuania" whose job was to sabotage efforts of the new government to rebuild.

In 1950, when the Korean War broke out, the Nationalist fascists took the outbreak of hostilities with Korea as the beginning of the long-awaited WWIII and intensified their resistance in Lithuania. American "Project X"—the creature of the CIA—had already arranged to parachute armed bands into Lithuania in a kind of grotesque imitation of the way in which the Lithuanian partisans had been parachuted behind the Nazi lines during the war. They began burning down farms and schools. Their prime target was school teachers, many of them serving isolated villages where no schools had been before. One of them was Ona Sakakiene, of whom more later.

WAR'S END: DEVASTATION

The fascists run, and endless rows
Of crosses by the roads they leave,
And in the future times no foes
Will ever venture past my grave.
                          Our Lucky Star— Paulius Sirvys, 1947

At the end of the war, the three Baltic countries were, one could justly say, economic and social basket cases. Not only had the Germans destroyed, consciously and according to plan, most of the country's physical resources. That loss to Lithuania alone amounted to 17 billion rubles. Factories were gutted, or carted away, homes were shattered, hospitals and public utilities rendered almost useless. This was devastation enough. But livestock was driven off to Germany or slaughtered. Cattle head were reduced to 53.6 percent of what had been; pigs, 63.9 percent. Indeed, people were killed *like* pigs. In a country of less than 3 million, 700,000 would never see a blue sky again.

The Nazis destroyed 90,000 buildings, which included homes, schools, and other enterprises. Cultivated land was laid waste by 20 percent. Looking the scene of destruction over one could have understood how the heirs to this destroyed country might have lost heart. They had inherited a graveyard.

But physical destruction was not all that the Nazis left behind. They had consciously tried to destroy the minds and souls of the people as well. It would be pleasant to be able to report that the Church had resisted the spreading of anti-Semitic poison over the minds of the people. But the Catholic Metropolitan Archbishop Juozas Skvireckas confided to his diary (June 30, 1941):

> The thoughts of *Mein Kampf*, concerning the poisonous Bolshevist influence exercised by Jews on the nations of the world, are worthy of note. The ideas are interesting, indeed. They are true to life and present an insight into reality. Whether they belong to Hitler himself or to his associates is hard to say. But all this testifies to Hitler being not only an enemy of the Jews, but to the correctness of his thoughts as well.[57]

The Ninth Fort was not far from the Archbishop's windows, and on a windy day the odor of corpses most likely could reach his nostrils. Nor could his assistant, Bishop Brizgys, possibly avoid that mephitic odor, nor, if he glanced outside his window, fail to see the columns of prisoners being herded to the Fort, from which they would never come out again.

Anti-Semitism has been in-built in Catholic doctrine for centuries, and only lately have half-hearted attempts been made to erase the texts which "justify" it. Writers for the American-Lithuanian *Darbininkas* to this day re-echo the old anti-Semitisms and invent new ones. Allowing the ideas of Nazism to penetrate the schools and churches was encouraging the corruptive spread of a poison which all mankind has joined in denouncing. The tragedy is that once planted, anti-Semitism not only grows but even when pruned back, or cut down, it continues an underground life that waits only for the positive moment to re-emerge.

Nationalism lived off anti-Semitism, and no matter how many times the official spokesmen moved their lips in a disavowal of murderous anti-Semitism, those who were entrusted with the down-to-earth obligation of carrying out Nationalist policy paid no attention. Nor did the infection stop at anti-Semitism itself. Nationalism also taught the doctrine (learned from the Nazis) of racial superiority of the Nordic race (though Lithuanians themselves were not Norse), and inculcated an attitude of contempt for science, education, humanist principles. We see the reemergence of these tendencies today.

In any case, though they were confronted with endless devastation, the generation that had survived the war—not passively but actively—now set themselves the heroic task of rebuilding their country—and, in the process, rebuilding the soul of the country.

Recovery was nothing less than miraculous. Nor did they have a Marshall Plan to help them do it. In the process of reconstruction, the nature of the people themselves changed. The Communist Party that emerged from the war had 3,536 members—though it had a greater membership now literally underground, in the cemeteries. It was primarily on their shoulders that the responsibility for reconstituting the country now fell.

If, looking at the resources and measuring the dimensions of the task ahead, Antanas Snieckus, secretary of the Lithuanian Communist Party since 1926, had thrown up his hands and surrendered, anyone facing the same problems would have understood. But this was not Snieckus' way. He had been in political charge of the resistance movement in Lithuania and had acquitted himself well. He put the problem on the table: the Party was not only obliged to give leadership in the physical reconstruction of the country but in reconstructing the severely damaged minds and souls of the people.

Snieckus himself had known the inside of Smetona's jails, and he had helped engineer a dramatic breakout of 26 prisoners from the Ninth Fort one Christmas eve when the Lithuanian jailers were drunk. He had a reputation for courage that was not limited to the battlefront. He crossed words with Stalin himself and managed to present the Lithuanian point of view in the Kremlin in a persuasively logical and Marxist way. It is he who is credited with saving and protecting innumerable Lithuanians unjustly accused of treason, including the Jewish doctor who had attended to Petras Cvirka's final days, and who was accused by an anti-Semite of having poisoned him. A modest man, he lived only for his people—but fully understood that his people could not hope to develop and grow cut off from the inspirational sources of the world working class movement. And if, instead of cooperating, Lithuanians were persuaded to pit themselves against the working-class forces, their fate would be to degenerate into a pathetic mouse of a nation which flattered itself that its squeaks were lion's roars....*

War had been the cruel master. It had destroyed not only physical but social Lithuania as well, and destroyed were not only bridges and railroads but people's minds. Regardless of what social system had followed the war, the monumental task of rebuilding the country would have confronted any system with the same problems. There was the bourgeois way, which institutionalized exploitation and saw in the prosperity of the few the success of the nation. And there was the way of the then socialism.

The bourgeois way would have certainly created a social system, and reconstructed the nation along classic capitalist lines. Adopting capitalism, it would also be prey to the vagaries of capitalism, with its periods of acute stress, expressed in dramatic episodes of the class struggle—strikes, mass demonstrations, the appearance of thousands of the homeless, the unwanted, the superfluous, the sick, the mentally unstable, the criminal. And— always the threat of war.

Inspired by socialist goals, the Communists, with the cooperation of the entire nation (which is what actually happened), set out not only to eliminate the tragedies of war but the tragedies of the class war by striking at the root. It matters little that the actual struggle evoked far greater difficulties than had been imagined, and that the hypothesis on which they set forth turned out to be too schematic. Here it's not out of place to note that there is no such thing as absolute defeat or absolute failure for the working class. Only experience. Only lessons. Defeat is the great teacher.

The battle of figures rages. Comparisons are made. Finland becomes the Shangri-La of all utopias. Nations are judged not by the kind of human being they produce but by how many cars they put on the road. Or how

---

* The author met Snieckas on various occasions, always parting with a pleasant impression. When he died in January 1974, the whole nation (with the usual exceptions) genuinely mourned this modest and devoted man. Henrikas Zimanas planned to write his biography but died himself before he could manage to do it.

many new millionaires can be pointed to each year. Greed is rediscovered and hailed as the true spur to human progress.

But even by the standard of quantitative factors alone, the record is an impressive one. Before the war, 73.8 percent of the population was raising cows and pigs and hens. Only 7.3 to 7.5 percent were in industry. And the products manufactured in those small factories and shops had no real value to others and could not readily be sold. "In 1940, Lithuania's per capita industrial output was only a third of that of the USSR, not to mention Sweden."[58]

When Smetona came to power his clique could hardly wait to sell off whatever was saleable in Lithuania to foreign "investors." Some 43 percent of the nation's natural resources and industry were precipitately "sold." "Stolen" is just as applicable a word. The process of disposing of the country's assets, such as they were, began by breaking off relations with Russia, thus destroying Lithuania's small metal and leather industries, but the best they had. Electrical power was turned over to a Belgian firm, which promptly raised the rates, forcing the people of Kaunas to resort to candles and oil lamps rather than pay the exorbitant rates. The match industry was turned over to Sweden, so that matches which sold for the equivalent of 2 cents in Sweden sold for the equivalent of 10 cents in the country of their manufacture. Land, temporarily in the hands of the few lucky benefactors who, though not rich, had managed to scrape together enough to hold title, promptly lost title and investment and saw it return to its original owners—the big landowners.

At no time, under bourgeois conditions, did Lithuania rise to a level where it could successfully compete on the world market. The war had destroyed even what had been achieved up until that point. In fact, without the active assistance of the rest of the Soviet Union, which sent money, supplies and workers, Lithuania would not have been able to recover half as quickly as it did.

Workers answering a call from Lithuania streamed into that country from all over the Soviet Union. Indeed, many of Lithuania's factories were patchwork quilts of diverse nationalities, as at Elfa,* an electrical component, which had workers of 33 different nationalities working for it. Incidentally, the only way they could communicate with one another was through the one language they had in common—Russian. (So much for forcing Russian on the population.) Between the end of the war and up until recently, the Union as a whole invested over 50 billion rubles in capital construction. Indeed, one of the serious points of contention today is the question of who owns what. Is the huge all-Union investment in

* Which I visited in 1965 et. seq.

industry to be uncomplainingly yielded to the newly-hatched entrepreneurs who ache to sell socialist-built property to foreign capitalists? Or to themselves as newly minted capitalists? Or is one permitted to demur?

In fact, one could make out a case charging that *all* of modern Lithuania belongs to those who invested the funds and labor to transform it from an agricultural nation to an industrial one. Instead of its remaining a source of raw materials in a classic colonial relationship to the more powerful industrial states, the Soviets consciously planned to establish the means by which Lithuania could achieve a certain national independence within the socialistic system on the realistic basis of a strong industrial foundation. It was, in fact, settled Soviet policy for many years to bring all the backward republics of the nation to the level of advanced Russia, and this could be accomplished mainly by establishing the infrastructure of industrial plants and factories to guarantee that. At no time did Lithuania, or any other republic, enter into a relationship with Russia in which one held the whip and the other jumped to command.

The postwar history of Lithuania is nothing less than the record of how it made an abrupt change from a primarily agricultural nation to a primarily industrial one. The progress was spectacular, and at the time, was what the people boasted of, and show-cased to visitors, with the refrain endlessly repeated: "Before the revolution, there was only wasteland here. Now we have a cement factory..." Or "Now we have a textile plant ... factory that makes radios...etc."

They would quote you figures before and after that never failed to impress you, the visitor, no matter how sophisticated you were nor how little you cared about factories breaking records making washing machines. By 1989, Lithuania was producing 88 times more industrial goods than in 1940—just before the war. It brought into existence a system that was tooled to further its settled industrial direction and spoke of a future in which it seemed that the whole nation would be cybernetically connected up and run as if by itself!

They spoke of mills and factories that had never existed in Lithuania before. But they also pointed to vast housing complexes which also had risen from barren ground as if by a miracle and by which they were hoping to meet the promise of supplying every citizen of the Republic with his own flat by the year 2000. Such huge residential production, it must be remembered, from a capitalist point of view, is a total loss. There is no profit in low-cost housing! Nor in other social constructions meant solely for the pleasure and health of the people and not of the banks—well-appointed sanitoria, special resorts for special kinds of illnesses, particularly of children, modern schools, etc. All this, from an investor's point of view, is loss—throwing money away.

That must always be kept in mind when making comparisons between the present and past and with foreign countries. A high Lithuanian official* once told me: "All we heard once we came to power were complaints about lack of housing. Strange: during Smetona's days there were no such complaints. And you know what? Such complaints are a tribute to socialism. Under socialism the people know it's possible to improve housing and even to get their own home. Under Smetona, they knew it was useless to even dream about it."

There was also the acute critic from abroad who comparing before and after figures concluded that more people got sick under socialism than under capitalism because under socialism there were more hospitals built and more people in them!

One might say, the people in power brought it on themselves. Since class distinctions, with their privileges, were abolished everyone was therefore legally entitled to share in the productive wealth of the country. The only trouble is that producing housing doesn't produce wealth: it absorbs it. It produces only people.

. Nevertheless, in Lithuania, as in all the Baltic countries, huge housing projects were launched which strove valiantly not only to make up for past losses (mainly military) and official neglect but to create a level of habitation that met civilized standards. The aim was not merely to erect a "concrete box" in which a person could exist. But to create a home in an environment which added to his pleasure in living. It was the plan to build no city so large that one could not reach the countryside in just a half hour by bus or trolley. And, within the concrete complexes, little parks were interspersed among the buildings. And the architecture, too, was of great concern to the city planners—architecture that not only dealt with the building per se but extended to and blended in with the entire environment.

In Lithuania, new housing had been almost non-existent in 1940—12 sq. meters per 1000 inhabitants. By 1988, that figure had advanced to 545 meters per 1000 inhabitants. Indeed, old Vilnius was itself rebuilt taking care to maintain its medieval character, preserving its narrow cobble-stoned alleyways and rehabilitated facades that perpetuated the atmosphere of a Vilnius that once charmed Napoleon.

But if the old was preserved, the new was not discouraged. Comparing maps of prewar and post-war Lithuania, one comes across many entirely new cities and new towns that had been built after the war. And not haphazardly—but according to a well-thought-out plan whose reigning motif

* Henrikas Zimanas, member of the Central Committee of the Lithuanian CP and editor of *Tiesa* and the *Komunistas* as well as a number of books on nationalism and other matters.

was to integrate the towns into a correlated system of social services, health care, education, recreation.

Libraries hardly existed for the masses in 1940–201 in the entire country. In any case, why did peasants need books? But by 1988, there were 2,000–and counting. There were only 2,000 doctors in 1940, and those concentrated in the bigger cities. There were 16,600 in 1988, with the entire population being served. Hospital beds multiplied from 8,900 in 1940 to 46,800 in 1988–thus proving to the skeptical visitor that more people got sick in postwar Lithuania than in prewar.

A telling figure is the one dealing with national income and consumption. Between 1966-1988, Lithuanians consumed through imports from the rest of the USSR products that far exceeded their income. Lithuania's economic ties with the rest of the USSR were extensive and wide.

Lithuania depends for fuel almost entirely on imports. All its non-ferrous metals and ores must be imported. When the Polish miners went on strike in the '80s, Lithuania, which imports much of its coal from Poland, had to cut electrical consumption nationwide by 3 percent. In 1988, Lithuania imported 7.5 billion rubles worth of products while exporting only 6 billion worth of goods. The balance of payments, which so bedevil other countries, has played no hobbling role in Lithuania's economy. Such a debt (1.5 billion rubles) with interest compounded, has sunk many ex-colonial countries which found themselves permanently and totally in thrall to Western (i.e. American) banks, and unable to pay not only on the principal but even the accumulated interest. "Independence," among other things, means that the entire economy would be put on a hard convertible currency basis, and in order to do business at all, one had to have credit, and the "credit system," whose operating strings are in the hands of the big banks of the West (and now Japan) worked more like the spider proposing in the child's poem: "Will you walk into my parlor?"–and never coming out again. Not only that, but to be at the mercy of the ups and downs of the international vagaries of the world economy, with one force, or a handful of forces, moving irresistibly toward world monopoly, in the process of attaining which not only small countries but even some large countries would become total sacrifices, mere appendages to a power over which they had not the slightest influence. When the world depression began in 1930, with the collapse of the Stock Market in New York City in 1929, it wasn't long before faraway Lithuania was registering the effects in shut down factories and unbought products. How was it possible?

In post-war Lithuania successes were marked up on an entire series of production charts, especially energy. Lithuania, with its access to energy sources outside Lithuania proper, eventually began to consume as much electricity as did France and more than Italy. Great domestic electrical

enterprises were built between 1940 and 1980, like the huge hydro-electrical station on the Nemunas at Kaunas, creating a 20-mile long "Kaunas
Sea." A thermal power plant was started in 1960 and is now one of the key
plants producing electricity–Elektrenai–for the industries and homes of
Lithuania. But it took the cooperation of 20 Soviet nationalities to do the
job. Indeed, hardly a major project in all the Baltic countries was created
without all-Union help and all-Union funding.

A case very much in point is the artificial silk plant in Kaunas, with
some 4000 workers. It had literally been bought–the whole plant–from
England in the '60s, and had cost 50 million rubles to finance it. Lithuania
didn't have 50 million rubles just like that. The money had to come from
the all-Union treasury. Moreover, the plant itself had to be paid for in hard
currency, that is, in English pounds, and the Lithuanians certainly didn't
have pounds tucked away somewhere just for such an occasion. It cost
money to send workers to England to learn how to operate the plant. They
came back to Kaunas to pass on their acquired skills to the local workers.
But, in the end, it all paid off. Artificial silk, which performed every bit as
well as real silk, proved to be so popular that the entire cost of installation
and maintenance was recouped in just two years.

Ambitious plans existed to put all of industrial Lithuania on an auto-
mated basis. An announcement in March 1978 would state that "by 1990,
Lithuania's entire national economy will be controlled by a cybernetic
system... It will combine in a single complex the existing and newly created
similar systems of enterprises, research institutions and industries. To this
end, a network of computer centers is being created, which are being
equipped by third generation computers and connected among themselves
by a multilateral automatic communications network." But 1990 came and
went, and there was no more talk of a "cybernetic system." Nor of the
"automation of management of the national economy" which was "necessi-
tated by the high rates of its development. In postwar years, industrial
output increased fifty fold. According to economists' calculations, the volume of managerial work will increase approximately four times each ten
years. By 1980, it will become practically impossible to manage the economy efficiently without computers." [59]

But the Lithuanian cybernetic complex was to be integrated into the
all-Union system, for "the republic complex is an integral part of the
countrywide automatic system of managing the national economy which is
under development in the USSR." [60]

All this has disappeared in schemes to make Lithuania the "Hong Kong"
of Eastern Europe!

There is no need to idealize postwar Lithuania. And even if one "cor-
rects" the positive accounts of their accomplishments which quite naturally

came out of their understandable euphoric visions of their future—they saw a Lithuania which would, by the year 2000, have solved the main social problems facing them; first in line, housing, and then followed by acquiring all the amenities of a civilized life—much that confronts the eye of any skeptical visitor is enormously impressive.

No doubt, if it had remained bourgeois, it would also have been able to register certain successes as well. Critics always pointed to Finland across the bay, which had also made a spectacular recovery after the war. And, of course, there was Japan. But both countries (and others) based their "successes" on a system of exploitation which had led them in the past into becoming part of the criminal war, and by accepting a role in the international order of things, where the bloody imperatives of imperialism continued to operate, they became hostage to that same demonic force which had caused so much devastation and pain in the world and which—as one watched disbelievingly—was relentlessly laying waste to rain forests, to the air, to the soil, to the very ozone protecting mankind from the deadly rays of the unscreened sun.

The "recovery" of a number of non-socialist countries after the war would have been impossible without massive loans from Western (mainly American) banks, and enough experience exists today to show that once indebted to Uncle Sam, always indebted. As we write, we are witnessing before our very eyes the economic trussing-up of Poland which is down on its knees before the Group of Seven industrial nations begging to give it new loans on top of old loans (which cannot be repaid) in an effort to turn back the historical clock and re-introduce raw capitalism—under the code phrase "market economy"—into a country which had been so close to transcending it altogether. The utopia of the future—Polish "theoreticians" now claim—rides on the creation of a "middle class"—a discovery which boggles the imagination, it is so philistine, so even ludicrous, and flies so blatantly in the face of economic reality, not to say historic experience, that one wonders why it isn't laughed off the political scene in one great gust of laughter. "Our intention," says the 39-year-old Prime Minister of Poland under Lech Walesa, "is to move to a market economy as fast as possible." His aim is to create a middle class by privatizing shops, restaurants and other small businesses, whose managers "will be the natural supporter of economic change."

But unless one has been entirely deaf and blind to recent history, how is it possible not to remember that the *support* of Hitler came precisely from that "middle class" of small shop keepers and penny-pinchers that is now so glorified? There are no people's heroes to be found among them; on the contrary, it was from them that Hitler recruited the bloody thugs of his regime. Poland is being sold bit by bit to foreigners, and the reality is all summed up in Bielecki's reply when he was asked if he envisioned any hope for the inevitable thousands—at the moment, later, a million—unemployed, "saying they would be encouraged to start businesses and find jobs themselves," for "he had no plans to expand Poland's safety net for one million unemployed." [61]

The cruelty of this statement rivals all the contemptuous dismissals of the poor that saturate Western upper class social comment, which sees in poverty not a breakdown of the system but of the person—poverty is the punishment for one's lack of ability.

In any case, this formula of Bielecki's is a prescription for future bitter class battles. And at a moment when even the USA is caught in a new depression with thousands losing their jobs, banks failing and closing, with a stupefying increase in the visible homeless—in the "richest nation in the world"—the model before them of the "market economy" par excellence should ring all kinds of warning bells.*

What is so surprising to an older generation is what seems like the emergence of a new generation that knows no history, does not believe in the laws of cause and effect, and actually seems to rely on magic. Its spokesmen talk as though their discovery of buying and selling is something unique and original. Their recklessness is breathtaking. At the base, however, of their "daring," one can see a philosophy, after all: it is reducible to the formula, power is everything. They have raised lackeyism to international capital to a transcending virtue. Resort to the International Monetary Fund and the World Bank does not serve to "cure" economic ills but merely to shift the cost of them even more massively on the shoulders of those already victimized by economic laws these institutions do nothing to change.

True, provisions for guaranteed work, health, educations, vacations, housing, old age, etc. cost such an enormous amount of the GNP that some feel the sum of it drags back the economy of the nation like an anchor. But a society which serves the needs of the people, and guarantees them a life of dignity, has been the utopian dream of mankind for centuries. One understands that it's nice to have cars, many-roomed houses, country homes, trips abroad, latest-model clothes, etc., but no civilized human being will accept these privileges for himself and his class at the expense of his fellow humans. Recognition of responsibility for each other marks the high-water mark of civilization, and the opposite—"*sauve qui peut*"—save yourself!—each for himself—has always been seen by the great moralists of the times as the epitome of human evil.

---

* In December 1991, Poland's parliament got rid of Bielecki, whose administration had created 10 percent unemployment and an almost stalled industry.

One of the great discoveries of Marxism has been the realization that the "spiritual" must have a material basis, or it will not soar. Until society had accumulated a surplus of food and goods and could liberate a certain number of its own from the all-consuming necessity of finding food was it possible to create a class who could think—who had the leisure to contemplate the meaning of what they were doing and to *plan*.

The "million unemployed" which the Polish ex-Prime Minister accepted with such complacency, certainly will have the time to think and leisure to create great works of art. But they will not. Their time and thought will be absorbed by the problem of how to survive. In fact, their "leisure" is a mockery.... In 1990, Warsaw was being called "the prostitute capital of Europe."

If the object of society is to provide the optimum means for the development of the human personality, this cannot be done by draconic measures, by accepting Darwin and Malthus as social guides. Yet the development of the human personality is obstructed by the low economic and cultural level of society. The question remains: how to raise the standard of living without creating a situation in which one's own development depended on the exploitation of others, resulting in their stunted cultural development?

It cannot be credibly denied that workers' power in the Baltics, which transformed the economy, also set about transforming each nation's "soul." The formula "national in form, socialist in content" was well suited to the creation of art on a humanist basis. Education flourished. The last remnants of illiteracy in a country notorious for its widespread illiteracy were soon ended with Soviet power. Thus, by equipping additional thousands of illiterate Lithuanians with the ability to read their own language, socialist Lithuania was not only deepening their spiritual lives but increasing, literally increasing, the scope and depth of culture, *of the language itself,* obliging it to grow, and, with new readers, provided an audience for Lithuanian writers they could never have ever dreamed of having before. (Not to speak of the sudden opening to other languages by translation: Russian, in particular. Larger editions of Lithuanian authors appeared in Russian, with a population of tens of millions, than in Lithuanian, which, after all, had a limited potential audience.) For centuries, Lithuanians had suffered from the fate of being "a small nation with a large vocabulary whose language the world does not understand."[62] The reverse also happened: more foreign authors were translated and made accessible.

In February 1979, the Minister of Education, Henrikas Zabulis, announced that the complete transition to a secondary education was now a fact in Lithuania. This was, indeed, a historic achievement. In 1940, the last year of bourgeois power, there were 300,000 illiterates or functional illiterates. Important to note was the fact that rural Lithuania no longer remained the bulwark of Lithuanian backwardness. Some 1,500 schools had been erected in Lithuania after the end of the war. Some 500 with boarding facilities were added. More than 400,000 children of peasants now went to secondary schools in Lithuania. This is ten times more than the best the bourgeois regime could show.

Zabulis would note that "the number of students in Lithuania doubled each five years after the war." He added that with a population of some 3 million, Lithuania had 150,000 specialists with higher education and 70,000 students in colleges. Jobs after graduation were assured and, of course, there was no charge for education at any stage. There are 13 higher educational establishments which train students in more than 100 professions, Zubulis noted. Many students were exempted from work on farm or factory to study. Colleges were turning out experts in electronics, cybernetics, engineering, physics, and ultrasound acoustics as well as lasers, etc.[63]

At a conference in Vilnius in September 1979, members from all the then-Socialist countries, plus Sweden and the USA, discussed ways and means of meeting the growing interest in Lithuanian literature from abroad. Lithuanian books—146 of them—had already been translated into 60 foreign languages, and plans for expanding both the number of books and translations were discussed.[64]

To be able to absorb culture one has to be physically healthy as well, and along with the elimination of illiteracy went the elimination of a whole list of diseases, accepted as chronic and inevitable, the result of poverty alone. In order to become cultured, one needs a social system which is able to allow a goodly portion of its citizens to remain outside the productive process until they are adults and concentrate only on learning—they needed leisure that had to be subsidized by the society itself. When a boy was expected to do work in his early teens, for what he could earn was needed by the family, he had no time or leisure to learn even how to read. But to learn to read somebody had to feed him and house him. Over and over one heard stories of how, born poor and illiterate, the revolution literally saved one from a life condemned to hard work and ignorance... What was true of boys was triply true of girls.

Mass diseases, scourges, etc., could be eliminated only by action of the state itself. Mass social scourges, like prostitution, chronic alcoholism, child labor and child sale, the oppression of women, the oppression of minorities, were also either eliminated, curbed, or suppressed.

Culture flourished. As Eduardas Miezelaitis put it: "It has brought us, poets of Soviet Lithuania, to a sort of poetic Renaissance. This was aided, of course, by the great poetic experience accumulated over the centuries and by the layers of creative energy, awakened by the new life, which had been hidden in the depths of our numerous lakes, in the hearts of poets, and by the propitious creative atmosphere that today prevails in the lands of the Niemen. What does this Renaissance mean? Its meaning seems to me to be quite clear: our poetry has focussed its attention on Man and in our poetic laboratory a bold experiment has begun which in its quests and discoveries resembles the greatest scientific experiments of the mid-20th century. In this laboratory, poetic culture has grown to maturity, philosophically thought has gained strength and the lineaments of man have appeared. Poetry has deeply probed the anatomy of the human spirit—intensive work is being done on perfecting man and modelling an integral personality."[65]

This was no mere salesman selling his wares. Miezelaitis, writing at 64, was looking back on not only 38 years of a nation striving to create human (i.e. socialist) milieu but also he was intimately aware of the old, bourgeois society in which he grew up in a worker's family, and so had the experience with which to compare one with the other. He had been an active revolutionary since his teens and had fought at the Front during the war as a correspondent-with-gun. His book of poems, *Man*, won the Lenin Prize in 1962, awarded to him for work inspired by "the philosophy of socialist humanism."

Miezelaitis' views, expressed here so succinctly but also repeatedly in other contexts, were essentially the views of the generation of artists who came to fruition after the war in a socialist-striving setting. There were others with reservations about the actual process of creating a socialist society and "perfecting man," who hailed the "new" Lithuania announced with such fan-fare by Sajudis in 1990—though their jubilation proved to be short-lived.

Before that, however, it must be noted that culture bloomed in all the Baltic countries, with art and artists of every variety springing up out of the ground. Book production soared. Theater prospered—including opera and ballet. Folk music was rescued from the scorn of snobbery, and enormous folk festivals became part of the national holidays. Cinema, an entirely new (as far as Lithuania was concerned) art form, was born and prospered and indeed produced artists who won world renown. Special schools for cultivating special skills and talents were set up (in one of which Landsbergis studied music). The work week was shortened. Efforts to eliminate heavy manual labor were encouraged. A plan existed to make every part of Lithuania close to some center of culture—in the effort to eliminate the age-old antagonism between city and country, between manual and intellectual labor. Hardly a home existed which did not have its own "personal" library, and hardly a household which did not subscribe to several newspapers and magazines, including the farm households.

More successful in some respects than in others, nevertheless the total result of many separate efforts was to create a social climate whose heart was indeed the concern of the State for man. That this "concern" had its shortcomings no one denies. That its reach perhaps exceeded its grasp was, as Robert Browning pointed out, "what a heaven's for." In the contest between the unfettered desire and finite fact, the fact always loses. The death of the dream is its realization. For some people the fact that they awaken to mere daylight is disillusion enough.

But the important thing is that the concept of the centrality of man—converting it into flesh and blood man—as the object of all social activity, of the main reason why the State exists, was openly announced as State policy. Some interpreted that to mean that now they, the people, were to be the passive benefactors of the actions of the State, which, in a sense, would become a kind of eternal waiter bringing them their breakfast in bed and lunch on the piazza. The only effort required of them was to open their mouths.

Caricature, perhaps. But enough truth in it to account for the psychology of a certain segment of the population which could justly say that no matter how I malinger on the job, get to work late, take time off for "sickness," perform sloppily so that my work has to be redone, *still* I'll always be on the payroll and take home (or to the wine shop) my guaranteed pay. Only extreme misbehavings jeopardizes one's job.

This was the price socialism had to pay for giving up the single potent weapon ensuring production in capitalist countries—the fear of the loss of one's job. How to motivate workers to perform well and honestly, and keep at it, was a prime concern of the Party and social planners. Moral incentives were not enough. And, even cash incentives—though of great help—were not sufficient if there was a lack of consumer items that could be bought with that added cash. During the Cold War, with the breaking out of hostilities always imminent, people understood the need for continued sacrifice, going without consumer items. But the moment the Cold War was declared over, the years of restraint, going without, simply burst the dam.

The cornerstone of the Leninist concept of the national question, which was destined to play so great a role in the postwar years, is the recognition, and the guarantee, of the complete equality of all peoples within the Union, ensured by their voluntary agreement, as Lenin had so clearly specified.

Indeed, this was the policy instituted by the Marxists and enshrined in the several Constitutions that were drawn up in the ensuing years. The assumption on which the policy rested was that, once free, the nations previously oppressed under Czarist rule would then voluntarily (more or less: there was always opposition) continue to remain united under soviet power, whose actual reality was still in the process of being formed.

Inequality between nations was ultimately due to economic inequality. One nation—one people—did not oppress another people simply because of a difference in skin color, or religion, tradition or culture, although all these played a role as pretexts of the class in power. One nation (or more accurately, one nation's ruling class) oppressed another in order to exploit the people. In order to exploit them more easily and efficiently, it helped to classify them as inferior in one way or another and thus deserving their fate. (The story of the dehumanizing and oppression of the American Indian, and African slaves, provided classic courses in how to rationalize and justify the subjection of one people by another.)

Central to the policy of the Soviet Union before and after WWII was the perceived need to make a special effort to raise the economic and cultural level of the backward nations in the USSR to the level of its most developed nation—Russia. Much was done toward that end. Numerous observers of the Soviet scene have attested to the fact that nations, once sunk in poverty, rent with disease and facing extinction, were practically rescued from the very edge of oblivion by the Revolution. Indeed, it's possible to visit the Buryats and other once-dying small peoples and note their extraordinary progress, both economically and culturally, under the aegis of Soviet power. Comparisons with neighboring countries—Uzbekistan with Persia, Armenia with Turkey, Kirghizia with Afghanistan, etc.—highlighted the difference in progress due directly to revolutionary changes. The essential humanity of the revolutionary changes could be seen especially in the dramatic leap forward made by women.

THE LATVIAN VARIANT

"From Latvians you come, you Latvian!"
(characteristic insult toward "barbarous" Latvians)

Latvia—similar yet different. Sharing many of the same experiences of Lithuania, yet putting its own spin on them. Its language is a first cousin to Lithuanian, for at one time in their history, both peoples had been one and shared the same language. Latvian is a variant of the root Lithuanian. Latvians shared many *dainos* with the Lithuanian, with their own particular twist.

But, like the Lithuanians, there are more unknown, teasing and tantalizingly promising periods in their history, whose contours it is difficult to distinguish or capture before they merge with myth. Facts dim around the edges. Enormously fascinating and equally frustrating, is the fact that though they are geographically tucked in between the Teutons and the Slavs, they are neither Teutonic nor Slavic. Their languages share many common roots with the Sanskrit—implying that in the dimmest of pasts both the Lithuanian and Latvians had a previous life far from the shores of the Baltic Sea. Could it have been Indian? Nobody has satisfactorily answered the puzzle, nor the equally tantalizing suggestion that at one time Lithuanians and Latvians had been part of the Roman empire. Again, their language shares words with the Latin, and there was a period in Lithuanian history when a section of the nobility sought for their roots in ancient Rome and favored the use of Latin over Lithuanian which, in their elevated view, was "the language of peasants."

When did the Lettish tribes come north? There is no written history to tell us. In any case, since no land, except the deserts and arctic wastes are entirely uninhabited (and even they have some habitation), the Latvians from the south found the Liva already on the banks of the Baltic and, after a series of wars, conquered and replaced them. The only evidence that once the Liva existed is to be found in the changes in the language, shifting the accent to the first syllable, like the Finns do, and as do the few hundred Livs who survived into modern times as fishermen on the border between Latvia and Estonia.

Hardly had the Latvians focussed historically as a people than they were torn apart again by the neighboring Teutons, who invaded Latvia in the

12th century. The power of the Teutons rose and fell in the ensuing centuries through the period when Lithuania enjoyed its greatest power (the 15th century) extending its domination over large areas of Russia, Poland and Latvia. Latvia, in due course, would fall under the sway of Sweden and of Russia under Peter the Great. But whoever held the formal reins of power, it was always the German barons who ruled. The power of survival which the German barons showed was due entirely to their function of direct rulers in the interest of the autocracy. The rule of the barons continued up to and through World War I.

Wars followed wars. Wars of foreign conquest. Peasant wars, desperate, bloody but always doomed. So grim had the history of the Baltics become that the 18th century philosopher and historian Johann Gottfried von Herder (1744-1803) protested:

> The lot of the illiterate Baltic nations constitutes a sorrowful page in the history of the human race. Humanity shudders, horrified at the blood there shed, in long and savage warfare, till the old Prussians were nearly annihilated; till the Jurlandese and the Livs were reduced to slavery under the yoke, under which they still languish. Perhaps there will come a time when they will be set free, and as compensation for the atrocities committed on these peaceful people and the robbery of their land and liberty, they will be re-established, and for humanity's sake enjoy a better freedom than they know.[66]

Indeed, the lot of the peasant seemed doomed to eternal slavery. Even with the end of serfdom in 1861, as in Lithuania, the freed Latvian serf was as helpless to contend with the forces in power as he was when he was directly bound to them. In any case, real, historical freedom was impossible for peasants, as the social perspective of peasants could not go beyond replacing only the masters, not the system. At best, they dreamed of a communal system in which all shared alike. The trouble with this utopian concept was that it was based on an economy of subsistence and lacked the historical spur to develop beyond. That historical spur was capitalism.

Not until the coming of industry which brought the working class into existence did the possibility also arise (at least in theory) of replacing one system with another. Capitalism as a mode of organizing the productive forces in society opened up the whole world to exploitation and in the process changed the world. But even at its birth "oozing blood and dirt" its historical limitations were discernible. Indeed, as anyone who has reviewed the literature of the period can attest, the transition from agriculture and artisan manufacture and mercantile capitalism to the erection of huge, congested cities into which yesterday's peasants, now landless, were forced to live, packed into sunless, inhuman tenements like animals, prey to new diseases brought on by poverty and unsanitary living conditions, as well as prey to crime, appalled sensitive spirits of the day. Here is how an American writer, Samuel Hopkins Adams, after a visit to Pittsburgh (in whose mines and steel mills thousands of Lithuanians would end up) reacted. It would be better, he wrote in 1909,

> for the unfortunate and innocent victims themselves, and certainly for the community at large, that this puny, helpless breed of human filth and misery which creeps about the city's man-made jungles, should succumb in infancy to the conditions that bred but cannot support them.*

Indeed they did "succumb in infancy" like flies in workingclass America. From the ages of six to thirteen, life expectancy in the working class areas fell. Childhood was a perilous time and most children who died, died of diseases traceable to unsanitary living conditions. But their fathers, too, died earlier. From 1921 to 1927, the life expectancy of a 22-year-old worker decreased from 44.95 to 43.86, a drop of 1.09 years—the working class was being systematically killed.

What was true of the USA—then and now held up as a haven for the "wretched" of the earth, a "land of opportunity"—was even more true of those countries, like the Baltics, in which the prospects for entrepreneurs were limited. The working class came into being as wage slaves, helpless before the great and arcane power of capital, which operated as a combination of impersonal forces—as helpless as they had been before the power of the land-owning masters.

The "wretches" of the city also dreamed of a better life. And, for the first time in history, the possibility of achieving it through their own efforts, in their own way—a heady vision brought down to earth—was raised in a practical sense by those two remarkable men: Karl Marx and Frederick Engels.

With the appearance of the working class on the scene came working class ideas. And, for the first time as well, in the vision of freedom for the worker, the peasant, too, could discern his own true freedom. By the turn of the century, Marxist ideas had already penetrated Latvia and the modern era began.

The first truly revolutionary party, the Social-Democratic Labor Party, was founded in 1904, and soon it joined with the Russian Social-Democratic Labor Party, which was the forerunner of the Bolshevik (Communist) Party.

Whether in the eyes of the die-hard Nationalists, joining with the Russians tainted the purity of the new revolutionary's character or not, the fact is that as part of Czarist Russia, Latvian revolutionaries understood that in order to free Latvia they had to join with Russian revolutionaries. "We are

* Ray Lubove, *Twentieth Century Pittsburgh*, N.Y., 1969, p. 1

for a free Latvia in a free Russia." They saw their fate, even when free, as intertwined with the fate of Russia itself.[67]

The 1905 revolution had its repercussions in Latvia as well. Demonstrations protesting the shooting of workers in St. Petersburg ended in a general strike in Riga. Revolutionary forces came to the fore propelled by the dynamics of the struggle, and though the revolution was suppressed, the lessons it had taught the workers were not lost on them, nor on Lenin. This "defeat" only underlined the permanent laws of revolutionary development: there is no such thing as an absolute defeat, as long as the working class itself exists. All "defeats" find their positive application as lessons. Marx learned from the defeat of the 1848 French revolution, and Lenin from the defeat of the 1905 revolution.

Suppressed, revolutionary fires were not to flare again until the end—or almost the end—of WWI, following the revolution in Russia in 1917. The victory of the Russian proletariat, the ending of the war, the execution of the Czar, the beginning of the monumental task of setting up the first, primitive elements of socialism-to-be, even though in a setting of intense hostility of the bourgeois world, which immediately set to work to undermine and eventually overthrow it, fired the imaginations of workers not only in the Baltics but the whole world over. Many in the ruling circles of the West feared that the world really did stand at the edge of world revolution, which they spelled Armageddon.

What was liberation to the oppressed, was a "spectre" to the ruling cliques. Terrified by the prospect—which was magnified by their guilty fears—the imperialist West closed ranks, or tried to. Uncomfortable victors in a war with one of their own, Germany, they feared a revolutionary Germany far more than the old Germany restored. The revolution for which Karl Leibknecht and Rosa Luxemburg were sacrificed was drowned in German workers' blood. A renewed Germany was looked on as a barrier to the spread of the "red plague." The notorious British spies, the Russian-born Sidney Reilly and Boris Savinkov, expressed not only their own opinions but the opinions of the British, when Reilly cried: "The Germans are human beings. We can afford to be even beaten by them. Here in Moscow there is growing to maturity the arch enemy of the human race. If civilization does not move first and crush the monster, while yet in time ('Strangle the baby in its crib'—Winston Churchill), the monster will finally overwhelm civilization."[68]

He had tried, putting 2 million rubles to work, to overthrow the newly arrived Soviet government, having bribed (he thought) the Latvian head of the Lettish guards in charge of guarding the Kremlin, Colonel Berain, and who—for a price—had agreed (he thought) to arresting the Central Committee of the Bolshevik Party. But Berain was a loyal Communist and worked with the head of the Cheka, Derzhinsky, to foil the plot, though the plot to assassinate Lenin almost succeeded when Fanya Kaplan, a Social Revolutionary, managed to shoot him twice.

The hard agreement reached at Brest Litovsk, which conceded hegemony to the German army in the Baltics, and the defeat of the Germans by the Allies some eight months later, changed the revolutionary situation in the Baltics for the worse.

On December 17, 1918, Latvia's first soviet government took power. It was headed by Peteris Stucka and, like the Lithuanians, moved quickly to institute socialist relations in the country. The new government was recognized on December 22 by the Russian republic. At the 1st All-Latvian Congress of Soviets in Riga on January 13, 1918, the Congress finally formed a Soviet Latvian government.

Like the Lithuanians, it launched a new social program that was calculated to change the relationships of power within the country, replacing the hegemony of national capitalist and international capitalist power with workers' power. The new government nationalized the banks, turned over land to the peasants, adopted laws to advance science, education, culture, separating the church from the state—in fact, carried out democratic reforms (like the extension of suffrage to women) that had been delayed and denied for so long that only a revolutionary movement could fulfill them.

But it was all destined to be short-lived. The allied powers (USA, Britain, France, etc.) using the remnants of the German army deliberately left behind and intact even after the end of the war, opened up an offensive on the new workers' government. The Latvian socialist government was finally overthrown by the decisive help of the German military forces after a few months in existence. Lacking an organized army of its own, with beleaguered Russia proper unable to come to its assistance, the new Latvian government succumbed.

A national government was announced on November 19, 1918, with Karlis Ulmanis at its head. In many ways, Ulmanis was a kind of clone of Smetona of Lithuania. Both depended on German support. One of Ulmanis' first moves, after gaining power, was to grant Latvian citizenship to the 40,000 German soldiers who had been the core of the counterrevolutionary forces that had succeeded in overthrowing the fledgling socialist government. He recognized and honored the peculiar special position enjoyed by the German Barons who were ceded land and their own *Landwehr*—an autonomous area, immune to the laws of the state.

The history of Latvia in the next two decades is one of intrigue, plotting, Byzantine maneuvering, the shifting from one master to another, the frantic search for favorable deals with Western powers that preserved the appearance of national independence while concealing the pathetically little reality in fact. The key question before Smetona of Lithuania, Ulmanis of Latvia and Paet of Estonia was: which of the Western powers—England, Germany or France—could most reliably support us (meaning the group in power)? It was as basic, as unadorned as that. The three Baltic states had come to power for one reason only: to serve as a barrier to the spread of Bolshevism westward. Those in the seats of power were judged solely on their ability to fulfill this assignment.

Ulmanis, seeing where real postwar power had shifted, shifted his own loyalty from the Germans to the British. The Germans promptly got rid of him and replaced him by one of their own, so universally recognized as an abject servant that nobody took him seriously—Pastor Niedra. Ulmanis had meanwhile taken refuge on a British warship in the Baltic. But the Germans were scoring victory after victory over the revolutionary forces, under the leadership of General Count Ruediger von der Goltz, whose opinion of Ulmanis he expressed quite succinctly: "Ulmanis was to have entered the government and his adherents were to receive seven-twelfths of the ministerial chairs. Niedra (his choice) was to have been sacrificed..."[69]

Governments were made and unmade at the will of foreign forces. Indeed, the Entente which willed these governments into being, at the same time had so little respect for them or their "presidents" that, even with Smetona at the head of the Lithuanian government, and Ulmanis installed in Latvia and Paet in Estonia, and the revolutionary forces defeated, they still withheld formal recognition. The truth was that the Entente powers expected the newly instituted government headed by Lenin to fall momentarily. In fact, the *New York Times* would announce its fall, the flight of Lenin, etc., all of 91 times. The powers in the West expected all three Baltic countries to be reconnected with Russia proper, once the Bolsheviks were gotten rid of.

The U.S. Secretary of State, Robert Lansing, put the American position quite clearly when he said that "the Baltic provinces of Lithuania, Latvia, and Estonia shall be autonomous states of a Russian Confederation."

Added to this was the statement of Evan Young, in 1922, when he was High Commissioner in Riga: "It is not improbable that through the operations of fundamental economic laws these countries will become part of federated Russia, or will retain autonomous powers that will be linked with the Russian government through close economic and political treaties and agreements."[70]

Even as late as July 25, 1922, Charles Evans Hughes remarked: "The United States has consistently maintained that the disturbed condition of Russian affairs may not be made the occasion for the alienation of Russian territories, and this principle is not deemed to be infringed by the recognition at this time of the governments of Estonia, Latvia and Lithuania, which have been set up and maintained by the indigenous population."[71]

It is worth noting, not without irony, that it was not the Western Powers which hurried to recognize the independence of the Baltic states, but Soviet Russia, even though their bourgeois regimes came into power as a result of counterrevolutionary activity, spearheaded by the Germans.

Between 1920 and 1940, all three Baltic republics were ruled by the bourgeoisie—which meant, by the power of banks, international financial powers, by the clergy and landowners. At the very outset, those who called the tune took steps to cut not only political ties with Russia—to which they had been attached for centuries—but economic ties. Then, as now, the economy of the Baltic countries was intertwined with the economy of Russia. Industry had advanced noticeably in Latvia, with Riga, the capital, having 90,000 workers in a city of less than 500,000 population. The industrial plants manufacturing textiles, shipbuilding, canning, rubber and metal were supplied raw materials from Russia and it was to Russia that the finished products were largely exported.

Obsessed by the drive to separate from Russia, the new rulers of Latvia abruptly cut vital industrial ties, disregarding the catastrophic consequences bound to follow. It was a case of the blind leading the blind—of cutting off their noses to spite their faces. Once the separation was made, key plants immediately shut down. In Riga, the Dvigatel car building plant laid off, or put on short time, 15,000 workers. The Becker wire-drawing factory which had employed 15,000 workers also fired most of them, leaving only less than a thousand on part-time. The Krenhold mills in Narva were cut from 12,000 workers to less than 2,000.

Naively, the new lords of the nation had turned to the West, believing that what they had lost in the Russian market they could recoup in the West. But there is no charity in business. He who lags or falls behind is devoured by the wolves. And, although the West was ready to spend millions (not their own money but the people's) to support an intervention-ist army, when it came to business, even class loyalty had to yield to what the profit and loss columns said.

Suddenly it was discovered that Latvia (and Lithuania and Estonia) weren't meant to be industrial nations after all. Except for Estonia's shale, they lacked all the necessary sources for building an industrial society—no deposits of coal (peat, yes), no deposits of iron ore, no inexhaustible sources of energy to power industry, no vast prairies for growing grain. Their natural bent was bucolic. It seemed—they were now told—that they had an inborn talent for raising pigs and cows. They were "potato republics."

The mass movement of poor peasants and landless workers to the cities had denuded the countryside of cheap manpower and severely begun to limit food production. Legislation to return the land to the peasants was passed in all three countries. Indeed, this action of granting land to peasants who would till it is cited as proof of the progressive nature of the several governments now in power. Even though it was a move forced on them, the truth is that the "grants" were so hemmed in by restrictive conditions that before long—the way water seeks its own level—the land the poor peasant acquired found its way into the hands of the rich peasant once again.

The strategy of returning the impoverished worker to the country (who had once been a peasant or had been born in a peasant family) was calculated to compensate for the loss of income from the closed factories. But, as matters transpired, even Baltic agriculture could not truly compete on the world market against traditional suppliers of dairy products, timber, hemp, and other indigenous raw materials. In any case, only the well-to-do farm owner could afford to hire additional labor, sowing and harvesting machinery, to sell or withhold a crop to take advantage of the market.

Dissatisfaction of poor peasants and unemployed workers led to demonstrations and ultimately a threat to, in Latvia, the Ulmanis government. But by 1934, with the dramatic triumph of fascism especially in Germany, the Ulmanis government, like the Smetona and Paet, believed that Hitler had found the formula—the bourgeois' Philosopher's Stone—by which the working class could be constrained and the revolutionary movements suppressed. He openly instituted a fascist government, as did Smetona in Lithuania and Paet in Estonia.

By then, there were some 70,000 unemployed in Latvia. Some 26,000 small farmers (thus ended the glorious adventure of luring the farmers back to the land) lost their holdings between 1935 and 1939. Unpaid taxes, and a low income for their crops, were the main instruments by which the land was returned to the "government" which then allocated it to the richer farmers, who were the political mainstay of the fascist government.

Like Smetona, Ulmanis did not bother to hide his aims behind either "socialist" or "democratic" slogans. He, like Hitler, had only contempt for the effeteness of parliamentary democracy. If the Baltic leaders did not go so far as to cultivate the myths of "folk" as the Hitlerites did, they invented their own myths, mainly based on nationalist themes. All progressive organizations, all periodicals and newspapers of the Left-progressive trend, trade unions and the Communist Party were suppressed. The concentration camps began to fill up with working class and democratic opponents of the regime.

The road to fascism had not been smooth. Not everyone in the bourgeois camp had been happy about the forced cut-off of not only markets but cultural contact with Russia. In 1926-27, forces made up of the Social

Democrats and bourgeois Democrats formed a coalition which brought them to power. One of their first acts was to sign a trade agreement with Russia, with provisions that restored and improved commerce between the two parties on key products from the metal, leather, glass, etc. industries. The trade agreement was considered favorable to Latvia, and it was precisely this positive aspect to it that was anathema in the eyes of reaction. The general policy of peaceful and commercial coexistence with Soviet Russia was unacceptable to bourgeois forces not only in Latvia but in all the Baltic countries. After all, the "assignment" given to them by the Entente Powers at the close of WWI was to block off revolutionary Russia, not to facilitate political and commercial relations with it. The West had never given up its dream of "strangling" the Bolshevik baby even when it no longer was a baby. Inspired by the British, who were the main political machiavellis in Europe for the two decades between the wars, the opposition went to work to undermine the relatively mild government brought to power by legitimate political means. It was British money which paid for the newspaper that became Ulmanis' mouthpiece, publishing articles like the following:

> We cannot fail to take into account that England will watch closely the conduct of the Baltic states. Recently, an English capitalist combine proposed to enlarge considerably its investments in local industry. Representatives of certain Latvian firms have even been invited to London for negotiations. It is evident that the situation with regard to obtaining large English credits is now more favorable than ever before. By entering the sphere of Russian influence, we risk the loss of this opportunity.[72]

Both the carrot and the stick are plain enough here. But even more plain is the incident in Geneva at a session of the League of Nations, at which Felix Cielens, then foreign minister of Latvia and a conservative Socialist, was snubbed by Austin Chamberlain, half-brother of the later and better known Neville (whose father was the Tory Joseph Chamberlain), chief architect of the Munich Pact in 1938 which, among other things, gave Hitler the go-ahead signal to take over Lithuania's Memel, and by implied extension, Lithuania itself.

Cielens had delivered a speech at the League which set out the principles of independence his government then championed. The speech was barely listened to in a half-empty chamber. His was only one of the pathetic appeals made by small nations (most notably by Emperor Haile Selassie appealing to the League to condemn the Italian invasion of Abyssinia in 1935). England's position was paraphrased succinctly by a Latvian reactionary commentator: "England will not tolerate the policy of a bridge between the USSR and Europe. If Cielens wants to try this policy, he can only do so against the will of England. To speak of any neutrality for Latvia in a conflict between England and Russia is childishness...."[73]

Indeed, Cielens' voice was a voice in the wilderness. He had held that position since 1927 and it proved to be prophetic. If followed, it would have avoided the reckless extreme to which Latvia was being driven. Cielens had counseled that "If we permit any state hostile to Russia to establish its political influence in our territory, we can with mathematical certainty forecast political pressure from the East. If we permit such places as the terminals of the Russia-bound railways, the harbors of Riga, Venspils, Liepaja and the Stratetic Dagoe and Osel Islands to become bases of operation hostile to Russia, I say emphatically that under such circumstances, counter-operations from the East are inevitable. Russia will strive to eliminate influences hostile to herself and seek to establish her own political hegemony." [74]

Connections between Latvian reactionaries and Hitlerites were all but open. Karlis Ulmanis and Karlis Balodis, heading the Latvian government delegation, made no bones about traveling to Berlin in 1933 and conferring there with Alfred Rosenberg.

Ulmanis took over power by a combination of stealth, demagogy, trickery, threat and open force. His first demand was that the sitting government that had been duly elected (and for the last time in Latvian modern history up to the war) should resign and confer on him the mandate to form a new government. The formula was hauntingly similar to the formula by which von Hindenburg legally handed over the chancelorship to Hitler despite the fact that Hitler's party wäs a minority party. Ulmanis was given power all the more readily since he promised to do no more than reshuffle the already well known, if not shopworn, personality elements in the power pool. Instead, he installed his own trusted followers, who by then were confirmed fascists—not "just" nationalists, but *fascists* inspired by and patterned on Hitler's Nazi party.

With this confronting them as a *fait accompli*, the still-functioning Latvian Diet protested, even going so far as to dismiss the fascist appointees. At this, Ulmanis ordered the police, and the Civil Guard, now under his direct control, to carry out mass arrests. All the actual opposition, and all the possible opposition, was arrested and sent to the Liepaja concentration camps, and with their going went the last possibility of a truly bourgeois-democratic state in Latvia. *Sic transit gloria.*

The coup succeeded. But it should also be noted, even if only in passing, that Ulmanis had kept a plane ready to take him to Berlin if the plot failed. But if the plot did not, in fact, fail, it was not because the opposition first of all failed: there was a large component of hara-kiri in their half-hearted efforts to both oppose and appease the would-be dictator. The success of

Mussolini in Italy and, even more spectacularly, of Hitler in Germany was a paralyzing factor in their effort to organize the will to resist. And, just as Smetona in Lithuania gave himself the title of "Tautas Vadas," which was the Lithuanian equivalent of Hitler's "Der Führer," so Ulmanis now named himself the Leader of the People.

With Ulmanis at its head, Latvia moved to come closer to Hitlerite Germany. Latvia's foreign minister, William Munters, was an all-but-open German agent. When the Nazis marched into Memel in 1939, no move was made by the Latvian government to protect its borders, now fluid to Nazi penetration into Memel. Instead, Latvian troops remained concentrated on the Lithuanian border, at Kurland, ostensibly to cow Lithuanian opposition. No Latvian troops left the Soviet border, and in view of the USSR's known offer to Lithuania to defend Memel, it was clear that these troops on the border were meant to serve as a barrier to Soviet troops, a sign that the Latvian troops would join with—not fight—the Nazis if it came to that.

The many treaties, both open and secret, reached by the Estonians, Latvians and Lithuanian governments at the time (now all fascist to one degree or another) with Hitler were nothing but paving stones on the road to the final moment when the issue of defending the Baltics came to the fore in negotiations between the USSR, France and England in 1939. It is interesting to note that when Franklin Delano Roosevelt inquired in April 1939, whether Hitler would guarantee non-aggression against the USSR and other countries, particularly with reference to the Baltic countries, Hitler had already signed non-aggression treaties with Latvia, Estonia and Lithuania—now headed by fascist and direct agents of Nazi Germany. In fact, so committed were the ruling cliques of these governments by ideology and treaty to the "protection" of Hitler that when they were approached during the 1939 crucial negotiations by the allied negotiators, they refused, as Poland, under the sway of the Colonels also refused, to enter into any agreement that included *Soviet* assistance. They were not so much allies of Hitler's Germany as total puppets.

In any case, where the USA was concerned, some of its more "far-sighted" diplomats were looking far ahead. One of them, William C. Bullitt, ambassador to the USSR from 1933-1936 (crucial years), had his own scenario, which he revealed in a conversation with the Polish ambassador to the USA who then reported it back to his own government. "Bullitt," the Polish ambassador Jerzy Potocki wrote (November 21, 1938) "had regularly informed President Roosevelt about the international situation in Europe and particularly about Soviet Russia, and President Roosevelt, as well as the State Department had treated his reports with great attention ... As regards Soviet Russia, Bullitt spoke of it with disdain, pointing out that the latest purges ... had brought about complete disorganization of the Red Army, which was incapable of active military operations....

"Bullitt replied that the democratic states would undoubtedly need at least another two years to rearm themselves completely. In the meantime, the German Reich would probably direct its expansionist drive towards the East, and for the democratic states it would be desirable that there, in the East, matters should reach the point of war between the German Reich and Russia...." [75]

Consistent with this attitude is the fact that when Bullitt was ambassador in Moscow he had as his file clerk a certain Tyler Kent, who later, working for Joseph P. Kennedy, ambassador to England and a notorious Hitlerite appeaser, was exposed as a German spy who interpreted and passed over to the Germans the confidential correspondence between President Roosevelt and Winston Churchill.

Bullitt's cynicism about the Soviet Union was by no means a minority position among those in power. It was shared by the Cliveden set in England, the "200 families" in France, and the America First set in the USA, and poisoned the diplomatic atmosphere which the corps of diplomats and politicians breathed daily. By 1939, it was accepted dogma in Western political ruling circles that the Soviet Union was mortally weakened by its internal purges and, as Hitler had already written in *Mein Kampf*: "The giant empire in the East is ripe for collapse. And the end of Jewish rule in Russia will also be the end of Russia as a state." And he added in conversation to his generals: "We have only to kick in the door and the whole rotten structure will come crashing down."

This estimate of Soviet Russia as a giant with clay feet was accepted as the conventional wisdom of the times. What the masters asserted with great bombast, the underlings echoed reverentially. No mere Smetona, Ulmanis or Paet could possibly imagine a point of view which differed with that one, held not only by the Germans but by all the allies, from Churchill and Roosevelt on down through powerful newspaper magnates like William Randolph Hearst.

It's necessary to emphasize how overwhelmingly dominant in most of Europe's centers of power was the view that fascism was certain to triumph in all of Europe in order to explain why the political factotums, so miniscule as forces, acted with such bravado and arrogance, which normally was not natural to men of such cautious opportunism that had made it possible for them to reach the positions of power they now held. Feeling sure that in the coming, inevitable war with the Soviet Union, Germany would quickly triumph, they felt no inhibitions about playing their roles as quislings in their own native lands. Episodes smacking of treason multiplied. Already in 1939, when Klaipeda was menaced, General of the Latvian

Army, Berkis, and his chief of staff, General Hartmanis, had absented themselves from the scene—they went to Finland. The commandant of the Latvian garrison at Laiepaja, General Oscar Dankers, went to Berlin in 1938 to attend Hitler's birthday party. Once the war began, he emerged openly as a German agent.

Irresponsible and criminal exploitation of the natural resources of Latvia, already well-advanced, now accelerated with the full dictatorship of Ulmanis. Almost literally the country and its riches were sold to the wealthiest foreign entrepreneurs at bargain prices. One favorite trick was to nationalize an industry, pour (by subsidy) the peoples' money into it, and then sell it at a cut-rate price to a private investor (with the usual bonus to the in-betweens to be deposited at the bank of most convenience, usually located in Switzerland). Money not hidden under mattresses was now considered to be at the service of the state—i.e., the Ulmanis' freebooters. Indeed, the State was literally looted into bankruptcy.

Since Latvia, like Lithuania, looked to Nazi Germany as its model, it quickly instituted many of the most odious features that characterized Nazi Germany, particularly stepping up anti-Semitism: 90,000 Latvian Jews became non-persons. The whole battery of persecuting devices used by the Nazis against the Jews was now repeated in Latvia and Lithuania (Lithuania had about 150,000 Jews). The demonically evil creed of racism—the barbaric assertion of the superiority of one people, one race, over another—impossible to justify on any scientific basis, not to mention moral—was now injected into Latvian life. The social structure was stripped clear of all Jews, and everything "Jewish" that could be so labeled in culture, was expunged—reaching and exceeding the borders of the preposterous. Jewish workers lost their jobs and Jewish businessmen lost their businesses. What was ironic—if only in a grotesque way—was the fact that while upper class Latvians took over the Nazi concept of a superior race—*Übermensch*—the Germans did not share the Latvians' high opinion of themselves. They looked on the Latvians as an inferior people whose fate was to be, at best, "germanization," but in any case, the loss of specific national features.

As the days passed on, Latvian fascists became bolder. In fact, there came a time when it was considered chic, in the upper class salons, to compete with one another in displaying their total fealty to the Germans, who, in their eyes, were the "defenders of Western civilization against the Bolshevik colossus." At one point, the wife of Latvia's foreign minister, William Munters, and the wife of General Balodis, could be seen gathering signatures to petitions begging the government not to resist the Germans at any point.

Latvian Chief-of-Staff, General Hartmanis, attended Hitler's birthday parade on April 20, 1939, in Berlin, along with Estonia's Chief of Staff,

General Reek. Lithuania's General Rastikis, commander-in-chief of the Lithuanian army, who played the role of strongman in Smetona's government, also attended. This attendance was not a mere protocol formality. It signaled a genuine admiration for the achievements and philosophy of the Nazis, and especially their leader, Adolph Hitler.

More and more often Latvian Nazis, in their white-stockinged dress, appeared openly in the streets. Former military men who had fought with the Germans in 1919-1920 "against Bolsheviks," along with people like Rudolph Hoess, the future commandant of Auschwitz, who cut his anti-Communist teeth in the merciless killings of what he himself called "destructive madness," were honored.* Nazi papers like *Rigasche Rundschau* and the *Revalsche Bote* appeared openly. The notorious sports unions, the *Kulturverbund*, organized by the Nazis as fifth columnists, carried on their parades with brazen insolence, and, very quickly, became less and less "sports" and "culture" and more and more military. Indeed, so insolent had they become, and so sure that they were untouchable, that they conducted provocative military maneuvers in full view of the Latvian army, and within sight of the Red Army on the other side of the frontier. Air fields, capable of accommodating dozens of planes, far more than the Latvian army needed or could handle, were suddenly built. General Franz Halder, the German chief-of-staff, even made an open visit to Latvia, and this open visit was more than what anyone needed to know which way the wind was blowing.

Opposition to encroaching fascism was raised by those Socialist forces that still dared to show their faces, and by the still-illegal Communist Party. In Stockholm, in early 1939, these and other forces met and issued a statement in which they declared that "The Red Army is the only real force capable of waging a successful struggle against the imperialist aggression of Germany in eastern Europe." They went on to say that "only conscious traitors to their country can renounce this sole and natural way of self-defense...."

They declared the need to unite all the opposition forces in a Peace Front. "Only common struggle to preserve peace through a Peace Front with the USSR and the western powers could maintain Latvia's independence."

The crisis in all the Baltic countries was enormously intensified with the act of betrayal by the Smetona government whose premier, the priest, Vladas Mironas, having given up his role of chaplain in the army and

---

* As though the present was literally mimicking the past, not only have such "anti-Bolshevik" creatures raised their heads again but even demand pensions for their past "services" as anti-Bolsheviks!

assumed leadership of the Lithuanian Nationalist Union, surrendered Klaipeda with barely a murmur of protest, much in the same spirit with which he had connived at the loss of Vilnius.

The surrender of Klaipeda, which came after the Smetona government had refused the offer of the USSR to defend it, was sprung on the Lithuanian people as a *fait accompli*. The abject surrender, carried out in secrecy, aroused widespread indignation. It was seen as the prelude to the complete surrender of Lithuania itself—therefore, Latvia and Estonia—to the Germans just as soon as they chose to make the demand.

In a transparent effort to draw a red herring across the trail, Smetona "threatened" the Germans by hinting at the possibility of concluding a non-aggression pact with the USSR—a gesture that fell of its own weight. But it's on such flimsy evidence that the Nationalists later built their claim that they had opposed "both" the Germans and the Russians. In fact, they had opposed *only* the Russians; that is, opposed their own people, for the hope of Lithuanian independence lay only with the cooperation of the Red Army—as indeed events would eventually prove.

But meanwhile, the drive toward self-destruction seemed to be mechanically set. Arrests of all opposition forces took place in all three republics.

The stage was prepared for a historical betrayal.

LATVIA CHOOSES

All of those did not return
Who went forth to war.

              –Traditional *Daina*

The signing of the Nazi-Soviet non-aggression treaty in June 1939 was followed in October with similar non-aggression treaties with Lithuania, Latvia and Estonia.

Although these treaties and the treaty with Germany have been assailed in diverse quarters, not least in quarters which had concluded all kinds of treaties with Hitler (and Mussolini before him), such an imperious judgment seems unbelievably unreal to any serious student of the times, who examines the times free of the corrupting influence of 45 years of the Cold War. It seems even more unreal to living contemporaries of the times who experienced truth not in books, no matter how learned, how thickly adorned with footnotes and bibliographic lists, but breathed it from the air tense with fear. With the signing of the Munich Agreement in 1938, everyone aware of the political forces in motion at the time understood that this Pact with the devil was nothing less than a go-ahead signal to Hitler—he was to go ahead Eastward—*Drang nach Osten*—his final goal the Soviet Union. No hidden clauses gave away Czechoslovakia. Czechoslovakia was delivered to Hitler in full view of the entire world.

With the example of Czechoslovakia and Austria and the Sudetenland before them, added to now by the "voluntary" cession of Klaipeda, it's clear to anyone still in possession of a modicum of objectivity that the small Baltic states simply had no margin in which to maneuver. What's more, the leaders of the three Baltic states—the three who by now were open fascists —were well aware of where German policy was moving. In fact, they were privy to this knowledge—and when the Germans actually crossed the border, the Nationalist forces inside these three countries met them waving Nazi flags, all prepared to carry out their orders.

It was absolutely decisive to the Soviets that they fortify their borders. They had no illusions about Hitler's intentions and prewar Soviet literature abounds with references to the "inevitable" war. The Communist International had repeatedly warned the world of its imminence. If the Soviets entertained any illusions at all, it was the hope that the Western Powers, in their own interest, would see their way to forging a military alliance which would effectively stop Hitler in his tracks. Litvinov's plaintive cry, "collective security" remains an accusation starkly frozen in time, along with his warning that "peace is indivisible."

The outbreak of the Finnish war (November 1939-March 1940) complicated the political situation enormously. War in Europe had officially broken out on September 1, 1939, when Hitler invaded Poland (after staging a crude provocation). Up until the invasion of Poland, the West, mainly France and England, had been conducting what was satirically referred to as a "sitzkrieg," or "phoney war." France was then the strongest financial power in Europe and, on call, could bring up an army of six million. Its navy was all-powerful. But its military thinking suffered from sclerosis. To prevent invasion from Germany, the French High Command simply organized to re-fight the last war. It built a powerful line of fortification—WWI had been a war of rigid trench warfare—stretching all the way from the Belgian to the Swiss borders. The Maginot line. Behind it, 110 French and British divisions sat and waited.

Across from them the Germans had also built their own line—the Siegried. This line was defended by 23 divisions. The monumental irony of this plan for war that was never destined to come (it had already come and gone in 1914-1918) was that the Germans simply chose not to replay the old game—which they had lost. Instead of attacking head-on, they simply went *around* the line.

More than that. Why did Hitler need tanks and armies when everything he wanted was handed to him on a diplomatic platter by those supreme political *maîtres d'hotel*, Daladier and Chamberlain?

Czechoslovakia had been an Allied gift to Hitler who, at the time, did not have the forces to take it militarily. Czechoslovakia had 35 divisions of superbly trained and highly motivated soldiers ready to lay down their lives in the defense of their homeland. But the leaders of their country did not have either their patriotism or their courage. Once they were delivered an ultimatum by England, they broke at the knees. Not only did they have an army of their own. France had promised 100 divisions to bolster their defense, in addition to Moscow's promise also to come to her defense militarily if she but chose to fight.

Hitler had only 50 divisions available for taking Czechoslovakia, and there is no way of knowing today that he would have been able to defeat the Czechoslovak army if it had resisted. As it turned out, he had no need to try. He didn't need a *single soldier*.

But Hitler hardly needed more to march into the Rhineland earlier. Subsequent accounts from German sources now reveal that the German High Command had agreed with Hitler's demand to march into the Rhineland fully prepared to turn right around and march out again if there was any show of resistance from France's 6 million strong army. Indeed, every move of Hitler's that might involve an armed clash was viewed with trepidation by the German High Command, which knew that it could not put up a successful military opposition to any determined allied attack. The High Command viewed events from a rational point of view. Unlike Hitler, they did not fully understand that at the heart of the Allied "resistance" was a mock-up, a pretense, that at all times the leading circles in France and England always regarded the main enemy to be Soviet Russia and not Nazi Germany. There is no other explanation for the ease with which Hitler gained concessions that had cost so much blood to earlier generations to acquire. No "genius" was Hitler; just a blackmailer with the morals of a pimp.

But with the outbreak of the Finnish-Soviet war, it was astonishing to see how the otherwise lethargic, semi-somnolent military high commands and their political guides sprang to life. They saw in that new war their golden opportunity to change the whole nature of the old war—*against* the Soviet Union, which was their sometimes openly expressed, but always profoundly held aim through every up and down of political changes.

What was implicit in Western governing policy became explicit among the underlings—Smetona, Ulmanis, Paet. In fact, some half-hearted efforts were made to send volunteers to help the Finns. As Latvian author Vilis Lacis notes in his book:* "In the winter the most reliable Aizsargs and reserve military instructors were invited to join volunteer groups and go to Finland to help Mannherheim. Alvar Taurin [son of the landowner] was also invited to join, but he had not the least desire to shed his blood for the ideals of some unknown Lapps. Only a few Aizsargs went off from their district..." (Aizsargs were paramilitary terrorist groups.) But two or three thousand Estonian "volunteers" did go.

The legend was launched then and, despite the grossest kind of proof that the ruling circles of Finland were fully in cahoots with Hitler, still persists in some circles even today that "little Finland" was put upon by the Soviet bully because ... because it was put upon by the Soviet bully.

Actually, as became all too evident in the trials that followed the end of the war, "neutral" Finland at no time was truly neutral. The notorious Barbarossa Plan, Hitler's plan for invading and occupying Soviet Russia, had the clause added to it:

The tasks of the Finnish army: rapid and secret mobilization. Participation in the offensive from the Rovaniemi area, preferably with picked forces. Two Finnish divisions to be assigned for the purpose (there will be no room for a larger force). The offensive to be conducted on both sides of Lake Ladoga, toward the Ladoga

* *Towards New Shores.*

Canal and the Svir. Finland's main forces to be brought into action for this purpose.[76]

Intimate contacts with Nazi political leaders was constant and ongoing. For domestic political reasons, especially with one "small" war behind them, and knowing that the Finnish people had no stomach for what they knew would be a major, destructive war, Finland's political leaders—the Ryti-Tanner clique—tried as best they could to keep their machinations as secret as possible from their own people. This reticence did not include the Germans, however. On July 2, 1941, Vaino Tanner was telling the German people via radio that he was with them and that "for the sake of the future of mankind, it is necessary that this noxious system (i.e., Soviet) be destroyed." This was backed up by the word of Finnish Chief of Staff General E. Heinrichs that Finland had ten divisions ready to invade the USSR.

The Finnish ruling circles also dreamed of a "greater Finland" at their neighbors' expense—mainly the USSR. The Nazis had made it abundantly clear that they intended to wipe Leningrad off the map of Europe, as an order of the day from the chief of staff of the German navy candidly put it: "The Führer has decided to wipe the city of St. Petersburg [he could not make himself say the hated word 'Lenin'] from the face of the earth," to which aim the Finnish masters had already dedicated themselves.* In a document signed by Martin Bormann, we read: "The Reichsmarshal asked the Führer what areas had been promised to other states. The Führer replied that the Finns wanted eastern Karelia, but that in view of its big nickel output, the Kola Penninsula should pass to Germany. The Finns claim the Leningrad Region. The Fuhrer wants to level Leningrad and then turn it over to the Finns."[77] A force of 40,000 Germans were concentrated in Finland on the eve of the war against the USSR. Most of the Finnish army was already under the command of Gen. Nikolaus von Falkenhorst from his post in Norway.

The Soviets were well aware that in dealing with the Smetona, Ulmania and Paet governments they were dealing with confirmed fascists, who had already made several "secret" deals with fascist Germany. About them they had no illusions. But they could not let these men, who were so quick to sell their country's independence to whoever came by—England, France, Sweden, Nazi Germany—now confront them with cries of "independence" when it was a matter literally of life and death—of the life and death of their own countries, first of all. Latvia, too, had its "fifth column" of Germans, as the American Ambassador to Riga, John C. Wiley, reported. Today, we

---

* It is ironic, indeed, that one reads that the present mayor of Leningrad and his confederates changed the name of Leningrad back to St. Petersburg, an action Hitler's ghost fully approves.

know the Germans intended to subjugate the three Baltic countries totally, and, indeed, it was no real secret even then. The decision of the three Baltic leaders to oppose the entry of the Red Army to man the borders facing Germany amounted to a preliminary maneuver in favor of Germany—that is, against their own countries.

The gap between the rulers of the three Baltic countries and the people had widened enormously—it had always been wide—in this crisis. What frightened them far more than the sight of Red Army troops moving through Vilnius or Riga to the western borders was the sight of the people cheering them on. For by this time it was clear to everyone that next on Hitler's list was most certainly the Baltic states. If they had any doubts, just a look at Klaipeda now under Nazi control was sufficient.

But the appearance of the Soviet troops did not mean the overthrow of the existing governments. Indeed, it won them a new lease on life. But soon enough, the people were disabused of the notion that letting in the Red Army meant extending friendship to them. In fact, the governments in all three republics now launched a storm of anti-Soviet propaganda, against the Red Army specifically, and "incidents" involving clashes with soldiers began to multiply. Demonstrations by working class forces in support of the Red Army were suppressed by the police, as in Riga where police opened fire on just such a demonstration, killing several and wounding many. Toward all of these provocations, the Red Army remained stoically detached, arousing in some the suspicion (rife in the rumor mills) that the Soviets had decided to leave the Latvian working class to its fate.

Actually, Red Army personnel had been given strict orders to keep out of local affairs. Nevertheless, their very presence discouraged the more blatant fascist activity, and hurried the exodus of some 53,000 Germans from Latvia, some 50,000 from Lithuania, and some 12,000 from Estonia. The sight of these Germans leaving for Germany lifted the spirits of the people who had had to suffer them and their arrogance for years, actually, as German Barons, for centuries. The treaty of mutual assistance concluded with the USSR "released the revolutionary dynamic forces of the people that had been held in check for 20 years. These forces have started moving and there's nothing that can stop them anyway," exulted *Cina*.[78]

Some idea of how the political scene was viewed by the upper and lower classes in Latvia at the time can be gleaned in the prize-winning novel, *Towards New Shores*, by Latvia's revolutionary writer, Vilis Lacis, who knew the old regime well:

> The commanders and instructors constituted a well-knit body of men who were ultranational in outlook, and they did everything they could to influence the rank-and-file soldiers... They gave lectures on home and foreign affairs, in which the main stress was on the two great powers, Great Britain and the Soviet Union.

They depicted Great Britain as a powerful state, both economically and militarily, which was vitally interested in the so-called Baltic area...

Organized in the paramilitary Aizsargs, the young bloods of the rural kulak rich periodically set out on hunts for Communists, much in the way animals were surrounded in the forest and shot down:

"We're going hunting for Communists tonight," said Stelp in a whisper. "They are having some kind of get-together in a wood, and one of our Aizsargs, who has infiltrated into their organization, knows the time and place exactly. We must take them by surprise, all at once. My job is to surround the wood from the north. It'll be great fun. Why don't you come with us?"

Yes, it would be "great fun"—not too much later the "fun" became even greater with the slaughter of thousands of Latvians by the Nazis. But this was still before the war, and the upper-class officers "drank vodka, nibbled lampreys and told each other about their conquests with women." But they also believed that "If we stick together, no one can overpower us... The Communist agitators haven't any prospect of winning over the mass of the workers and labourers. The Latvian is a born individualist and you're not going to lure him into any kind of commune. He loves patriotic customs; he regards his master and employer just like a father, the head of a great family to be loved and respected...."

"Hunts" for "Communists" were occasions for celebration:

That winter Aivar [a leading character] took part in several hunting expeditions, where he became acquainted with many well-known people—senior foresters, merchants, doctors and agronomists. Each of these hunts ended with lunch and a thorough carousal, during which the conversation was centered on hunting stories and world politics. Immense hatred towards the Soviet Union and unconcealed contempt for the common people were the main themes... Any kind of progressive idea, any mention of democracy, social justice and revolution drove them into a frenzy...

And then:

From time to time Taurin [a kulak] received circulars and information bulletins through which the Aizsarg headquarters strove to maintain a militant spirit among the commanders. These bulletins turned up particularly frequently at the beginning of 1940 in connection with the so-called Finnish campaign and the quartering of Soviet garrisons in the western district of Latvia. Their contents resembled the rude bellowing of a mad bull. In every bulletin there were allusions to the impending war with the Soviet Union, indications that Britain and France were on Finland's side and hints regarding the decisive role of the three Baltic states in the future conflict....

This was a strange and uneasy time. As before, it was clear to the working people that only from the East, from the Soviet Union, could they expect liberation; from the West they could expect nothing good. The Germans, or the English, could only become the oppressors of the Latvian people. It was more difficult for the governing clique, the rural and urban bourgeoisie of Latvia, to define their position. It was obvious to them that great events were about to take place and that they could no longer sit on the fence. The presence of Soviet garrisons in Latvia irritated them all the more because it rendered the working class and progressive intelligentsia bolder and more restive. When, on the instigation of Britain and France, Mannerheim's Finland provoked armed conflict with the Soviet Union the Latvian bourgeoisie were prepared and eager to follow in Finland's footsteps....

Upper-class bloods who enjoy hunting and carousing are not overly inclined to endure the rigors of a military campaign in which the other side is shooting bullets at *them*.

The account of the transfer of power from the Latvian Ulmanis' landowners clique to the people—we say "the people" advisedly—remarkably parallels the account given by the American Anna Louise Strong in Lithuania. Independently of each other, Miss Strong and Vilis Lacis describe a similar process. Writes Lacis:

> And suddenly everything changed. It only needed the appearance of a few Soviet tanks on the streets of Riga to arouse all the working people of Latvia. They rose, cast off the yoke of slavery, and with a mighty blow, shattered the chains which had held them in bondage. They came out on to the streets of the capital and after prolonged years of silence began to speak with the voices of masters—the real masters of their country.
>
> The structure of oppression and deceit collapsed like a house of cards. The Government of Ulmanis was no more and a new era had begun in Latvia.
>
> The news of the fall of the Ulmanis regime swept over Latvia with lightning speed. Its approach had been apparent for several days before the actual downfall of the old order—in the anxiety of its representatives, both great and small, and in the columns of smoke which rose through the warm June night above the chimneys of the government offices. On its way out, the regime overthrown by the people, was hurriedly destroying the evidence of its evil deeds and the innumerable proofs of its oppression and its crimes against the people. They could burn the papers, but no fire could obliterate from the people's memory the injustices which they had endured.

A scene to be repeated many times—baskets of incriminating documents thrown into the flames, or to bring the process up to date, fed into shredding machines, and *then* consigned to the flames. (No government office today in the West is complete without its shredding machine.)

Once the landlord class and its army of hirelings fled, literally leaving their offices vacant, the new, revolutionary forces were confronted with a problem daunting in its proportions. And yet the moment now faced by the Latvians would be repeated over and over in the coming years ... as Ngo Dihn Diem's factotums left Saigon, sometimes too quickly to destroy incriminating documents, finding a haven on the American destroyer in the harbor, the oncoming "pantless children" of Ho Chi Minh entered the city from the other end and named it Ho Chi Minh City—and the first problem they faced was the problem donated to them by the previous regime: thousands of prostitutes, thousands of unemployed, children with no schools to go to, thousands addicted to drugs whose leisure-time reading material was the flood of pornographic novels fresh from the USA.*

What did a Ho Chi Minh peasant know of typewriters, computers, the rise and fall of interest rates? In Kabul, the street boy who exchanged Afghanis for black market dollars, calculated to the precise decimal, was better instructed in international finance than the men suddenly given authority over banks and commercial institutions. In Latvia, too.

Nevertheless, the workers required *were* found. They came from the people. Farm laborers and landless peasants took over authority from the kulaks in rural areas. Workers became government commissars, in the mills, factories and shops. The progressive intellectuals, who had been unemployed under the previous regime, began to take the lead in cultural life. The auxiliary service, recruited from the people, looked after public order, and became the nucleus of the "People's Militia," which was in process of being organized.

Confusion, mistakes, injustices were inevitable. It was no great problem for the bureaucrats from the old regime left in office to lose valuable papers, misroute others, "forget" still others. Disputes over the division of the land were many. As in Afghanistan, there was also the psychological problem to overcome: ingrained for centuries with the conviction that the lord of the manor was also a servant of God (which the Church did not contradict), the ordinary peasant could not grasp what had happened.

---

* I had personally witnessed the transformation and its problems in Vietnam and Afghanistan.

LATVIA STRUGGLES TO FIND ITSELF

The strong man hit the weak man
The wise man mocked the fool
The rich man torments the poor
The idler scorns the workers.

—Latvian *daina*

One of the unappealing characteristics of small nations, indeed of all the weak, nations or individuals, is that, unable to defend or enforce their wills by their strength, they have to resort to cunning, wiles, subterfuges, flattery, endless compromises. They develop Machiavellianism to a high art. Their whole aim in diplomacy is to maneuver among stronger forces, hoping at best that the main contending powers will block each other. Thus, their "security" lies in the hope that their possible enemies will knock each other out. They also invest their hopes in the services they can render, which are needed by both or all contending parties, like the services the Swiss were able to extend to both sides in the war. The precincts of their banks were as holy as was the area of the Vatican.

This, without sentimentality, is the best "independence" a small country can hope for in the real world. Lacking banks and services of use to all parties, the Baltic countries were denied the fact of neutrality in 1940 for the same reason that they were denied it in 1914 and before that in 1812 with Napoleon. As the bourgeois cliques in charge of the nation saw it, their hope lay not in some utopian concept of maintaining an island of peace and concord in the middle of an inferno, but of choosing the winning side. They chose Hitler.

Communists did not dominate the elections of 1940. In Latvia, for instance, out of 30 members of the presidium of the Supreme Soviet and the Council of People's Commissars, only seven were Communists. Three of these had been previously elected in the pre-1934 (before open fascism took over) Diet, and one of them was Latvia's greatest living writer, Andrejis Upitis. Heading the government was Dr. A. Kirchensteins, professor of microbiology, famous for his resistance to Ulmanis. Bruno Kalnins, a Socialist, a past opponent of the Communists, was chosen to head the army's

173

political department. General Dambitis, who had been ousted as chief of staff in the Ulmanis takeover of 1934 for his anti-fascist activities, was appointed to head the army.

Although little credit today is given to the Soviets in this period, the fact remains that Soviet response to national sensitivity extended to the smallest details. In those instances where the too-enthusiastic partisans tore down the national flag (which they had every personal reason to hate), and replaced it with the Soviet, they were sharply rebuked by the Latvian Communists themselves who, in their paper, *Cina*, wrote: "Such actions are to be severely condemned since nobody can be allowed to insult the national flag. Instead it should be raised together with the red flag of the working class."[78] Indeed, liberalism toward past enemies was extended on a broad basis. Despite the picture of rampant oppression painted by nationalist diehard opponents, whose nationalism merged so easily with fascism both domestic and foreign, every attempt was made to conciliate yesterday's foes, even the most cruel. The national armies were not disbanded, only reorganized, with reactionary officers who had hopelessly compromised themselves encouraged to retire.

In Latvia, Generals Klavins and Dambitis were given high posts, despite their past history of opposition to revolutionary change. Policy was stated clearly as published in *Cina*:

> During the 20 years of reaction, the working class has learned that its economic demands must not be directed against property rights of the small and moderately prosperous peasants and productive bourgeoisie of the towns. Small peasants and artisans who themselves work on their farms or in their workshops, and also those somewhat more prosperous persons, who although hiring labor to assist them also work under the same conditions. Workers have no interest whatsoever in opposing the peasant's rights to his land or the artisan's rights to his workshop and means of production. Moreover, with respect to large enterprises of a capitalist nature, it is a mistake to believe that sweeping experiments are now in order. Such experiments would only cause disorganization of economic life and difficulties in the supply to the population.[79]

There spoke reason. Only the largest enterprises were nationalized. Nationalization by itself, in any case, is not to be taken as equivalent to socialism, since hardly a country exists today which has not been forced to nationalize some industries essential to the general welfare.

In Latvia about 800 such enterprises were nationalized at this time. True, the wealthiest individuals in the nation whose income was overwhelmingly acquired by excess exploitation were parted not so much from their ill-gotten gains (which were all salted away in American or Swiss banks) but from the source of their gains—the factory and the workers in it. Since it is inhuman—still an exotic thought in some parts of the world—to deny people a roof over their heads because, in the obtaining situation, they cannot afford it, the state moves in and guarantees housing for everyone. This means expropriating some of the largest property owners. And not incidentally, by expropriating the property owners, and leasing homes at below the cost of maintenance, the socialist order dealt a blow to the kind of statistics gathered by bourgeois statisticians to graph the national income. Rent from such homes and businesses is always part of the profit statement of the bourgeois owners and is pointed to as proof of the wealth of the nation. But this considerable source of profit was eliminated by workers' power—and its loss was cited as proof in the drop in the GNP, that socialism had failed.

The middle section of the population which had only a moderate income was left untouched. Indeed, in Latvia where small industry and private entrepreneurship had been well advanced, almost nothing—unlike in the USSR proper—was changed. Indeed, so much of industry remained in private hands that a People's Commissar of Labor was instituted solely to protect the interests of the workers in private industry.

Consideration was given to the fact that ownership of land differed in Latvia from old Russia. Although the small landholdings which had been the result of the land reforms of the earlier, more progressive regimes, had in fact, disappeared at an ever-accelerating pace into the hands of richer landowners and speculators, still enough remained to justify measures to ensure that they continued to remain in the hands of their present owners. The average farmer had no or little land. The new regime promptly granted additional land to about 200,000 farmers very soon after it took power. Some 50,000 landless farmers were granted *free* land, amounting to something like 1,087,000 acres altogether. Some 23,000 farmers on substandard farms were granted an additional 227,000 acres. "Half of Latvia's two and one-half million acres of state lands were distributed in the first six months."[80] Similarly, in Lithuania and Estonia.

Those who picture the behavior of the revolutionaries now in power as anarchists gone berserk, rushing through the country burning down churches right and left and roasting millionaires on spit fires, need to be reminded that the actions taken by the revolutionary governments of all three republics were soberly considered and judiciously administered. A clause in the Constitutions of all three republics reads: "Every attempt to encroach on the private property of the peasants or compel working peasants to organize collective farms against their will will be severely punished since such attempts injure the interests of the people and the state."

Each of the Baltic countries' new Constitution contained the following: "Land occupied by the peasant households within the limits set by law is secured for their use for unlimited time"—anticipating 50 years ago some of the ideas about the ownership of property in a socialist state now being currently debated.

Already established cooperatives in the three Baltic countries, which had proven themselves over the preceding 20 years, were freed of parasites and distortions and allowed to function once again as they were meant to—as instruments through which goods were exchanged, free not only of the anarchism of the 'free market' but of the stranglehold on commerce which developed with monopoly control.

Also, in view of the virulent propaganda and ceaseless intriguing against the socialist countries instigated by the Church, it is important to emphasize that the new regime trod very gingerly around this issue. Marxism is and has always been extremely clear on the question of religion. Although Marxists are materialists, and have no belief in forces outside the laws of physics, they do not compel believers to give up their religious beliefs. But it is true that particularly in Lithuania, the Church (and here we mean the Catholic Church, which did not have the same power in Latvia and Estonia) had acquired enormous power, not only politically, but materially. It owned vast tracts of land—80,000 hectares—from which it garnered a huge income, out of which it was able to subsidize a considerable cadre of priests and (in the other two countries) ministers who, quite naturally, propagated their faith and defended their privileges.

Most of Latvia, with the exception of the province of Latgale, is Lutheran, as is Estonia. Antagonism between the two faiths—Lutheranism and Catholicism—has deep roots, dating from Martin Luther's open challenge to the absolute power of the Catholic Church in the 16th century. Lithuania did not benefit from the Reformation, which was fiercely fought in Lithuania by the Jesuits, except by indirection. Martin Luther remained (and remains) an apostate in the eyes of Rome and his teachings are heretical.

Nevertheless, while expropriating the huge estates and dividing them among the needy peasants, the new socialist-oriented regime made sure that the Catholic priests and Lutheran ministers were granted enough land (7.5 acres) on which to raise food. Land already owned by the clergy (up to 30 hectares) remained in their possession.

It is not to be assumed that this reasonable policy toward a sworn enemy (after all, as victors the atheist Communists had at least theoretically the victors' right to abolish *all* religion) did not have its critics. It was criticized from "the left," as being not only too lenient but actually betraying the cause of the revolution. And, of course, it was criticized from "the right."

Obviously, for men whose lands had reached to the horizon and whose property was worth millions, who controlled the educational institutions and dictated the substance of what the young were to be taught, and who sent their own men directly into government—some becoming prime ministers—the loss of their former power was seen as a great blow indeed. It is understandable if they confused their secular power with heavenly power: their wealth and power were taken to be material witnesses to their spiritual ascendancy. It is no doubt naive, and is reminiscent of the forthright statement of the Right Reverend William Lawrence, Episcopal Bishop of Massachusetts in 1901: "There is a certain distrust on the part of our people as to the effect of material prosperity on their morality. We shrink with some foreboding at the great increase of riches, and question whether in the long run material property does not tend toward the disintegration of character... in the long run, it is only to the man of morality that wealth comes... Godliness is in league with riches."

The reconciliation of God to capitalism—indeed, a famous book claiming that Jesus was the first salesman was a best seller at one time in America—could hardly be put more bluntly and with more brazenness.

But despite the fact that in the West (and particularly in the USA: its dream, model, goal) the church had long been separated from the state and from public schools, still such a separation in Lithuania, 200 years after the Americans had first performed the lobotomy, was seen as a purely Communist blow at religion itself. The Church has never forgotten nor forgiven, and the most virulent of the present-day have their ideological origins in—not teachings—but in the *behavior* of the Church.

LATVIA UNDER THE NAZI BOOT

Oh, my lord, my master!
Do not whip me in the evening
Whip me in the morning after sunrise;
Let the sun weep bitterly.

— Latvian *daina*

None of the three Baltic states was to be given what they needed most—time. Hardly had the outlines of a new socialist system been drawn, and the first tentative steps taken to implement them, than the Nazis struck.

The first to engage the Nazi armies as they crossed the borders of Lithuania, Latvia and Estonia were precisely those Soviet Red Army troops garrisoned there over the protests of the governments then in power. The resistance of the Soviet troops in the Baltics, though heroic, could not stem the advance of the Nazis but it could and did slow it up, thus gaining time. Thousands of refugees in all three countries fled East along with the retreating Red Army. Others did not. Of those, some went underground and became part of the resistance. Others met the German troops at the village border with bread and salt.

Despite fifth column treachery, resistance to the Nazis was spontaneous, heroic, and eventually widespread. The substance and moral content of the word "guerrilla" or "partisan" was forged in the three years of bitter battles behind the lines, of an existence of "forest brothers," of underground resistance inside the cities and towns and even inside the ghettos. It is one of the most gallant and heroic chapters in the history of mankind's struggle for freedom and liberation. It is one of the grotesque deformations of language, and therefore thought, that these words, coined in the struggle against fascism and its blood brother, nationalism, should be used today by those against whom the heroes fought.

In Latvia, at Dvinsk, the railway workers blew up the ferry crossing—holding up the advance of the Germans, forcing them into house-to-house fighting. In Krustpils, Riga, in Liepaja, the native resistance to the Wehrmacht was fierce, and involved hand-to-hand combat in battles that raged for days. What was true in Latvia had its counterpart in Lithuania and Estonia as well.

Lithuanians and Latvians with historic memories now saw the old drama repeated: the modern Teutonic Knights who, like the Crusaders, and yet not entirely like, came also with crosses—with crooked crosses. But they came by the same route. And their message was delivered by fire, sword and rape.

Resistance was organic. The Latvians who escaped eastward eventually formed a separate Lettish Division of the Red Army and fought in the Battle of Moscow, near Staraya Russa, and in the Demyank salient. Indeed, there were Latvians at the fall of Berlin. Along with the invading Nazis came thousands of Baltic Germans (whose precipitate fight only months before measured the depth of their fear of the Red Army). These connected up with the native collaborators (not all had been deported) and now literally took over command, as a first step in the ultimate liquidation of the Baltic states as entities, and where they had been, now existed only *Ostland*.

The Germans were well aware that in order to pacify and mislead the people, they had to put on a patina of national, indigenous identity, even if only superficially. The native Baltic landowners were given back the land they had lost. Indeed, they had always depended on German support. The director of the Chamber of Commerce in Kaunas put it succinctly: "If the Germans come, they will destroy the Lithuanian nation but leave our houses and property intact. While the Soviets will leave the Lithuanian nation intact, but will confiscate our houses and property. I prefer the former."

Readers of Balzac will easily recognize this as the moral core inherent in the gallery of personalities he draws from among the bourgeoisie. Owning property, being rich, having a "position in society," constituted the substance of their existence as human beings. At the root of their personalities was the psychology of owning property and they so closely identified "owning property" with being a person that they literally felt that if they lost their property, they died as a person. Without their bank accounts, seats on the Bourse, their heavy ledgers with their long columns of figures in black and red, without the servants who gave them the only respect they ever knew, they felt naked but not only naked—ravaged, ransacked, reduced to zero, shamed and humiliated. The fact that literally millions of people—peasants and workers—had no property, no land, no respectable status in society at all, and yet loved their children and worked for their families and defended their countries (though they would never own more of it than the six feet it took to bury them) did not constitute for them, the rich, a moral problem. But it was they, the rich landowners, who betrayed their country to the invader, who sought the invader's protection, who danced to his tune, who bent his knee, who learned to speak in the invader's tongue.

How explain otherwise the willingness of men who had had all the benefits of culture, education, the "easy life" to kowtow to a foreign invader, stand aside and watch the invader torment their own people, and indeed, join in tormenting them?

Today, as attempts are being made to revise and glorify the past, this fact cannot and should not be ignored or forgotten. Domestic betrayal by the upper class, in any case, was typical of all the upper classes in most European countries as they cheered on Hitler's easily won early victories. They feared their own people more than they did the foreign invader, whom they looked on as a rescuer. France fell in six weeks, and Czechoslovakia between cocktails. Few missed breakfast the day the Austrians accepted *anschluss*. Poland's colonels were armed to the teeth for war with the Soviet Union but had only token and futile resistance to put up against what was after all their ideological brother, the Nazi Hitler.

In Latvia as well, the same formula operated, with only a few local deviations. It was not the Latvian upper class' sons who escaped into the forests and there, in cold and rain, set up resistance to the invaders. On the contrary, the sons of the rich joined the bands that hunted these "forest brothers" down. It is ironic that many of the elements of the programs of the present Nationalist regime were first applied to the Baltic countries by the Germans in 1940 et. seq. Farms given to the poor peasant were returned to their previous owners. Factories that to some extent had come under workers' control—that had had to observe civilized standards for work, health, payment—now abandoned all that. For just a moment in time, the workers and peasants who had experienced the incalculable pleasure of feeling that they had become masters of their own lives, now saw it snuffed out again. Not only were the factories returned to their original owners. The best of them were transported, almost stick by stick, to Germany itself.

Latvians, in their own land, were declared second-class citizens. Nothing could drive the reality home more vividly than the fact that native Latvians were paid only one-third the wages of Germans. Food was parceled out with the same logic. A Latvian received 1,750 grams of bread a week, and a German 3,500. A Latvian received only 200 grams of meat from his own slaughtered cows and hogs, while the German received 700. As in Lithuania, all papers and periodicals published in the native language were banned, or appeared only in translation from the German. Schools taught German, the so-called law was conducted in German, and here the last word in justice, as with everything, was marked *German*.

Jews, of course, were directly targeted for the most extreme horrors, which began immediately. Jews were driven into ghettoes and they left those ghettoes only for the crematoria—or to join the partisans. On November 30, 1941, some 8,000 Latvian Jews were driven into the woods at

Bikernek, near Arnickas and there exterminated. And this process was repeated until there literally were no more Jews to kill.

If ordinary, and "law-abiding" Latvians were spared the crematoria immediately, this was only because they had some value as slaves. Thousands were shipped to Germany proper.

In the *Black Book* (1946) we read:

> Wehrmacht Field Marshals von Model and Schoerner and 86 other Germans were named responsible for the death of 577,000 persons in concentration camps in Latvia and the deportation of 175,000 others as slave labor, in a report by a Soviet investigating committee.
>
> The committee reported that the Germans methodically destroyed factories, public utilities, libraries, museums, hospitals and homes, had ransacked libraries and art galleries and slain many Latvian intellectuals. At least 170,000 civilians, including women and children, were slaughtered in mass extermination camps near Riga, it was charged.
>
> "In the central prison in Riga," said the report, "they murdered more than 2000 children whom they had taken away from parents, and in Salaspils camp they killed more than 3000 children." In this camp the commission said it found nine grave pits covering an area of more than 3600 square yards, and had established that the Germans tortured to death more than 56,000 civilians there....
>
> "The Germans also killed residents of Riga and its suburbs in Bikernek, Dreilin and Rumbul Forests," the report continued. "In Bikernek Forest, located on the outskirts of Riga, the Nazis shot 46,500 civilians..."
>
> A witness was quoted on the shooting of Jews saying: "People with little children, old men and women, poured out into the streets where they were lined up ... In endless columns the Jews plodded along the streets. The exodus lasted from 5 p.m. Saturday all through the night and ended on Sunday evening.
>
> "The streets were covered with ice, and people fell and were shot on the spot... As people traveled their last road to death, the German beasts snatched small children from their mothers' hands, seized them by the feet and killed them by dashing them against poles and fences."[81]

Some 120,000 Latvians were slaughtered outright, almost ten percent of the entire population. But these are the statistics only of the immediate dead. Thousands more were herded into camps where they also died.

What is most appalling about this unprecedented mass slaughter of the population—hundreds of St. Batholomew Eve massacres rolled into one—was the fact that, though ordered and organized by the Germans, they were eagerly carried out by the Latvians—all of them already conditioned to serve the Germans by years of Nationalist propaganda. What was equally shocking was the fact that these genocidal murders were carried out with the connivance of the churches in the respective three Baltic countries.

It wasn't the low-brow, mentally retarded village idiots of the country who were recruited to commit such murders. In their various guises, some directly, some indirectly, some by turning away their eyes, *all* of bourgeois and bourgeois-influenced Latvia connived at the murders. It was Latvia's

General Oskar Dankers, representing Karl Ulmanis, and accompanied by Alfred Voldmani, a minister in Ulmanis' cabinet, who attended Hitler's birthday party on the eve of Munich, in 1938. A year later, April 20, 1939, again Hitler's birthday, high-ranking officials like the Chief of Staff of the Estonian and Latvian armies, General Reek and General Hartmanis, and General Rastikas, the Lithuanian Commander-in-chief and the 'strong man' in the Lithuanian government, were sent to attend.

The myth has been fabricated and widely circulated in the West, particularly in the USA, that the Nationalists opposed both the Germans and Russians. Aside from the fact that it was absolutely physically impossible in the middle of such a fierce war to oppose *both* antagonists, the truth is quite different. Perhaps for what might be called nothing more compelling than aesthetic reasons, some Latvians would have wished to see as little of the Germans as possible. But their *angst* about Germans did not amount to a positive *hatred* of them, leading to resistance gun in hand. Granted there were some who cringed at the sight of German soldiers goose-stepping along their streets. But they confined such subjective opposition to polite protests, if that, and subversive gossip. That is, the best of them. The others had no compunctions about cooperating with and carrying out the orders of their German masters. And even if they, too, were to be ultimately proven to have been nothing but shallow fools, this stupidity born of greed, racial hatred and profound lackeyism can arouse no sympathy. And yet, today—though it seems like an episode in a surrealist nightmare—some of these same "guerillas" have come out of hiding and demanded that they be paid pensions for their services during the war in the struggle against the Russians!

Their supposed animosity to the Germans in no way could be compared to their open hatred and bloodthirsty hostility to the Soviets, or anyone they dubbed "Communists"—even if it meant shooting the village school teacher in full view of her children in class!

Meanwhile, though quisling Latvians, Lithuanians and Estonians cooperated with the Germans, in the very nature of their function they could not be depended on even by the Germans. Their position was objectively contemptible—morally intolerable. And indeed, the Germans learned soon enough that they, themselves, would have to take over the reins of power directly and administer the new "province" through orders to their Latvian underdogs.

But true Latvian (and Estonian) patriots (now abused), in the little time they had to do so, managed not only to escape eastward, but to take with them whole university faculties, which were then set up again in various parts of the Soviet Union itself. Scientists from Tartu and Riga and the Tallinn Polytechnical Institute reconvened their resources in exile and resumed their work. Wherever they reassembled in the Soviet Union—some behind the Urals—they constituted the nation-in-exile. There the native tongue was spoken and newspapers appeared in their own language. Indeed, it was the express policy of the Soviets to preserve the identity of the overrun republics as completely as possible, encouraging the setting up of schools and universities. The crowning act which proved the viability of the nations and their true independence was the formation of national armies as part of the Red Army. It was the assignment of the national armies to lead in the liberation of their homelands, which is precisely what they did, finally. The first soldiers many Latvians, Lithuanians and Estonians would see, after three years of seeing only German soldiers, would be their own boys and girls whom they greeted in a delirium of joy and gratitude as they marched triumphantly through the ruins of their cities still smoking and still cluttered with corpses. These soldiers did not come to liberate their own countries from the Nazis only to hand them over to the Russians. In any case, "Russians" had become inapplicable: by this time, the entire nation with all its hundred nationalities had risen as one to repel the invader. They had moved from "Russian" to "Soviet."

Some idea of the scope and depth of the Latvian contribution to the anti-Nazi struggle can be learned from these eloquent statistics: 20,000 Latvian soldiers and partisans were awarded medals and orders, while 28 won the highest order of all—Hero of the Soviet Union. As already mentioned, the Latvians who had escaped to the east had formed a separate Lettish Division and fought in the Battle for Moscow and all the way to Berlin. The 201st famed Latvian Rifle Division was awarded the title of Guards Division, the 130th Rifle Division and the 308th Latvian Rifle Division received the Order of Suvorov (Second Class) and the Order of the Red Banner. Over 3,000 of the Lettish Division's soldiers and officers were decorated.

The victors liberated a country that was almost literally a vast graveyard. Almost one out of three Latvians had perished. The Nazis, with Latvian Nationalist assistance, had set up 48 prisons, 18 ghettoes, and 23 concentration camps on Latvian soil.

All over Latvia, Lithuania and Estonia, monuments commemorating the sacrifices and the victories of that heroic generation have been erected. It is to the dishonor of the present people in power that they have allowed gangs of fascist hoodlums to destroy so many of them!*

The total damage to Latvia has been put at 20 billion rubles. As in other republics, the Germans had driven into Germany or slaughtered on the spot

---

* At the foot of the monument at Salaspils camp, near Riga, where 100,000 were murdered, including 7,000 children, flowers are laid every day and the mournful tick of the metronome marks the numbers of the dead in an endless and "monotonous" reminder.

most of Latvia's cattle and hogs. They had wrecked farm machinery and stripped factories of all machines that could be transported. They destroyed bridges, ports, railways—whatever could be blown up, they blew up.

Along with the cattle driven to Germany went the most notorious of the quislings. The flight westward at the end of the war in the Baltics (1944), was a dramatic reversal of the return eastward in 1941 of these same quislings at the outbreak of hostilities, locked in step with the Nazis. This time the criminals did not stop in Germany itself. Nazi Germany was doomed, and at Potsdam the allies would swear to pursue the criminals "to the ends of the earth." They sped—not to the "ends of the earth"—but to West Germany where the Americans managed to give them an "understanding" welcome. In due course, the worst of the Nazi and native collaborators were provided with false passports, false names, and handed the aptly named "ratlines" along which they escaped justice in their homelands and entered the "land of the free and the brave." Some became American citizens in due course and voted in the same free elections with Jews who had managed to escape Europe, and in the vast homogenization of "refugees" from Europe, criminals along with their victims, were manufactured into typical Americans who understood nothing and boasted about it!

ESTONIA IN DEFEAT

You must row for the boat you are sitting in.
—Estonian saying

Estonia is different. Miniscule as a state (45,000 square kilometers), its entire population of about a million and a half can be contained entirely in many cities in the West. Its history, too, is the history of a small nation and of a people who were always inevitably the pawns of the ambitions of other nations and peoples. At various times, it was under the power of the Danes, Swedes, Germans and finally, after Peter the First defeated the Swedes, it became part of the Russian empire in 1710, and so it remained until 1917-18.

Again, unlike its Southern neighbors, Lithuania and Latvia, it has its own specific origin—it rose from the Ests, a Finno-Ugric people who seem to have been the first of the tribes truly inhabiting the area. But the area itself could hardly be less inviting to alien tribes. Estonia must also be understood by the fact that it is 800 islands, and its position at the peak of Europe looking into the Baltic, which opens into the Atlantic, makes it also the beneficiary—or victim—of a quixotic climate. Though generally temperate, the weather can be capricious indeed and bring premature snows and frosts in the fall and premature warm spells in winter, when the country is practically shrouded in fog and the inhabitants grope their way from home to work like immaterial ghosts. There is almost nothing, geographically speaking, to see: Estonia itself is one long plain, with dunes and rocky shores, green hills and marshes everywhere. It has 1500 lakes and 420 rivers. You will find few or no forests of great oaks and thick pine in which the creatures of legend live. Instead, the land is largely covered by shrubbery. And even so, the land is not fully cleared: it is dotted with huge boulders deposited by the Ice Ages. So rocky is the land that farming has always been a heroic feat.

Nevertheless, Estonia has great reserves of minerals, and possesses huge deposits of combustible shale which is used as fuel. In addition, the country's wetlands had rotted the previous century's vegetation and turned it into peat. Peat covers one-fifth of the country's area.

And yet, no spot on earth is so bleak that it cannot arouse the love and loyalty of those born in it. To the northern Eskimo the vast horizons of

185

snow and ice nevertheless contain a charm invisible to the southern eye. So, too, with Estonia. Its poets find it incredibly dear to them.

> *My native land!*
> *With thee I am unhappy,*
> *Without thee sadder still!*
>   Junan Liiv—(1864-1913)

And:

> *My native land, my dearest love,*
> *I'll never thee forsake,*
> *And should I die a thousand deaths,*
> *That fate I'll take.*
> *Let jealous strangers say their part,*
> *They'll never tear thee from my heart,*
> *My native land...*
>   Lydia Koidula (1843-1886)

And, cries another poet:

> *Why should not my country's tongue*
> *Soaring through the gale of song*
> *Rising to the heights of heaven,*
> *Find its own eternity?*
>   Kristjan Jaak Peterson (1801-1822)

And yet:

> *Nought but a roof overhead*
> *and work for one's hands,*
> *A mouthful of bread and a foot of earth*
> *—my country!*
>   Anna Haava (1864-1957)

Beloved, nevertheless for some it was a harsh and ungenerous land. Where there are rich, there are poor. Where some prosper, others suffer poverty. "We are poor because you are rich"—Cuba's Castro summed it up.

Under Russian Czarist rule—although the phrase Czarist rule seems ominous—the truth was that Estonia began to prosper. It prospered simply because it was under the protection of a power strong enough to resist all other foreign intrusion. It was particularly then that the development of modern commerce would bring some prosperity to Estonia which, situated as it is on the commercial crossroads, benefited from the trade that passed through its ports and along its railroads and rivers.

Nevertheless its history proved to be no different, essentially, from that of its southern neighbors. Though it prospered, it prospered as a result of capitalist development and capitalism cannot itself grow except by expropriating the labor power of the people—particularly of the workers. The appearance of factories also signaled the appearance of workers and, with the appearance of workers, also came the consciousness that as workers they produced the wealth but did not receive it back in equivalent wages or living conditions. This consciousness which grew out of—at its primitive level—the simple observation of the worker (as before him of the peasant) that he lived in a humble hut, if not a slum, while the factory owners for whom he worked (slaved) lived in a mansion. Indeed, it was not Karl Marx who said it but the 16th century John Bull:

> *When Adam delved and Eve span*
> *Who was then the gentleman?*

What was clear to the 16th century English peasant was even more clear to the following generations' workers. And if the peasant revolted from time to time, and was always defeated, this would not be the inevitable fate of the workers.

At best, the peasants could—and did—force the Czar to grant them their freedom from serfdom. If the average peasant of the times saw in the end of serfdom and the right to own land all he asked of freedom, it was in ignorance of the laws of capitalist development which, while freeing the serf from slavery to the land, confirmed his slavery to the factory and mill, now as a worker. The small peasant, as a "landowner," might have experienced the intoxication of the feeling that in *owning* land he at last owned himself, but this moment was historically extremely brief: a match lit for an instant in whose light he saw a world with expanding borders!

For the deadly fact was that something entirely unknown to him—indeed, unknown to most, even the profoundest thinkers of the times—was at work which stripped these newly born farmers of their small farms and cast them into the anonymous ranks of the propertyless worker, who traveled from countryside to city in the often vain attempt to sell his labor power at whatever price he could get for it. This secret, unknown law of economic development, which was remorseless, was an objective working-out of forces over which no one had more than temporary control (and even that was imagined). Historically, the peasant was doomed to give way to the town—to the mill and factory—to the finance-capitalist, and to the forces that made of him that typical product of the 19th and 20th centuries—the propertyless worker.

Relentlessly, the countryside was emptied of independent peasants and the cities were filled with unemployed farm hands. Like some mindless Molech let loose on the land, capitalism, born in "blood and dirt," made its ineluctable way. Its voracious, cannibalistic appetite forced more and more out of what, after all, is a pool of human energy which is finite.

When the war broke out in 1914, none of the Baltic countries were spared its devastation, nor were any spared German occupation, during and for some time after the war. When the Bolsheviks took power in Petrograd in November 1917, this event ignited not only revolutionary workers in the Baltics but inspired workers in Europe and America and in even remoter parts of the world.

The Estonian Communist Party was headed by Victor Kingissepp, a Bolshevik, who would lead the Estonian working class to power. Meanwhile, the Germans re-invaded Estonia, and were not ousted until 1918 by the Red Army. On November 29, 1917, however, socialist power was instituted at Narva.

As in Lithuania and Latvia, the revolutionary Estonian government immediately instituted a series of progressive social reforms that swept away the old state infrastructure altogether. Once the new government formed, it was recognized as independent by the Soviet Government, which, among other aids, granted the new state a credit of 60 million rubles.

But the euphoria of victory and the heady wine of directly experiencing revolution itself did not last long. The Estonian bourgeoisie was defeated but not conquered. Typically, it turned to foreigners for help, unable to find it among its own people. The British immediately responded by sending warships to Tallinn, where they sat in the bay with guns pointed shoreward. But when this did not prevail, White Guards and Estonian counterrevolutionaries, along with the Germans, launched new attacks on socialist forces. The Red Army was itself hard pressed everywhere. The combined forces of counterrevolution managed to drive the Red Army out of Estonia and the new government of the Estland Working Commune collapsed.

In power again, the bourgeoisie turned its eyes westward, cut off economic relations with Russia, destroying in one reckless act immense domestic markets, and for the next 20 years, Estonia was a pawn in the anti-Soviet machinations of France, England and the USA.

Turning to the West for markets, Estonia quickly encountered the grim realities of international finance. Nothing is given for nothing. In order to do business, Estonia had to acquire credit—and credit meant debt. By the middle '20s, it was deeply in debt to France, England, the USA and Sweden. In effect, a good portion of Estonia's working class was working for foreign masters.

Foreign capitalists moved in and took over control of Estonia's major industries and sources of energy—particularly its one valuable source: its shale-oil deposits. German companies soon had control of 46 percent of one of Estonia's major shale-oil sources. The British also moved in. Typically, Estonians wound up with only 12 percent of the shares of their own Port Kunda cement works, which were controlled by the Swedes and Danes.

Wood-working, pulp manufacturing, paper and textile industries were also foreign-controlled. By January, 1939, Estonia owed foreign investors 60 million kroons—exactly half of its industrial and agricultural assets. In the ups and downs of the business cycle, as always, the workers paid first and most harshly—not only in lower wages but in the loss of jobs. By the mid-30s, Estonia's main trading partner was fascist Germany. By 1940—before the socialist period—the Estonian GNP (Gross National Product) was below 1913 levels.

From 14,000 unemployed in 1932—when the world Depression finally hit the Baltic countries—the number of workers out of work rose to 26,851 in Estonia. Estonia's entire major work force added up to less than 50,000. Between 1920 and 1925, the first years of the bourgeois period, over 100 political trials were held in Estonia.

In 1924-25, there were 86 secondary schools in the entire country with 18,700 students. In 1933-34, ten years later, the number of schools had dropped to 67 with 11,800 students. In the first year of socialist power—1940—121,000 children were in school—which number dropped precipitately as the Nazi-Estonian collaborators came back into power. But once the Nazis and their Estonian hirelings had been disposed of, the nation promptly sent its children back to school again, and by 1950 there were 156,000 children studying. Education did not stop at the primary or secondary levels. Higher education became available to further levels of the population—workers and poor peasants who could only dream of university educations before the war. In 1932-33, only 15.5 percent of the enrolled students of Tartu University could be classified as originating in working class and poor peasant families.

Estonia, too, had its own fascist interlude, when all the social gains, so briefly won in 1939-40, were reversed. But resistance to a return to pre-revolutionary Estonia arose everywhere. Trials of Communists and suspected Communists continued for two decades on what seemed like an endless conveyor belt of trials. Sentences were always harsh. Victor Kingissepp, the Estonian Communist leader, was sentenced to death and executed in 1922.

Even so, it was impossible to keep the workers cowed. On December 1, 1924, the workers rose with arms in hand in Tallinn and though the uprising was put down, it eloquently restated the fact that the interests of the workers and those who exploited them were irreconcilable. Today's generation has to make an effort of the imagination to understand why, in the '20s and '30s, the image of Benito Mussolini loomed so large in the bourgeois world and why he was virtually hailed there as a hero. Winston Churchill waxed ecstatic (no less) when speaking of Mussolini, whose bogus "March on Rome" had inaugurated fascism in Italy in 1922. It is worth while to ponder this phenomenon for a moment.

No one had suffered the revolutionary tides rolling over Europe with greater agony than did Winston Churchill. Thus, in 1927, he would rhapsodize, after meeting Mussolini for the first time: "I could not help being charmed by Signor Mussolini's gentle and simple bearing."[82]

The murderer of Socialist leader Giacomo Mateotti in 1924 (and 4,000 militant workers) was seen by Churchill, who had had a hand in putting down the 1926 general strike in England (and had nightmares of revolution ever after), as having found the formula he had himself been seeking. "Italy has shown that there is a way of fighting the subversive forces which can rally the masses of the people...."

And to an Italian audience in Rome, January 20, 1927, he orated: "If I had been an Italian I am sure I would have been whole-heartedly with you."[83]

Later, in 1938, to prove that his first ecstatic reaction to Mussolini had not been a wayward result of too much Beefsteak gin, he added Hitler to his roster of "great men" who had found the key to stopping Bolshevism. Churchill's later record of opposition to Hitler's attempt to take over all of Europe, including England, has tended to becloud his initial warm reception to both of the dictators. In a *Collier's* article in 1938, he wrote that Hitler has "revolted against the crude Marxist catch-words," and had "felt himself born to greatness." And the key to this "greatness" was the ever-recurring and fundamental class *motif*–for Hitler was "great" because he had defeated "the Bolshevik fever (that) threatened to spread beyond the bounds of semi-Asiatic Russia" and "by a supreme effort defeated Germany threw it off."[84]

"Adolph Hitler," Churchill went on to explain, "is Führer because he exemplified and enshrined the will of Germany ... The German people observed with growing anxiety how one key opposition after another passed under the control of the Jews.... The Jewish war profiteers and the Jewish socialist adventurers obtained control over the lifestream of the nation....

"Any objective examination of the aims of German foreign policy ... ought to calm those who are apt to fear Germany's intentions. Her aims are limited to [Labensraum] for the German people. Her foreign policies do not aim at undiscriminating territorial aggrandizement."[85]

Impossible to be more wrong. That confident and trusting statement, made by such a shrewd class-conscious politician as Churchill, revealed either monumental class blindness or the effects of an *idée fixe*–the single modern *Carthago delenda est*–Moscow must be destroyed. This was *one year* before the outbreak of the most devastating war in human history.

Churchill was not stupid. Nor is it merely coincidental that Joachim von Ribbentrop, at his trial at Nuremberg, used the same defense, even the same language, to justify the Nazi barbarities: "Today the key problem for Europe and the world still remains: will Asia dominate Europe or will the Western Powers restrict the influence of the Soviets to the Elbe...."

Churchill's position was no more than England's set policy toward the Revolutionary East since 1917. At no time did Churchill abandon or even soften his oft-quoted statement that he had not assumed the Prime Ministry of England in order to liquidate the British empire. The difference between him and Ribbentrop was quite simple and quite clear: both wanted what only one could have....

What the lion purred in its sleep sounded like a fearful roar to the jackals listening at the door. Britain constantly kept her hand firmly in Baltic politics and understood the underling types that the politics of the times produced. While courting Hitler, the politicians of bourgeois Baltic countries also feared him, and as a "counter-balance" they kept an ear cocked for advice from Great Britain. There is nothing heroic in such a position. For it's based on fear of one's own people, who remained a constant threat.

In Estonia, fascism found its "native" form and spokesmen. The fascists' organization was "Vabs" which, exploiting the complaints of the peasants, succeeded in winning a large proportion of them. In fact, its power grew quickly and enormously; by 1933, when the world crisis had reached its nadir and Hitler his apogee, Vabs forced the not-too-unwilling government to order a referendum on fascist amendments to the democratic constitution.

With the amended constitution as his justification, Konstantin Paets moved for absolute power. His first act was to dissolve the troublesome Vabs, which had become too much of a rival, but he also moved to undermine and make helpless democracy, such as it was, in Estonia. The army backed Paets and all opposition was crushed. Nazi Germany, too, made it clear that it supported Paets and preferred Vabs to support him too.

Treachery, double-dealing, constant suspicion and panic—these were the forces operating on the men who "ran" Estonia. General Laidoner, who had helped bring Paets to power, and who was the Commander-in-Chief of the Army, with his adviser, chief of the Estonian military intelligence, Colonel Maasing, conspired together, and conspired with the Germans—especially with German intelligence—for, in their hearts, they expected the Nazis would win in the coming inevitable military showdown, and they planned to win with them.

They had to hedge their bets, however. For in June 1940, the working people of Estonia overthrew their German-imposed government, which by

now was led by a bloody dictator, deeply involved with and in political debt
to Hitler, with those Estonian agents with which the Germans were in
constant contact. These "leaders" had degenerated to nothing but errand
boys for Hitler.

Swiftly the new forces, through their newly elected Duma, proclaimed
Estonia a Soviet Socialist Republic. Just as Lithuania and Latvia had done
at about the same time, the Estonians appealed to the USSR Supreme
Soviet to accept them as a full member of the Union, and were so accepted.
With Hitlerite Germany breathing on their necks, the Estonians had no
illusions about what their fate would be once the Germans decided to
march east.

Immediately, too, the new Estonian government put into practice a new
constitution along with a whole series of decisions that swept the political,
economic and cultural landscape clean of its overburdened past, and instituted a people's government. One should pause here and ponder the fact—
that for the first time in human history, the *people*, those great amateurs in
self-administration, those eternal governmental outsiders, those faceless,
nameless, anonymous masses existing hitherto for no other purpose than
to haul water and hew wood for their "natural" superiors—for those who,
on grounds that had no historical justice—nevertheless had arrogated the
power of life and death over them.

The new republic would not last long enough to wear out its enthusiasm
or suffer a letdown from its first euphoric transportations. It was brought
abruptly to a close—if temporary—on June 22, 1941, when the Nazis invaded. Those who resisted—and the resistance was often spontaneous—died
heroically. Those who had time and organization retreated further into the
USSR and there reformed themselves into the Estonian National Corps and
fought as part of the Red Army until Estonia was finally liberated in the
autumn of 1944.

There were—as was true in Lithuania and Latvia—many who collaborated
with the Nazis. Others truly wished to remain neutral—neither Red nor
Brown. But these were dreamers. Their wished-for "neutrality" had no
ground to stand on: everywhere the earth was scorched. In any case, in the
eyes of their conquerors, their "neutrality" was not recognized.

But others were deeply implicated in crime. These fled (they always
knew when to flee) with the Nazis back into Germany as the tides of war
rolled westward, particularly after the German defeat at Stalingrad.

The Nazis reached the Estonian border on July 7, 1941, where they
were checked for some precious days. Resistance was spontaneous but by
January 1942, between 35 and 40 thousand Estonians were enlisted in the
Red Army's 8th Estonian Infantry Corps, led by Major General Lembit
Parn.

During the German occupation, which was as ruthless in Estonia as it was in Lithuania, the Germans, with their Estonian collaborators, managed to kill 125,000 people, including 64,000 Soviet POW's.

But by 1942, the partisan movement organized and headed by Nicolai Karotamn, Secretary of the Communist Party, consisted of more than 60 armed groups. Although there is a drive today to obliterate the role of the Communist Party in the defense of their homeland, the fact is that many Communists were martyrized in that period. At a time when Estonian history is being rewritten, it's even more timely to recall that courageous and advanced individuals turned to the Party, which alone held up a banner of intrepid resistance to the invader, one based not merely on some kind of visceral hatred of aliens but on a confirmed knowledge of the reason for the war and how to win it. It was no surprise to Communists that their peacetime enemies, the Nationalists, automatically collaborated with the enemy. The Party grew during the war, many individuals taking out their applications on the eve of battle.

The supreme contempt that Nationalism held for its cultural figures is to be seen in the names of those who perished and those who enjoyed the patronage of their new masters. During the occupation, playwright and journalist Evald Tammlaan was sent to a concentration camp where he died. Such, too, was the fate of the short-story writer, Johannes Ruven, who was executed in Tallinn. The poets Juhan Sütiste and Aleksander Antson lost their health in the fascist jails. Valmar Adams, Rudolf Sirge, Osvald Tooming were imprisoned. Of course, books by revolutionary writers were taken out of the bookstores and libraries and destroyed, presumably today as well.

There were, on the other hand, writers who collaborated. If in the unspoken definition of a poet, a writer, an artist is the underlying assumption that his or her function in life is, to put it simply, to defend life, to struggle to make these beasts, people, into human beings, we know differently today. We know that in every country, confronted by the stark choice—remain loyal to your creative self, and die by our hands; or flatter us and we will give you honors and awards—some of the most eminent, or at least prominent, writers of Western Europe chose the road of national and artistic betrayal. In Germany, Gerhart Hauptmann—a proletarian playwright—caved in. In Norway, it was Knut Hamsun. In France, Ferdinand Celine, Jean Cocteau, Andre Gide, the not yet known but to be known, Jean Genet. In England, it was the writer of comical books, P.G. Wodehouse and, more slyly, the American ex-patriot, T.S. Eliot. America could also point to Ezra Pound in addition to Charles Lindbergh.

The Estonian writers who collaborated with the Nazis were also—as was typical of most of the top collaborators—extremely keen sniffers of the shifting winds. They had caught a whiff of what seemed like the wind of the future when Hitler came to power and installed his own henchmen into leading positions in the Baltics—Paets in Estonia. However, when the winds shifted once more and they could smell the odor of retribution coming on the wind from the east with the sound of guns as the Red Army approached, they fled westward, to safety. Nazi Germany as a haven does not immediately spring to the mind of most civilized human beings. But for these writers, and many other collaborators, it did indeed. For even if Nazi Germany too was destined to collapse, they had learned by that time that a real haven had meanwhile been erected in Western Germany by the Americans and there, as though being serviced by a travel bureau, they were issued passports and tickets to many of the safe "havens" in the world—to Latin America, Spain, Portugal, and the USA. They were given what has been unappetizingly tagged as "ratlines," to facilitate their exits. Now, ratlines are no more than the hawsers by which ships are tied in ports, and down them crept rats at night, many of them infected with bubonic plague, and in their newly acquired free zones they infected everything they could reach with their poison. Rats, too, are known to leave sinking ships. Captains, on the other hand, go down with their ships.

So they were rats. Many of them, with new names and new identities, became solid citizens of their acquired countries, like Karl Linnas in the USA, and during the Cold War, particularly in America, they felt totally at home. Most of the writers who collaborated with the Nazis made their escape in good time.

But Karl Linnas should not pass off without special mention. In 1962, the Supreme Court of Estonia, sitting in Tartu, found three notorious Estonian collaborators—J. Juriste, K. Linnas and E. Viks, guilty of crimes against humanity and sentenced them to death. They had been in charge of one of the most notorious of Estonian concentration camps—the Tartu Concentration Camp. Of those found guilty, only one suffered the extreme penalty. E. Viks had escaped to Australia. And Linnas was safe in the USA.

Linnas had started his collaborative life with the Nazis as duty officer in the Tartu Camp, but was "promoted" to commandant when the camp was transferred to Kuperjanov Barracks in Kostan Street, Tartu, though he was only 22 at the time. As commandant, Linnas had reached the peak, not only of his career, but of his psychological imperatives—he was a confirmed sadist. Now, as commandant, he could indulge his sadism to his heart's content, and feel no remorse. It was he who interrogated prisoners and passed sentence on them, often personally carrying the sentence out at Jalaka Line where he stood on the edge of a ditch there and shot those victims who showed some signs of life after having been executed. Later at the trial, Hilda Jalkas would testify:

In December 1941, I was sent to a concentration camp in the former Kuperjanov Barracks. We estimated that there were 1000-1500 inmates in the camp at any one time...

In January 1942, I was lashed on the orders of Linnas, the camp commandant, for striking a guard who tried to rape me. They beat me till I began to bleed. I was pregnant then and soon produced still-born twins.... In 1942, I saw a red bus taking four- and five-year old children out of the camp. They were told they were being taken to a bath for a wash. Karl Linnas accompanied them. Later we learned that these children—nearly 100 in all—were shot at the anti-tank ditch.[86]

Altogether, about 12,000 inmates were slaughtered at this camp in Tartu.

Earlier, Major Franz Kurg, who headed the Omakaitse, the punitive organization that rounded up "Bolsheviks," boasted that during his time with it, the Omakaitse in Tartu had captured 12,200 "Bolsheviks" and killed 4,812... "I wish to express my gratitude to my closest assistants Hauptmann, J. Juristed and Ensign K. Linnas."

Linnas's history was eventually uncovered and measures were taken to annul his citizenship, which he had acquired by lying. Indeed, his citizenship was revoked on July 31, 1981. The Soviet government again raised its demand that Linnas be returned to Estonia to stand trial. But compliance with this decision was delayed time after time. Linnas had acquired defenders, most notably the Joint Baltic American National Committee, which included the Estonian American National Council, the American Latvian Association, Inc., and the Lithuanian American Council.

They launched a campaign to prevent deportation, citing as one reason why Linnas should not be deported to Estonia the fact that the United States did not recognize Soviet authority in the Baltics. Among some notables they managed to persuade to back their cause was Senator Alfonse D'Amato (R. NY) who wrote a letter to the President asking for a stay. Senator D'Amato was himself in deep trouble, facing charges of misusing his influence to benefit himself and his relatives, and in dire straits reached for any straw to save himself. But as luck would have it, his letter also proved to be an embarrassment as Linnas' guilt as a war criminal was fully exposed, and D'Amato denounced the Joint Baltic Committee for "lying" and "deceiving" him and his staff.

However, proven to be no wiser, but even more desperate as he felt the hot breath of justice on his neck, D'Amato reached for another straw—this time the Lithuanian issue. To newspaper headlines in the tabloid press, he announced plans to come to the unspecified help of "heroic" Lithuania, but was refused a visa by the Soviet authorities in Poland, and had to return ingloriously home without any kind of negotiable "success" that could be translated into a form that would discourage further investigation of his shady financial deals. Senator D'Amato is not the only, but is perhaps most typical, of both Estonia's and Lithuania's defenders—men so desperate themselves that they grab for any lifeline to save their necks.

The Nazis left behind a devastated country. The Nazis had destroyed 2500 factories, 41 power stations, 21,000 homes, and the workforce decreased by 3.5 percent. In Tallinn alone, 2,400 buildings were destroyed, including historical sites. Everywhere one traveled one came across little shrines by the wayside, each with its small bouquet of flowers, and the legend that so-and-so had been killed here by the Nazis.

But the Nazis, too, died here though their graves bear no devoted legends. More than 20,000 Estonian soldiers and partisans were decorated for bravery. More than 200,000 Hitlerites with 42 generals were taken prisoner.

At the end of the war, facing the monumental task of rebuilding the country, the USSR gave 300 million rubles—half the state's budget—to Estonia to help it rebuild. Food imports, mainly from Russia proper, exceeded exports by 1.6 times and the importation of industrial products exceeded exports by 10 times. Parity between exports and imports was reached only in 1956.

The Government gave back to the peasants in 1947 some 868,000 hectares of land that had been owned by the kulaks. Some 34,000 peasants got land.

We read in *The Plot Against the Peace*:

When advance Red Army units reached a German labor concentration camp of the Todt organization near Klooga, Estonia, in the fall of 1944 the troops were sickened by a smell of burning flesh which came from the surrounding forest. The Red Army men discovered in the forest four huge funeral pyres which were still smoldering. The pyres contained the bodies of some 3000 men, women and children who had been butchered a short time before. Many of the victims, as an investigation subsequently established, had been intellectuals from Vilna, Riga and Tallinn...

An English correspondent visited the terrible site of the pyre, accompanied by Jeremiah Ratner, a former Lithuanian prisoner in the Klooga Camp. With tears streaming down his face, Ratner pointed to three of the bodies. "Look, that's the body of my fifteen-year-old boy, Mathias," he said. "There's my wife and my sixteen-year-old daughter."

Then Jeremiah Ratner said to the English correspondent: "Will people believe what you wrote of the things you've seen here? I know that the Russians will show no mercy to the criminals who burned my fifteen-year-old boy, but can we count on the people in Britain and America to show the same determination?"[87]

Grateful to the Russians of the Red Army who died to liberate Estonia, the people erected a monument at Valga—an assault tank in memory of the 8,000 Red Army's 51st Armored Division who were killed here.

In July 1990, former collaborators with the Nazis planned to hold a reunion in Tori, near Parnu—a reunion billed as a rally of "fighters for Estonia's freedom." Due to take part in it were members of the notorious 20th SS Division and the Omakaitse "police," perhaps among them men who could have told Jeremiah Ratner exactly how his wife and children were murdered.

Surprisingly, the rally was permitted by the now "liberated" Estonian authorities, on the argument that both the Soviet Red Army and the Nazis were equally guilty of fighting "for the interests of the great powers and the implementation of their ideologies."

But if the Estonian parliament—the *free* parliament—with the exception of a few Communist members who refused to go along—were prepared to "forget" and put the murders and the murdered in the same pot, the Estonian people themselves were not. A storm of protest forced the liberated MPs to cancel the Nazi rally. An Estonian one-time prisoner of Buchenwald, Emil Karlebach, speaking from Bonn, declared: "The fact that this band now dares to demonstrate in Estonia is an outrage, a blow to the struggle for human rights, and humanism, and a provocation not only with regard to the Soviet public but the world public as well."

But in the USA, the Senator from New York, Alfonse D'Amato, raised his voice in protest against the proposed deportation of a convicted Estonian mass murderer—Karl Linnas.

They say that those who forget the past are condemned to repeat it....

SOCIALIST ESTONIA

*The working masses of Estonia ... are not always
able to recognize a wolf in sheep's clothing.*
—Victor Kingissepp, Estonian,
general secretary of Communist Party,
executed by the Estonian bourgeoisie.

The Estonian Socialist Constitution, which had been in force up until
the late 1980s, states, among other things:

Citizens of the ESSR are equal before the law, without distinction of race or
nationality.

Exercising these rights is ensured by a policy of all-round development and
drawing together of all the nations and nationalities of the USSR, by educating
the citizens in the spirit of Soviet patriotism and socialist internationalism, and by
the right to use the native language and the language of other peoples of the
USSR.

Any direct or indirect limitations of the right of citizens or the establishment
of direct or indirect privileges on grounds of race or national exclusiveness,
hostility or contempt, are punishable by law.

It is the internationalist duty of citizens of the Estonian SSR to promote
friendship and cooperation with peoples of other lands and help maintain and
strengthen world peace.

Article 69 also reads: "The Estonian SSR shall retain the right freely to
secede from the USSR."

In this small country of hardly more than a million and a half people,
there are nevertheless 104 different nationalities. Indigenous Estonians
make up the majority (900,000); Russians—(600,000); Ukrainians—2.1 percent: Finns—1.4 percent, and so on. By 1980, most of Estonia's people lived
(mainly the Russians) in the cities.

It had always been the pride and even the boast of the socialist countries of the USSR that they had solved the national question and, therefore,
the ages-old national antagonisms which had caused so much misery and
shed so much blood were things of the past. The principles of socialism—
the economics of socialism, in which exploitation of man by man had been
eliminated (exploitation which often took the form of the stronger nation
exploiting the weaker one)—were given credit for achieving at last the
utopian dream of national harmony.

Marxists had pointed out, persuasively, that historically, the strongest weapon used by the oppressor to keep the oppressed in bondage was nationalism—the unthinking, irrational hostility of one people for another based on no just reason. The USA was the classic example of how one people—the Africans—were kept in subjection for hundreds of years with no better justification than the fact that their skin color was different. And this was carried on under the slogans of freedom and liberty!

The Marxists saw in the pattern of oppression based on national grounds the real purpose for it and its real roots. Dividing peoples against one another on the basis of race, nationality, religion, etc., had only one aim in view—keeping those in power *in* power. It's doubtful that any weapon has proven to be more powerful in the hands of reaction—of the backward ruling classes of the world—than nationalism, blind, in-growing, mindless nationalism. Marx early explained it, particularly in his famous statement about the American working class, divided on a racial basis: "Labour cannot emancipate itself in the white skin where in the black it is branded." He also pointed out that as long as England can oppress Ireland, then the British worker will remain impotent....

Marxists believed that basic injustice in society would be eliminated by taking the ownership of the means of production and distribution out of the hitherto owning, capitalist class and returning it to the hands of those who created the wealth of a nation by their labor.

This, too, was a great revelation and stands as an inviolate monument to the power of human thought.

And yet, as we now know, this proposition and others stemming from it, are under fire, challenged, and in some former socialist countries are disowned.

But there was no inkling of the shadows ahead when the Baltic countries adopted the principles of what was then understood as socialism, and prepared to change society and themselves in the process of implementing them. Indeed, in the first postwar years, when the first Five Year Plans were being tried out, the successes that ensued were impressive. Almost immediately, the standard of living began to rise. Production rose. Farms prospered. The health of the nation noticeably improved. Its educational level leaped ahead. The Baltics began to create a culture that commanded world attention—books, paintings, architecture, music, and particularly the cinema.

In 1975, Estonia celebrated the 450th anniversary of book printing. During this time, 85,000 titles were published in the Estonian language—more than half of them were published during the Soviet period. In order to make such large editions feasible, an audience that could read books was needed, and toward that end, Soviet power eliminated illiteracy and raised the educational level of the people to the highest level in its entire history. By the late '70s, the government could claim that the entire Estonian people enjoyed at least secondary education, while many thousands—for the first time in Estonian history—went on to higher education. Free!

In 1978, "more than a million folk songs, legends, and proverbs will be included in a folklore edition prepared by the scholars of Estonia. It will consist of 40-45 volumes with summaries in Russian, English and German," according to a Tass announcement (May 30, 1978). Similar collections were launched in Lithuania, as well as Latvia—testifying to the tremendous respect in which socialist authorities held the people's past, recognizing in folk culture the basis upon which every national culture must be built.

And although today this is no longer mentioned, the fact is that being part of the Soviet Union opened the world to the Baltic peoples—certainly one-sixth of the world. An Estonian could travel thousands of miles from his little pocket of a country in northern Europe and, using his second language, Russian, as a *lingua franca*, he could feel at home anywhere—speaking to strangers unreachable hitherto—in the words of the one language they held in common. For a small people like the Estonians, whose language nobody else knew or had to know, it was absolutely essential that they acquire a second language, or remain boxed off not only geographically but socially as well.

With the falling of hostile borders, little Estonia, too, became accessible to many more peoples of the Soviet Union than had been possible under Czarist Russia. The end of the war had left her ravaged and, like Lithuania and Latvia, she sent out a call to the rest of the USSR for help. "Help" meant mostly from Russians, for they were the most numerous, and indeed they (along with many others) answered the call, and did it consciously as a patriotic duty. They didn't come as merchants to set up shops where they bought cheap and sold dear. They came mainly as workers. It was with Russian (non-Estonian) help that Estonia was largely restored.

For years intermarriages between Russians and others (of all the republics in the USSR) were hailed as a homogenizing process which, as it grew, would begin to eliminate not only geographical borders but the borders of blood: the children of intermarriage were—what? At 16, they themselves could choose to put down on their internal identity cards what nationality they belonged to: their mother's or their father's. But more and more of them just said they were "Soviet," raising the perspective finally of a nation so intermixed racially and ethnically that "Soviet" was the only way to identify themselves. Some 70 million "ethnics" lived outside their national borders, for instance, and inter-mixed even if they did not intermarry.

Estonians, too, settled down in other parts of the USSR, and married, and raised children who also could only be classified as "Soviet." Even so, they did not surrender their feelings of national origin, preserved their language and customs—but only visited the land of their birth.

Even the most hostile of Western critics of the Soviet Union can come up with no impressive evidence that Russia "exploited" its smaller republics, in the classic way in which the great Western empires exploited (and exploit) their vassals. Wealth was not extracted out of Estonia like gold out of Mexico and diamonds out of South Africa, and carted to Moscow. The flow went the other way—so much so, in fact, that, in the late '80s, one could hear murmurs of resentment in certain quarters in Moscow that they had sacrificed enough. Suffice it to note that while, in Lithuania, the average annual consumption of meat came to over 60 kilograms a year, Russians had only something like 40 kilograms.

With undoubted successes in almost every social field that, summed up, certainly justified all those who believed in living socialism—and they called it that—it seemed to any unbiased visitor that the people of the Baltics were indeed, and the word is advisedly used—lucky. In fact, it's not too quixotic to say that their very success gave them—some—the basis upon which to launch their demands for political independence. Forget for the moment that, at least in the case of the Lithuanians, when they sought for symbols to dramatize their "ideals" they returned to the middle ages, when feudalism was in flower.... The truth is that their new "perspective" is fraught with danger, for it launches itself from an unreal base both in history, philosophy and science. True, Marx and Engels, although they set before the philosophers of the world the task, not merely of explaining the world but of *changing* it, they did not draw up a blueprint. In 1893, Engels speaking for himself and the dead Marx, had stated: "Pre-set opinions regarding the details of the organization of the future society? You won't find even a hint of them in our works."

As scientists, and not utopian dreamers, they understood that no man is so mighty of intellect that he can draw up a scheme for living well and then force it upon the people, ready or not, and, even if they accept it, as various colonies of utopians did, time proved that such artificially constructed societies never endured. Socialism, in Marx's view, was the natural outcome of capitalism, once capitalism had exhausted its main possibilities for growth. True, there were occasions when coming out of feudalism and even tribalism, some peoples opted to skip the capitalist stage altogether, as now being artificial, and passing directly into socialism. As for socialism itself, Marx and Engels left it to the men and women whose task it would be to build it, once the main requisite was established: the ownership of the means of production and distribution coming into the hands of the working class.

Nobody knew precisely how to build it. Those who claim that "socialism has failed" are much too naive. "Socialism" has not failed; one of the means for establishing it has outlived its usefulness. In a sense, all of the USSR was in "prison" from its birth: it was surrounded by hostile forces openly plotting to overthrow it and, under such constrained circumstances, it had to try to build a society which erected the material basis for freedom in a context which was unfree.

That so much was possible under the unpromising circumstances is what should be noted and out of which inspiration should be drawn.

But to make it possible for children to study far beyond the point where "normally" they were expected to work and help support the family, the society had to: (1) choose to sacrifice other material values in order to obtain the leisure for study; and (2) it had to provide the generation that was readying itself to administer socialist power with decent living conditions. Again, to do this a large percentage of the national wealth had to be segregated—separated from production—in order to construct hospitals and train doctors to build schools and train teachers, etc. The expense was borne by the society as a whole.

But basic to everything was the fact that in order to create the necessary wealth which would make it possible to support all those services which do not directly contribute to making a profit, indeed, to create an intelligentsia, the industrial base of the country had to be erected. Socialism is unthinkable in a nation that has no working class. In order to change a nation of peasants into a nation of workers, one had to build factories, mills, mines, laboratories, ships, machines, etc. In order to be able to use all these industrial resources to the fullest, one had to have a large, highly-educated population. In the goal of transforming Estonia into an industrial nation, Russia (and the other republics), but mainly Russia, made a great contribution. Lenin had long before established as policy the aim of bringing the backward nations of the USSR up to the level of the most advanced. If "Russia" (under socialist leadership) had been truly an imperial power, the last thing the beneficiaries of imperial power would have wanted was to industrialize and educate "their" colonial vassals. Great Britain, France, the USA, Japan, Italy etc., did not conquer foreign nations in order to abolish poverty and illiteracy. They conquered them in order to make money out of them, and poverty and ignorance—at least for a hundred years—were absolutely necessary allies in that exploitation.

History shows no precedent here where great nations voluntarily made genuine sacrifices of their own resources in order to help a backward neighbor. Socialist Russia had no colonies, and later references to her "empire" in Eastern Europe came out of the same poisoned stew with which some of the people of the world were fed for so many years. Even the most malicious anti-Sovieteers researched the record in vain in an attempt to establish a Soviet economic relationship of exploiter and exploited, which is typical with the classic imperialist nations. "You are rich because we are poor," Castro has commented, speaking to the bourgeois representatives, noting that 40,000 children in the Third World died of preventable diseases as daily sacrifices to the Molech of Imperialism. For these 40,000, questions of "rights"—right to vote, right to education, etc.— did not exist. Only socialism made them real.

There is no need to glorify or idealize the past. And yet it is absolutely true (and confirmed by numerous observers) that under socialism all of the one-time subject nations took on a new lease of life—all experienced a cultural revolution, all of them added years to their people's life-spans, all of them shared in the joy of accomplishments which appeared as if by magic in front of their eyes.

Probably the most precious "gift" that socialism brought to them was the vision of a world without war, a dream that at last it seemed was within reach of mankind, and only in our "socialist" era.

A NATION FLEES

Hundreds of thousands of Lithuanians are leaving, but none are returning. Return to your homeland, Lithuanians! Save your country from ruin, sons and daughters. Do you see what hardships Lithuania suffers? Do you see the earth is slipping out of Lithuanian hands? That precious land watered with our ancestor's blood is now grieving for its sons.
—Kazys Gineitis, 1925, *Amerika ir Amerikos Lietuviai*

There is another Lithuania that exists outside the geographic borders of that country, but in some eyes, it seems to be the tail that wags the dog. Although "little Lithuanias" exist in a number of countries,* there is one country where that other Lithuania exists and wields power, perhaps even decisive power, on its "home" country, and that is the USA..

It is impossible to speak of Lithuania without thinking of America-Lithuania. Landsbergis' thoughts always go westward to Washington, and it is there that he comes for support (money) and what might be called inspiration. American politicians who have a Lithuanian constituency were loud in their "support" of Lithuanian independence, though not until yesterday were they quite sure where Lithuania really was on the map of Europe.

So the "cause" of Lithuanian independence has found dubious supporters, and yet it exists as a political force in the USA.

But exactly who are these American Lithuanians who have come to the rescue of their home country (though many had never seen it and few want to return) with gifts of money, with tons of "literature," with fax machines, and even with the loan of a one-time law clerk of Supreme Court Justice David Souter, to advise Landsbergis on how to present his case for independence?

Altogether over the years, some 1,650,000 (estimated) Lithuanians emigrated to the USA. It's difficult to say exactly, since before 1918 they quite likely were classified as "Russians" or "Poles." In any case, over the years they largely disappeared. The 1970 census notes 76,000 foreign-born Lithuanians and 254,976 native-born, second-generation Lithuanians. But most

* In 1974-75, 35,000 in Argentina, 40,000 in Brazil, 24,500 in Canada, 10,000 in Australia, Poland and Germany, and 400,000 in the USA.

of these "second generation" Lithuanians, although the figures are not available, are most likely married to non-Lithuanians, and already their children have no notion of their Lithuanian ancestry. Indeed, if one was motivated that way, one could see in the utter disappearance of so many Lithuanians a monumental tragedy—as, indeed, from a national, truly patriotic point of view, it was. It was a kind of genocide, initiated by poverty and oppression at home which drove them into emigration, and ended by a process of assimilation into a soulless Americanism which left no trace of their national origins. At most, such Lithuanians appear on "national holidays" in costume—as living museums. If their children are interested at all, they have to learn Lithuanian as a foreign tongue.

But still they exist. And today they represent a political force which—in the political turmoil still going on—they could even represent a critical force. It's important to know who they are and where they come from.

They came over the centuries, with the first Lithuanian recorded as coming to New Amsterdam in the middle of the 17th century. He was invited to teach boys Latin. His name was Alexander Cordus Curtis. He didn't stay. Presumably once he had convinced those distant Hollanders that "all Gaul was divided into three parts," he felt free to return home, which he did.

We do not hear of Lithuanians again until the Revolution. We must be reminded that the generation of the American Revolution of 1776—with its stentorian Declaration of Independence—bears little resemblance to the grandchildren that grew up under its aegis. We shall not linger here to point out that in that same Declaration that declared "all men are created equal" did not see, or did not choose to see, (under its breath, so to speak), there also existed another unwritten clause which might have read, "except Blacks, Indians, indentured servants, men without means, women, etc."

Let that go, too. There is no such thing as purity in the world—only innocence, only the state of non-being before engaging in struggle, only choices between bad and worse. The resounding rhetoric of the Declaration sped around the world, exactly the way Emerson claimed the shot fired by the embattled farmers at Lexington "was heard around the world." The framers of the Constitution, the leaders of the revolution itself, those who shaped and fixed its ideology, were men of great intellectual stature whose ideas escaped the social confines of the society they helped to bring into being. Not only did the ideas of the American Revolution, combined with the ideas of the French Revolution, reshape the thinking of mankind, they helped reshape the world. Indeed, they remain potent to this day, so potent, that to champion them too faithfully makes one a marked man.

It was the power of attraction which these ideas generated that brought Thaddeus Kosciusko to help the embattled revolutionary army under Washington—a most extraordinary general who won the war by losing almost every battle but the last.

Kosciusko, a revolutionary from a noble background, was born in Lithuania, but a Lithuania that wasn't sure it was Lithuania. Perhaps it was Poland? In any case, inspired by the revolutionary winds crossing the Atlantic and stirring the minds of men all over Europe, he offered his services to General Washington, and served indeed in several campaigns. His name still lingers in the names of some streets and schools here and there in the USA, although (it must be added) to this day most Americans stumble in the effort to pronounce it.

Actually, the first mass migration of Lithuanians took place after 1860, after serfdom was abolished in Russia, which meant also Lithuania setting "free" tens of thousands of former serfs. But "free," they were more unfree than ever. If before liberation, their master was compelled to provide them with food and shelter, though he appropriated their labor without compensation, now he was no longer obliged to supply them with anything. They could, and they did, starve—free.

Two famines in succession had decimated the population. In the eyes of the starving, the image of the USA as a land of untold opportunity begging for settlers, especially after Congress voted the first of the great Homestead Acts (1862) that made 160 acres available free to those who tilled it for five years. That image shone with an extraordinary lustre.... And, indeed, there was substance to it. True, the race would be to the swift, and to those who survived, who most quickly mastered the skills needed to survive, the cost would be considered cheap. But the cost to others, to those who did not survive, the cost was their lives.

America's story of immigration is generally represented in the language of success, opportunity, freedom—in Emma Lazarus's words engraved on the base of the Statue of Liberty, "Give me your tired, your poor, your huddled masses yearning to breathe free...."

But the generosity implied in that invitation did not exist in fact. Misrepresentation, fraud, downright robbery—the immigrants were the victims of all of it. They could hardly make a move which they did not have to pay for in some way. Still desperate at home, where famine stalked the land, they were in no position to choose. Any promise of rescue seemed miraculous. Indeed, in the almost 100 years that followed until World War I (1914-1918), millions of Europe's workers and peasants abandoned their homes, as if abandoning a sinking ship, and made their desperate way to America. This huge emigration is eloquent testimony to the failure of European capitalism and perhaps headed off revolutions earlier than they occurred. The exodus was so great from Lithuania that many towns were literally denuded of eligible young men, a fact lamented bitterly by the single women left behind with no hope of marriage. A typical lament:

> ... Sad is the lot for Lithuanian girls. All the men have left or have been killed in wars. Some girls have already bought bibles and are preparing for the nunnery.
> Others will be left alone. I'll go across the ocean where the young men are. Even if I don't marry, at least I'll live well. There everyone wears silk hats and everyday I'll have a different young man. Others are saying that if they fatten their dowry, they'll get a man. But no more honest men are left in Lithuania.[88]

Between 1899 and 1914, it is calculated that 252,594 Lithuanians emigrated to the USA. Most of the emigrants were single men between the ages of 14 and 45. They added up to 170,699. Only 81,895 women emigrated—leaving a disproportionate number of men to women of two to one. It is interesting to note that though most of the immigrants were listed as farmers in the country of their origin, almost none of them took up farming in America, rejecting a quixotic offer by Buffalo Bill Cody to settle them in Wyoming.* They had had enough of farm-peasant life. Instead, they became largely workers, and in the beginning, concentrated in mining and steel.

Again, only 20,185 were children under 14. Children were legally allowed to work at age 14 in America and it is after this age that we see the greatest number of immigrants—from 15 to 45 there were 227,724 immigrants. The cut-off age of 45 was not accidental. At this age, workers were not generally hired for mining or steel work; the reason was simple: their stamina and health declined after 45. Of that age—over 45—there were only 4,795. The old stayed home.

Most of the immigrants in that period were functionally illiterate. The figures show 118,000 recorded as being able to read and write; 11,352 who could only read; and 122,777 who could neither read nor write. Even so, these figures are misleading, since often those listed as being able to read and write could do so only on an elementary level and only in Lithuanian. Most of them never adequately learned English.

Although most Lithuanian immigrants were poor, the myth that they were totally impoverished and brought nothing to America but their hopes does not stand up to reality. For one thing, the law obliged every immigrant to prove that he had at least $30 to $50, and that he would not be an automatic charity case. For the period 1860–1900, it is estimated that immigrants brought $3,518,445 to the USA in cash, not counting the value of gold wedding rings, personal jewelry, or undeclared monies.

But the real wealth they brought with them was not in the few pennies they had been able to borrow or save. Their real wealth was themselves. It lay in their ability to work. Immigrants in this period amounted to a huge

---

* Only 82 Lithuanians lived in Wyoming as of 1970.

bonanza to American capitalism, for they came ready to work and at no cost. The expense of raising a native worker to the age of 16, calculated as between $1,700 to $2,000 before WWI—the expense of schooling, for instance—was saved, for most of the young men who came to America were over 14--16—and with no need for school.

Thus, for the 300,000 workers who came to the USA between 1860 and 1900, not a cent was spent for schools for them, for health or housing, for compensation when injured, or for pensions, running into billions. When they arrived, they tended to congregate in those areas where they had been promised jobs, and where colonies of Lithuanians already existed. In the beginning, the jobs were mainly in the coal mines of eastern and western Pennsylvania. There they were crammed into jerry-built shacks; or, if single, into boarding houses where they often shared the same bed—the day worker had the bed in the night but the night worker had it in the day. Other housing was mainly what was proferred by the companies they worked for—company houses. Those who scraped up enough money to make the down payment on a mortgage that entitled them to "their own" house, would be yoked to the bank for the rest of their lives as they kept paying off—finally able to pay no more than the compounded interest which grew like a cancer and took over and superseded the original amount.

Whole towns were nothing but company towns, whose every function was controlled by the company, which determined the rent, the price of goods, the payment for a ton of coal. Miners never saw real money but only company scrip, redeemable only in company stores. The company often instituted a check-off system of payments for the church of one's choice (whether one had chosen it or not). And, come election day, the worker found his poll tax receipt in his pay envelope—already paid for by the company. (It's little known that the poll tax was required, not only in the backward South but also in many of the company towns of the North.) Working conditions in the mines and mills were notoriously hazardous and unhealthy. Indeed, as far as the mine owners were concerned, it cost nothing to replace a killed miner. It cost $50 to replace a killed donkey.

At every stage of their lives in America they were preyed upon relentlessly by a variety of thieves: con men, politicians, salesmen, and priests. From the golden-voiced promise of an easy life with a well-paid job sung to them by company agents in their home villages (now but an aching memory) to the day when they died under a fall of caved-in rock, or choked on methane gas in mines with no safety, second exits, nor air ventilation, or disappeared in a flow of molten metal from a furnace break in the mill, human leeches stuck to their bodies and sucked the blood out of their veins. Accident rates in mills and factories were incredibly high. In Allegheny county, for instance, which contains the city of Pittsburgh, 525 men were killed in industrial accidents from July 4, 1906 to June 6, 1907. That is, one in four workers was either killed or seriously maimed by accidents for which he received no or only token compensation. Embarrassed by the sight of armies of men without hands and legs , with crushed-in faces, the company often volunteered to pay their passage back home—but not out of compassion. More justly, one has to say it was to clean up the environment, and to pass back to the mother country the expense of maintaining a hopelessly crippled and, therefore, useless worker.

Meager company insurance policies, paid for by the worker out of his own wages, but controlled by the company, barely paid for his modest burial expenses, his death usually directly or indirectly having been caused by his work in the mine or mill. Pneumonia was the chief cause of death among working miners and steel workers. The illness was due to the fact that at work they breathed in polluted air (often made up of bits of sharp steel dust or coal dust) which weakened their lungs and made them vulnerable to pneumonia. But since pneumonia was not directly attributed to work conditions, these deaths were not listed as industrial deaths.

Indeed, many were the towns up and down the three rivers meeting at Pittsburgh (Ohio, Allegheny and Monongahela) where the people lived in conditions lacking primitive protection against sewage pollution and contaminated water. For years, the Health Department of Allegheny County kept no records on sickness and death. To have done so would have revealed a pattern of neglect that underlay the appalling statistics of early deaths of men who came to this country with red cheeks and bulging muscles, the result of a life in the open and clean country air, from air pollution and typhoid.

These workers, who were not citizens—and couldn't become citizens unless they could prove literacy, or their vote was especially needed—had absolutely no rights whatsoever. They took no part in the social or political life, and indeed working 12 hours a day, seven days a week, hardly left time for anything after work but sleep. Nor did the record of deaths and illnesses, which always came like an epidemic in these towns each winter, taking off a crop of one-year-olds, impress those who ruled. Foreign-born workers were hardly more than a cut above the native-born Africans who, however, had been brought to this country over 200 years before and could speak English (though it did them no good).

To exploit others, to profit from their deaths without suffering a twinge of conscience, needs some kind of rationale—some philosophy which absolves one of guilt while in no way interfering with the cruel and inhumane way in which one used them. The most successful formula that ensured the dominance of one class over another was (and is) the ability to rationalize the superiority of one people over another. "Inferiors" had no rights, were not people. When a steel official was asked why he worked men 12 hours a day, seven days a week, with a "long" day (24 hours) in between shifts, he answered a Congressional investigating committee in 1912 that *he* didn't set the hours, the hours were set "by the laws of nature."

> The accident rate for non-English-speaking employees at the South Works steel mill from 1906 to 1910 was twice the average of the rest of the labor force. Almost one-quarter of the recent immigrants in the works each year—3273 in the five years—were injured or killed. In one year, 217 Eastern Europeans died in the steel mills of Allegheny county.[89]

Their deaths were hardly noticed. Writer Arno Dosch, in *Everybody's Magazine,* November 1911:

> "To think," I exclaimed, "that not a man was killed." "Who told you that?" asked the young assistant. "Why, it's here in this report sent to the newspapers by your press agent. He makes a point of it." The young assistant smiled... "Well, yes, I guess that's right," he replied. "There wasn't anyone killed except wops." "Except what?" "Wops. Don't you know what wops are? Dagoes, niggers, and Hungarians—the fellows that did the work. They don't know anything and they don't count."

And so one could murder them anonymously and even the statistics of their deaths would not appear publicly.

In this period, Andrew Carnegie—of whom Mark Twain quipped that he bought fame with cash—won international notice for giving libraries "free" to a number of towns in western Pennsylvania, where anyone could borrow books if he could read English and, after putting in a 12-hour day in Carnegie's mills—had enough energy or interest to do so.

It was on the "free" working power of the millions of European immigrants—as well as the total exploitation of the African slave—that American capital built its enormous industrial empire. Cheap. Nobody has worked out the cost in dollars and cents, and there is a good reason. If the total cost of building America in the early 19th and 20th centuries was calculated (including the wealth accumulated by stealing the lands of the Indians) one might possibly discover that the cost of building the Egyptian pyramids shrinks in comparison. At least, those slaves were fed by their masters.

It was in this set of circumstances that the Lithuanian Catholic Church, which played and plays so great a role in determining Lithuanian life in America, found its function.

CATHOLICS IN AMERICA

In every country and in every age, the priest has been
hostile to liberty. He is always in alliance with the despot...
—Thomas Jefferson, 1814

The future of Catholicism is in America.
—Cardinal Henry Edward Manning, 1808-1892

Who wants to cross swords (even crucifixes) with priests, bishops, cardinals and popes?

Thomas Jefferson, the architect of the revolutionary theses that were embodied in the American Constitution, wrote in 1802:

I contemplate with sovereign reverence that act of the whole American people which declared that their legislature should make no law respecting an establishment of religion, or prohibit the free exercise thereof, thus building a wall of separation between church and state.[90]

The very syntax of reason speaks from the following passage which he wrote to his nephew on August 10, 1787:

Do not be frightened from this inquiry by any fear of its consequences. If it ends in a belief that there is no God, you will find incitement to virtue in the comfort and pleasantness you feel in its exercise, and the love of others which it will procure you.[91]

And further to his nephew:

Shake off all the fears of servile prejudices, under which weak minds are servilely crouched. Fix reason firmly in her seat, and call on her tribunal for every fact, every opinion. Question with boldness even the existence of God, because if there be one, he must more approve of the homage of reason than of blindfolded fear.[92]

To another correspondent, Van der Kemp, he wrote in 1820:

It is not to be understood that I am with him [Jesus] in all his doctrines. I am a Materialist; he takes the side of Spiritualism; he preaches the efficacy of repentance toward forgiveness of sin; I require a counterpoise of good works to redeem it....[93]

Nevertheless:

Among the sayings and discourses imputed to him by his biographers, I find many passages of fine imagination, correct morality, and of most lovely benevolence....[94]

But also:

> ... of so much ignorance, so much absurdity, so much untruth, charlantism, imposture, as to pronounce it impossible that such contraditions should have proceeded from the same being.[95]

Jefferson was one of those great bourgeois revolutionaries, who in Engels' view, transcended their class limitations and "had anything but bourgeois limitations." Jefferson's way of thinking easily blends into Marx's and Engels' though he had never heard of Marx or Engels. It might be said of him, as with Moliere's *gentilhomme* who discovered to his surprise that he had been speaking prose all along, that Jefferson had been "speaking" Marxism all along.

And yet, though an atheist (or, as they put it, a "Deist"), who had no belief in "spiritualism," he nevertheless championed the right of any citizen to hold whatever religious views he wished and to be protected in holding and espousing them. Indeed, if it had not been for Jefferson, the Catholic Church (of which he had no high opinion) probably at this very hour would still be at bay as it was in America for most of America's 200-odd years. As late as 1884, it would be denounced in company with two other execrations "rum and rebellion," connected in the troika: "rum, Romanism and rebellion." "We are Republicans and don't propose to leave our Party and identify ourselves with the party (Democrats) whose antecedents are rum, Romanism and rebellion," thundered Samuel Dickinson Burchard in October, 1884, heading a delegation of clergymen to meet with James G. Blaine, presidential candidate.

The KKK listed Catholics among its enemies—which included Blacks and Jews. The climax of anti-Catholic sentiment in the USA came, perhaps, in 1928 when the Democratic Party nominated Al Smith, a Tammany Catholic, to run for the presidency, and untold thousands of free American voters literally believed that if Smith were elected president he would see to it that a tunnel was built between the White House in Washington leading to the Vatican in Rome.

Taking heed, the Catholic primates saw to it that the Church kept itself clear of politics, at least visibly. This fear of underground but relentless prejudice against Catholics was laid to rest—or at least, alleviated—with the election of John F. Kennedy to the presidency. A Catholic, Kennedy nevertheless made it clear that he believed in the separation of the church and the state.

Among the masses of emigres who poured into the USA after the war (1945) were many from one-time Catholic countries who not only retained their Catholicism but their fanatical hatred of all things "Communist." So extreme, so immune to all democratic amelioration of their views that they nurtured in emigre colonies for decades, with undiminished bitterness, that their fanaticism set them apart and in fact alienated normal public opinion. Probably none were as extreme as the Catholic Lithuanian fanatics. Their one-eyed view of life bred fantastic rhetorical monstrosities, like the following: "Towards the end of the Second World War a large number of musicians withdrew to Germany before the invading Russian forces entered Lithuania...."[96] Again: "A considerable number of Lithuanian artists ... felt they could only work in freedom, so in 1944, they fled to the West."[97]

But in 1944, to "flee" to the "West" meant "fleeing" to Germany, which nobody in his right mind mistook at that time as a haven of freedom. In fact, thousands of Lithuanians had already come to Germany even before 1944, but they were *driven, forced* to go, and ended up in concentration camps and—as the U.S. War Refugee Board noted (November 25, 1944), 50,000 of them ended up in Auschwitz. Writers like V. Montvila and T. Tilvyte, I. Simonaitigte, J. Butens were either shot or tortured to death or died in the camps.

One struggles to understand the mind that saw in the Russian Army, with its Lithuanian 16th Division, before whose advance the Nazis fled pell-mell also "to the West," only foreign "invaders," "occupiers." One did not read anywhere that the French called the American army an "invading" army when it entered France.

The hatred of all things "Russian" goes so deep that this hatred replaces every other function of the mind and even the body. It *becomes* the mind, the body.

Pathology has played a distinct role in the Cold and the various hot wars. We do not normally wish to dicker with people who make lamp shades out of human skins. But in the last big war we found a use for them. What they offered was an absolute fixation that needed no additional persuasion, was immune to doubt or logic, and functioned in the dead air of suspended morality. In anti-Communism, all the underground streams of national resentment, racial hatred, petty-bourgeois jealousies and envies meet and find expression, sanctioned by a Higher Power (church or state). The *Kapo* who carried out diabolical tortures on his helpless victims before dispatching them, knew, however remotely, that his actions were privileged and—*needed.*

Among the colonies of Lithuanians in the USA, the Church played a distinct role. It not only offered religious solace to the Lithuanian immigrants but also those forms of social activity, limited as they were, open to them. The Church baptized one's child, and came to anoint it when it lay dying, and officiated at its burial. It was the confidant of personal secrets and sins. Although the men often men worked on Sundays in the mines and mills, their wives and infant children did not. (Boys worked with miners and in mills.) For the wives, churches were the only haven, the only diversion, outside the home. And around the Church grew up the only form of social life the immigrant was to know for years, and which his children—and most certainly his grandchildren—finally broke with.

The Church also ran parochial schools in which Lithuanian children, though born in America, were taught as though they had been born in Lithuania. The parochial schools existed apart from the public schools, and though parents had to pay tuition to the parochial schools, this did not exempt them from paying a "school tax" in support of the public schools. Catholics paid for other church "services" as well: for special masses, blessings, grave rents, etc. Those families who wanted to take advantage of free public schooling were anathematized from the pulpit, threatened with excommunication and with the loss of certain benefits—especially the loss of burial in "sacred" soil.

All churches enjoyed the support of authority. This included the Catholic Church though by and large, up through World War I, it was clear that most members of the ruling class (a term objected to but nevertheless inevitable) were Protestant, or Episcopalian, and Catholics were looked down on and merely tolerated. Often the corporate officials of the mine or mill made donations or outright gifts to the churches (all denominations), which included even such practical "gifts" as directly financing a new roof for the church, painting the walls, or making repairs of all kinds. In some instances they supplied the churches with electricity from their own sources. In return, corporate America expected the Church to use its influence to bank down working-class anger and resentment, and, indeed, this service the Church sedulously supplied.

The children who were sent to parochial schools were as distinctly separated from children who went to public schools as were *they* from upper class children who went to private schools. Such distinctions bred hostility. Early, the children of the "foreign-born" learned that they were aliens, pariahs, and because they were easily identified by their names—names that ended in "ski" or "ciwz," etc.—they changed their names as soon as they could change their home addresses. One of the problems in tracing Lithuanians in America is the fact that, by the second generation, they had new names.*

They suffered not only from ethnic discrimination, but from the fact that the education given in parochial schools was manifestly inferior to that given in the public schools. Parochial schools were staffed with under-educated, emotionally starved nuns, who had chosen the Church rather than

* For instance, the actor Charles Bronson's real name is Casimir Businskis; the British Lawrence Harvey was born Laurynas Skinkis.

an early marriage with a doomed mill worker, or a life of prostitution, and who taught the children not so much how to read and write but the crucial difference between venial and mortal sin. Laggards were speeded up by beatings with rattans, pointers or heavy straps.

Harassment took overt and sinister form. The KKK included Catholics with "niggers and Jews" and "foreigners" as mortal enemies. Before and after WWI, the KKK had enormous influence, a large membership, and its "invisible empire" literally dominated the social scene. At one time it included among its members Senators and even one president (President Harding). In 1925, they were able to stage a march of 40,000 along Pennsylvania Avenue in Washington, D.C., making the (Italian) fascist salute as they went. In the Company working-class towns all over America, and not only in the South, but especially in the mine and steel towns of Pennsylvania, they maintained visible organizations to which members of the American Legion belonged, as well as officials of the mills and of the city councils, and all those who depended on them or feared them.

Foreigners were endured on sufferance. The myth that America was hospitable to foreigners is built largely on retelling the success stories of the usual handful of the exceptionally gifted, determined, ruthless or opportunist (as is typical today of African Americans). During the infamous "Palmer raids" of the 1920s, something like 10,000 aliens were summarily rounded up as possible subversives, held in prison without a hearing, and hundreds were deported to the country from which they had emigrated, forced to leave (often) an American-born wife and children behind. This ruthless attack against foreigners was based on principles anticipating Hitler's racism. The then attorney-general, A. Mitchell Palmer, who masterminded the raids, explained it this way: "We must purify the sources of America's population." During the postwar period, the McCarran-Walter Act effectively kept 10,000 "subversives" from entering the USA even for a visit.

Persecuted for simply being "foreign," those immigrants before and for some time after World War I, who were also workers (and most were) and found themselves involved in a strike or in illegally helping to build a union, or joining one (which most did), suffered a kind of double jeopardy—as aliens (therefore suspect) and as workers (therefore, potential revolutionaries).

The great steel strike of 1919, which was the first nationwide strike in American history, involved a majority of the "foreign-born," among them many Lithuanians, and this, of course, made them most suspect of all. Wrote William Z. Foster (1920), who organized and led the famous steel strike of 1919:

Everywhere American-born working men, unfortunately, are prone to look with
some suspicion, if not contempt and hatred, upon foreigners, whom they have
been taught to believe are injuring their standard of living. The companies made
the most of this. Dubbing the walkout a "hunky" strike, they told the Americans
that if it succeeded the latter would have to give over to the despised foreigners
all the good jobs and shop privileges they enjoyed. Their slogan was, "Don't let
the 'hunkies' rule the mills." They openly circulated handbills inciting to race
war....

In towns where often the foreign population is three-fourths of the whole,
such propaganda was most inflammatory. The newspapers did all they could to
make it more so. They solemnly warned of the danger of a foreign uprising and
advised a campaign of militant, 100 percent Americanism; which meant, on the
one hand, for the local authorities, gunmen, and businessmen to set up a reign of
terror, and on the other, for the workers to go back to work at once. The courts
and so-called peace officers did their part. They jailed, clubbed and shot the
foreigners and left the Americans, even if they were strikers, in comparative
immunity....

But if the Americans and skilled workers generally proved indifferent union
men in the steel campaign, the foreign, unskilled workers covered themselves
with glory....

This attitude of the foreign workers is a bitter pill for the Steel trust. For
many years it had scoured the countries of Eastern and Southern Europe, and
packed its mills with poor, dispirited, ignorant immigrants of three score nationalities, in the hope it was finally supplanting its original crew of independent
American and Western European workers by a race of submissive, unorganiz-
able slaves.... [98]

Among the strikers were many Lithuanians, and Foster records that
"suddenly the Lithuanian Society deposed its President, who was friendly
to the steel company, and voted to give its hall to the unions, permits or no
permits." (To speak anywhere one had first to get a permit from the
Mayor's office, inspiring the famous declaration made by the mayor of
Duquesne, James F. Crawford, that "I wouldn't give Jesus Christ a permit
to speak for the AFL in Duquesne!" After all, Christ was a foreigner and
agitator to boot!)

Historically, the church acted as a center of attraction and social cohe-
sion among emigrant Lithuanians. Small worlds were created around the
church as the hub. One could be born, christened, educated, married, and
buried without, so to speak, touching "America" except as a worker. Knowing no English or knowing it badly, most immigrants found that the church
was the only place where Lithuanian was used both in Mass and in social
affairs. In this respect, the church served as a preserver of the language,
and a curator of native customs and traditions, keeping alive the national
consciousness, though always in the context of religion. Although the
church was located in what was undeniably America, it existed as though it
was located somehow still in Lithuania. As noted, it was the curator of

Lithuanian custom and the language. But it was also the breeder of a strange provincialism.

Most Lithuanian immigrants, either openly and definitely, or as a secret dream, planned at some point to return home. Once they had saved enough money for passage back, and a bit more to buy land with, they expected to return. Their stay here was tentative. That being so, they made little effort to learn the language or adapt to the customs of America. America was "them." Yet, though they dreamed of going home, few actually could save enough money to do so. Between 1899 and 1914, of about 250,000 Lithuanian immigrants, only 19,000 returned, some of these maimed or sick.

The church was powerful among Lithuanians, but among other Catholics it was weak. For even among Catholic churches there was a pecking order—a ladder of authority and influence. Classified as second-class citizens (if they became citizens at all), the church Lithuanians attended was also classified as second class. The Irish Church (as well as the older German) wielded much more influence than the Lithuanian could, and only because, in the case of the Irish, though immigrants no less lowly than the East Europeans, nevertheless they had the advantage of speaking English. Indeed, knowing English was a distinct advantage to Irish workers, for they were the first chosen to become straw bosses, foremen, policemen, etc. In the cities, particularly New York and Boston and Pittsburgh, they entered politics in a big way. Tammany was an Irish invention, and for years determined New York politics, openly in league with the Catholic Church, which meant that in New York State it was almost impossible to obtain a divorce, and for years it was totally illegal to have an abortion. Not for just Catholics—but the whole citizenry.

The typical company town in Pennsylvania contained 30 or more separate religions, each with its own church. Even among Catholics, the Irish, Germans, Poles, Lithuanians, Slovaks, Italians, and, later, the Hispanics had their own churches, with corresponding prestige or lack of it—determined not by their degree of piety but by their political clout.

The towns were veritable Towers of Babel, and that was reflected in the work force of the mines and mills. Typical was Duquesne, a company steel town of some 12,000 located 12 miles south of Pittsburgh, which employed 6,075 workers from 33 different nationalities, most of whom could not communicate with one another, except through a kind of mill pidgin "English." In that mill there were 201 Lithuanians (only three Latvians and no Estonians). This gallimaufry of nationalities was a conscious corporation policy, the idea simply being that workers who could not talk to each other could not "conspire."

Although the Lithuanian church was the center in many towns of Lithuanian immigrant life, it did not totally monopolize it. For one thing, in the beginning, there were not enough Lithuanians, or churches (Duquesne had no Lithuanian church), or priests to serve the people, and often Lithuanians shared churches with the Poles, creating a situation that continued in religious garb the historical antagonism of Lithuanians for Poles, for power. Bitter, often bloody battles broke out among parishioners for ownership of the church. Priests fought priests.

The other Lithuanian force that opposed the would-be monopoly of the Church arose from non- and often anti-religious sources, many of them strongly influenced by socialist ideas. They were bitter opponents of the Church hierarchy, not so much on strictly religious grounds (even some atheists chose to have at least their children baptized) as on political and ideological grounds. They had a certain (sometimes more, sometimes less) influence among the conscious workers and established their own newspapers and publishing houses, choral groups, theater, literary, fraternal and insurance societies. Lithuanians played a significant role in the founding of the American Communist Party. On September 1, 1919, of eighteen Lithuanian delegates, two were elected to the executive committee. In New York's Brooklyn, they published *Laisve* (Liberty), and in Chicago, *Vilnis* (Vilnius), both newspapers with a socialist orientation. The movement produced outstanding personalities like Anthony Bimba, of *Laisve*, Lithuanian born but brought to the USA in 1913 as a child, a noted authority on labor history in the USA. He also authored the standard work on the Irish underground miners organization, the so-called Molly Maguires, which remains a basic study of that part of the American miners in Eastern Pennsylvania. Roy Mizara, also an outstanding immigrant Lithuanian, wrote a number of novels dealing with life in America for Lithuanian immigrants. But he wrote, unlike Bimba, in Lithuanian. At his death, his ashes were buried in Lithuania—as were Bimba's.

Another outstanding personality was Margaret Cowl (Kavaluciate) who became a member of the Central Committee of the American Communist Party in the '30s and '40s.

In fact, there is no aspect of American working class life, its struggle to grow, its struggle for recognition, where Lithuanians did not play some role. One of the four martyred marchers in the Ford Hunger Strike of 1932 was a Lithuanian youth, Joe York (Yorkus). Lithuanians were part of the struggle to organize the miners, the steel workers, the auto workers—wherever the struggle was, there was a Lithuanian there, too.

Needless to say, none of the working class heroes are even noticed in the various books purportedly reporting the activities of Lithuanians in America. Those noted are the already accepted, the "Americanized," the orthodox.

So, as in all social questions, there were at least two trends—the non-conformist, revolutionary, working class. And the other: those who accommodated themselves to the powers that be, and learned precisely how to render to Caesar that which was Caesar's, and to God, that which was God's. But in the case of the Lithuanians their God, borrowed from Rome, never quite lost his pagan predecessor's aspect—Perkunas, god of thunder and lightning.

Those Lithuanians before WWI who left their homeland never left it in their hearts. Those who fled Czarist-oppressed Lithuania to the USA, initiated and pursued a struggle supporting those still in Lithuania. They sent in smuggled books and periodicals printed in Lithuanian at a time when nobody in Lithuania was allowed to read Lithuanian.

When World War I ended, they saw in the meetings of the Four Powers at Versailles the hope of Lithuanian independence, particularly as President Wilson had so often and so loudly proclaimed his support of "small nations" and of their independence.

But Lithuanians abroad were divided over how or if to support the infant socialist government set up in Lithuania in 1918 as an organic part of the Russian revolution the year before. The roar of the cannon on the battleship *Aurora* in St. Petersburg was taken to be the signal for not only the rising of the Russian workers, but of workers the whole world over. Indeed, revolutions appeared, if not all at the same time, in the Baltics, in Hungary, in Bavaria, and movements for revolution flourished everywhere.

Advanced Lithuanians, like immigrants from most Eastern European countries, hailed the revolution and on news of it, there was dancing in the streets of New York City. Indeed, the revolution had the fervent support of all of progressive America, and the statement of Eugene Debs, leader of the Socialist Party and opponent of America's entry into WWI for which he was imprisoned, wrote: "The world stands amazed, astounded, awe-inspired, in the presence of Russia's stupendous achievement."[99] He would also declare: "From the crown of my head to the soles of my feet, I am a Bolshevik, and proud of it."[100] Helen Keller, who would soon become world-renowned for her extraordinary and indomitable will that conquered blindness, deafness and muteness, denounced the hypocrisy of the American policy of opposition to the revolution "half-secretly and in the dark with the lie of democracy on their lips...."[101]

The Church did not see in the liberation of Lithuania from the Czarist yoke hope for itself, and backed those groups which opposed revolutionary Lithuania. Nevertheless, so widespread was the support for the new revolutionary government that an attempt to raise a Lithuanian contingent—Knights of Lithuania—to fight the "Bolsheviks" shoulder to shoulder with the Germans (who, though defeated in Europe were encouraged to continue fighting in the Baltics)—was ignored.

Nevertheless, pro- (as it turned out) Smetona groups were active in America supporting those forces in Lithuania which were destined to rule that country for two bloody decades. Led by the Lithuanian American Council, a bourgeois organization violently opposed to socialism in any form, they lobbied in Washington for American recognition of their counterparts in Lithuania. Although wishing to meet with Wilson himself, they were shunted off to meet with "Commissioner of Public Information," the notorious George Creel, who is credited today with being the father of the modern technique of disinformation.

It was Creel who invented the tale of the German Huns cutting off the hands of Belgian children, a totally fabricated tale which played a key role in turning American public opinion, which had been overwhelmingly neutralist, into an anti-German, pro-war direction.

The American Lithuanians were generally disappointed in President Wilson's reluctance to take an open stand for Lithuanian "independence." Wilson, like the other allied leaders, did not really believe in the viability or even desirability of "independence" for any of the Baltic states. In his and their view, the Baltics had only one role to play—as buffer pawns against the spread of Bolshevism. In any case, Wilson held that the Baltic states were organically part of Russia, and once Lenin was disposed of, and *The New York Times* kept telling him daily that he was about to be, and a proper regime, like Kerensky's, was installed, then the Baltic nations would once again resume their natural positions within the Russian empire.

But George Creel was much craftier, and whatever he believed about the future fate of the Baltic nations, he understood the value of putting such reactionaries as those now petitioning him in political debt to American power. And America had a distinct stake in a future Russia, and to ensure that there would be a stake there, the administration sent an army of 9,000 to Archangel to suppress the revolutionaries who had taken over power.

Nevertheless, the Lithuanians got nowhere with Wilson in Washington as Voldemaras would get nowhere with him (and the others) at the Paris Peace Conference in 1919.

But the American Lithuanians did not rest. In their zeal to popularize Lithuania's cause among the American people along nationalist lines—and the American people couldn't care less—(they never did clear up in their own minds whether the Baltics were the Balkans, in northern or in southern Europe)—they were not too squeamish where they went for help.

They contacted Carl Byoir, Associate Director General of the Committee on Public Information, one of those "publicity organizations" which later would flourish to such an extent that no public figure felt clothed without the protection of one. Then, however, Byoir was still somewhat in a pioneering position, needing to fight the prejudice that some diehard Americans clung to in wanting public figures to speak straight out in their own voices and not through in-betweens who wrote their speeches, and set up "photo opportunities," as later they would be quaintly called.

In 1919, future Nazism was still no more than a diseased gleam in Nietzsche's eyes and a festering microbe in the heads of a few Germans. But Carl Byoir was already deeply involved in secret dealings with extremely dubious forces in Europe. The task given to him by the Lithuanians appealed to him on ideological grounds. Byoir was associated not only professionally but ideologically with George Sylvester Viereck, an exposed and convicted German agent, indeed a spy for the Kaiser, who nevertheless enjoyed remarkable immunity in the USA, ultimately taking on U.S. citizenship—and continuing to spy, now for Hitler. As an American citizen, along with the equally notorious "information publicity" agent, Ivy Lee, Viereck busily promoted pro-Nazi propaganda in the USA when Hitler came to power, again being convicted, again serving short time, and again being sprung to go on spying as before.

In the early '30s, Byoir would be paid $108,500 by the German Railroad Information Bureau, which engaged in espionage under the guise of a tourist agency.[102]

Carl Byoir's career reeks of corruption, cynicism, even of espionage. Here, according to George Seldes, is what Carl Byoir "a confessed... agent of Nazi Fascism" was really like:

> In September, 1933, the firm of Carl Byoir and Associates was hired, according to testimony before the McCormack-Dickstein Committee, to present the Hitler viewpoint in America. It sent its junior partner, Carl D. Dickey, and a wartime German-American propagandist, George Sylvester Viereck, to interview Hitler, Goering, Goebbels, Frick and Schact in Berlin for the purpose of preparing a series of "unbiased and unprejudiced" articles for American readers. The contract called for $60,000 a month and was nominally for the purpose of stimulating travel in Germany by propaganda for the German (Government) railroad system. Defending himself before the investigators, Viereck declared that "there is not the slightest touch of impropriety in the contract between Byoir & Associates and the German railroads nor in my connection with that distinguished firm...."
>
> The investigating committee, however, learned from Mr. Dickey that in 1933 his agency received $4000 from the German Consul General in New York, Herr Kiep, to "explain" Hitler's attack on the Jews in well-written publicity releases....[103]

Byoir had worked during WWI for "the American propaganda machine (the committee on 'misinformation' as it was generally called by journalists) presided over by George Creel, and after the war he moved to Cuba where he became publisher of *Havana Post* and the *Havana Telegram*." There he functioned as a propaganda apologist for the bloody Machado regime, for which he handed out "globs of free stuff," which hid the reality of the bloody dictator whose record for murder and torture was second to none.

Viereck was sentenced to prison not as a Nazi agent in 1941, which he was registered with the Justice Department as being, but for suppressing vital information about his motives and actions. Carl Byoir escaped such indictment and continued his ways—getting paid $500,000 from the Pennsylvania Railroad in the 1950s for his work in their campaign against the truckers, in which he saw to it that at least five members of the Pennsylvania legislature were bribed.

Byoir's record was well known for years. But although the book which boasts of how helpful Byoir was to the cause of Lithuanian "independence" in 1919 was published in 1975, no hint of disapproval, embarrassment, let alone shame can be found anywhere in it in connection with his name. Byoir was an open supporter and spy for the Nazis. The American Lithuanian Nationalists couldn't care less.

Indeed, their attitude toward Byoir was part of a pattern. Any enemy of "Communism" was friend to the Nationalists. Nazi Germany was never excoriated in the ultimately reductive terms of denunciation that the Soviets were. Actually, of course, the Nationalists cooperated with them—the documentation is overwhelming. They came back into Lithuania from exile with the German army and departed again from Lithuania with the German Army. It was conceivably possible that the trains that brought them into Lithuania from Germany in 1941 passed long freight trains coming out of Lithuania and into Germany loaded with Lithuanian cattle—and with Lithuanians. The cattle ended up on the tables of the German hausfrau, and the Lithuanians in the crematoria of Auschwitz. Even so, they—the cremated— quite possibly also ended up on the tables of the German hausfrau, for their ashes were used as fertilizer to grow the fat German cabbage.

All of Lithuanian emigre church literature reeks of hatred, blind, unforgivable, to-the-death hatred, and where such Nationalist and religious hatred exists together, anti-Semitism is not far away. Example:

> Dr. Bielskis made a similar report. Socialists pressing about him urged him to "tell the Lithuanian Socialists in America about our situation and activity. With Bulota at the head, the American Socialists must have gone out of their minds. They collect donations for impoverished Lithuania but do not transmit the money. The little they do send goes only to a Jewish organization." "Lithuanian Socialists told me many things and asked that I let the American Socialists know, but I explained to them that the Lithuanian Socialist in America is a creature with whom it is very difficult to communicate."[104]

Indeed, in 1916, when this episode occurred, the very reference was to "socialists," not yet Communists, for the Communist Party was yet to come, is marinated in an acid of anti-"communism." Dr. Bielskis had been a Nationalist delegate from the USA to Vilnius in 1916 and had made his organization's opposition to "Bolshevism," not yet in power in Russia, clear from the start.

Already quite explicitly stated, Nationalist (*cum* Church) anti-socialism meant hostility to all progressive and advanced social measures. As for the Church, it had a materialist stake in a social system that allowed it to own large areas of land and coin profits from the unpaid or low-paid labor of its workers. Although there were exceptions, and by no means monolithic agreement inside it, the operating fact remained that the Church was to the oncoming Nazis an ally, not an enemy. Driven by this one-dimensional obsession, the Church turned a blind eye to the unspeakable horrors and endless monstrosities committed by the Nazis which the Church, in its own right, and through the Nationalists, aided and abetted.

The record is clear, and 50 years later amply documented. Even the flight of some 300 Lithuanian priests westward to Nazi Germany, which was by then nothing but a huge death camp for all democrats of whatever stripe, is eloquent testimony of where they felt safe.* To see the liberation of Lithuania in 1944 by the Red Army, led by its 16th Lithuanian Division, as an "invasion" is the ultimate in self-mutilation.

Most of the Lithuanians who in one way or another had compromised themselves during the Nazi occupation fled, hopefully to the USA, but in any case beyond the reach of justice. Readers should be reminded that a secret, unpublicized policy of smuggling war criminals into the United States, and elsewhere, was operating and effectively supplying ratlines not only to the big criminals like Klaus Barbie and Joseph Mendele (helped to go to Latin America) but to literally thousands of smaller ones, and others not so small.

Following the vow adopted at Potsdam to pursue Nazi criminals "to the ends of the earth," the Displaced Persons Commission had sought to weed out just such criminals from the 400,000 displaced persons who applied for entry into the USA between 1948 and 1952. But in 1950, a sharp turn was made in this policy. Among those who benefited from American "liberalism" toward previous Nazi criminals was the Baltic Legion, known in Eastern Europe as the Baltic Waffen, directly connected with the German Waffen, Hitler's elite guard, guilty of numberless crimes. The justification for absolving the Baltic Legion was the U.S. governmental "finding" that "the Baltic Legion not to be a movement hostile to the United States..."

---

* Of these 300, "almost 200" came to the USA but proved to be a problem to the Church for not enough Lithuanian Catholic Churches existed in the USA to absorb them, and most were given non-Lithuanian assignments.

The imperatives of the Cold War had turned all former enemies into friends, bloody tyrants into "democrats." It was from among these specially anointed criminals that the ranks of American Lithuanians, Latvians and Estonians found their ideological leaders, and who today are active once again in their home countries, now posing as "democrats" who believe in "pluralism," but who are supplied with huge amounts of money from the National Endowment for Democracy with which they buy up as many "democrats" in these countries as they can. Lithuanian "democrats" of the Landsbergis variety in particular have benefited enormously from this largesse.

Of 84,400 suspected German war criminals against whom legal proceedings had actually been instituted in West Germany, only 6,430 had been sentenced in the 20 years following the end of the war. Most cases were dismissed by the same judges who had passed death sentences on more than 5,000 anti-fascists for their opposition to Hitler. Thousands of others were summarily executed by decision of the Nazi "special courts."

But when it came to bringing the guilty to justice, the wheels turned with agonizing slowness. SS men who had been in charge of Maideneck concentration camp and carried out innumerable acts of bestiality on the helpless prisoners were brought to trial at Dusseldorf. The preliminary investigation took 15 years! Of the 17 criminals indicted, eight escaped trial altogether, and four were let off "for insufficient evidence." The rest of the trial lasted another five years and seven months, resulting in a single life sentence and token sentences to the others.

Most Germans (which included the collaborators in the Baltics) managed to "escape" to Western Germany where they found "understanding." Thousands fled the country, many of them—one of every 10 Nazi criminals, it has been estimated—ended up in the USA, often with new names and new biographies arranged for them by the American special services.

Writes Christopher Simpson in his well-documented *Blowback*:

The most important Western ratlines that have come to light thus far, including those that smuggled Nazis, operated in and through the Vatican in Rome. Unraveling the reasons why and how the Catholic Church became involved in Nazi smuggling is an important step in understanding the broader evolution of the post-war alliance between former Nazis and U.S. intelligence agencies. One organization is worthy of close scrutiny. It is the prominent Catholic lay group known as Intermarium. During its heyday in the 1940s and early 1950s, leading members of this organization were deeply involved in smuggling Nazi fugitives out of Eastern Europe to safety in the West. Later, Intermarium also became one of the single most important sources of recruits for the CIA's exile committees. This can be said with some certainty because about a score of Intermarium leaders ended up as activists or officials of Radio Free Europe, Radio Liberation, and the Assembly of Captive European Nations (ACEN), each of which the U.S. government has since admitted as having been a CIA-financed and controlled organization.[105]

LATVIANS IN AMERICA

Make a sled of dog bones
Carry off the forester.
Look, you people!
Dogs are carrying a dog.
                    —Latvian folk song

It is a matter of historical record that many Nazi-collaborating governments in Eastern Europe were Catholic-led. Before the war they had followed ultra-reactionary policies, which led without a hitch into open alliance with Hitlerism once the war began. They served as the native, cooperating governments when occupied, as with Slovakia, where Father Monsi-
gnor Josef Tiso willingly served as puppet for Berlin, justifying and sanctify-
ing the ruthless murder of 75,000 Slovakian Jews. In their antiSemitism
they were given at least implicit moral support in Catholic teachings going
back to the Middle Ages, in which Jews were held directly and forever
responsible for the death of Christ.

The Vatican set up various agencies to handle the flow of "refugees,"
many of them "refugees" only from justice. In Rome, the Lithuanians had
Reverend Jatulevicius, through whose hands passed most if not all the
Lithuanian priests who fled justice.

Reveals the U.S. State Department intelligence report of May 1947,
(cited by Christopher Simpson) "... the Vatican ... is the largest single
organization involved in the illegal movement of emigrants...", and in those
Latin American countries "where the Church is a controlling or dominating
factor, the Vatican brought pressure to bear which has resulted in the
foreign missions of those countries taking an attitude almost favoring the
entry into their countries of former Nazis and former Fascists or other
political groups, so long as they are anti-Communist...."[106]

Simpson also reveals, citing declassified U.S. State Department and army
intelligence records, that Intermarium was rooted in "an alliance of mili-
tantly anti-Communist Catholic lay organizations from Eastern Europe established in the mid-1930s. The Abwehr (German military intelligence service) used Intermarium contacts as prewar 'agents of influence' abroad, as
well as reasonably reliable sources of information on the large emigre
communities of Europe. By the time the Nazis marched across the Conti-

nent, Intermarium had become, in the words of a U.S. Army intelligence report, 'an instrument of the German intelligence....'"

The aim of the organization was to "unite nations 'from the Baltic to the Aegean' in a common front against the USSR." Since their aims and ideology coincided, the mathematics of life itself ("things equal to the same thing are equal to each other") arranged for organic cooperation, and "a number of its leaders actively collaborated with the Nazis."

After the defeat of the Nazis, Intermarium, through its *Bulletin*, issued in January 1947, called for "amalgamated common armed forces of the Intermarium" whose ultimate aim was to destroy the USSR by "crushing her military strength and partioning her into ... free states in their ethnical borders...."

The present (1991) drive to dismember the USSR is an almost faithful reproduction of what was already a well-developed scenario, not the sole possession of Intermarium, but of all the Western intelligence services, and most notably the American.

Intermarium functioned as a conduit for criminal escapees. It provided numerous ratlines down which the aptly named "rats" escaped in droves, carrying their anti-democratic bacillus with them, with many of them winding up in the USA, which facilitated their entry into this country by conspiring to evade the law. The law explicitly refused entry to Nazis and Nazi-collaborators. The CIA, State Department, Immigration Service, etc., not only conspired to smuggle criminals into the USA but gave them false identities and smoothed their path to becoming citizens. It is of more than passing interest to note that among the several Attorney Generals in charge of executing this policy of bringing Nazis into the USA was Tom Clark who, while with one hand he aided Nazi criminals, with the other he set into motion the legal machinery to crush the Left in America, starting with the plot against ex-vice president Henry Wallace and his Progressive Party, as well as the Communist Party itself.

Not only were the Lithuanian priests who had, in one way or another collaborated with the Nazis and Nationalists allowed to enter the country, but many other equally criminal Nationalists of a whole series of countries were also helped. It's estimated that some 10,000 criminals or possible criminals were given special entry permits into the USA. Only the most notorious of them were ever identified and exposed, and only a mere handful were ever sent back to their home countries to stand trial.

To cite Simpson again:

> The Latvian component of Intermarium was among the most deeply compromised by its services to the Nazi war machine, yet a number of its most prominent members entered the United States. They went on to play leading roles in what are now known to have been CIA-funded emigre projects inside the country.

The Latvian Fascist Perkonkrust Fuhrer Gustav Celmins, for example, had organized a Latvian SS unit in 1941 and served as a Nazi agent inside nationalist circles throughout the war. He went on to become an officer in the powerful Rome branch of Intermarium. Celmins entered the United States as a displaced person in 1950 and was quickly hired as a teacher in a Russian studies program in Syracuse, New York; a state college with a history of ties to American intelligence agencies. Celmins eventually fled to Mexico following a newspaper series that exposed his efforts to organize anti-Semitic activities among Latvian exiles in the United States.

Other Latvian emigres in Intermarium include Alfreds Berzins and Boleslavs Maikovskis, both of whom were wanted on war crimes charges and both of whom ended up on the payroll of CIA-financed organizations during the 1950s. They served as leaders of the Committee for a Free Latvia and the International Peasant Union respectively, which were bankrolled with agency funds laundered through RFE/RL and the related Assembly of Catholic European Nations (ACEN)....

CIA money paid for the ACEN's political congresses, provided substantial personal stipends to emigre leaders like Berzins, and in some cases, published transcripts of their speeches in book form. Many Intermarium activists became guests of RFE/RL broadcasts, and the radio stations aggressively promoted the organizations they represented throughout the 1950s. CIA money laundered through Radio Free Europe ... also financed the publication of the book *The Assembly of Captive European Nations* which presented the proceedings of the first ACEN congress in New York and included commentaries by Berzins and the Albanian Bloodstone emigre Hasan Dosti, among others. This text was distributed free of charge to virtually every library, newspaper and radio station in the United States and Europe....[107]

Latvian Nationalist activity in the USA did not have as great scope as the Lithuanian, for the simple reason that there were fewer Latvians (and fewer still Estonians) in the USA. The 1970 census noted 41,707 Latvian-born, while 44,706 were already of the next generation, American-born, with only 86,413 altogether identifiable as Latvians. (Like Lithuanians and Estonians they tended to disappear into the general population by inter-marriage).

But as with the Lithuanians, the only qualification that any Latvian criminal needed to enter the USA was Allen Dulles' very simple one, which he cited to explain why he dealt so hospitably with the head of German intelligence, Reinhard Gehlen: "He's on our side and that's all that matters."

Even so, as events would later demonstrate only too graphically, there were different interpretations of what "on our side" meant; for the Pentagon Papers and later the revelations of the Watergate scandal and the Iran-gate scandal, opened up a quick view into another interpretation of what "our side" meant: "our side" was a hidden, secret and underground "side" which ran the visible government invisibly (until exposed), behind the scenes.

A U.S.-adopted program labeled "Bloodstone" put into operation before even the end of the war an extensive plot—and here "plot" is used advisedly—to destabilize and hopefully to destroy the Soviet Union from within. Important to this scheme was the dedicated help of emigre nationals from the various Eastern European countries, including the Baltic, which, once they were passed through the porous immigration barrier, which let them in and kept Picasso, "a Communist" out, they set up anti-Soviet programs or took over already existing ones. Directly under the funding and tutelage of the CIA, they became sources of endless propaganda and agitation against the socialist regimes in their home countries. Organizations like the Committee for a Free Latvia and United Relief Fund of America and other "religious" organizations were the beneficiaries of a $100 million CIA slush fund between 1950 and 1960. In the early '80s, the functions of the CIA were taken over by the Reagen-installed National Endowment for Democracy which then funnelled additional millions to organizations staffed with out-and-out war criminals, as well as their American-born counterparts.

A notorious case in point is the Daugavas Vanagi (Hawks of the Daugava River), which was an organization run totally by Latvian escaped criminals but funded by the CIA. Vanagi had started out life by helping Latvian SS veterans in Germany, who had "escaped" to that country at war's end. Many of them had been active fascists in prewar Latvia and when the Nazis invaded Latvia they became active collaborators, making up the bulk of the extermination squads. Many had become officers of the Latvian Waffen SS division and, by all the standards for determining war guilt, they over-qualified. Indeed, to them fell the "honor" of committing such excessive barbarity that even some of the Germans recoiled. Instead of being hung from the end of a rope by their fellow Latvians, which they richly deserved, they "escaped" to eventually the USA where their particular skills were newly appreciated, where their nights were cozy and meals sumptuous. As for their consciences, just as they had turned them over—the way one turns over one's coat for someone to hold for a moment—to Hitler when Hitler ordered them to, now they turned them over to the Americans. The Americans told them that their killing "Communists," even "Communists" in their mothers' wombs, was okay, and that was A-okay with them too! So much so that today some of them have had the unbelievable arrogance to return to Latvia and even demand pensions for their sufferings in the war against the Communists!

In the USA, members of the Vanagi spread throughout the Latvian community and eventually came to dominate the native organizations, other than their own, like the National Federation, and the Committee for a Free Latvia which, however, already was nippled by the CIA. Many of the Latvian emigres were known criminals, especially men like Vilis Hazners,

Boleslavs Markovskis, and Alfreds Berzins. Their entry into the USA was paved with lies. If you pressed on one of those lies blood would gush forth.

Especially notable among Latvian exile groups is the World Federation of Free Latvians, which is affiliated with the Coalition for Peace Through Strength, a violence-oriented anti-Soviet organization. The "Free Latvians" speak of branches in six other countries. "Its U.S. branch, the American Latvian Association, is active in the campaign against the Justice Department's Office of Special Investigation ... The book *Inside the League*, describes the ABN (Anti-Bolshevik Bloc of Nations) Latvian affiliate as a band of Latvian leaders who assisted the Nazis in exterminating the Jews of their Baltic homeland."*

The ABN is not shy about admitting its connections with Hitler. In a booklet published in 1960, it says:

> That many of us fought on the German side against Russian imperialism and Bolshevism, was in our national interest ... the fact that some of us fought on the German side against Russia can be justified from the national political and moral point of view.**

---

* *Old Nazis, the New Right, and the Reagan Administration*, by Russ Bellant, Political Research Associates, Cambridge, 1988, p. 51

** *The Truth About ABN*, by Molp Malasjodze, ABN Press and Information Bureau, Munich, 1960, p. 14

AMERICAN-LITHUANIAN REACTION

*The great sun of democracy which Whitman sang is
setting on this continent (North America). Today it rises
over the Old World from the continent of socialism.*
  —Eduardas Miezelaitis, from *Niagara Falls,
  or A Walk with Walt Whitman,* 1962

Similar to what happened to the Latvian community also happened to the Lithuanian community. (Estonia, small to begin with, had an immigration colony of only 26,000 in 1980). War interrupted emigration to the USA and indeed, united most Lithuanians in the common hope of seeing their homeland liberated from Nazi occupation. Most American-Lithuanians, like most Americans in general, looked upon the Soviet Union during the war not only as an ally but as a liberator. They did not draw the strange and appalling conclusion that the liberation of Lithuania by the Red Army meant that Lithuania was being occupied!

But things changed after the war. Hope in Nationalist ranks that Lithuania could survive as an "independent" country with the same semi-colonial dependence status as before evaporated when the Provisional Government of Lithuania under Juozas Ambrazevicius was dissolved by the Nazis after a mere three months during which it existed on rations, carrying out Nazi orders and committing unspeakable crimes against the population in general and the Jews in particular.

At war's end, Ambrazevicius "escaped" by a convenient ratline to the USA, where he changed his name to Brazaitis and resumed life as a newly-coined "democrat" of the American variety as though no blood had ever stained his "independent" hands. An idea of just how deep runs the moral corruption of so many of the leaders of the American-Lithuanian community, one need go no further than the book, *Lithuanians in America*, written by Dr. Antanas Kucas, who is described as a "historian, educator, writer, Professor Emeritus of the University of Scranton, obtained his Ph.D. at the University of Kaunas, Lithuania; he also studied at the French Universities of Grenoble and Nancy."

It is said of him, in his self-written biography, that he had been "arrested in 1943 by the Gestapo, (and) was deported to the slave labor camp at

Stuffhof, East Prussia. Liberated [by whom—doesn't say: it had to be the Red Army], after two years, he published a poignant account of his experiences. After a year in Paris, Dr. Kucas emigrated to the United States. From 1947 to 1970 he taught history and modern language at the University of Scranton. Author of several books on historical subjects, Dr. Kucas is one of the editors of the *Encyclopedia Lituanica*."

His book about Lithuanians in America is recommended as being written with complete candor including "pimples and warts and everything," and so his account may be taken with confidence that it is truthful.

But read how he treats Juozos Brazaitis! "Juozos Brazaitis mentioned before as a member of the *Darbininkas* editorial staff, was a dedicated resistance leader against Bolshevik and Nazis alike."

An extraordinary claim! Not only is no mention made of the fact that Brazaitis is really Ambrazevicius and that the so-called "Provisional Government of Lithuania" was set up completely to cooperate with the Nazis and in the short three months it was allowed to exist, it supervised the murder of 46,692 Jews!

In his own doleful account of the demise of his puppet—if ever the word was justified it was justified here!—government, Ambrazevicius indicted himself as a Nazi collaborator over and over, and indeed, it was as a war criminal fleeing from justice that he made his way, like many other war criminals, to the USA through especially prepared ratlines that brought him to safety. In his swan song, as "premier of the Provisional Government," on August 5, 1941, he would say, among other damning admissions, that "on June 23, at 9:30 a.m. the Activist Front [a secret prewar organization of Lithuanian fascists with headquarters in Berlin] standing at the head of the nation and determined to restore free and independent Lithuania, emphasizing friendly relations with Germany and their will to become part of Europe under the new regime of Adolph Hitler, proclaimed the Provisional Government of Lithuania ... As early as the first sitting of the Cabinet of Ministers the headquarters of the Lithuanian Armed Forces was established. It took steps to establish close contact with German troops with a view to cleaning the country of the savage Bolshevik bands that were active in many parts of Lithuania up to the very end (an effort was made to get the consent of the German military headquarters to organize a national Lithuanian corps which might take part in the struggle against Bolshevism)."[108]

Where was resistance to Nazis here? In fact, Ambrazevicius boasted, when he felt his future was still bright, that "...when, with the outbreak of war, the German troops would turn against the Bolsheviks. According to the plan [concocted in Berlin] on the very first days of the war the activists and partisans started fighting the Russians..."

When did the Nationalists start fighting the Nazis? The record shows no such moment. Indeed, one of the leading partisan commanders in Lithuania, whose resistance to the Nazis was a lengendery example of that form of resistance, Henrikas Zimanas, who was well aware of who fought and who did not fight, remarks: "The Lithuanian nationalists took no part in the struggle against fascism. They justified this inactivity by saying that the fascists were not against Lithuania—they were just against the communists. The nationalists worked at German offices and establishments, helped the Gestapo catch members of the underground and partisans, and watched on indifferently as the fascists sent thousands of Lithuanians, Jews, and Russians to the gallows, to prison, and the concentration camps. The nationalists were actually betrayers of their people."[109]

The only "resistance" to which the Nationalists can point, and it was inspired and organized, not by Lithuanian patriots aroused to struggle for their homeland, but under the auspices of the American secret services, was the one-time well-known Project X. "Guerrillas"—recruited Lithuanian fascists who had found sanctuary in Germany during and after the war—were parachuted into the forests and countryside of Lithuania where they hoped to find support among the Lithuanian peasants. They failed to get it, but before finally surrendering—taking advantage of the government amnesty—they wreaked a great deal of havoc and murdered many collective farmers. Their favorite target however was the teachers.

"They would hide," she said,* "in the woods. Then, when it got dark, they would sneak out of the woods and shoot at us..."

"At *you*?" She was a school teacher, barely then out of her teens, but still as apple-cheeked as she then was.

"Oh, yes. I was a village school teacher. They particularly hated us. They particularly wanted to murder us."

"Why?"

Her still-virginal blue eyes rounded. "Why? Because we were Socialist teachers."

"What did you really teach?"

"ABC's, of course. Reading, writing, spelling. The Lithuanian language."

"And for that..."

"But it was we who were teaching them—we Socialist teachers. The struggle in the countryside was fierce. We never expected to survive. After the Nazis were driven out, and we started to rebuild, you must realize—the Nationalist gangs..."

"Gangs?"

---

* To the author, 1965.

"Oh, they had prettier names for themselves! They called themselves patriots, but they served the Germans. They were murder gangs."

Sometimes the assassins waylaid them on lonely roads, attacked them, left their bodies lying broken and violated where they fell, often with a "message" attached to the wounds. In other instances they shot them to death in full view of the children, as they stood with wooden pointers in front of the school blackboard.

One they murdered in cold blood was named Ona Sukakiene. She had been given several warnings to leave the territory, or be killed. Instead of leaving, she sat down one evening not long before her death, to write a letter that proved to be her last will and testament. It was the 9th of February, 1946, and the first post-war election to the Lithuanian Supreme Soviet that would consolidate socialist power, was about to take place.

> The tenth of February is drawing near. Then my fellow citizens will decide their and their nation's fate. I know that February the tenth will bring a bright future for our people.... If you learn that I am killed, know that I love only my Motherland, only she was worth my life and my love.

And they did kill her, these boasters of slaughter today in their Chicago and Brooklyn "havens." Indeed, in cooperation, the Nazi and Lithuanian fascists killed more than 1,000 Lithuanian teachers like Ona. But they failed to win over these young martyrs or the farmers. Why?

"What defeated them?" The man being asked that question was himself a collective farmer (a Jew, incidentally) who had been attacked, shot, left for dead, but survived. "It was not their bullets," he replied, "but their ideas which were helpless against our socialist system."[107]

The prize-winning movie, *The Last Shot*, gives us a vivid view of the types engaged in this bitter and merciless battle, in which the Nationalist forces hated beyond the reach of reason everything for which Ona Sukakiene was murdered.

It boggles the imagination to believe that the Lithuanian people have knowingly re-accepted these murderers "back into our country...."

Not only have we seen the transformation of the Lithuanian fascist Ambrazevicius into the American democrat Brazaitis, but we saw in him a phenomenon that was not restricted to him alone. Let the Church of Rome boast of its powers! Its powers dwindle to bird seed in comparison with the power of America to transform a murderer into a democrat by passing him through a process which gives him a new name, a new personality, but lets him retain his old conscience. He is obliged, as a new-minted American, to learn a new vocabulary. If, in Lithuania, he looked upon all democrats as nothing but Communists, he had to learn in America to lipsync with all rhetoric in America that praises "democrats." Difficult as that is, and some newly arrived, and newly anointed "Americans" never learn to do the trick with any plausibility, still it has to be mimicked. Lithuanian Nationalists in America use the word "democracy" in the same spirit as the Nazis used the word "socialism," and (with apologies to the oldest profession in the world) as whores use the word "love."

Let us take a close view of this modern-day miracle as it developed through the personality of one Bishop Vincentas Brizgys. In Lithuania, during the war, he was the assistant to the Catholic Metropolitan Archbishop Juozapas Skvireckas in Kaunas, he who earlier had approved of Polonizing Vilnius. The notorious Ninth Fort is located on the outskirts of Kaunas. Used as a prison for Lithuanian dissidents before the war, its facilities were expanded during the war, and about 80,000 prisoners, from all over Europe* as well as Lithuania, passed through its portals as human beings and emerged as corpses hastily buried, and then unburied and burned as the Red Army approached, in an attempt totally to destroy even the fragments of bones.

Although he witnessed the almost daily roundups and killings not only of Jews but of "Communists," Brizgys "saw" nothing. Instead, according to a diary entry of his superior, Archbishop Skvireckas, On July 1, 1941, Brizgys made contact

> ... with the representative of the German government for the Baltic states (Dr. Greffe, former head of Gestapo in East Prussia, who) ... proposed ... that he (Brizgys) should make an appeal to the people to behave quietly and pursue their daily business with confidence, without any fear that they might be harmed.[110]

On June 30, 1941, the archbishop had recorded in his diary: "The ideas of *Mein Kampf* on the question of the Bolshevik--Jewish contagion are splendid... they prove that Hitler's not only an enemy of the Jews, but generally speaking has the right ideas."[111]

Not only did Skvireckas, Brizgys, Archbishop Mecislovas Reinys, and Prelate Kazunieras Siaulys officially welcome the Nazis to Kaunas, but they also signed a telegram of thanks to Hitler for "Lithuanian liberation," sent in the middle of July 1941. Possibly the same one Landsbergis' father did. He too had signed a telegram of gratitude to Hitler.... As the Nazis and their collaborators implemented the diabolical logic of *Mein Kampf,* Brizgys, "set an example for the entire population by forbidding the clergy to aid the Jews in any way."[112] He also urged from the pulpit, and via radio and newspapers, that Lithuanians cooperate with the Nazis.[113]

---

* Scratched on the wall of one of the cells is the poignant message: *"Nous sommes 900 Francais."*

When the Soviet army, led into Lithuania by its 16th Lithuanian Division, drove the Nazis out in 1944, Brizgys fled to safety in Germany. Then, by a process which has become all too familiar by now, he was passed swiftly through the many barriers usually confronting would-be immigrants. The Immigration Service that kept Pablo Picasso (and many other—10,000—anti-fascists) out of the United States let the Bishop in without blinking. "Invited" by Bishop Stritch of Chicago to come to Chicago, Brizgys found a welcome there. Almost immediately he resumed from Chicago the same "war" he had fought in Lithuania.

Although leading a marginal existence on the political scene—supporting reactionary Congressmen from areas with some Lithuanian constituency, as in Chicago—Lithuanian Nationalists in the USA nevertheless persisted in the never-dying hope that their opportunity to regain power in Lithuania would one day strike.

Indeed, it did. Today not only do certain politicians curry favor with Nationalist Lithuanians, but their representatives have been received by both President Reagan and Bush in the White House itself.

Ensconced in the United States, Brizgys was not one to retire to a rocking chair. He was a very busy man; indeed, a driven one. He, like the reborn Ambrazevicius, resumed in the USA where he had left off in Lithuania and West Germany. He helped launch the Lithuanian Catholic Religious Aid Society in 1961, and later inspired the creation of the Lithuanian Information Center which would play so large a role in supplying what it called "information" about the Lithuanian "underground."

However, its past clings to it. The present Lithuanian Information Center is a clear echo of the Lithuanian Information Bureau, organized and located in Berlin (1939), from which the Catholic opposition also conducted "underground" work on socialist Lithuania. The Berlin Bureau, under the guidance and auspices of the German Gestapo, was privy to the plan for the invasion of the USSR in June 1941, and in anticipation of that day sent the following message to its "underground" organizations, particularly the Savandoriai, the Nationalist paramilitary organization, to which the father of the present "president" of Lithuania was actively attached:

> ... liberation is close ... uprisings must be started in the cities, towns and villages of Lithuania ... communists, and other traitors ... must be arrested at once ... (The traitor will be pardoned only provided he proves beyond doubt that he has killed one Jew at least.)[114]

The present Information Center located in Washington and New York openly boasts of the praise garnered from Voice of America and Radio Liberty, indifferent to (or perhaps flattered by) the fact that they were (and are) CIA-funded.

They were no doubt right to cite such authoritative auspices for praise from them proved to be no obstacle when it came to obtaining funds from the National Endowment for Democracy, set up by the Reagan administration in 1983, and quite blandly and with little attempt to conceal, stated their aim of overthrowing the socialist governments of Eastern Europe, (and succeeded) but most importantly of all, the USSR itself.

Indeed, during the two years (1990-1989), NED had granted $70,000 to Lithuanian Catholic Religious Aid Society and the Lithuanian Information Center. Founded in 1961 to provide the "Church under the Soviet oppression with spiritual and material assistance..." Lithuanian Catholic Religious Aid's parent organization was the Lithuanian Roman Catholic Priests' League, probably at some point touching hands (if not more) with Intermarium. In any case, LCRA's executive director, Father Casmir Pugevicius, served in 1983 on an advisory committee for Senate Charles Percy (R. Ill.), then a member of the powerful Senate Foreign Relations Committee. Pugevicius was also welcomed in Reagan's White House in 1986.

According to LCRA and LIC, its 1990 grant application to the National Endowment for Democracy requested $618,300 and outlined its ambitious proposal as follows:

> ... five separate pro-democratic organizations (in Lithuania) would receive technical and material aid. The first, a coalition of democratic parties enjoying broad support in Lithuania and capable of assuming leadership roles in the new legislature would receive computer and audio-visual equipment ... Communications and video equipment will also be transported to the Sajudis Information Agency...
>
> The second part of the project would ensure a continuous supply of much needed paper for independent publishers and organizations. The dramatic increase in the number of democratic groups in Lithuania in the past year has caused severe shortages in the very limited pool of resources. Because of the greater degree of liberalization in Lithuania, this republic has emerged as the publishing center for the independent groups throughout the Soviet Union....[115]

Within weeks of the arrival of this hard-to-get technological equipment (fax machines were unknown in Lithuania as in most of the USSR, for instance), traditional sources of information in Lithuania were suppressed or taken over by Sajudis, which had first come on the scene, not as a political party, but as a "movement."

Nationalists moved to take over all sources of information, cutting off broadcasts from Moscow over USSR-owned TV national circuit, later temporarily retaken by the Soviets, and flooded the airwaves with anti-Soviet propaganda, which began to mimic the same lines and themes of the anti-Soviet propaganda of the pre-war Nationalists headquartered in Berlin.

So influential indeed is LIC that it supplied Landsbergis with American advisers, significantly the 34-year-old William J.H. Hough, III, who does not speak Lithuanian but whose value to Landsbergis obviously lay in the fact that in 1985 he edited the *New York Law School Journal of International and Comparative Law*, which devoted an entire issue to the "Baltic question," purporting to back up with authoritative citations the assertions that the Baltics were "annexed" illegally to the USSR in 1939-40, and thus, Landsbergis could claim a just basis, not for secession, but simply for the resumption of independence. More about Hough later.

In any case, the Church, despite having compromised itself so heavily during the Nazi occupation, seems to have forgotten nothing and learned nothing. It is worth reviewing its history in socialist Lithuania, and for that I present a first-hand account.

THE CHURCH IN LITHUANIA
(1965)

The closer you live to the Church,
The less you know of God.
                                        — Lithuanian saying

Here, as written in 1965, based on visits to churches and interviews with priests all over Lithuania, is the author's report on the status of the church in Lithuania. Shortened somewhat, the article is otherwise reproduced exactly as it was originally published.*

There's a war. Somebody wins. Somebody loses.

I go now to meet some of the losers (it's now 1965).

They'll all deny that they're losers. But they've been in a "war"–that they will not deny.

Father Jonas Zemaitis, whom I interviewed in his home on the shores of the man-made "sea" of Kaunas, was preparing to leave Lithuania for Rome to attend the last session of the Ecumenical Council. His duties there, he explained to me, would be modest; he was not "high enough"–he raised his hand–to sit in the policy-making councils. No, he would serve humbly as a "tongue"–an interpreter.

Father Zemaitis is a tall, totally bald-headed man with great vitality, despite his 62–or perhaps because of his 62–years. In his youth he had ambitions to be an operatic tenor, had studied voice in Rome. But later he became an officer in the Czar's army, and then entered the Church. He was a seminarian in Paris where, he said, as a young student–and he clasped his hands and lowered his eyes piously–he used to go through the street avoiding the sight of pretty legs and bosoms. But now, he cries riotously, he looks at pretty girls without fear whatsoever that the sight will jeopardize his soul!

His opinions are a mixture of candor and non-reply. He is quite at peace with the government, he assures me; the virtue of the new state of affairs, to him, is that now only the true believers come to church and the spirit of

* In *Beyond the Borders of Myth*, PRAXIS Press, 1967.

piety is uncorrupted by social and political motives. He sees no reason why the Church and the state cannot get along.

It was no secret to anyone that Radio Vatican, as well as a whole battery of radio broadcasting stations in the West—Radio Free Europe, Radio Liberty, etc.—broadcast daily not only the standard propaganda cliches of the Cold War, but also specially beamed propaganda with priests, "refugee" priests, reading lines all drumming on the single theme of resistance to "red tyranny." The barrage was continuous and the reception in the socialist world not jammed. But year after year, the effect of the broadcasts grew weaker and weaker, as the tirades grew shriller and shriller, and for a very simple reason: not only promises delayed become promises denied, but also because the broadcasts revealed less and less knowledge of the real life within Lithuania and exposed themselves, and their aims, more nakedly, therefore.

Unreality persisted in too long, especially in the face of mounting contrary evidence, becomes pathology. I had traveled this same valley in 1959. It was being cleared then for the coming "sea." Entire villages had been shifted to other ground, like this very church. Birds flew above me. I interviewed the chief engineer of the dam that was even then being constructed, and had a merry conversation with the workers who roared at the notion that in my part of the world it was commonly held to be impossible to build anything so big as a huge hydro-electrical complex without financing by the Rockefellers or Morgans, or any of the City's big banks. "But we're doing it!"

That winter I met a "displaced person" (DP) in New York who asked me about my trip to Lithuania, and when I told him that they were building a huge dam in Kaunas, his open skepticism showed me that he considered me a dupe, hopelessly brain-washed, or a clumsy liar. In his Article of Faith, the socialist Lithuanians could not—must not—dare not—succeed in anything positive, otherwise where would he stand? So, to his mind, it was evident that I had not placed real feet on a real dam, of real concrete. It had been *papier maché*—hastily dragged out and propped up for a visiting simple-minded American, and manned with a cast of "workers" recruited from the local theatre.

Next year, I returned to Kaunas, and this time where the birds had flown fish now swam. The deep valley was filled with water for 20 miles. I skimmed over it on a hydro-foil boat—not touching the water itself, but riding on a cushion of air. The electricity which was generated by the great turbines fed a power grid which served not only Lithuania but parts of Latvia and even Leningrad.

But this could not be. For the DPs, it *must* not be. And it is at this point a curious moment arrives in the psychology of the dissenters. They have come to a great Dividing Line between what might still be called 'honest' opposition to socialism as they understand it, and what objectively, if pursued, amounts to madness, to a species of insanity.

An attitude of antagonism toward socialism was far harder to maintain on the scene than in exile. Pranas Smuksta, a priest from Kaunas, in answer to the question: "How are you as a priest evaluating the social changes?" would say: "It is pleasant and at the same time unpleasant to speak about it. Though I am not personally responsible for what went on during the last five years of the Smetona regime, because I was only an ordinary parish priest, it is nevertheless hard for me to state that such social problems as large families, care in case of sickness and old age, social security, and similar things, were solved in our fatherland not by us Catholics but by the Bolsheviks."

This repeated and insistent reminder that you dissociate them, specifically *them*, from the past, from the priests who took up arms against the people, under Smetona and then the Nazis, is also sounded over and over to me. It is misleading to think that these disclaimers are not sincere. They are utterly sincere.

Over 300 priests fled with the retreating Nazis. Over 900 did not. Why did some flee and some stay?

I asked this and a variety of other questions of all the priests I met, which included these basic ones: Are you happy with the state of affairs now existing between you and the Government? If not, what are your complaints? How do you see the future of Catholicism in Lithuania? How do you feel about the new current in Catholic thought expressed most impressively by Pope John in *Pacem in Terris*, which proclaimed the possibility of a dialog between Catholics and Marxists? What is your attitude toward the priests who fled and are in America now? What is your opinion of Cardinal Spellman and the "American" wing in the Catholic Church?

It was no easy matter to interview Father Antanas Pavilonis. His name was already familiar to me from a *New York Times* story which reported his arrest, trial and punishment. He consented to be interviewed, among other reasons, to show the world that he was a free man, and insisted on taking photographs with me as further proof.

But this, by no means, signified that he had fundamentally changed his views. He had been convicted of currency speculation, and the charge was that he had solicited dollars from Americans on the plea that the church had no resources. Since Lithuania's economy is not based on dollars, these dollars had to be changed into rubles—and here the rude snout of speculation entered. Since he is not a bank, how did he change dollars into rubles? And at what rate? In any case, he made a pile, and from it, resorting to less-than-legal methods, he procured scarce building material, built a rather impressive structure in Klaipeda, and in doing so greased a few palms, cut a few corners, fractured both moral and civil law. Apparently Father Pavilonis solved the ethical dilemma of ends-and-means in his own way. The surplus building material he was accused of selling for his own personal profit; he was brought to trial, convicted and served out half his time. Now he was free, living in a two-room apartment on the upper floor of a house set among vegetable and flower gardens, with the services of a housekeeper. He regularly said Mass in a church in Vilnius now.

I found no embittered man, though no penitent either. Here was a tough, unsentimental, Rough Rider of a priest, a kind of shock-trooper in the crash battles of the Church. He had seen and witnessed and knew too much to be impressed by lace-curtain ethics; and this crusty realism he pointed up with his tart reply when I asked him where in his judgment the fault lay—with him or the state? "They had their opinion. I had mine. Meanwhile, the church was built."

For him this was enough. Pragmatism had overtaken the slow feet of Faith. One of the surprising aspects of the case was the fact that he was able to engineer so great an undertaking, involving so many workers, so much financing, contracting black marketeers in rubles, with no interference from the police until long after the fact. How was that possible? The answer I got seemed almost austere in its severe contrast between fact and fancy.

"Because," the high official I queried told me, "in spite of your newspapers, and Congress, we are not a police state. We have to have evidence of crime before we can take action. There is nothing illegal about building a church in our country, if the funds are raised legally among the parishioners, and if the land and material are legally obtained. Under those circumstances, the state cooperates with the church."

There's no need to take his naked word for it. An independent examination of the conditions of the churches in Vilnius, for instance, shows the care with which these buildings are protected and preserved, and even the casual stroller through the city is more apt than not to come upon little fly-men stuck to a high steeple fastening gold leaf on to one of the onion domes, or repainting the facade of a baroque 16th century cathedral, or, inside, restoring old frescoes of saints and sinners, faded with time and violence.

I had a rather pleasant but no-nonsense talk with Pather Pavilonis. He had gripes against the government, and made no bones about expressing them; but it was also obvious that he was satisfied too that he could come and go and function as he wished.

When we came to questions of Catholic life at home and abroad, it seemed to me that he really did belong to that hard core of resisters to change. In this respect, he would be in the minority, not only in general, but within his own Church. When I asked him why it seemed that Catholicism flourished best in backward, feudal and semi-feudal societies, but where the industrial revolution had progressed and capitalism had come into being, Catholicism had lost ground, he snapped back at me: "Isn't Catholicism most popular in America?" Since this was right after the death of President John F. Kennedy, and the well-advertised "conversion" of one of President Johnson's daughters to Catholicism, I felt that he had scored a point, though perhaps not for quite his reasons. For Catholicism had almost become chic in America among the rootless middle-class, and the dramatic conversions of glamorous movie stars and public personalities had become a full-time industry of the television matine idol Bishop Sheen.

"We coexist here," Father Algirdas Gutauskas, pastor of the Ausros Vartai, the famous Vilnius cathedral many centuries old, told me. "Life is normal. We have the full possibility to work. Believers are real believers now. We practice real religion. I work as a priest, and nobody bothers me. All our churches carry on services in Lithuanian or Polish. Enough money is raised from our parishioneers to carry on our work, and the State provides funds for major repairs, as it did to repair the famous St. Peter and Paul Cathedral, for example...."

He had been ordained priest in 1945—right at the end of the war—and so he was still in his forties, and had a view of both societies, Janus-like, past and present. He was not perturbed at anti-religious propaganda. "In Old Lithuania we also had atheists who published their literature. Live and let live...."

His assistant, a puckish fellow who seemed much too lively for the solemn regimen of the Church, kept snapping pictures of us all the time and making roguish remarks that stopped just this side of impropriety. He seemed more preoccupied with "pretty girls" than with the austere demands of a priesthood into which he had to be only a late-comer. The older priest looked on his antics with indulgence.

"The Church," Father Gutauskas insisted, "is always for peace. Leaders of our Church belong to the Committee for Peace...."

"Cardinal Spellman," I said, "does not believe that you are free to function here."

This was the first heat he showed. "It would be good," he said holding himself in, "if Cardinal Spellman were to come here and see with his own eyes!"

I had visited the shrine of Mater Misericordiae, to which the old women came crawling on their knees, and there before a wall covered with silver replicas of legs and arms, heart and head, bent their bodies to the floor and prayed for health. "How can you reconcile this medieval superstition," I asked him, "with true teaching of religion?"

He denied that there was anything equivocal here. "The Church does not claim that they will be healed. But they are devoted...."

We supped and drank and posed for pictures, and I left him with the impression that here the *modus vivendi* between Church and State had been satisfactorily if gingerly worked out.

I visited the Catholic Seminary in Kaunas, and spent most of the afternoon with the fathers there with whom I had meat (or rather fish: this was Friday and before the Pope's dispensation), drink, song and merry talk.

Those who imagine that one meets only gloom and despair among the churchmen "behind the Iron Curtain" are far from the mark. Although the atmosphere of medievalism saturated the stones and environment of the Church, including the school and the surrounding grounds, the priests themselves were young (though there were some older ones) and the seminary was supervised by Father Victor Butkus, who was perhaps in his late thirties or early forties. He was not only frank with me but eager to be understood and to convince. He made it immediately clear that no obstacles were placed by anyone in his way to recruiting youth for seminary training, but he did admit ruefully that the number of applicants had fallen off sharply, especially this year, and his total enrollment was only 25. I had already encountered these novitiates in their afternoon meditations, some already in the robes of monks, reading their breviary; some in civilian dress, having just lately arrived, and, I noticed to my surprise, several were no longer in their first youth.

Yes, they had problems, Father Butkus cheerfully admitted. It wasn't an easy thing to get recruits now. Church was strictly religion, and no ladder for social or political advancement. Without state support, it was strictly on its own. Almost unanimously, the priests I talked to assured me that now the really devout came to church, whereas before many came for social reasons. The faithful were truly faithful. The Church had found—or been restored to—its original purpose, purged of all but spiritual concerns.

Later, when I interviewed a young man who had been an ordained priest since 1945, but then had left the Church, I was to get some insight into why so few youth now applied for seminary training and why, to be frank about it, those who did apply seemed to have so little real quality.

Even here, when I visited the dormitory, I noticed several empty cots, and these empty cots, I was informed, were "waiting" for novitiates who had enrolled but as yet—and time was growing short—had not arrived to begin their training. Were they having second thoughts? In any case, I found little in the life that was reserved here to attract any warm-blooded youth. Up at 6:30 a.m., they worked their way through the day's regimen of prayers, chores, studies, contemplations, and pious thought which brought them back, by 11:30, to their bare rooms of five and six narrow iron cots (like, I might add, irrelevantly, the narrow iron cots Lenin and his wife, Krupskaya slept on, with seaweed mattresses, in the Smolny Institute, right after winning power.) It was interesting to me to learn that their curriculum of study also included study of "Marxism-Leninism," and the history of the Communist Party.

"Oh, yes," Father Butkus assured me, "we try to understand dialectical materialism, though of course we are not materialists...."

It seemed almost fey to me to be hearing this—much as I had felt that I was in the same sort of reversed wonderland when I listened to a "capitalist" in Tientsin solemnly assure me also that he was a conscientious student of "Marxism-Leninism."

We foregathered in the big dining room and there amongst the wine and cognac, between toasts to one another's success and continuing prosperity, we managed to touch on a whole array of subjects, both sacred and profane, in which all five or six priests (a number of gray-haired ones) freely, sometimes wittily, participated. Some had read my first novel, *Burning Valley*, which deals with the moral crisis in the life of a Catholic boy whose religious beliefs come into conflict with the social reality of the poor. They gave me their interested reactions.

There was a strong "anti-Americanism" among them. This anti-Americanism sought its specific target: the American Catholic hierarchy: the bid for power which they felt it was making. They owed the American hierarchy no special loyalty; that loyalty belonged to Rome. Their anathema was Cardinal Spellman. His support of the "right" of America to use atom-bombs against "Communism" of course placed them—literally them—straight between the cross hairs of the target. They had no respect for those priests who had "run away" to America, and had even less respect for them when only their disembodied voices returned to Lithuania via the airwaves. After all, *they* had not run away! On the other hand they had not been guilty of crime, either.

Obviously anybody dissenting against political matters was automatically propelled into collision with the Church itself.

So when the Church was forced to attend strictly to God's affairs, it did not accept this re-assignment joyfully. On the contrary, the restriction of its function to religious matters was for it a painful new experience. So it seemed to the Church leaders that their golden opportunity had struck when, on June 22, 1941, the Nazis began the war by raining bombs on children in their vacation camp at Palanga. Nazis? It didn't matter: they were Christians, and the Communists were "godless atheists." Moreover, who should question the instruments God chooses in his mysterious wisdom his wonders to perform?

The Church officially encouraged the people to support the Nazis. Some priests, like the notorious Lionginas Jankauskas (Jankus), now living in America, joined the Nationalist bands and took part in the butchery. But it must be noted, too, that not all priests followed this course—and how they behaved under Nazi occupation has served since as an absolute line of demarcation between the Lithuanian clergy, both at home and abroad.

The Church during the Hitler occupation heavily compromised itself. It gambled on the expectation that the Nazis would win the war. It gambled wrong.

So it is this Church, whose reputation is so tarnished, that the people know. Therefore, it's not to be wondered at that its influence had fallen so low. Unlike the Catholic Church in other countries, where it refused to cooperate with the Nazis, and so retained its credit with the people, the Church in Lithuania suffered a profound loss of popular confidence. Not "Communist propaganda," nor the suppression by the State, but its own misdeeds and miscalculations are the cause for its position today.

But that position is far from hopeless. New winds have been blowing through the Catholic world. New ways of cooperation, ecumenical forces, dialogs between ancient foes: nothing like this has been seen for centuries. Before the overriding problem of problems, shall we survive? Both Communist and Catholic are joined by history in mutual responsibility.

Lithuanian Catholics know this, and have cast their lot on the side of progress and peace. That is the sure road back from Calvary.

Novosti Press Agency Interview (Aug. 9, 1965)

French author Jean Paul Sartre and Madame Simone de Beauvoir spent several days in Lithuania. They visited Vilnius, Lithuania's capital, Kaunas and other cities as well as the maritime towns of Neringa and Palanga.

Before Mr. Sartre's departure an APN correspondent asked him several questions.

"Question: On coming to our Republic you said that you have long wished to become acquainted with Lithuania and its culture which, in your words, is part of the Soviet and European culture. Have you gained any interesting impressions from your trip?

"Answer: I think that LIthuania is an example of an original culture displaying the profound intrinsic unity of history, traditions, landscape, the work of artists of the past, folk arts and of what to now is being created in Lithuania by artists, writers and architects whose works I have seen. I was greatly impressed by the connection between traditions and the present-day searches of modern art which preserves its folk character.

"Question: We know that Western propaganda pictures the Lithuanian people as an 'enslaved nation., What is your opinion on this score?

"Answer: All Lithuanians whom I met exemplified complete freedom... I also met Lithuanians from America who came on a visit here and author Phillip Bonosky who had already been to Lithuania before. They would hardly come to meet slaves. When in Vilnius, Kaunas and other places we visited one sees people, one gets a clear impression that it is a free nation."

THE 'GOLDEN PERIOD' OF LITHUANIAN ART

For I am Man, the Eighth Wonder of the world.
—Eduardas Meizelaitis, *The Wonder*

For those who do not accept religion to fill their spiritual life, there is art. This same year—1965—(again to be personal), Lithuania was in the midst of what artists themselves called a "renaissance." By 1965, Lithuania had succeeded in forming an image, a national image, mainly through art, that had begun to attract attention, first in Russia and the other Soviet republics, and then in Europe and the world.

Every visitor to Lithuania sooner or later came to see on the road to Pirciupe, standing by the wayside, a stone image of a woman. She stands for the widows and stricken mothers of all Europe, and yet the quality of her grief has survival and even triumph in it. She was carved by Gediminas Jokubonis for which he received a Lenin prize. Pirciupe is a name that stands for a town all of whose inhabitants were herded into a barn and set on fire by the Nazis.

Sculpture plays a large role in Lithuanian life. It is stimulated by a broad program of promoting monumental, commemorative and decorative sculptures. The demand almost outstrips the means. Such sculptors as P. Vaivada, who created the statue of the revolutionary veteran, Vincas Mickevicius-Kapsukas, and the late J. Miernas, and Petras Cvirkas, the Lithuania writer. All of them have been since torn down.

Many artists have made their mark in the graphic arts, appearing widely in books and magazines and especially in children's literature as illustrators. Known throughout the USSR was Vytautas Jurkunas as was S. Krasauskas. A. Makunaite's work derives from folk sculpture and wood carvings. Vytautas Valius draws the life of the working people and the landscape of his native Zamaitija (Samogitia).

Contemporary painting, realistic in spirit, is infinitely varied in style. We have the dramatic landscapes of A. Savickas, the psychologically-penetrating portraits of A. Gecas, the expressive works of A. Gudaitis, the dreamy, lyrical landscapes of A. Zmuidzinavicius, who was also the founder of the museum of devils in Kaunas. There are many, many more.

Exhibitions of art are frequent, not only of easel work but of all the applied arts as well: book-illustrations, posters, purely decorative art. Ceramics play an important role in Lithuanian art, combining in their patterns modern motifs and themes taken from folk tales. Lithuanian ceramics often win prizes at international exhibits.

A special word must be reserved for those who work in amber, Lithuania's "northern gold." Amber carving has been brought to a higher art in Lithuania, and a special museum was built to contain the most striking examples of them at Palanga. The museum was robbed lately and most of the art, truly priceless, stolen, exactly in the spirit with which the Nazis looted the amber room in the Czarina's palace outside Leningrad and, to this day, the stolen amber has not been recovered.

Lithuanian artists working in stained glass have produced remarkable works, many of them windows installed in public buildings. Many also work in wood, carrying on the folk tradition and lifting it to a consciously artistic level. They are united in the Artists Union of Lithuania which (in 1965) had 335 members. A museum in Kaunas is dedicated the great Lithuanian artist, who was also a composer, M. K. Cirulionis (1875-1911). Special attention is paid to children of talent in Lithuania, as in all the Soviet republics, and special schools to nurture them exist. Artists living unknown and half-starved in bare garrets are today a thing of the past. The demand for art is so great that today—at least up until recently—every artist with any talent can easily make a living.

Theater, too, has flourished. In 1965, Lithuania had 11 professional theaters, which together produced 55 *new* plays each season. Modern themes, today's life, the problems of growing Lithuania—these concern the playwrights. In the last few years, the Lithuanian stage presented such original plays as *Professor Markas Vidinas* by J. Grusas; *Herkus Martas* and *Wedding Anniversary* by the same author. *Mustaches Did Not Help* by A. Gricius. *How Am I Guilty?* by S. Kosmauskas. *The Boy with the Devil's Hair* by J. Skliutauskas. *Don't Leave Me,* by V. Miliunas. And many more, including revivals of classics, especially Shakespeare.

New directors and new actors have come on the scene as a result. Indeed, as they themselves remark, Lithuania has never before seen so much new talent on its stages.

One must also mention the Lithuanian puppet theater, led by S. Patkevicius, whose fame extended far beyond Lithuania's borders.

Opera, ballet, choruses, everything connected with music, has taken on a new, vivid life. New operas and ballets are created and given their chance. A striking new opera house (whose architect was a woman) was to be opened in Vilnius in 1965.

The Lithuanian movie industry (in 1965) is still young. There was no film-making industry in prewar Lithuania (only some newsreels, mostly about government officials). Under socialist power, the film industry grew dramatically. Much help was received from other Soviet republics, particularly the Russian, whose own movies had already been acclaimed all over the world. Thus far (1965), 15 full-length movies have been made. They bring Lithuanian reality, past and present, to the people. Such films as *Ignotas Returned* (based on the novel, *The Truth About Blacksmith Ignotas*) by A. Guaditis-Guzevicius. *Julius Janonis,* a biographical film about the tragic life of the presocialist Lithuanian revolutionary poet, who died so young. *Adam Wants to Be a Man,* about life in Lithuania under the old regime and the struggle for freedom, (there are different definitions of freedom). *The Living Heroes,* about the lives of children; *Strangers,* about the conflict between the old and new morality; *Steps in the Night* about the underground struggle of the anti-fascist youth against the old regime.

The Living Heroes won a prize at the International film festival in Karlovy-Vary, in Czechoslovakia. The film director was the then unknown V. Zalakevicius, who since has become quite famous not only in Lithuania but in Europe everywhere, for a series of remarkable films.

But most probably the Lithuanian creative spirit finds itself best in poetry. Poetry has taken on a new life and Lithuania's leading poet, Eduardas Miezelaitis, was awarded the Lenin prize for poetry in 1962 for his book, *Man.* Justinas Marcinkevicius, just coming into his own, was already making his mark, with *Blood and Ashes* and *Contemporary Poems,* and would in due course be heralded as the poet of the national spirit of Lithuania. It was quite logical for him to support Sajudis in its early stage, since he took the movement to be the realization of his poetic concept of Lithuania in state form. He was to be disabused.

Mention should be made of Teofilis Tilvytis' heroic poem on the death of the poet, Vytautas Montvila, who was killed by the Nazis.

Also renowned as poets are Algimantas Baltakis, whose *The Devil's Bridge,* won wide interest. *The Wheel of the Full Moon* by Vacys Reimeris is full of romantic vigor and the feeling of the pathos of life. Janina Degutye, Alfonsas Maldonis, Alibinas Zukauskas, Eugenijus Metuzevicius, Paulius Sirvys, Bronius Macevicius, Vincas Giedra, Antanas Driling are only a few who have won notice lately. But it should also be recorded that the president of the republic, Justas Paleckis, a journalist in the past, is also a poet, and has lately published a book of poems.

Novels burst upon the scene almost at the same time with quite a few new (and old) novelists. The old is being woven into the new. Leva Sinmonaityte, a leading writer of the older generation, published an autobiographical work called *Under Another Roof,* compared to Halldor Laxness' work.

K. Marukas published *Streets Are Swept on the Green Hill*. Jonas Simkus, a writer of the older generation, published a book of short stories, *Tomorrow Will Be Beautiful*, and Juozas Baltusis, another writer from the older generation, would live to see his books nailed to a tree by Sajudis thugs in Kaunas. *Silver of the North* is by Antanas Venclova, minister of education, a travel book. *The Near Remoteness*, by B. Pranaskas Zalionis, an old revolutionary, recalls the past in unforgettable images (as the reviewer put it), illuminating the road along which progressive Lithuanian literature has developed. Books by A. Bauz, M. Eglinis, Aldona Baltruniene, Jonas Dovdaitis, Vladas Dustrartas, Algirdas Pocius, I. Jeras, Vytautas Misevicius—all of them short story collections—came out. A novel by Vytautas Sirijos Gira, *That Is All* was published in 1963. New novels were also written by Vincas Mykolaitis-Putinas, Mykolas Sluckis, J. Paulstelis, Aleksas Baltrunas, Jonas Dovyditis, J. Avyzius (whose later novel, *The Lost Home* (1974) would win him much fame and prizes), books by A. Bielauskas were also published. American-Lithuanian writers, still abroad, were published in their homeland, and every effort was made to establish a bridge between the emigres (the old ones and the new ones).

This period has been called, and with some justification, the "golden period" of Lithuanian culture. But most of the cited artists, and certainly those closely connected with the socialist ideals of the Communist Party (in which most of them held membership) are no longer published, and indeed have become instant non-persons, if not directly assaulted and persecuted like the late Juozas Baltusis.

Vitautas Petkavicius would assail the sudden turn to "nationalist themes" in what handful of literature has come into existence in the last few months. "We Lithuanians seem to be beset by delusions of grandeur, or the 'European Syndrome.' Instead of the 'historical basis' we are all so tired of, our critics now all tend to view a writer's work through the prism of nationalist revival. But what, after all, is nationalism?"

And he goes on: "It has become fashionable to see it as an antidote to great-power chauvinism, but that is only the political aspect. What about the spiritual side? I see it as patriotism taken to the point of folly, which has nothing in common with nobility and morality, it will never turn into nationalism...

"Many today adopt the trappings of nationalism to make their politics more attractive, turning our sacred patriotic feelings into a propaganda gimmick, into the fray go the ready-made phrases our glib politicians need to arouse the public, but nobody looks ahead to the consequences...."

He sums it up: "Talent is confronted by organized mediocrity—that's an old, old story."[116]

WAVING THE BLOODY SHIRT

*A stork on the roof like the day just passed stands
on the look-out. The gates are wide open for all to
come back home.*
— Justinas Marcinkevicius, *Brother*

In his book, *Russian Silhouettes*, published in English from a Russian translation in 1984, Albertas Laurenciukas, editor of *Tiesa*, member of the Central Committee of the Communist Party of Lithuania, delegate to the Supreme Soviet of Lithuania, long-time foreign journalist, Chairman of the Lithuanian Union of Journalists, and winner of various prizes for his writings, summing up his impressions of Russia over which he had traveled for many miles and many years, wrote: "I looked for ordinary people in Russia, and didn't find any." He goes on to say: "I have seen much of the world, and in recent years almost all of Russia, a kind, spacious land."

Every bit of ground here (in Orel) is soaked in blood. Every bit of the ground has heard the "hurrah" that the Russians shout when rising to the attack, and it is also heard the Lithuanian "vailo." This is where the 16th Rifle Division, a Lithuanian unit of the Soviet Army had its Alexeyevka on the 20 February 1943, and on 24 February at 09.30 hours together with other Soviet units, mounted its first attack. And failed to crash through the Nazi fortification. In March, the Lithuanians mounted one more attack. And from 23 July to 11 August, counterattacking, they advanced more than a hundred kilometers, liberating 54 villages and towns, including a village called Litva (Lithuania). But the real Lithuania was still far away, languishing under the Nazi boot.

Not until a year later, on 13 July 1944, was the Red Flag raised again on the Gedimin Tower in Vilnius. Lithuanians welcome their liberators with bread and salt, flowers and tears of relief.

Monuments are not put up for people not yet born or for exploits not yet performed. Standing on the untilled green field, I thought of the evil intents nourished by the Western imperialist powers. They falsify history, defame the Soviet way of life, misrepresent the fate of my own land, Lithuania, the face of my people. But lies, as people say rightly, have short legs.

He goes on a bit further:

At the center of Zemaitija, a historical area of Lithuania at the intersection of the Riga-Kaliningrad and Kaunas-Klaipeda motor roads, stands an imposing monument—a woman holding an oak-leaf wreath, the symbol of victory. It was put up by the grateful Lithuanian people to the Soviet Army, its liberator. Soviet soldiers brought us our freedom. And as long as clouds float over the Lithuanian land, as long as Lithuania's amber shores are washed by the Baltic, its people will never forget their brothers, those who liberated them.

And further still:

My Lithuania is little, like a drop of pure amber. That is how our great poetess Salomeya Neris, described it. But Lithuania is also immeasurably great because it lives and breathes with the Russian and the brother nation of the Great Soviet Union. We share the joys, the fruits of our labor, our bread and our songs. Lithuanians went off to plough up the virgin lands, are building atomic power stations....

The path of progress is neither smooth or straight. I remember the days when our Russian brothers sent the first combine harvesters to Soviet Lithuania to help our collective farms bring home the first collectively grown harvest. The former rich farmers spread the rumor that combines kill life in the grain and that the following year it will not grow. And there were those who believed them....

We Soviet people are making good headway in peaceful construction, putting into effect the plans charted by the party and government. It does one good to stop and look around: how much have we achieved, how much have we done, how much have we created? With pride....

On the border post is the state emblem of the Soviet Union. "Why the hammer and sickle on your state emblem?" a journalist asked me one day in Brazil....

I explained that the hammer and sickle were not meant to symbolize technical standards, but the fraternal alliance of workers and peasants.

The Soviet state emblem. A globe. The hammer and sickle. Fifteen twists of red ribbon—to equal the number of Soviet republics—wound around ears of wheat. A golden sun.

And finally:

The plane was steadily reducing its speed... The gangway arrived, the door opened, I took a step into the open, and stopped for an instant... And I bowed to the land whose roads I have walked and whose people I have met, and to the ever-present birch trees of Russia.

During the Days of Culture of the Lithuanian Socialist Republic in Moscow, Eduardas Miezelaitis, renowned and many-time honored poet, winner of the Lenin Prize, who has been chairman of the Writers Union of Lithuania, a war correspondent, a secretary of the Young Communist League from 1954 to 1959 and elected deputy premier in the early '80s, declared: "We love you, Russia! We love you for being the first to build a new world after casting off the fetters of slavery, for extending the hand of assistance to all the people of our vast country in the years of disaster, for opening them unprecedented horizons of freedom and happiness. We love you for the great humanistic tradition of your culture, the culture of Pushkin and Dostoyevsky, Repin and Tchaikovsky, Tolstoy and Gorky. We love you faithfully because you are the land of Vladimir Illyich Lenin, the greatest revolutionary of all times and peoples, who brought up a guard of fearless revolutionary champions...."[117] Miezelaitis has written: "I hate fascism on principle. I don't care in what way it is dated or what documents it uses for cover. I know its face too well, it will never escape my scrutiny ... I know even if it wears the most innocent, the most liberal mask, I have scars on my skin to prove my first-hand knowledge of this 'punishment of God.'

"Revolutionary thought has become part and parcel of me from my youth. That thought imbued the very air in our working class suburb. No surgeon's pincers can tear that thought out of me ... For me, the creative act is also a revolutionary act."

"More than anything I am afraid of perfidy, the demagoguery pointing in one direction and the practice, in another, sometimes diametrically opposed. That's when real fear comes, for you don't know when the mortal blow will be dealt, and from what quarter. I cannot stand spiritual fascism which can become real fascist practice at any moment...."[118]

He speaks of the "new man": "The man modeled on the scale of mankind in general. No great people can expect any special privileges in this respect, and no small people can expect any allowances to be made. There's one measure, one criterion, one norm for all. All people are equal. The national balance must not be disrupted under any circumstances. A member of a great people must treat a member of a small people as an equal member of the human race, of one family—as a brother. And a member of the human race, of a fraternal family. That is the only way to international harmony and true humanism...."[119]

One could gather what would amount to an anthology of statements such as these by two of the most prominent personalities in Soviet Lithuania before 1990. These are statements made by men already mature, who had formed soberly considered conclusions about life.

Indeed, from all appearances and in terms of formal logic, theirs seemed to be the majority opinion at the time. True, an alternative point of view existed. But it found expression only on a primitive backward level. Shop girls were openly rude to Russian customers. During a soccer match played in Vilnius between a Russian and Lithuanian team in 1978, the natural rivalry of the game exploded into "hooligan" actions among the Lithuanian fans against the Russian players and other Russians. Certainly, anti-Russian jokes were passed among one another. Anti-Russianism led a busy clandestine life, but at the level of gossip.

That was all. It seemed to any casual observer that the cause of nationalism was in the hands of the most backward, narrow-minded and ignorant sections of the population where, indeed, one supposed would be its natural habitat.

Even now, searching for immediate or recent causes of anti-Russianism, one comes up empty-handed. The classic cause for national antagonism—the imposed rule of a foreign power, expressed by the foreign power enjoying special privileges over the indigenous people, occupying the key areas in the economic life of the nation, exploiting the people, appropriating its wealth, corrupting its youth, etc.—simply did not exist.

The Russians came as liberators. *True* liberators. Erecting statues in commemoration of their sacrifice was a natural and, indeed, quite normal thing to do. Tearing down these statues forty-five years later—that is the abnormal, inexplicable thing, indeed. Russians did not come to exploit the nation. On the contrary, not only did Russians, poor and devastated themselves, come to equally devastated Lithuania (and Latvia and Estonia) right after the war to help in rebuilding the nation—with no special compensation—but in moments of crisis thereafter, they continued to come to Lithuania's assistance, with fraternal generosity. "Moscow" not only extended credit, including international convertible valuta, but brought machinery, technical knowhow, and continued assistance and cooperation in every field, from helping to drain swamps to sharing the most advanced and developed medical knowledge then available.

A case in point. In 1978, Lithuania suffered a natural disaster brought on by too much rain, by floods. In western Lithuania, crops of cereals were destroyed and thousands of hectares of sugar beets and potatoes began to rot in the ground. Fifty years before, in 1928, Lithuania had suffered a similar disaster, known as the "Black Year." Hunger spread everywhere. Cattle were killed because there was no fodder to feed them. Many small farmers had to sell their farms or see them taken in payment of debts. About 50,000 peasant families emigrated, never to return. The loss to the nation in human labor was even greater than the loss of goods.

But this year—1978—was utterly different. Once the danger was understood, the entire nation was mobilized to meet it. Thousands of volunteers from the cities went into the countryside to gather whatever wheat crops they could save. Factories speeded up production to turn out better machinery to cope with the water-logged soil. Planes were used to sow new crops.

Nevertheless, not enough fodder was salvaged to feed the cattle. In 1928, that meant the slaughter of cattle. But in 1978 fodder was sent to Lithuania on an emergency basis from almost every other republic in the Union, saving the cattle. Other republics also provided fertilizer and specialized machinery.

As a result, with the concerted effort of the entire Union, few cattle were lost and a substantial portion of the crop was saved.

The entire nation recognized the event as a dramatic example of the superiority of socialism over capitalism, where it would have been every man for himself and the devil take the hindmost.

According to the testimony of leading cultural personalities, becoming a part of the Soviet Union benefited artists enormously. In 1982, Arvydas Valionis would note that: "More than 500 Lithuanian books were translated into Russian and published in the post-war years." He would further note: "Today Lithuanian folk-lore and works by Lithuanian writers have been translated into 36 languages of the peoples of the USSR, and 28 languages of other nations. About 1500 Soviet and more than 400 foreign translators have been working on translations of Lithuanian literature. Before 1940, that is prior to the restoration of Soviet power in Lithuania, only about a dozen books by Lithuanian authors have been translated into German, Latvian, Russian, Polish and Swedish." And: "Today almost all the best works of Lithuanian classical and Soviet writers have been translated into Russian ... Lithuanian literature is widely translated into the language of the peoples of the other republics of the USSR. Almost a hundred Lithuanian books have been translated by our neighbors, the Latvians, and a large number have been translated into Estonian, Byelorussian, Ukrainian, Moldavian, and Armenian."[120]

An oppressing power typically slights the native language or suppresses it altogether. Soviet power expanded the Lithuanian language. In fact, Soviet power *increased* the spread of Lithuanian first of all to Lithuanians themselves by eliminating illiteracy. Thus, "In 1939, Lithuania had 190,000 people with secondary or higher education, while by 1979, their number had increased to almost 1,600,000."[121]

Charges of Russification simply do not stand up to an examination of the reality. Russian was, in Lithuania, as throughout the Union, a second language through which diverse people all over the Soviet Union had a means of mutual communication. If Alfonsas Maldonis, Chairman of the Writers Union, could say in 1982, that "half a century ago one of our poets said with anguish that 'We are a small nation with a large vocabulary whose language the world does not understand,'" by the late '70s this was no longer true of Lithuania, Estonia or Latvia. Almost miraculously their voices, known to no one but their own people, expanded through Russian to reach the world. Editions of their works, which in their own native language necessarily had to be modest, became (in numbers alone) what in the West would have been considered best sellers when published in Russian and in the other languages of the republic. The expense of these huge publications was borne by the state. Whatever one might otherwise have said about the quality of writing, no one could point to Soviet literature as promoting pornography, war, or chauvinism.

What was true of literature was equally true of art, music, theater, architecture, ballet—and most notably, cinema. Lithuanian cinema, practically unknown before the war, reached a remarkable level in the post-war period, particularly in the work of Vytautas Zalakevicius. With film subsidized in Lithuania, the artist and directors were freed of the onerous burden of watching two "scripts" as they worked: the script of the movie itself and the "script" of the accounting office. Needing to make sure-fire "hits" which made a great deal of money did not concern them.

All this—and much more—is quite true, as many visitors from all over the world have testified. Indeed, in many ways, Lithuania seemed to be working out since the war a kind of contemporary version of a utopian dream of socialism. Lithuanian socialism was characterized by an advanced, civilized approach to humanity. It lacked no spiritual riches. It did lack automobiles, a stock market and fat bank accounts.

How then, explain what happened?

A visitor who had last been in Lithuania in, say, 1986, and returned in the summer of 1988, would have been astonished to see the difference. At first, he, too, might have felt himself swept up by the heady wine of what seemed like a newly liberated people. The air was full of all the grand words—freedom, independence, sovereignty, etc.—and he would even perhaps hear these same sentiments expressed to the pounding beat of a rock band:

> *Hey, you, you're curious in the West*
> *About the Soviet Union? Listen, that's okay*
>
> *Come in, smart guy, but don't forget*
> *This isn't Russia yet, Russia's miles away.*
>
> *Hey you, you spiffy visitor from Europe*
> *Aboard the Paris-Moscow friendship train*
>
> *The map you've got of us is, oh, so screwed up—*
> *It's missing all the Baltic names!*
>
> *The State of Lithuania: pronounce it, try!*
> *The State of Lithuania: new day is breaking*
>
> *The State of Lithuania: to live or die.*
> *The State of Lithuania, hey, world, we'll make it!*

To the American visitor the sound, the beat, the drive of the music, the slang, the air of bravado—all of it was familiar. He would be flattered that Lithuanians expressed their independence and native character in American Rock, and would wonder for perhaps just a moment whatever happened to the Lithuanian *daina*—which was so unique and so indigenously Lithuanian that it is known to the world only by its own name, *daina*? But this greeting by the Lithuanian youth, sporting long hair, "crazy" clothes and already privy to marijuana (smuggled into the country) twanging their guitars and proclaiming their independence, bearing a strongly nihilistic character, nevertheless seemed, despite the air of topicality and insolence, curiously *used*–secondhand. Rebellion expressed in American Rock and obscenity which–in other songs–reached into the bowels of pornography for inspiration, seemed (to the American who had gone through the '60s) somehow old hat–an imitation. Is it possible to have an imitation independence? Was "independence" also to mean a drug culture, organized prostitutes of both sexes, and invariably the scourge of AIDS?

What happened? Indeed, the more he looked, the deeper he searched, the American visitor would be impressed over and over by the odd quality of this new experience as one *that already had happened.* It was independence–but an imitation independence.

So one goes back and retraces one's steps–the country's history in the search for the genuine and the true. How did it happen? What changes, how and why?

In a way, what happened–its speed, its scope–remains from a purely logical point of view a mystery. Lithuania (and what was true of Lithuania was equally true of Estonia and Latvia) had developed remarkably over the four decades since the end of hostilities in 1945. Not only had the nation been rebuilt–war had almost literally reduced it to ruins–but, beginning in the '50s, and extending through the '60s and '70s, it was seized by a national creative elan that looked forward confidently to a nation which, by the year 2000, would practically run itself. Everything was to be mechanized. The sources of energy were secured, and with the planned building of atomic plants, seemed to promise a complete solution to that problem for all time to come.

To fulfill its grandiose plans, Lithuania trained a whole new generation of intellectuals, engineers, scientists of all kinds, cultural workers, administrators, etc., so that by the early '80s a visitor found a nation hard at work, humming with activity, and, most striking of all, apparently totally in the hands of the generation in its 30's or early 40's, with the generation in its 20's coming up hard behind.

It was accepted as self-evident that Lithuania's progress and prosperity (it was one of the most prosperous of the Soviet republics) was due to its socialist system, as shaped and given substance to by its Communist Party. At war's end, 1945, the Communist Party had a membership of only 3,536. In a country of little over 3 million by 1984, the Party had a membership of 186,885 and the Young Communist League, 495,400. A breakdown of the Party's membership showed 97,681 professional or office employees– mainly bureaucrats–26,081 peasants, and for a Party ostensibly by and for workers, only 63,073 classified as such. By 1990, the Party would be split and its membership radically reduced. Indeed, it would be stripped of most of its former power, including its central offices and various publications, as well as leadership in many organizations and institutions. In August 1991, it was suppressed altogether.

How did it happen?

One can perhaps start in April of 1985 at the 27th Congress of the Communist Party of the Soviet Union. The main report—given by Mikhail Gorbachev—summed up the world situation thusly:

> The progress of our time is rightly identified with socialism. *World socialism* is a powerful international entity with a highly developed economy, substantial scientific resources, and a reliable military and political potential. It accounts for more than one-third of the world's population; it includes dozens of countries and peoples advancing along a path that reveals in every way the intellectual and moral wealth of man and society. A new way of life has taken shape, based on the principles of socialist justice, in which there are neither oppressors nor the oppressed, neither exploiters nor the exploited, in which power belongs to the people. Its distinctive features are collectivism and comradely mutual assistance, triumph of the ideas of freedom, unbreakable unity between the rights and duties of every member of society, the dignity of the individual, and true humanism. Socialism is a realistic option open to all humanity, an example projected into the future.

By 1991, the same Gorbachev who summed up in such confident terms the world and socialist principles and options, stood in the midst of the ruins of "world socialism," as seen and constituted then, and was announcing the fact that within the Soviet Union itself a struggle for power had erupted between forces supporting socialism as modified by perestroika and forces wanting to destroy socialism, every aspect of it, altogether. The class struggle, banned in the USSR for 70 years, suddenly came alive.

The change was indeed so sudden, so widespread, so devastating to socialist power that it left part of the world stunned and part of it celebrating the "end of communism." Repercussions in the Baltics were not long in coming.

In Lithuania, events took on a course that began as one thing and ended as another. In June, 1988, an hitherto unknown musician—Vytautas Landsbergis—who had benefited as his whole family had benefited from the special services extended by socialist free schools to gifted children—was made head of the Initiative Group of the *Sajudis*, which then rapidly changed from an amorphous "movement" to a more organized but still unspecific political force. In March, 1989, Landsbergis was elected by the city of Panevzys to represent Lithuania in the USSR Supreme Soviet, which sat in Moscow. Apparently, the Soviet system was functioning well enough, and fairly enough, so that it was possible for Landsbergis to be elected to its Supreme Soviet. But that was not enough. In February 1990, Landsbergis was "elected" to the Supreme Council of Lithuania, and on March 11, presided over the session of the parliament that "voted" (but not unanimously) to "proclaim" the "restoration" of what it called an inde-pendent Lithuania.

The wording was peculiar—"restoration." In the explanation that accom-panied the declaration, it was now revealed that it was not really necessary for Lithuania to secede from the USSR since it had never been legally part of it! It had been forcibly annexed, and "all" that the parliament (which contained a number of certified criminals) had chosen to do was to reaffirm its former "independent" status.

This was quite a striking formulation and needed exploration. Where did it come from—since nobody had questioned Lithuania's organic unity with the USSR before in quite those terms? True, the USA had never formally acknowledged the move of the Baltic republics in 1940 to join the USSR, and had kept the issue alive by referring to those countries as "captive nations," and periodically issued formal declarations of support for their "independence."

But why now? Some hint of what was happening behind closed doors came out in April 1990, when the Soviet Union apparently refused to renew the visa of an American citizen, William J. Hough, III. Nobody knew who Hough was. He was chastely described as being a close confidante of Landsbergis, on "various international and domestic matters" and that he was only 34, an American lawyer. He knew no Lithuanian. In fact, it was quite strange that a 34-year-old American lawyer, noted for absolutely nothing except that he had been a law clerk to the then New Hampshire Supreme Court Justice David Souter, later to be lofted to the Supreme Court by President Bush.

But what was even more surprising was to discover that this non-Lithu-anian had been sponsored and presumably recommended to Landsbergis by the New York-based Lithuanian Information Center, which was the creation of Catholic Religious Aid. It was even more interesting to discover that the man who was identified by the *New York Times* as nothing but a "friend" of Lithuania, had been the protege of the Lithuanian Information Center, which was organized by one Bishop Vincentas Bryzgys, who had been operating out of Chicago for 25 years.

But Hough had one advantage few other "friends" of Lithuania could boast. He was editor of the *New York Law School of International and Comparative Law*, which, in the winter of 1985, ran a book-length article entitled, "The Annexation of the Baltic States and its Effects on the De-velopment of Law Prohibiting Forcible Seizure of Territory."

In this long, turgid collection of data, Hough describes the interwar period of Lithuania under Smetona as one of "political and constitutional stability" which promised "progress toward the restoration of full democracy." Here is how that same period is described in the *Columbia Encyclopedia* (Third Edition, 1968):

> The virtual dictatorship (1926-1939) of Augustus Voldemaras was succeeded (1929-1939) by that of Antanas Smetona, and an authoritative constitution on corporate (fascist) lines became effective in 1938.

So Hough's "friendship" to Lithuania becomes quite clear. Mobilizing all the legal minds he could gather together, Hough built up a case for secession, based on the assertion that Lithuania (and the other Baltic countries) had been forcibly *annexed* and, therefore, its status as a Soviet republic was illegal. Useful friend!

But in this, as in almost every other aspect of the political struggle that now began, reliance on America become more and more pronounced, and just as the rock 'n rollers greeting visitors at the airport sang about Lithuania in American terms, so did Landsbergis. His mentors were Americans. His independence was dependence on America.

On March 11, 1990, the Lithuanian Soviet—it was still a Soviet—voted, not to secede, but—and here we detect the fine hand of the American sinister lawyers—merely to "redeclare the independence" of Lithuania.

This session of the parliament had been hurriedly called together and, in just a few hours with practically no debate, "voted" (if that is the word) 91-38, not to secede, which would have involved them in a long, law-prescribed process, taking at least five years, but simply to restore the *status quo ante*. It was a trick too slick by far. (To show how firm this motley group of adventurers were—and they included several convicted criminals— they just as hastily suspended for 60 days their decision to "redeclare" during the oil crisis.)

On the same day, March 11, 1990, the knocked-together parliament elected Landsbergis "President" with less than 133 delegates voting, and also voted for a new Constitution, which expressly annulled its socialist character, although in its provisions it did not dare to spell out in full detail just what a return to "market economy" really entailed. On the contrary, those gains made and ensured by Socialist Lithuania, and integrated into the character of the nation, were left undisturbed, at least on paper. But adoption of the new rules was taken as a signal for the Sajudis thugs to launch a reign of terror in the nation, and for would-be merchants to start setting up businesses to make them millionaires in the American way.

By no stretch of the imagination could the Congress, presumably voted into power in March, be considered *democratic*. Not only did it come to power on a wave of unparalleled demagogy, but, even statistically, it could not honestly claim to be representative of the will of the people. The Supreme Soviet was elected by only 41.2 percent of the votes, of which only 30.4 percent went to Sajudis. Nor could one claim that even all those who voted for Sajudis, or who represented Sajudis, shared its political aims—indeed, *could* not, since those aims were kept secret.

The vote was widely reported in the Western press as a vote for "independence." In December, 1990, a public poll had shown that 70 percent of those responding supported continued socialism. Had this changed by March, and if so, why?

There are polls and there are polls. And very often polls do no more than report the extent to which a previous campaign of demagogy and misinformation has succeeded in confusing, persuading, or disgusting the public. In any case, all this was a novel experience for the people who, with the abdication of the Communist Party, had no guidelines.

The Constitution was not offered to the people for discussion and adoption. No referendum was held. It was "adopted" by a show of hands of less than 200 men (and some women) in the new parliament! So much for democracy. Later, many referendums were held in the spirit of: do you want to be free or slave? What are called "ice cream questions:" do you like ice cream? But the main referendum, held on a Union-wide basis on March 17, 1991, Landsbergis was afraid to hold. He ordered it boycotted and, advisedly, for over 80 percent of the Soviet people voted to remain a Union.

To forestall the March 17th nationwide referendum, whose results could be catastrophic to secessionists, Landsbergis ordered a referendum of his own on February 9th. The Lithuanians were asked the "Do you like ice cream question?" That is: "Are you in favor of an independent democratic republic?" Is there anyone on earth who is in favor of a *dependent*, undemocratic republic?

In any case, asserting that the Lithuanians had spoken—for 90 percent of the 80 percent who voted of course voted affirmatively—Landsbergis refused to allow Lithuanians to vote in the March 17th referendum, which asked whether they wished to preserve the Union as a renovated "federation of equal sovereign republics."

Nevertheless, though forbidden to vote, and often having to run a gauntlet of jeering, threatening Nationalists, over 600,000 Lithuanians braved the dangers, present and future, and voted in booths set up and administered by the army and other Soviet safe quarters exactly the way elections were handled by the Union Army in the defeated South: soldiers ensured the right of Blacks to vote in America in 1865 and in Lithuania in 1991.

THE BATTLE OF THE CONSTITUTIONS

We hold these truths to be self-evident...

In Latvia, 125,000 voted against secession. In Estonia, a bit more.

For every citizen who came to the polls, several others dared not. And who knows how many who had voted for an "independent democratic republic" found any contradiction in voting for a Union of "equal sovereign republics" at the second referendum?

Indeed, it is a question whether they knew by this time whether they were voting for God or the devil. The Lithuanian TV, radio, and press had been saturated for weeks and months with a volume of anti-Soviet propaganda that had not been equalled since the occupation by the Nazis. In addition, the Communist Party, and particularly its leader, Algirdas Brazauskas, failed them in this crucial moment, leaving them leaderless. The Party broke in two, one supporting Sajudis, the other defending socialism.

In any case, voting, referenda, saying "yes" or "no" did not in itself reflect knowledge or reality, or even their real wishes, if they had known them. What the Baltics were to be remained in dispute, in conflict. As we were to see, a gradual sobering up began to take place and forces that had originally supported Landsbergis in the first fine frenzy of perestroika and glasnost now began to think again.

In practice this meant the disfranchisement of all minorities in the country, especially those of Russian origin, as well as of Polish origin, who were now stigmatized as pariahs. From them absolute fealty to the Lithuanian Nationalist concepts was demanded, which meant also adopting a hostile attitude toward Russian nationals, even pressuring them to give up their Russian to learn Lithuanian. Before long, both Russian and Polish would be branded as "local languages," thus pinning on those who used those languages an invidious label. No longer would Russian and Polish be spoken out loud and in public, and schools in which those languages were taught would be closed. All this meant the institution of a minority as a permanently despised sect. This included Poles and Russians who had lived in Lithuania for generations.

Changes in the Constitution were accompanied by threats. Thousands of Lithuanians opposed secession and a mass meeting of 180,000 in Vilnius on March 18, 1990 denounced the move to secession as "an unconstitutional coup."

Moves in parliament were aimed at those opposing secession warning them "not to participate in actions directed against resolution of the Lithuanian parliament and ordinances of the government." It threatened those who continued in opposition as "placing themselves beyond the pale of Lithuanian civil society and stand unprotected against negative legal, economic and social consequences," in the words of a Tass dispatch."[119]

Strikes were outlawed and Sajudis moved to levy heavy penalties on anyone calling for violations of the republic's territorial integrity, especially through the use of the mass media and copying equipment.[120]

Ethnic Poles and Russians stood in peril of losing their Soviet citizenship if they remained in Lithuania.

The new "Constitution" made many radical changes, beginning with dropping the words "Socialist" and "Soviet" from the name of the country. It went on to change the entire character of the country itself, eliminating the most typical and definitive elements which made it distinct as a socialist country, and left it vaguely characterized as a "democratic republic."

Significant among the changes now made in the Constitution was the change in the definition of a citizen. In the old constitution, Article 31 read: "Under the uniform citizenship established in the USSR, every citizen of the Lithuanian SSR is a citizen of the USSR."

Not so, says the "new" Constitution. "The republic establishes citizenship ... The essence and condition of and procedure for acquiring or forfeiting citizenship ... shall be defined by the law on Citizenship of the Lithuanian SSR."

The gist of the changes in the new Constitution was contained in Article 70 which, in the old Constitution, read: "Citizens of the Lithuanian SSR enjoy in full the social, economic, political and personal rights and freedoms proclaimed and guaranteed by the Constitution of the USSR, the Constitution of the Lithuanian SSR and by Soviet laws....

"Enjoyment by citizens of their rights and freedoms must not be to the detriment of the interests of society or the state, or infringe the rights of other citizens."

And: "The laws of the USSR shall have the same force on the territory of the Lithuanian SSR."

These Constitutional principles were universally accepted by every republic in the USSR. But the Lithuanians now amended them to read:

Article 70. In the Lithuanian SSR shall operate only the laws adopted by its Supreme Soviet or by a referendum. The laws of the USSR and the legal acts of bodies of state government and administration of the USSR shall operate on the territory of the Lithuanian SSR only upon their endorsement by the Supreme Soviet of the Lithuanian SSR and registration according to the established procedure. Their operation may be limited or suspended by a decision of the Supreme Soviet of the Lithuanian SSR.

That was May 1989, when Lithuania was still referred to as a "soviet" nation, and part of the USSR, with the social content of the nation still socialist. Secession was not yet on the agenda. But before many weeks, the question no longer remained one of autonomy but of secession.

In this process, the role of Algirdas Brazauskas was key. As general secretary of the Communist Party of the Lithuania, in addition to his other positions, he was factually the most powerful man in the country.

In any case, in 1989, he would be writing that despite certain periods in Lithuania's relations with Russia that he condemned sharply, mainly the way in which Lithuania joined the USSR and the policy of deportations before and after WWII, nevertheless, "In the exceedingly complex historical situation of 1939-1940, when the destiny of the Lithuanian people was being decided, Lithuania's Communist Party and its farsighted leader Antanas Snieckus advocated the entry into the Soviet Union. History has confirmed the correctness of this decision. The Lithuanian people could only have survived and did so only with the aid of the Soviet Union."[122]

This was Brazauskas early in 1989. Then, he would say, from a position of confirmed power (as the leader of the largest and best organized party in the country) that the Party "interacts with independent public organizations and movements, in particular, with Sajudis, the Lithuanian movement for perestroika. It actively interacts with them for common aims."

He approved resuming the singing of the "national anthem" which Nationalists had never given up singing, and going back to the "old" flag with its national symbols, replacing both the flag of the Soviet Union and the flag of socialist Lithuania. He did not put on record his feelings later when the organized crowds surged into downtown Vilnius and tore the hammer and sickle symbols from the headquarters of the Communist Party, which were closed, and later padlocked. (Landsbergis had set himself the goal of destroying the Communist Party.). He clung to the belief that the Party and Sajudis still shared "common aims" in support of perestroika. He still believed, too, that "Lithuania's full independence is unrealistic for many reasons—both political and economic. The economy of our republic is too deeply integrated into that of the entire country. And we maintain close political ties. Many Lithuanians," he, an economist warned, "live under the illusion that if Lithuania were to become an independent state, its separation from the Soviet Union would produce immediate and beneficial results."[123]

He would go on to say:

> As a historical example they refer to the events of 1918, when our republic gained the status of a state and nothing terrible happened. But it must be borne in mind that in those days Lithuania had a self-sustaining economy, which did not require either the present degree of integration or the present economic potential. But our industry is oriented mainly on manufacturing end-products, which necessitates a great number of ties between enterprises, associations, and ministries. Our republic receives all the raw materials needed for the normal functioning of production through established channels. Oil and gas, for instance, come from the Tyune Region. One-third of the social product is involved in a continual exchange. As an economist I can say that there is a very high level of integration .... When I hear paens to private ownership of the means of production and the advantages of private land-ownership, I find it difficult to believe that in those times over a thousand peasant households annually went under and that many peasants, despairing of making a living on their own land, set out to earn their daily bread across the ocean....[124]

He goes on to assert that "Our idea and aim is the sovereignty of our republic within the Soviet Union. Our key political task now is the self-reliance of Lithuania's economy."

And: "When all is said and done, how do we visualize our future? We want to speak the language of our ancestors and to own the lakes, rivers, fields, meadows, forests and sea they have left to us. We want to survive and live in Lithuania." And he ends on a note which becomes an essential and implicit surrender to the Nationalists. "For a long time," he says, "we were even too intimidated to say: 'Lithuania is our motherland.'" Instead of which, he insists, for "Lithuanian Motherland" Lithuanians were taught to see the entire USSR as their "motherland": "Motherland to us then was something boundless—the tundra, and the taiga, and volcanoes, but Lithuania was merely our native land. Now our people's pride for its glorious past is reviving, and from its revival we are drawing strength for today's accomplishments."[125] If so with Brazauskas, who envisioned a "sovereign" Lithuania within the Union, it was not so with Landsbergis, who had only contempt for the Communist Party and considered its existence a "myth."

Early on, in 1989 in fact, before his aims were quite clear, and Sajudis was projected as no more than a dissenting movement whose role was to correct the excesses of government policy, much like "the Greens" in Germany, Landsbergis gave an interview to the *Washington Post*,[126] in which he was perhaps somewhat indiscrete; in any case, premature.

While still maintaining that Sajudis was nothing more than an expression of perestroika, he made it clear that full secession and a return to capitalism was his goal, and that all minorities had better toe the nationalist line or get out. By this time he was already referring to the Communist Party of Lithuania as a "myth," and in his several trips to the USA, he established close ties to the CIA-funded American nationalist organizations, as well as the forces representing National Endowment for Democracy, from which he received thousands of dollars in "aid." He paid visits to some of the most reactionary forces in the capital, like the Heritage Foundation, "think tank" of ultra-reaction, where he was warmly received, and from whose "thinking" he presumably benefited.

Interestingly enough, these statements of Landsbergis had the support of a J.V. Paleckis, then the ideological head of the Lithuanian Communist Party, who, citing the notorious proposition that "human values" took priority over "class," entered into an alliance with the confirmed enemies of Lithuanian democracy, like Kazys Bobelis, Chairman of the Supreme Committee for the Liberation of Lithuania, a pro-fascist Nationalist organization centered in the USA.

Through NED (National Endowment for Democracy), set up in 1983 to funnel Congressional funds to political groups overseas, Washington helped finance, train, advise, and equip the region's "democratic oppositions." In fact, according to NED'S public information officer Peter Kosciewicz, "it pumped nearly $15 million into Eastern Europe and the Soviet Union in 1990 alone...."

"It has supported political organizations accused of neofascism—like Sajudis in Lithuania and the Hungarian Democratic Forum ... All its beneficiaries are dedicated to free market capitalism, the complete dismantling of the Soviet bloc, and the eradication of class analysis ... [in 1990] NED also funded opposition forces in the Baltics..."[127]

It is not too extreme to suggest that many such "democratic" candidates, who are thus directly sponsored and funded by the CIA (NED is a mere camouflage) have attained key positions in the new governments in Eastern Europe including the Baltics. Few living Lithuanians had ever seen Smetona fascism up close, had never been in a bourgeois prison, or had even ever participated in a strike. They were a generation of professionals, born since the war, raised in conditions of peace and class harmony, taught a socialist morality in the abstract, while witnessing it being violated (often by themselves) in daily life. In fact, they were a naive generation, almost totally inexperienced in politics, who had become Communists, not as a result of struggle, but as a kind of reward for work in which not their lives were at stake, but just their careers.

In the pre-Congress meetings, Communists who did not favor secession, and mainly they came from the older, veteran generation who *had* been alive in prewar Lithuania, *had* spent time in Smetona's prisons, and *had* gone through the war in which the best of them perished, were bullied, mocked, denounced as "Stalinists," as stooges of Moscow. They were pictured as the last of the sinking ship, called "Marxism-Leninism" which, the neo-Marxists contended, was implied in Gorbachev's new policies—in the elevation of "universal human values" over the class struggle, which Shevardnadze would champion with such disasterous results. In a world which had suddenly been cleansed of the class struggle, why did anyone need a Communist Party?

These Communists did not make it to the Congress. Later, they would issue a composite letter in which they renounced the revisionists and post-fabricated version of events in Lithuania during and after the war, and they would move to form a separate party with an initial membership of 40,000. But it was their sons and daughters, for whom they had created a social milieu based on socialist morality, that judged them now.

These young men and women were, in a paradoxical way, products of the success of socialism. Most of them had been peasants or their parents had been peasants just one generation before. But the socialist state had taken them out of the countryside and educated them—equipped them with the vocabulary with which to denounce socialism as imperfect, as having failed. They had long ago forgotten the smell of manure. They had never known work—work as their fathers knew it, as sweat, as grunt, as blood— and their membership in a Party dedicated to the working class took on an unreal quality.

It was in this highly rarefied atmosphere of pure morality—of life perceived from the aesthetic distance of art—that they seized on the revelations that a "secret codicil" to the Non-Aggression Pact which the Soviets had signed with the Nazis in 1939 contained provisions determining the immediate fate and, therefore, the future of Lithuania. They were not even alive then when their very future hung so desperately in the balance, and every wind across the border from Poland brought the stench of burning bodies. They condemned "Stalin"—no longer a real person, but now a myth—and equated him with Hitler. They had no grasp of the real politics of the times when there were no second chances—where the choices were not between vice and virtue but between bad and worse, between survival or death. It is extraordinary, to anyone who had witnessed events at the time as they unfolded—1933 to 1939—that those who attack the Soviets for dealing with Hitler, magnanimously pass up or excuse the far more secret, devious and criminal dealings which England's Chamberlain had conducted for years with Hitler, all with the aim of directing his military machine against the Soviets. Indeed, as we have seen, when the British were asked by the Soviets if they would actively defend the Baltics in case of Nazi attack, the British refused to give that assurance—which meant, in the reality of the time, that they accepted in advance—and (Hitler so understood it) any move that Hitler might make against the Baltics. Britain (and France) had already turned over Czechoslovakia, Austria, the Sudetenland, Klaipeda, etc. to Hitler. Why not the Baltics?

This generation has no gratitude to extend to the Russians for having returned Klaipeda, and most significant, for having restored—not once but twice—Vilnius as Lithuania's capital. Nor, for that matter, helping to rid the country of its most notorious quislings and traitors, the fascist Smetona and his crew, and with their going ending the power of the class they represented. To cover that period so bitter to the workers and peasants in a glow of fictional nostalgia is no favor to the young. Under those bourgeois conditions, the law that ruled was to buy and to sell—and, when it came down to it, it was their country they bought and sold to international capital. Nor were they free to decide at what price to buy and sell. They bought and sold human souls at the price dictated by the Stock Markets of the capitalist world.

The delegates functioned under the spell of perestroika and glasnost, as first defined, which seemed then to open up for the whole socialist world a new era of unbuttoned freedom; and a life unburdened with toil. So swept away were they by this new perspective that when cadres were needed to harvest the potato crop, the liberated Lithuanians couldn't be bothered to go into the country and dirty their hands digging them up out of the soil! (Soviet soldiers had to go).

When David Stockman, President Reagen's budget director, was asked whether he had made provision in the new budget for social "entitlements," he snapped: "You [the poor] are entitled to nothing." None of the Lithuanian delegates would have understood this. *They* were entitled to *everything*—from the cradle to the grave: medical care, education, housing, work, vacations, old age care.... They took all this for granted and assumed that "freedom" in the "market economy" still meant all that—plus capitalist goodies.

Brazauskas had encouraged the Young Communist League to abandon Marxism-Leninism and (with huge losses) to reconvene as a pale shadow of its former self with a mission no firmer than to echo the line now set by the enemies of Socialism. (And finally to disband altogether.)

As for Brazauskas, "firmly" opposed to secession only weeks before, and cogently pointing out, as an economist, how disastrous secession would be to Lithuania's economy, now as a member of Lithuania's parliament (to which he was elected by courtesy of Sajudis, which chose not to contest his seat) with what is indecent haste voted for full secession, because, he explained, he would have otherwise been branded a traitor. "We chose the people," he claimed, meaning he had accepted Sajudis as "the people."

He no doubt envisioned a continued leading role for the Party which had led the country from devastation and despair to where it was one of the most prosperous in the USSR, but in surrendering to Nationalism and accepting its claim to represent the true spirit of the nation, he discovered that there was no line he could draw beyond which he, as a Communist, could not go. Indeed, he went all the way, shedding his "Marxism" as he went.

His reward was to be made deputy premier, a position with no power whatsoever. His trade-off was to drape Sajudis with working-class, even "Communist" approval, thus surrendering to Sajudis the moral right not only to represent the will of the people but to lead them back to capitalism which the phrase "see(ing) the independent Lithuanian state restored" really meant. Soon, Brazausksas too, no longer spoke of a "socialist" Lithuania but only of a "democratic" Lithuania.

The position the Communist Party took amidst a storm of demagogy, distortion and a newly cobbled version of history now custom-made to fit present needs, differed in no essential way from the Nationalists, nor indeed from the position of international imperialism, which had now become solidified and reduced to a code.

Whatever illusions Brazauskas may have entertained about the role he and his split-off party would play in post-socialist Lithuania, he was soon to be disabused of them; though, by the time a rational person might have understood that he had outstayed his welcome, Brazauskas still clung on. His public comments became more and more fuzzy and disoriented. In the end, his voice disappeared entirely. When Kazimiera Prunskiene resigned as Prime Minister in 1991, her going was the unmistakable sign that the original principles of perestroika had all been strangled in their crib. As far as Landsbergis was concerned, not only was there *never* a legitimate Communist Party in Lithuania, but what did exist was nothing but a "myth." To him there was no place for a party of the working class.

Indeed, the real purposes of Sajudis were revealed slowly and step by step. Much has become clear in retrospect, particularly the key question of why Lithuania was chosen to start what was hoped to be a process of the disintegration of the entire Soviet Union. The process was helped along and inspired by the American secret services, working especially through quasi-religious organizations, which had conducted underground activity in Lithuania for years. The CIA particularly worked through the National Endowment for Democracy, pouring millions of dollars into Lithuania through various agencies all dedicated to a new-found passion for "democracy," "pluralism," and devotion to a market economy; as well as through the AFL-CIO, whose president Lane Kirkland is a militant anti-Communist with ties to the CIA, but no Lithuanian.

What could be more eloquent, for instance, than the "principles" of the Lithuanian-American Council, a branch of the worldwide Supreme Council Committee for the Liberation of Lithuania, a member of the Coalition for Peace Through Strength, and all of it under the umbrella of the Anti-Bolshevik Bloc of Nations, which makes no bones about its roots in violently fascist Nationalist groups like the Ukrainian Bandera? Its aim is the "liberation" of Lithuania, and it does not shrink from using the words "democracy," "pluralism," etc., which by now have become the well-worn coins of anti-democratic cant.

Landsbergis himself admits in an interview with Norwegian radio that Sajudis was not a spontaneous uprising of the people but a carefully cultivated organization that worked "underground" for years. He says:

> For those several decades, we (Nationalists) smoldered with the desire to survive. Alongside this, there was also the strategy of dissent, of open protest, of the underground press [financed by the CIA], which denounced the occupation [of the Red Army troops that had driven the Nazis out of the land and left over 200,000 of their own dead] called for resistance to Bolshevism, and for the protection of the religious rights and democracy....
>
> But there was that semi-official struggle, which was very visible, but could not be named—because that would have been like revealing your cards to your opponent—everyone more or less knew who stood for what, who tended towards conformism, towards being parasites in this huge state which bought intellectuals, which tried to buy our culture. Then, on the eve of Sajudis, clubs of intellectuals and philosophers began to meet for discussion....[128]

So, after all, there had *been* a conspiracy!

Here is how he sums up the whole process of distributing land to the peasants, the formation of collective farms, etc.:

> A man who, ten years before had his own small farm with a brook and trees and homeland—ten years later has nothing—only a ditch and a bare field remain of his former home, and he and his neighbors have been herded into a town, to live in concrete boxes. He still ostensibly lives in Lithuania, but the real Lithuania, the one in which he was at home which he loved, has been destroyed. The wayside crosses which dotted the countryside—destroyed ... He may live in a new housing block, with gas and hot water, but he has lost something which he perhaps cannot put in words, and begins to drink for some reason, sitting by his gas stove.
>
> Some kind of demonic power has devastated this land. Deformed children... Empty lives....

And, as for socialism itself, he would say:

> The existence of such a system is basically meaningless. It is a creature of Satan....

Nevertheless, the committee that was sent to Moscow to organize the inclusion of Lithuania in the Soviet Union in 1940, was made up of some of the leading writers and artists of Lithuania: the famed poet, Salomeya

Neris, novelist, Petras Cvirka, the poet and later Minister of Education, Antanas Venclova, as well as the outstanding journalist, who later became premier, Justas Paleckis, among others: an extremely distinguished delegation indeed.

But, this day when Lithuania was accepted into the Soviet Union, and which was hailed all over the country with great mass meetings of workers and peasants and intellectuals, appeared to Landsbergis, whose version was acquired from his bitter-end Nationalist father, as

> a day when Lithuania and its people were betrayed. And a great misfortune befell them. The so-called Peoples *Sejm*, convened in an atmosphere of terror unleashed by the secret services of a foreign occupying power, and deceived by the party of local quislings [the party now headed by Brazauskas] voted for a "voluntary" entry of Lithuania in the USSR, though it had not been authorized by the electorate to do that.[129]

A "reply" had already been drafted to this highly-distorted version of events by 124 survivors of the period, long-time Communists, now sneered at as "quislings," though it seems difficult to imagine anyone fitting that term more snugly than Smetona and his gang who are today's heroes in the Landsbergis' mirage. Said these survivors:

> Under the banner of the struggle for the restoration of Lithuania's sovereignty, anti-socialist and anti-Soviet forces are striving to put an end to its socialist sovereignty. Their aim is to destroy the Union and cooperative and fraternal relations between the Soviet republics and to sow enmity and mistrust among Soviet peoples, thereby eliminating the main economic, political, social and cultural advances of people living in Lithuania which have been achieved during the years of Soviet government. They want to restore a bourgeois system in Lithuania.[130]

It is worth noting, in view of Landsbergis' charge that Lithuania had been coerced into joining the USSR, that when it came to separating from the USSR, the decision, made by his handful of Sajudis followers *in a few hours*, was *sprung* upon the Lithuanian people whose wishes were not consulted. And although a number of "referendums" took place later, as we have noted, the propositions were couched in such a way that only the desired result could be produced. But when it came to letting the Lithuanian people vote in the referendum of March 17, 1991, on whether they wanted to be part of a federation of soviet republics or not, the Landsbergis forces refused to allow the voting to take place. This refusal was eloquent proof, indeed of just how "voluntary" the move to secede from the USSR had been....

The statement of the 124 survivors of the first struggles to establish socialism in Lithuania goes on to say:

Having first posed as supporters of perestroika, which was initiated by the Soviet Communist Party, they are doing their utmost to prevent the successful solution of its main tasks, and in particular, the filling of Lithuania's sovereignty with qualitatively new content.[131]

This was quite true. Sajudis had originally come on the scene, not as a political force, but as a kind of ombudsman—as concerned citizens monitoring the actions of the state. Specifically, it proposed to support the development of perestroika, encourage openness, further democracy, protect the environment by shutting down atomic plant construction, carrying socialism to a higher level. Their "support" of perestroika was camouflaged. It was all a fraud. They simply hijacked the program and turned it into its opposite.

As the melodramatic elements of the period of opposition to Soviet power began to recede and a more sober look at reality became possible, the intellectual poverty of Sajudis' advocates came even more starkly into view. The truth was that they had no ideas, only refurbished old ones. To advocate returning to a period when, as Brazauskas has pointed out, over a thousand small farmers annually lost their farms, and their "brooks," and spurning "gas and hot water," in what Landsbergis called "concrete boxes" (whose rental was minimal and from which nobody could be evicted) is to ask for what is in reality impossible. As matters turned out, when those ex-farmers, now suffering in warm "boxes," were offered farms to return to, they almost universally passed up a golden opportunity to return to the pleasures of their ancestors—to dark huts and impacted ignorance. In Landsbergis' eyes—the eyes of his Nationalist father—urban Lithuania is anathema to God—the work of Satan—and the sooner the people return to raising sheep and pigs and cows, the better. The system which eliminated illiteracy, poverty, created a new intelligentsia, a new culture, wiped out many diseases, etc., he sees as the work of "Satan."

So much for history, culture, progress, common sense.

What is so striking to any viewer of the scene today is this aspect of the opposition—its unbelievably low intellectual level. It has no new ideas. What ideas it does have merge with mysticism, a kind of Nazi return to the concept of "folk," of seeing in the land the mystical source of all human values, and in the city the degeneration of those "folk." "Folk," expressed in narrow nationalist terms, quickly emerges as a formal national exclusiveness, bordering on racism.

It is also eloquently revealing that when they wanted to replace the socialist flag, they had to go back over 500 years of history to find an acceptable symbol—the Knight on the horse *Vytis*. This symbol was an echo of the battle of Grünewald (1440), when the combined Polish and Lithuanian forces of the Grand Duchy, finally dealt a mortal blow to the invading Teutons. No one seemed conscious of the irony involved in such an historic leap back, that indeed when the Germans were to be rebuffed a second time, 500 years later, it was the *Russians* (with the help of Lithuanians) who repulsed them, and so, fittingly enough, the Lithuanian victors adopted for the symbols on *their* flag, the instruments of working-class rule—the hammer and sickle—symbols by the way, of peace among all peoples.

Typical too of the essential frivolousness and absence of connection to reality that the changes represented was the heated debate conducted in the new Lithuanian parliament for two days over how to depict the horse in the new insignia—with its tail up or down? (The faction that wanted it up seemed to have won out.) They took longer to decide whether the tail should go up or down than it took them to decide to leave the USSR and scuttle socialism!

Nor should it occasion too much surprise that in seeking for anti-Communist symbols the Lithuanian Nationalists should—as it were—helplessly repeat symbols couched in mystical phrases already used by the German Nationalists—the Nazis. Over and over, Landsbergis harks in his rhetoric to the "simple" folk of Lithuania who spent their lives in arcadian innocence—uncontaminated by any modern "inconveniences" like gas and electricity and inside toilets. To him, socialism means cities of houses that are "boxes," where modern plumbing reigns, and where children—who died like flies in that "arcadian" paradise—no longer die of diseases that clean water and proper medicine can prevent.

LITHUANIA IN CRISIS

At home, at work, in restaurants, on stage
We tear each other into little pieces.
While stage-lights burn, across the wall's wide screen
Our comic shadows go on leaping, ceaseless ...
Who knows how things will turn out finally?
—Alfonsas Maldonis, *Rhetoric*, 1963

By the end of the year—1989—things had begun to deteriorate so sharply inside the three Baltic republics, but especially in Lithuania, that Gorbachev felt compelled to pay a personal visit in January to Vilnius and speak to the Communists there. By now, the party had ideologically split in two, and the factions were no longer listening to each other.

The scope of the demonstrations that had taken over Kaunas and Vilnius—though countered by counter-demonstrations—nevertheless were alarming. Algirdas Brazauskas had become deaf and no appeals to what had always constituted the very essence of Communist principles could now move him. By this time he had forgotten his own, more cogent, analysis of the situation in which he understood the necessity of remaining within the Soviet family.

Gorbachev began his address to the meeting on a defensive note: "My stay in the republic and participation in this meeting, at which both wings of the Communist movement in Lithuania are present, indicates that you, comrades, have not yet got out of the state of euphoria and that is so far difficult to direct the process of the comprehension of what is happening in your republic into a deeper channel."

The "euphoria" had been almost mindless. After the unilateral declaration of independence, crowds, obviously following a previously arranged plan, surged through central Vilnius, stopped before the Central Office of the Communist party and tore down the hammer and sickle emblem as though totally eliminating the Communist Party from social life.

This had not been foreseen in the general exposition of perestroika and glasnost. At most, the Communist Party was to surrender its leading role in the nation and, in cooperation with all other positive and democratic organizations, move toward a fuller and more expansive and wider democracy, but a *socialist* democracy.

Deluding themselves that Sajudis was expressing a populist uprising, some leading Communists, as it were, threw away their Communist cards and symbols of affiliation and joined "the people," helping to give Sajudis working-class support. Almost overnight, membership in the Party declined. And within the party itself a deep split opened up. Other organizations of every stripe, (about 20) also appeared as if overnight, with aims and objectives varying from left to extreme right. In June, the Young Communist League had held a convention, at which it voted to secede from the all-Union YCL, and reconstitute itself as a vague, aimless organization which immediately began to disintegrate. Brazauskas—elected general secretary of the adult party only recently after the death of Petras Griskevicius, its former general secretary—had given the YCL his blessings to commit hara-kiri.

Now he was bent on repeating the same drama with the Communist Party itself. His aim was to cut it loose from the all-union party and to introduce a novel (though not new) proposition, which in his day Lenin had fought, making each party in each republic "independent" and "autonomous," choosing or not choosing to support the general policies of the Communists of the entire Union as it saw fit.

For a brief period, because of his perceived defiance of the "big" Party, Brazauskas became the most "popular" personality in Lithuania, and a poll taken in June 1989 gave him an 84% "approval rating," some 14 points above Vytautas Landsbergis.

Indeed, at this point, Brazauskas stood at the very peak of opportunity. He was in a position to turn the nation in the direction of support for perestroika in its original form with its original content—as expanding the real democracy of the nation along a socialist direction—but he was fated to choose otherwise. He chose the route of "independence," and in effect he handed over what authority he had to Sajudis. And in that act he committed political suicide.

In his plea to the Communists of Lithuania to stop and think, Gorbachev pointed out that the future of Lithuania lay not along the route of bourgeois democracies, that mere "pluralism"—many parties—did not in itself constitute more democracy. "We know dozens of states with 10 to 20 parties, but ruled by dictatorial regimes. And not all have been freed from them. Everything is determined, comrades, by the regime of political power, the level of democracy, the political process, public opinion, public movements that are capable of accumulating and expressing and making known public interests...."

He asked the assembled Lithuanian Communists—perhaps to remain Communists only briefly—"What is then the party for? Or do you want to bury it here at first and then spread the experience further? Then go ahead and say so. We shall not be able to do without the party." (Later he turned against his own words.)

He said to Brazauskas, in effect, that by cutting loose from the Union, the Party in Lithuania dooms itself to impotence. And as events mount up, "Comrade Brazauskas will be reading newspapers to learn what we have decided and what the fate of Lithuania should be in this connection."

Indeed, ominous events began to proliferate. Suddenly, in May, an organization calling itself the Lithuanian Freedom League erected a monument honoring the anti-Soviet "guerrillas" in Vilnius. Soon they would petition the parliament for pensions and compensations for their "patriotic" struggles against the "Soviets" during the war and after. Statues of Lenin were destroyed and cities and streets bearing the name of Lenin were renamed—and February 16 was declared national independence day. This date referred to February 16, 1918 when Lithuanian "independence" was first declared—under German protection, as it happened.

This was not "perestroika" or anything like it. It was open counterrevolution. On April 2, 1990, an article by Peter Schille appeared in West Germany's *Der Spiegel*, titled *"Angst vor Sajudis,"* in which Schille wrote that "Everybody fears Sajudis. Anyone who attacks Sajudis is declared an enemy of the people by Landsbergis, and that happens very quickly." In addition, the notorious Savandoriai—a paramilitary fascist organization—which had played so deadly a role during and after the war, and of which Landsbergis' father had been a member, was revived and suddenly the atmosphere in the country turned sinister, dangerous, and ugly.

In April, Gorbachev addressed an appeal to the Lithuanian people in which he declared that

> The attempts being made by the incumbent Lithuanian leaders is to break the republic's ties with the Soviet Union and its tactics of unilateral actions and ultimatums endanger the normal life and security of all peoples in the republic—Lithuanian and non-Lithuanian—and are a cause of grave concern in the country.
>
> Is it normal when amendments to the Constitution, resolving the destiny of the republic and its people and concerning the interests of the entire people, country, are adopted in haste, without consultations and discussions, actually *within one night?* [my italics—P.B.]

Indeed, everything had been done in haste, in an effort to confront the people with a *fait accompli.* The decision to cut itself loose from the Union had been made, in March, not after a prolonged discussion in the press involving the entire people, but by a small group of men (and women) elected for one purpose—but who, once elected, acted to enact an entirely different purpose. The vote which had historic implications was 91-38.

Gorbachev went on to say:

Attempts are being made to convince you that genuine sovereignty within the Soviet Union, without breaking away from it, is impossible. Simultaneously, old grudges are being purposefully kindled and the negative aspects of our life together are being emphasized.

Indeed, our past includes many things that we mutually reject. And this refers not only to the Lithuanian people. But no one can say that in the years of perestroika that any group of people in our country has been deliberately elevated or purposefully humiliated.

For years we have lived in one home. Does the past deserve only bad words? Have Lithuanian literature and poetry, theater and cinema, music and architecture, education and sports faded and become lost in the multicolored Soviet culture?

On the contrary, as any visitor or student of the scene would have to report.

Gorbachev—still a Communist—went on to remind them:

> Was it not through working together and with the fraternal aid of other republics that your industry and agriculture have developed? Did Lithuania itself not extend a helping hand to other people in times of trouble?
>
> Did the citizens of your republic not support the USSR Constitution, by which Lithuania abided for years honestly and strictly as a fully-fledged republic?
>
> The incumbent Lithuanian leaders are trying to convince you that their separatist actions will not affect economic, scientific, technical and other ties with the other republics of the USSR.

And, soon enough, what the case really was and would be, became clear when the USSR decided to eliminate the subsidy on oil it had extended to the Lithuanians (as to other non-oil producing republics) causing a crisis for the government immediately and the suspension of its declaration of independence for 60 days.

Events in Lithuania generally roused little foreign support in the beginning and, indeed, hopes that more active support would come in a dramatic way from the USA were doused with cold water. The *New York Times* advised "sympathy" ["Cheer Lithuania, but Don't Meddle," ed. March 17, 1990] but not much else, and when a direct appeal to President Bush was ignored, Landsbergis issued a bitter denunciation comparing the rejection to a "scenario that recalls 1940," as well as the Munich of 1938. It was in 1940 that the Smetona government, under pressure, had finally agreed to letting the Red Army take up border defenses—a moment in Nationalist mythology consecrated as the "betrayal." As for Munich, invoking the memory of it in present circumstances merely distorted the whole significance of it.

There were forces in the West who did not like the peaceful manner in which negotiations were being conducted by the Soviets with the Lithuanians. The ultra-reactionary columnist for the *New York Times* (a one-time speech writer for the convicted thief, vice-president Spiro Agnew) William Safire viewed the Lithuanian scene after the gas cut-off, which showed Lithuanian cars lined up at empty gas stations, and wrote that "to prick the conscience of the world, Lithuanians will have to do more than line up cars at gas stations." Such a scene lacked pathos, he implied. What Safire missed was the sight of broken bodies and bombed hospitals.[132]

Earlier, under the heading "Let Lithuania Go," Safire had waxed indignant that Gorbachev had ordered all Lithuanians to turn in their shotguns. He complained that Gorbachev "rips the shotguns out of the hands of peaceful Lithuanians (thereby inviting the violence leading to a crackdown)."

Indeed, attempts had been made to smuggle arms into Lithuania. That same April, customs officials had seized 250,000 hunting rifle cartridges on board the *M. Koslov* in Lithuania's Baltic port of Kiaipeda.

But in the columns of Safire, as well as in the speeches of other sudden converts to the Lithuanian cause, one could detect the yearning for a dramatic explosive episode that could be shown on international TV in the black-and-white scenario terms already agreed on: Russia, the handle-bar mustached oppressor, little Lithuania the pure maiden in distress. This image was enough for "middle America" which, two weeks before, did not know the difference between a Lithuanian and a lobotomy. As far as most Americans were aware, "captive" Lithuania was where Cole Porter, the song writer, had left it in the famous song from his 1928 Broadway musical, *Paris*: "Lithuanians and Letts do it, let's do it—let's fall in love...."

Almost as if following a script, the "violence" which Safire so patently yearned for finally broke out when the all-Soviet army already stationed in Lithuania, moved in Vilnius to take over the TV, which had been spewing anti-Soviet propaganda for weeks, calling on soldiers of Lithuanian nationality to desert the army.

Such events in Lithuania were a bugle call to "soldiers of fortune" all over the world. Answering was one, Andrew Eiva, son of a pre-socialist Lithuanian military man, who had become active in the Afghan war, inventing an organization called the Federation for Afghan Action—one of those organizations with no membership, a fund-raising letter with "impressive" names on the letterhead, and a shredding machine within easy reach. He saw no future in Afghanistan after the Soviets withdrew. Instead, he moved to the Supreme Council of the Liberation of Lithuania, an out-and-out fascist organization, subsisting mysteriously on invisible funds, but loud in its support of "democratic" Lithuania.

Stories of clashes in Lithuania called to Eiva, who saw in developments there "the newest growth industry for conservatives."

He turned up in Vilnius, whose borders for such as he are fantastically porous, in January 1991. The situation in Vilnius looked like this to an observer:

> Every morning now, school children come from class and tape up their harrowing watercolors of tanks crushing a crowd of people, stick-like figure soldiers firing on stick-figure Lithuanians. Adults bring their official symbols of Soviet citizenship—their passports, draft cards and Communist Party cards—and spike them on strings of barbed wire. Students throw copies of the "History of the Communist Party" and "History of the Great Red Army" into small bonfires near the wall....
>
> Inside the parliament, defense volunteers walk around in rag-tag uniforms, carrying ancient hunting rifles or knives. An American former Green Beret who helped the *mujaheddin* rebels in Afghanistan [obviously Andre Eiva] hands out advice to anyone who will listen....
>
> Rita Dapkus, a young Chicagoan of Lithuanian descent, was one of a dozen Americans [from NED?] who ran the parliament's press center ... They helped engineer a revolution by telex, video and facsimile machines [all unknown in Lithuania before] keeping correspondents and supporters around the world informed of every declaration and troop movement in Vilnius just minutes after it happened....
>
> Now Dapkus, like so many other volunteers and legislators, is sleeping in the parliament building. The building has changed remarkably: its walls are covered with religious pictures, caricatures of Gorbachev....[133]

These were the types of Americans (how many?) who came to "save" Lithuania from Bolshevism, carrying on a crusade laid down by their fathers 40 or more years earlier. A Senator just one step ahead of prison, and a Green Beret, whose savage career in Vietnam remains a bloody scar on the American conscience, "handing out advice" on how to defend Landsbergis' variety of "democracy," plus *New York Times* writer William Safire—these were the types who have come to the aid of "little" Lithuania!

Of Andrew Eiva, David Khybar would write:

> Andrew Eiva has the necessary conservative credentials; young and fervently anti-communist with a penchant for paramilitary operations. Eiva is also the grandson of Lithuanian General Kaziemieras Ladyga, who had fought the Russian revolutionaries at the end of WWI [as had Landsbergis' father]. His parents had taught him about post WWII guerrilla networks in Lithuania, which enjoyed CIA support and had been finally shut down by the Soviets.[134]

The euphoria Gorbachev spoke about finally disappeared. Kaziemiras Prunskiene came and went. Her appointment as Foreign Minister had been the last gesture Landsbergis would make toward those Lithuanians who still believed in the original aims of perestroika. She had come on the scene voicing approval of Gorbachev's new direction and had insisted that Lithuania would follow that direction, even as a separate country.

But it was not to be. When proposals to implement perestroika and for introducing the first elements of the socialist "market economy" were made and were turned down by Landsbergis, their paths parted.

As the paths of many were to part. In the beginning, as we know, strictly as a movement for greater autonomy for Lithuania but not secession, Sajudis had managed to get the support of many of Lithuania's intellectuals. As late as the end of 1988, poets in Lithuania were still writing:

> *My position is human,*
> *with no indulgence and no compromise.*
> *For I am that fellow who works at the furnace,*
> *he who sows grain on the bare fields in spring...*
>
> *I am that man who stood true, firm and fearless,*
> *who had achieved the great Revolution;*
> *not for some personal gains*
> *but to bring all the gain to others around...*
>
> *Thus as a Communist I am speaking,*
> *having acquired that name in the war.*
> *And the position I proclaim you can take up entirely*
> *or as quite alien, can decline it at once.*
>   *My Own Position*—Yuozas Macevicius[135]

This proud, forthright statement of a political and moral position was not to be seen again in the literary works after March, 1990. Now, the literary periodicals teemed with denunciations of Communists, the past, Communist aims, socialism, and the leading cultural figures whose works had been circulated in the thousands in little Lithuania (and thousands more outside Lithuania) were either now silenced, denounced as Russian agents, or went over to Sajudis like the much-honored Marcinkevicius. One no longer heard from Miezelaitis,* nor from other leading intellectuals, after their first ecstatic hosannahs to the 'new freedom' envisioned in perestroika and particularly in glasnost. With glasnost, they had believed they were now free to "say anything"—to create those great masterpieces which they flattered themselves they had suppressed in themselves before. They were sure that "freedom of expression" led to the wedding with truth whose progeny would be a unique, liberated literature soaring into the bluest of heights on wings of unfettered inspiration.

Nothing of the sort happened. What really happened was that, before they knew it, newspapers which published their opinions in the past no longer solicited them. *Tiesa*, once the leading paper of the Republic, shriveled into a shadow of its former self and was finally suppressed. Publishing houses turned down their latest manuscripts. TV was dark to them. Their

---

* After the death of his wife, Miezelaitis seemed to retire to silence and depression.

voices could not be heard on radio. Indeed, suddenly as if on a signal from nowhere, they found themselves to be 'outside society', pariahs in their own land, mocked by every schoolboy stoned on rock 'n roll, whose impudence was in direct ratio to his ignorance. The notion that with Landsbergis a government which honored culture—a living culture, not a 'culture' dug up out of the ruins of the Middle Ages—would be instituted on the highest moral level soon enough died of asphyxiation. In fact, freedom of expression died with Sajudis. In Sajudis' terms, glasnost meant solely the right to slander socialism.

One by one the dreamers—grownup men in their 40s and 50s whose grasp of reality would have shamed even a teenager—dropped off, until finally, almost no intellectual of any standing wanted to be associated with Sajudis.

IS IT DARK AT THE END
OF THE TUNNEL?

Be not deceived. Revolutions do not go backwards.
—Abraham Lincoln, May 19, 1859

In December 1990, a kind of climax was reached when one of the leading supporters of Sajudis, the writer Vitautas Petkavicius, finally cut loose. In a revealing interview with V. Zarovski, he not only gave his reasons for breaking with Sajudis but drew a picture of what had happened to the cultural and intellectual climate of Lithuania that left nothing more to be added:

A cold, cold wind was blowing, fluttering the "old" Lithuanian tricolor which had just been hoisted above Trakaisk Castle in Vilnius. Side by side, among the thousands of others uncovered, was one Algirdas Brazauskas, leader of the independent Lithuanian Communist Party, another the much-loved writer Vitas Petkavicius.

Just two years have passed and Brazauskas is still Deputy Prime Minister ... but the other is out of favor, renounced and even expelled by the Sajudis he helped to found.

What has changed? "Everything," says Petkavicius, recalling that the original Sajudis had proclaimed that it would always remain in opposition and fight for Lithuania's spiritual rebirth.

"It was thought of as a popular front, but we wanted to avoid the word front, which sounded too military, too confrontational," he recalls, adding ironically that confrontation had eventually swallowed up the movement.

"The group that created Sajudis was made up of people who had been talking openly for ten or even 20 years about the need to revive Lithuanian culture.

"There were also young people, who didn't hold 'important positions' but who were very active. At one of the first meetings of our movement I said to the poet V. Daunarasu: 'These people are very mediocre and therefore they will unite against us.'

"At the time nobody believed me, but that's exactly what happened—the only thing I didn't guess was who would be their leader.

"Vytautas Landsbergis was elected chairman of Sajudis by bending the rules, which contain principles of collective leadership and norms of decency. Not even all the members were present at that meeting of the council on November 18, 1988."

And now?

"Sajudis now consists of wicked and untalented people. The writers, sculptors, teachers, scientists—those who created culture—are now cursed simply because they were communist party members, they helped the 'occupiers.'

"At present, a 'cult of those who never took part'—and therefore did not sin—is being cultivated. Yet the worst sin for a human being is to do nothing."

New parties arose, like the Independence Party, which barred former Communists from membership.

"The division of society into Communists and non-Communists has begun. Out of three and a half million Lithuanians, 200,000 were Communist Party members. Add to that an average of four family members and you get around a million people. Is it possible to enter the European Home with such a load of hatred? Is it possible to be democratic?"

How did it happen?

"We wanted to unite the people, regardless of nationality and faith, but it all turned out the other way around... Only six months have gone by since Landsbergis became the leader, and never before has Lithuania been so impudently robbed and plundered."[136]

Sajudis had turned into a cover behind which out-and-out adventurers and thieves saw their opportunity to line their own pockets. Hare-brained proposals have become stock-in-trade of many men now suddenly vaulted into the seats of power. Ignorant of economics, even of the most elementary facts connected with running a business concern, if their ideal of a 'market economy' were actually to be realized, most of their enterprises would end up in bankruptcy. Decisions that affect the lives of thousands are made with scarcely any discussion and no debate, and merely with the raising of hands. Appalled, Petkavicius remarks that "it is impossible to destroy the economic structure that existed for decades with one stroke of the pen or by several hands raised in parliament.

"The destruction of state farm villages will be a great disaster for us. Between five and ten percent of the republic's residents are retired: who is going to pay their pensions?"

A question nobody in Sajudis ever stopped to consider, but in their silence, delivered their answer: nobody. The old could shift for themselves.

In the mad drive to condemn everything that went on before in the period of the "occupiers" the Sajudis wreckers are destroying the positive accomplishments of generations of sincere and hard-working Lithuanians. "State farm heads are now the most cursed 'masters' and 'slave owners,' but no one wants to know that they gave a lifetime of effort to drag us up out of the mud. Now we're heading straight back into the mire—face down." Says Petkavicius: "I am for an independent Lithuania, but what sort of independence is it that ties my hands, that prevents me writing and stops me working for my Lithuania? I am for the prosperity of my people and not for the bankruptcy of 1938."

How many of the present generation of Lithuanians remembered 1938, and what that "bankruptcy" meant? Lithuania then, after 20 years of bourgeois-fascism under Voldemaras-Smetona, stood with empty pockets before its own people, although foreign investors were constantly making profits from the people's labor.

Writes Doctor of Economic Science, V. Savelyev:

> Objective data show Lithuania, before joining the USSR, to have been one of Europe's economically most backward countries with an economy in which agrarian-raw materials branches prevailed. In 1938, 73.8 percent of the active population was employed in the agrarian sector, and only 7.3 to 7.5 percent in industry ... produc[ing] mainly unsophisticated agricultural implements and consumer goods. In 1940, Lithuania's per capita industrial output was only one-third of the USSRs, not to mention Sweden...
>
> About 50 billion rubles of state capital investment has been put into the economy over the Soviet period ... 55 percent of it in the last 10 years. The bulk of it came from the central government in Moscow.[137]

Setting gangs of hoodlums loose on the people has not only endangered the lives of those men and women still defending Lithuania's socialist choice but they have set about wrecking all of Lithuania's monuments to the defenders of Lithuanian soil from the Nazis. Petkavicius feels grateful to the Soviet army which protects these monuments from the Sajudis vandals. Says he: "So it now appears that for 40 years I was working for the occupiers, and now I am to be cursed for it. The poet J. Marcinkevicius, a most patient person and the last remaining founder of Sajudis, has been expelled, and even the prewar Foreign Minister, J. Urbsys has been intimidated."

Almost an exact reprise for Nazi atrocities now occurs everywhere. "Not long ago, I was in Kaunas, where I saw a crowd on the corner of Daukat Street and Laisves Avenue. One of Jouzas Baltusis'* books was nailed to a tree.

"I managed to break the nail, and they started shouting and threatening to beat me up. I said: 'Let's fight, but I won't allow you to mock the book. What did Hitler and Stalin begin with? With bonfires.'"**

Letters, he says, come to him every day filled with despair, calling for help. Famous personalities like "V. Statulvicius, the mathematician, have been driven to the grave. The president of the Lithuanian Academy of

---

* Since, Jouzas Baltusis, true to his Communist principles, and openly saying so—and being persecuted and slandered for it—has died.

** Petkavicius is in error here. There is no evidence that Stalin ever ordered the burning of books. On the contrary, Baltusis was hounded by the fascist elements of Sajudis and almost on his death bed, he defiantly flung back at them: "I am a Communist!"

sciences, J. Pozela [son of one of the four executed Communist leaders in Smetona's era—P.B.] the first to raise his voice two years ago against the dominance of bureaucrats and stagnators in the Communist Party—has disappeared from the scene."

Once the "new" type of parliamentarians, under Sajudis' auspices, came to power, they took this to mean that they were now free to plunder the state right and left. "One activist took 15,000 rubles, and when that was uncovered, he claimed he had been robbed.

"It takes these MPs days to decide whether the horse's tail on the state emblem should be up or down, while the harvest is rotting in the fields.

"Sajudis called for mobilization, and only three people came to dig out potatoes in the region of Prenaisk. However strange it sounds, the opposition army came to help, exchanging machine guns for buckets.

"The chairman of the state farm phoned me and asked: 'Shall I take the soldiers? Won't I be damned for it?' I said: 'Take them. If you are left without potatoes—then you'll be damned.' The MPs are running away from the people, trying to go unnoticed. Take Landsbergis' body guards: in less than a year they have cost 623,000 rubles. His doors and windows are being reinforced with bars—what for?

"Before, I stood for the withdrawal of Soviet troops from Lithuania, but I now think they are needed to stabilize the situation here.

"It wasn't such a long time ago that those who raised their voices against the totalitarian system were 'enemies of the people.' Today if you criticize Landsbergis you become an 'enemy of the nation.'

"Love of the Homeland has again become the monopoly of a small group of schemers. Their delving into people's pasts is the basis of every evil regime, with the old policing methods of recruiting criminals who will do the job not out of love but out of fear.

"Of course there are good MPs, but the others are quick to grab them by the throat. They have already created an Athens of the North for themselves: Landsbergis has given himself a monthly salary of 2,000 rubles,* and he awards his supporters with flats and foreign trips.

"The intelligentsia is again confronted with the job of writing, explaining, meeting. Why am I not allowed anywhere near the newspapers, the television? Because they are afraid of the truth."

Late in December, 1990, an "Appeal to the Lithuanian People," signed by "prominent Lithuanian community leaders and cultural figures" was published. "The Appeal warned: democracy cannot be built by undemocratic means. And that was three months before the Lithuanian parliament approved Lithuanian passports (to replace USSR internal passports) and

---

* The average wage was about 150 rubles a month.

passed amendments to the republic's Penal Code, specifying capital punishment for 'enemies of the nation.'"

Again, Vitautas Petkavicius spoke out through the pages of "Literary Gazette" (January 1991).

"Landsbergis," he said, "hasn't been in power for even six months, but collections of his speeches are already coming out in mass editions ... Writers who dared to criticize him are disgraced and blacklisted. Sinister pickets are staged outside the windows of those who had the courage to protest. The republic's radio and television networks taken over by Landsbergis pour dirt over dissenters, branding them 'enemies of the people.'

"What democracy, what law-abiding state can you talk about when the amended Penal Code of October 4 specifies imprisonment, expropriation and execution for dissent?

"How come the majority in Lithuania puts up with this situation? Because our ambition prevent us from admitting our mistakes.

"Evil ... and mediocrity and power are generally well-organized. Add to that the terrible envy that consumes the nonentity and the desire to be prominent, rich and powerful, and you can explain the appearance of all those people and understand their hankering after the power...."

And so, "farewell to Sajudis."

Toward the end of 1990, the amber museum in Palanga was broken into and robbed. For over a decade, the museum had been there, open to all, guarded hardly at all, but nobody thought to break in. Taken were amber specimens that are "priceless" and still others worth thousands of dollars. And, so, hail to the era of "market economy"!

And farewell, too, to Queen Juraite, and farewell to the mortal man with whom she fell in love, and farewell, too, to Perkunas, god of thunder, a jealous god, but whose power has had to yield to Greed.

But yes, the stroller along the beaches of Palanga finds pieces of amber rising from the depth of the sea—yes, those are still tears.

SUMMING UP: A GLANCE TO THE FUTURE

When a great social revolution shall have mastered the results of the bourgeois epoch, the market of the world and the modern powers of production, and subjected them to the common control of the most advanced people, then only will human progress cease to resemble the Hindoo pagan idol, who would not drink the nectar but from the skulls of the slain.

—Karl Marx, "The Future Results of British Rule in India."

On September 6, 1991, what was still the central government of the USSR, acting through its Supreme Soviet, recognized the independence of the three Baltic states, all of which had already declared their independence. In October, 1991, all three republics were admitted to membership in the UN.

Thus, independence of a sort became a fact.

Surely a historic occasion? And yet, once the momentary euphoria evaporated, what was left was a huge gaping black hole, an entrance to a dark cave out of which no one could see an exit. Once the political glue that held them together in opposition to Russia disappeared, they also lost what had become a convenient political scapegoat.

Once they had legal independence, they were forced to reveal precisely what independence realistically was to mean. Democracy had been the cry, but when the August 1991 ill-advised, ill-fated attempted coup failed so miserably, arguing that it was never seriously meant to succeed, all talk of democracy was thrown overboard, and with the coup as a pretext, they moved swiftly to suppress all Communist Parties in the Baltics and to shut down (and even padlock) those vestiges of independent and critical publications that still remained, taking over total monopoly control of the press, TV, radio, publishing houses, and cleaning out the libraries of subversive literature. With this as their moral imperative, they set about selling socialist property to the highest and not always the highest bidder. Thus, it became only too clear what independence meant in practice: monopoly control of the political process, and of all means of expressing dissident, alternative and opposition opinion. In short, counterrevolution.

The writer Vitautas Petkavicius, months before any kind of attempted coup, had already raised the cry: "how can you illegalize one-third of the nation? How is it possible to enter the European Home with such a load of hatred? Is it possible to be democratic?" Instead of "democracy" (vaguely left undefined), Petkavicius was to note that "only six months have gone by since Landsbergis became the leader, and never before has Lithuania been so impudently robbed and plundered."*

"New" Lithuania, while announcing that it would resume where "democratic" Lithuania had been interrupted in her development by the "invasion" of the Red Army (which entered by agreement to stop the Nazis at Lithuania's western borders) had little resemblance to the "old" Lithuania now so sentimentally recalled by the swarms of Nationalist would-be writers who seem to have sprung up out of the woodwork. For under Smetona, Lithuania had been an open fascist dictatorship not denied, nor disguised, but even proudly declared to be, Lithuania's "democratic" period had been fleetingly brief, and had proved itself ineffective, and had quickly yielded to the fascists Smetona and Voldemaras. The same applied in varying degrees, to the fascists Ulmanis in Latvia and Paet in Estonia.

The Lithuania which the Landsbergis forces took over was an entirely different Lithuania from the one Smetona had created. In the four-and-a-half decades, under Communist leadership, and as a secure member of the Soviet "family," Lithuania changed from a mainly agricultural-bucolic nation to a mainly industrial nation with an increasingly growing and better educated working class quite able to take over running the system. We have already seen how illiteracy, unemployment, and the main diseases that regularly devastated the population and shortened the life span of the average Lithuanian were wiped out. Lithuania also eliminated the class of parasites living off unearned income, but whose power dominated social life. In some ways they were worse than the bubonic plague.

What was true of Lithuania, which one suspects more and more was assigned the pioneering role of applying first the still-hidden agenda of counterrevolution, was true with local modifications in the other two Baltic countries as well. But Lithuania took the lead. In fact, it developed the tactics which were to prove successful, and instead of Gorbachev leading Brazauskas, it ended up that Brazauskas taught Gorbachev, though Brazauskas took his cue from the undercurrent implications of the perestroika and particularly of what turned out to be the camel's nose under the tent: "market economy." In the end, both were eliminated.

* See p. 283.

It all boiled down to property who would own what. And here they came face to face with the most stubborn problem of all. For the fact is that *all* of the property in the Baltic as well as the other ex-Soviet states was owned literally by the people. This is not a mere phrase. No plant, factory, mine or power complex exists in any ex-socialist country that was once owned by AT&T, or Ford, or Morgan and Rockefeller, and therefore could theoretically still be returned to them. There was nothing to return to them.

What conceivably might have survived the revolutions in Eastern Europe especially in the USSR, was entirely destroyed by the WWII as was indeed true in the Baltics. Peace found these nations nothing but smoking ruins. Everything had to be built from scratch with their own funds, their own labor, their own time. There were no investors, no shareholders, no coupon clippers, no infusion of capital from abroad. At most, funds were donated by the Central Government. Indeed, today property worth billions in the Baltic countries is (or was) claimed by Moscow.

Several generations have grown up in what used to be the Soviet Union with absolutely no experience in owning private property. By 1990, the overwhelming majority of Lithuanians, Latvians and Estonians also had had no first-hand experience in personally "owning" plants and factories, forests and farm land. They saw it all as *"nasha"*—ours. Indeed, this historic fact as it expressed itself in the culture and the human personality is what was the distinct difference between the Western, aggressive, money-minded personality and the socialist personality. "Socialist" psychology is rooted in the majority of the population and explains why the changes wanted so badly by Landsbergis and Yeltsin go so slowly and meet so much passive and active opposition.

Trying to create a nation of "property-owners"—of remolding the psychology of a whole people from cooperation with each other and with all into a people who ask: "What's in it for me?" is no easy task. Turning socially created and owned property over to individual promoters and financiers is probably the rock against which the present forces in power in the ex-socialist world will shatter. People who have worked, and been *guaranteed* work, all their lives are not schooled to assimilate mass unemployment as "natural." Current attempts to "sell" the property to individuals in the form of stock certificates which will entitle the individual "owners" to a share in the profits, and even to give them an extra incentive to work harder themselves, smacks of nothing more original than similar attempts even in the USA to create a people's capitalism by selling individual workers a share or two in their factories. Such attempts failed in the USA, as they failed in Yugoslavia, and as they are failing before our eyes in Poland, etc. Once the economy is opened up to vagaries of the capitalist market, it becomes the victim of those often unpredictable and catastrophic events which no capitalist country is immune from, and which indeed will eventually do them in.

Though raised in a Marxist society, most people knew very little about the realities of profit, where it comes from and what it consists of. Profit is unpaid labor. It comes out of the blood, sweat and tears of workers and from nowhere else. To make a profit, which *must* go ever higher, wages also *must* be cut. The single owner of a share in his factory can find himself in a position where one part of him is rewarded with a profit but the other part of him—his real self—is punished by a drop in wages, a rise in rent, in consumer goods and even in the cost of funerals. Lowered wages breed opposition—strikes—perhaps a factory close-down—and unemployment.

He learns then that nothing comes from nothing: if he profits, it's out of his labor or (better) some one else's. If he's a worker, then others profit from *him*, with all the consequences that the world is only too familiar with today.

Some will prosper. Some always do—even in building better crematoria or manufacturing a better Zyklon-B gas. And their prosperity will be pointed to with pride as an example to emulate. But such "prosperity," we know to our cost, is no reliable index to the economic health of the country, but goes hand in hand with a general moral and cultural corruption. When the cash nexus is all that connects people, then all social relations, all mores, all art, find its equivalent.

For just as water seeks its own level, capital seeks the highest rate of profit. If it is more profitable to manufacture guns than baby nipples—there will be no baby nipples. As in Yugoslavia, factory will find itself competing with factory in its own country and, more importantly, with factories abroad. Those that can will survive. Those that can't will go under—and they go under in America at an alarming yearly rate, where bankruptcy seems to have become the norm. Nor is it enough to say that it's right that the fittest will survive and deserve to survive.

Social Darwinism is the destruction of civilization. Society needs baby nipples, affordable housing, medical care, etc., and since there is no profit in those fields, they will inevitably be neglected, forced into the uncharitable and unwilling hands of whatever passes for "government" with predictable and already witnessed direst of consequences.

Even so, no matter how bravely they set out to distribute shares to the people, sooner or later, if those shares have any value at all, they will find their way into the hands of the great financial moguls and the people will end up at their mercy. Capitalism, my friends, is no utopia, as the Estonian economist academician Mikhail Bronstein tried to warn his people: "Market laws are tough...."

We have seen some of how "independence" works: each country has its own flag, own money, own representatives at the UN where they dutifully vote the way Washington wants them to, and nobody dares speak Russian in Vilnius or Tallinn or Riga. How does "democracy," which the people had been promised so lavishly, now fare? A good start was begun with the suppression of all opposition parties and their means of existence and expression. For one thing, Lithuania has its own "army"now—a force of 30,000, hardly more than New York City's police force. In outlawing the Communist Party, they have done nothing significantly different from what almost every Western country (most notably in Italy, Germany, Spain—and Lithuania), had already done at one time or another, and this act alone does not outrage even liberal circles in the West, which socially accept such measures as necessary to a liberated economy. These circles believe that the same force that drives the economy hung the stars in the sky. For them, "democracy" means "capitalism," sometimes called a "thousand points of light."

Landsbergis, as well as Yeltsin, also agrees that democracy means capitalism. But unschooled in the Byzantine ways of the West, especially of the USA, Landsbergis almost as his first "independent" act, committed a grave error. He assumed that the right people in the USA were privy to his private thoughts. He had every reason to assume so since they told him so in private conversations at places like Heritage House. But what he forgot was that what they said "between us" must not be publicly uttered. He forgot the Holocaust.

So, in all "innocence," he made his initial blunder. Hardly was Lithuania declared independent than he threw open the prison doors and let dozens of war criminals free. Almost at the same time, some 30,000 certificates of exoneration were issued to others, mainly Nationalists, who had been implicated in collaborating with the Nazis (and we've seen in this book just what that meant), or had fought the socialist government in the '50s under CIA inspiration.

Landsbergis "forgot" the Holocaust, of course, because his family—specifically his father—helped create it. In any case, the storm of protest and outrage that rose from mainly (but not only) Jewish quarters all over the world but most significantly from the USA, took the Landsbergis forces by surprise. Why the outrage? Wasn't President Nixon anti-Semitic, as his secret tapes revealed? Didn't Reagan stand at a cemetery at Bitburg in Germany and, in effect, "forgive" the fascists buried there? Didn't Bush have on his campaign staff "ethnics" who were wanted for crimes against Jews in their native lands?

His first reaction was resentment. The World Jewish Congress, and particularly the Wiesenthal Center, had led the outcry. They charged, producing documents, that indeed real criminals were being smuggled out of prison under the pretence that since the *Soviets* had imprisoned them they must be innocent. Landsbergis flared back, according to the *New York Times*, "suggest(ing) that the Wiesenthal Center's records were planted by the KGB in an attempt to discredit Lithuania."[138]

So he stubbed his toe. But hurried to New York to make amends, and since the main Jewish forces had been anti-Soviet all along, charging the USSR with anti-Semitism, be managed a meeting of the minds after all.

That's Lithuania. Soon after "independence," ads appeared in the American press, under the cheerful headline: "The Baltics: From Independence to Prosperity," presumably only a hop away.

In this key ad, the three countries show what they have to offer. But first they wanted to assure the Westerners how much they admired the West, now that they were free of socialist tyranny. In Estonia, we read, "the signs of Westernization are already evident in daily life."[139]

And just what are these reassuring "signs"? Now, "Mercedes and Audis... are becoming a regular sight on the city streets of Tallinn..." And: "pizza parlors and fast food chains..." are to be seen more and more, and to cap it all, "for a while it seemed that the lines for the multi-flavored Penguin ice cream were even longer than for bread." Add to their sleek cars and chemically-colored ice cream, American movies of the rip-gurgle-blood type and TV programs like "Friday, the Thirteenth" in which sadism and sex are dished out raw to teen-agers, and you certainly are right in believing you are about to enter paradise.

And yet even so there's a snake in this paradise. Though "grocery stores are better stocked than they were under the command economy system," the fact is that all the average Estonian, who makes an average $15 a month, can do is *look* at them, he can't buy them any more than he'll ever honestly earn enough to buy a Mercedes or even a Lada.

But not everyone. Hardly was the ink dry on their declarations of independence than those much-admired Western entrepreneurs descended on the Baltics in swarms. Before long one was reading in the Western press (*Panorama*, Milan):

> Wearing a Bond Street suit, gold Rolex watch on his wrist, a Valentino tie and with five bodyguards who do not leave him for a moment, Andres, 35, is the new boss of Tallinn. With his "stable" of 150 girls, he controls the most important of the nine Mafia organizations which shared the prostitution racket in the capital of Estonia.
>
> A few weeks after independence, Tallinn gained the slogan of 'true Bangkok of the Baltics': it drew swarms of fireflies coming from all of the Soviet republics to crowd the hotels Viru, Olympia, Palace. The prey is always the foreign tourist or businessman, who will wake up [come to] in his underwear in a neighborhood street, the victim of knock-out drops cleverly mixed in his drinks. The police

intervene only when it is a fatal matter [involves death, homicide, etc.] as happened with two Swedish trade unionists.

The Baltic Mafia meanwhile is preparing to expand its range of action. The *padrino* [godfather] Andres, for example, has rented out nine rooms in one of the best hotels in Helsinki and an equal number in Stockholm. Every 20 days he sends a gang of his best girls to round up clients. Preferably in this order: Arabs, Germans, Americans, Italians, Swiss.[140]*

Such bon-bons of freedom and independence became available "overnight" in all three Baltic republics. But even more serious than the rampant dissolution of the moral order that had created such a climate of psychological health in the socialist period is the added potentially unpleasant fact that with "independence" of the Baltics came the independence of neighboring states and increased power, particularly of Germany which had just swallowed up the hitherto friendly GDR–German Democratic Republic. Is it too cynical to suggest that a day will yet come (perhaps not too far in the future) when the cry, "Give us back Memel (Klaipeda)" will be heard again in Berlin? Or, from Warsaw, "Give us back Polish Vilnius"–which Poland had "owned" much longer than the Lithuanians ever did? Even Belorussia has hinted that it may want onetime Belorussian land, now in Lithuanian hands, returned.

And what about those large "minorities" *inside* the Baltics, who have been isolated by events, and in effect reduced to second-class citizenship? Forty percent of Latvia is Russian. Almost as many Russians exist in Estonia. A smaller percentage exists in Lithuania, but they exist. They have been told to shape up or ship out–to become instant Lithuanians, Latvians and Estonians (going to school to learn those languages better) or live from hand-to-mouth as aliens in a country in which many were born that scorns them now. Many have already fled in panic. Those who remain...remain....

And, then, what about the "model" on which these countries strive now to base themselves: the USA? Their timing could not be worse. The USA is in the throes of one of its worst economic depressions in decades, with millions homeless, millions more unemployed and more to come–with crime rampant everywhere and with social corruption now the norm. Suffice to say that in the USA there are an estimated 200 million handguns owned by 25 million households, who keep shooting each other at a rate of 30,000 a year, in a simmering "underground" civil war that seems never to end.

---

* In January 1992, the Estonian government resigned–the first of what will be many.

In Kaunas, there is a museum devoted to the works of Lithuania's only authentic painter, Ciurliones (1875-1911), whose mystic canvases, which attempt to capture in paint what music does in notes, have tantalized critics for decades.

In the same museum there is, or was, a section devoted to what can hardly be called sculpture unless one can accuse Nature of being a sculptress. It's a collection of tree trunks, but very strange tree-trunks: these tree trunks all have human faces. These faces were not carved by human hand. Nature carved them, creating in her own punning way a sardonic comment on humankind. At twilight one can easily feel that one is in a land of pagan Lithuania re-encountering in these tree trunks the lost souls of Lithuania's past. This to not unlikely. For it has not been too many centuries ago that Lithuanians in their *dainos* sang of man turning into tree and tree into man. Nor has that past escaped. For along the beaches of the Baltic sea, as we know, the stroller can still come across bits of amber, some of which contain remnants of the past, now frozen forever in this stilled sunlight, but which he can hold today in his cupped hands.

Trees are human and humans are godly or satanic. One can find oneself suddenly surrounded by tree trunks who are devils. And the *motif* of the devil is never far from the Lithuanian consciousness.

Behind the Ciurlones museum in Kaunas stands another museum—an entirely unique one: a museum of devils. The man who inspired it—Antanas Zmuidzinavicius—was in his 90's when I met him, and his collection of devils took up only his own apartment. But the collection became famous and a few years later (after his death) the entire house was turned over to the devils, and there are literally hundreds of them, not only from Lithuania, but from all over the world.

But devils, as we have seen, are not confined to the museum. You may meet them in almost any forest, where 2,000-year-old oaks still stand. But you will also find them in shops and offices, on the street, in homes.

But why the devil? Why does a country deposit so profound an element of its spiritual self in the image of the devil? The reason, I think, is clear. A country that has been oppressed and subdued as long as Lithuania has—absolutely deprived of any power to decide its own fate—which is so reluctant to let go of its mystic ties to a time when it felt at one with nature—has to find some means of expressing itself that is at once tolerated by the powers-that-be and at the same time is expressive of the latent rebellion that everyone instinctively feels. If God can't save us, we have, after all, the devil....

As we know, piety has only one face: passive, asexual, suffering, submissive—rather, one is reluctant to say, stupid, yes, stupid. But rebellion has many faces: they vary from the deliberately ugly when "beauty" is demanded, to the sly, the mocking, the impish, the hating, the angry. There is life there because there is discontent: discontent implies a critical judgment. The devil is caught in the center of the Lithuanian soul. It is caught in the amber of history. It is the eternal restlessness and the unsatisfied nature of man's seeking for harmony, grace, justice. It is the incarnation of nightmares, the face of fear and guilt and always it is threat. The devils of the Baltic state peer out at us through the resin haze of golden amber.

The tale is not over.

NOTES

1. *The Golden Bough*, by Sir James George Fraser, Colliers Books, New York, 1963, p. 186.
2. *The Daina*, Anthology of Lithuanian and Latvian Folk Songs, by V. Katzenelenbogen, 1935, Chicago, Lithuanian News Publishing Company, quoted from *Mitteilungen der Lituaischen Litterarischen Gesellschaft*, 1879, p. 15.
3. *Reactionary Prussianism*, International Publishers, 1942
4. "The Story of Lithuania Through the *Daina*," by Nora Bonosky, Senior History Thesis, Antioch University, 1980
5. *Capital*, by Karl Marx
6. *The Deserted Village*, by Oliver Goldsmith, 1770
7. *Selected Poetry and Prose*, Adam Mieckevicius, Polonia Publishers, Warsaw, 1965, p. 179.
8. *Documents Accuse*, selected Nazi and Nationalist documents during the Nazi occupation, Gintara Publishers, 1970, p. 93.
9. *Struggle of the Lithuanian People for Statehood*, by Prof. Kostas Navickas, Gintara Publishers, Vilnius, 1971, p. 21.
10. *Ibid.*
11. *Lithuania, 700 Years*, ed. by Albertas Gerutis, Maryland Books, N.Y., 1969, p. 60.
12. *Ibid.*
13. *American Labor Year Book*, 1929, Rand School of Social Sciences, N.Y., p. 243.
14. *Ibid.*
15. *Ibid.*
16. *The Struggle of Lithuanian People for Statehood, op. cit.*, p. 68.
17. *Witness to a Century*, by George Seldes, Ballantine Books, 1987, p. 111.
18. *Lietuvos Aidas*, Dec. 16, 1933.
19. *Commandant of Auschwitz*, by Rudolph Hoess, ed. by Windenfeld and Nicolson, 1959, Wydawotwo Printers, Warsawa, 1951, Random House, N.Y.
20. *Lietuvos Aidas*, March 22, 1938.
21. *Tiesa*, Oct. 1, 1938.
22. *Soviet Peace Efforts on Eve of War*, documents, Progress Publishers, Moscow, 1973, p. 219.
23. *How War Came*, by Donald Cameron Watt, Pantheon Books, N.Y., 1989, pp. 156-57.
24. *The New Way*, by Theodore Oberlander, 1936.
25. *The Nazi Legacy*, by Magnus Linklater, Isabel Hilton, Neal Ascherson, Holt, Reinhart & Winston, N.Y., 1984, p. 18.
26. *Hitler, Memoirs of A Confidant*, (Otto Wagener), Ed. by Henry Ashby Turner, Jr., Yale University Press, New Haven and London, 1978, p. x.
27. *Ibid.*
28. *Documents of German Foreign Policy*, 1918-1945, Series D, Vol. vi, London, 1956, quoted in *The Struggle of Lithuanian People...*, p. 125.
29. *Soviet Peace Efforts, op. cit.*, p. 587.
30. William Forrest, *New York Post*, *London Chronicle*, quoted in *New Masses*, Oct. 3, 1939.
31. *Documents of German Foreign Policy, op. cit.*, quoted in *The Struggles of Lithuanian People...*, p. 119.
32. *The Struggles of Lithuanian People..., op. cit*, p. 120.
33. *Tiesa*, Aug. 15, 1939.
34. *Right In Her Soul*, The Life of Anna Louise Strong, by Tracy B. Strong and Helene Keyssar, Random House, 1983, biographical note, cover flap.
35. Francis Hackett, "The Sickbed of Culture," (essay) in *A Modern Book of Criticism*, ed. by Ludwig Lewisohn, Boni and Liveright, N.Y., 1919, p. 192.
36. *Cinema In Revolution*, ed. by Luda and Jean Schnitzler and Marcel Martin, a Da Capo Paperback, 1973, pp. 92, 93, 99.
37. *The New Lithuania*, by Anna Louise Strong, Workers Library, N.Y., 1941, p. 27.
38. Craig Whitney, *New York Times*, April 4, 1990.
39. *The Struggles of the Lithuanian People for Statehood, op. cit.*, p. 134.
40. *In Fact*, Aug. 10, 1940.
41. *The New Lithuania, op. cit.*, p. 59.
42. *Ibid.*
43. *The Great Conspiracy*, by Michael Sayers and Albert E. Kahn, Boni and Gaer, N.Y., 1947, p. 46.
44. *Ibid.*
45. *Documents Accuse, op. cit.*, p. 123.
46. *Blowback*, by Christopher Simpson, Weidenfeld and Nicolson, N.Y. 1988, p. 25.
47. *Who Is Hiding on Grand Street?*, Mintis Publishers, Vilnius, 1964, p. 15.
48. *Documents Accuse, op. cit.*, p. 88.
49. *Who Is Hiding on Grand Street?, op. cit.*, p. 20.

50. *Ibid.*
51. *Commandant of Auschwitz,* op. cit.
52. *Ibid.*
53. *Documents Accuse,* op. cit., p. 93.
54. *Lithuanians in America,* by Dr. Antonas Kucas, 1975, pp. 313-14.
55. *Black Book,* published by Jewish Black Book Committee, NYC, 1946, p. 324.
56. *Documents Accuse,* op. cit., p. 88.
57. *Ibid.*
58. *Ekonomikai Zizn,* No. 37, 1990, by V. Slavelyev.
59. *Tass,* March 24, 1979.
60. *Ibid.*
61. *New York Times,* Feb. 4, 1991.
62. Alfonse Maldonas, quoted in *Soviet Literature,* No. 8, 1979, "This Land is Called Lithuania."
63. *Tass,* April 25, 1979.
64. *Ibid.*
65. *The Lithuanian Muse,* Introduction to Anthology of Poetry, *The Amber Lyre,* 1983, p. 14.
66. *The Daina,* op. cit., p. 96.
67. *Baltic Soviet Republics,* Gregory Meiksins, 1944, National Council, American-Soviet Friendship, p. 12.
68. *The Great Conspiracy,* op. cit., p. 25.
69. *Baltic Soviet Republics,* op. cit., p. 16.
70. *Ibid.,* p. 18.
71. *Ibid.*
72. *Ibid.,* p. 24.
73. *Ibid.,* p. 25.
74. *Ibid.,* p. 31.
75. "Letter from Polish Ambassador," *Soviet Peace Efforts on Eve of World War II,* Progress Publishers, Moscow, p. 84.
76. "The Trial of the Finnish War Criminals," by Otto Kuusinen, *Information Bulletin,* Feb. 16, 1946.
77. *Ibid.*
78. *Cina,* Secret Diplomacy, Bourgeois Latvia in the Anti-Soviet Plans of Imperialist Powers, 1919, 1940. Riga, 1968, by V. J. Sipols.
79. *Cina,* July 30, 1940.
80. *The Baltic Soviet Republics,* op. cit., p. 39.
81. *The Black Book,* op. cit., p. 329.
82. Quoted by Herbert Aptheker, *History and Reality,* Cameron Associates, N.Y., 1958, p. 181.
83. *Ibid.*
84. *Collier's,* Sept. 3, 1938.
85. *Ibid.*
86. *The Killers' Whereabouts Are Known,* by Vladimir Molchanov, Novosti, 1986, p. 33.
87. *The Plot Against the Peace,* by Michael Sayers and Albert E. Kahn, George Braziller Publisher, NYC, 1945, pp. 141-42.
88. Bonosky, Nora, *The Story of Lithuania Through the Daina,* op. cit.

89. Brody, David, *Steelworkers in America,* NYC 1960, Harvard University Press, pp. 100-101.
90. "Letter to Baptists of Danbury, Conn.," 1802, by Thomas Jefferson.
91. To Peter Carr, Aug. 10, 1787.
92. *Ibid.*
93. Letter to Van der Kemp, by Thomas Jefferson.
94. *Ibid.*
95. *Ibid.*
96. *Lithuanians in America,* op. cit., p. 228.
97. *Ibid.,* p. 240.
98. *The Great Steel Strike,* by William Z. Foster, B. W. Huebach Publisher, NYC, 1920, pp. 198-201.
99. *The New York Call,* April 21, 1918.
100. *The Class Struggle,* Vol. 11, Feb. 1919.
101. *The New York Call,* Nov. 10, 1919
102. *American Swastika,* by Charles Highman, Doubleday and Co., NYC, 1985, p. 41.
103. *Freedom of the Press,* by George Seldes, Garden City Publishing Co., NYC, 1937, p. 136.
104. *Lithuanians in America,* op. cit., p. 153.
105. *Blowback,* op. cit., p. 176.
106. *Ibid.,* p. 179.
107. *Ibid.,* p. 184.
108. *Documents Accuse,* op. cit., p. 93.
109. *The Real Truth,* from "Amongst the People," by K. Telyatnikov, Raduga, 1986, p. 131.
110. *Documents Accuse,* op. cit., p. 88.
111. *Ibid.,* p. 88.
112. *The Destruction of European Jews,* by Paul Hilberg, Harper and Row, N.Y., 1961, p. 201.
113. *There Shall Be Retribution,* by Vladimir Molchanov, Progress Publishers, Moscow, 1984, pp. 86-87.
114. *Documents Accuse,* op. cit., p. 123.
115. Internal Lithuanian Information Center Bulletin, Washingtonm D.C., Ja. 1990.
116. *Literary Gazette,* International, Jan. 1991.
117. Quoted in *Lithuania,* by Petras Griskevicius, Novosti Press, Moscow, 1980.
118. *Monologue the Third,* Soviet Literature, No. 2, 1987
119. *Ibid.*
120. *Soviet Literature,* No. 8, 1982.
121. *Ibid.*
122. *Sputnik,* 1990.
123. *Ibid.*
124. *Ibid.*
125. *Ibid.*
126. *Washington Post,* Aug. 20, 1989.
127. "Is Eastern Europe Our Backyard Too?" by Beth Sims, in *Loot,* May 1991.
128. Interview on Norwegian Radio, May 1990.
129. *Ibid.*

130. *Pravda*, March 15, 1990.
131. *Ibid.*
132. *New York Times*, April 23, 1990.
133. Washington Post Foreign Service, by David Remnick, Jan. 21, 1991.
134. *Covert Action*, "The Afghan Contra Lobby," by Said Khybar, Nov. 1988.
135. *Soviet Literature*, No. 11, 1988.
136. V. Zavroski, *Soviet Weekly*, Dec. 6, 1990.
137. *Ekonomika i Zizn*, No. 37, 1990.
138. *New York Times*, Oct. 17, 1991.
139. *New York Times*, Oct. 28, 1991.

Index

Zadeikas, Povilas 74
Zalakevicius, Vytautas, 249, 256
Zarovski, V., 282
Zaunius, Dr. Dovas, 72
Zemaite, Julia, 32

Zemaitis, Father Jonas, 137n, 140n, 238
Zimanas, Henrikas, 92, 111
Zmuidzinavicius, Antanas, 247, 294
Zuhauskas, Juozas, 92
Zukauskas, Silvestras, 58